ST. MARY'S COLLEGE OF MARYLAND

W9-CIG-988

VISIONS AND BELIEFS
IN THE
WEST OF IRELAND

General Editors
T. R. Henn, C.B.E., Litt.D.
Colin Smythe, M.A.

45316

VISIONS AND BELIEFS IN THE WEST OF IRELAND COLLECTED AND ARRANGED BY LADY GREGORY: WITH TWO ESSAYS AND NOTES BY W. B. YEATS

"There's no doubt at all but that there's the same sort of things in other countries; but you hear more about them in these parts because the Irish do be more familiar in talking of them."

with a foreword
by
Elizabeth Coxhead

NEW YORK
OXFORD UNIVERSITY PRESS
1970

Foreword copyright © 1970 Colin Smythe Ltd.

First edition published in 1920 by G. P. Putnam's Sons
London & New York
Copyright 1920 Lady Gregory
Essays and Notes Copyright 1914, 1920 W. B. Yeats

The volumes of the Coole Edition are to be published
by the Oxford University Press in the United States of
America and Colin Smythe Limited in Great Britain.

Acknowledgement is made to Miss Anne Yeats for permission
to include *Witches and Wizards and Irish Folklore* and the
Notes by W. B. Yeats and to Miss Anne Yeats and the
Macmillan Company of New York for permission to include
Swedenborg, Mediums and Desolate Places, from W. B. Yeats'
Explorations. Copyright © Mrs. W. B. Yeats 1962.

Library of Congress Catalogue Card No. 71–111492

Printed in Great Britain

FOREWORD

All Lady Gregory's non-dramatic works have been unjustly neglected, but two of them are seminal to any study of the great upsurge of dramatic and poetic talent which we call the Irish Literary Renascence. *Our Irish Theatre* describes the movements leading up to the foundation of the Abbey Theatre, and its early struggles. This book, *Visions and Beliefs in the West of Ireland*, is the principal record of the folk-lore-collecting which furnished the Renascence with so much of its inspiration and material.

It was Lady Gregory's third book of folk-lore, the much slighter *Poets and Dreamers* having appeared in 1903, and *A Book of Saints and Wonders* in 1907; it was not published till 1920. But work on it had been continuing since the turn of the century, and her diaries often speak of new items added to "my big book of folklore."

In fact, this was an interest reaching back to her earliest childhood, when, as the youngest girl in a vast, extrovert, hard-riding family of Anglo-Irish squires, she alone cared for the fairy stories told by Mary Sheridan, their Irish-speaking nurse. She longed to learn the mysterious language spoken all around her on her father's great agricultural estate, but "my asking, timid with the fear of mockery, went unheeded," she tells us in the Preface to *The Kiltartan Poetry Book*, (her translations of vernacular poems). It was not until she had been widowed, and was bringing up her only son and caring for his inheritance of Coole, that the opportunity came. Young Robert, having won a classical scholarship to Harrow, took a fancy "to learn a nearer language." Mother and son borrowed an Irish grammar from their neighbour Edward Martyn, and puzzled it out together.

At much the same time, in 1893, two slight books were published which caught her imagination: W. B. Yeats' *The Celtic Twilight*, with its folk stories of his native Sligo which at once made her jealous for Galway, and Douglas Hyde's *Love Songs of Connacht*, Irish poems handed down orally, which he had collected, and translated into an English dialect she was at once able to recognise—the English of people who are mentally translating from the Irish. She had heard it all her life, but now knew it for what it was.

Like many others, she began to look and listen. "This discovery, this disclosure of the folk learning, the folk poetry, the ancient tradition, was the small beginning of a weighty change. It was an upsetting of the table of values, an astonishing excitement. The imagination of Ireland had found a new homing place. My own imagination was aroused. I was becoming conscious of a world close to me and that I had been ignorant of. It was not now in the corners of newspapers I looked for poetic emotion, nor even to the singers in the streets. It was among farmers and potato diggers and old men in workhouses and beggars at my own door that I found what was beyond these, and yet farther beyond that drawing-room poet of my childhood (Moore) in the expression of love, and grief, and the pain of parting, that are the disclosure of the individual soul."

She invited Yeats and Hyde to Coole, and lifelong friendships ensued. On Yeats's recommendation she went out in the summer of 1898 to the Aran Islands, and found there an untouched peasant culture; indeed, following in her footsteps sixty years later, I found it very little changed from the charming description she gives in this book except for the advent of portable radio sets and bottled gas. And Mr Paudeen Conneely, then in his eighties, had a clear recollection of her appearance and manner, and of her good spoken Irish—in contrast to J. M. Synge, who was there at the same time, and could hardly understand Irish at all.

But this was her only trip to Aran, for it soon appeared, from her collecting rounds with Yeats or Hyde or alone, that there was a rich harvest of material nearer home. Her estate of Coole, with its eerie woods and swan-dappled lake, was a favourite haunt of the Sidhe; so were the limestone-plated hills of the Burren, and the lonely, desolate plateau of Slieve Echtge, all within driving distance for herself and her pony Shamrock, who has his small place in literary history. Her accounts of their sometimes alarming adventures add greatly to the charm of this book.

The Sidhe—"shee" is the nearest the English tongue can get to the word—are not like any English fairies, unless it be the mischievous Puck, Lob-Lie-by-the-Fire, whose self-portrait in *A Midsummer Night's Dream* accords well with their activities. They are beings much like ordinary people to look at, until they suddenly vanish, or lead you astray, or afflict you with violent pains in the back or hip, or fill your pockets with gold which turns to cow-dung in the morning. The seers and faith-healers who combat their malign influence do so by being, in some sense, in league with them, and able to steal their charms.

Her quest for stories of the Sidhe, and her good Irish, were for Lady Gregory a passport into the cottages. She was no longer a visiting Lady Bountiful, but a sympathetically received equal. She became the principal folk-lore collector of the group, for Yeats never learned Irish, and was mainly interested in stories which confirmed his own spiritualist and occult beliefs; while Hyde, who had excellent Irish, gave his main energies to the founding of his Gaelic League for the promotion of Irish as a living language. Also, it was Lady Gregory who lived on the spot, with the Sidhe clustering round her "thick as grass".

She had her geographic limitations, and perhaps also some limitations of sex and social class. Some of the tales may have been bowdlerised for her ear, and the wicked landlord, who loomed so large in peasant experience, is notably absent from her accounts. (The Gregorys had always been good landlords, and it goes without saying that she continued the tradition.) Nevertheless, the modern experts of the Irish Folk-lore Commission have the highest respect for her integrity and accuracy. She is in the best sense objective; probably a sceptic, who in the haunted woods of Coole "never met anything worse than myself," but it does not occur to one to question the point. One merely registers that this is what old Mrs. Casey or Michael Barrett said.

The chief benefit of the folk-lore collecting on her own work is not the supernatural element, never very comfortably introduced into her plays, but the deepening of her knowledge of the peasant mind. It can be classically comic, as in the conversation of the two old men in *The Workhouse Ward,* some of it taken word for word from the "Banshee" section of this book; or it can be deeply pathetic, as in the contrasted women of *The Gaol Gate.* And the assembling of a dramatist's material can almost be seen in the composite picture that is gradually built of up Biddy Early, the Clare wise woman and healer, twenty years dead but still a living presence in the folk memory. Biddy is a fascinating character, humorous, generous, humane, ("it's a thing you never should do, to beat a child that breaks a cup or a jug.") Her one weakness seems to have been a propensity for

7

marrying much younger husbands, and then letting them make free with the whisky brought to her by the grateful clientele.

Lady Gregory and her friends were fortunate to catch the last flowering of a great oral tradition. Already scepticism was setting in among the younger people—though I very much question whether all the "visions and beliefs" are outmoded today. But in any event, it would be a very superficial reading which regarded her book as a mere hotchpotch of quaint superstitions. For it is obvious that these stories are myths and symbols, and that through them we look directly at a life of much fear and hardship, with a high maternal and child mortality, mysterious sicknesses, (typhoid fever was endemic all along the western seaboard), sudden disasters by land and sea, and the ever-present memory of the Great Famine, when the Sidhe had turned the potatoes black in the ground.

And it may further occur to more readers than myself that these myths are uncomfortably valid still, just as are the Greek. Advances in medicine and the Welfare State have mercifully cushioned us against some of the disasters afflicting the Irish working people at the turn of the century, but the realities of suffering and death are inescapable, and we know it. We too consult seers and healers, and often less honest ones than Biddy Early, who would not take a poor woman's shilling when she knew there was no cure. We too are "away" when the tension grows too much for us, though we call it by names like nervous breakdown and neurosis. And we too seek shelter from our human condition behind a barrier of symbols; but it is very seldom we achieve the vivid poetic personification that came so naturally to Lady Gregory's untutored peasantry, living dangerously under their great rain-washed skies on the extreme edge of the western world.

Elizabeth Coxhead

PREFACE

THE Sidhe cannot make themselves visible to all. They are shape-changers; they can grow small or grow large, they can take what shape they choose; they appear as men or women wearing clothes of many colours, of today or of some old forgotten fashion, or they are seen as bird or beast, or as a barrel or a flock of wool. They go by us in a cloud of dust; they are as many as the blades of grass. They are everywhere; their home is in the forths, the lisses, the ancient round grass-grown mounds. There are thorn-bushes they gather near and protect; if they have a mind for a house like our own they will build it up in a moment. They will remake a stone castle, battered by Cromwell's men if it takes their fancy, filling it with noise and lights. Their own country is Tir-nan-Og—the Country of the Young. It is under the ground or under the sea, or it may not be far from any of us. As to their food, they will use common things left for them on the hearth or outside the threshold, cold potatoes it may be, or a cup of water or of milk. But for their feasts they choose the best of all sorts, taking it from the solid world, leaving some worthless likeness in its place; when they rob the potatoes from the ridges the diggers find but rottenness and decay, they take the strength from the meat in the pot, so that when put on the plates it does not nourish. They will not touch salt; there is danger to them in it. They will go to good cellars to bring away the wine.

Fighting is heard among them, and music that is more beautiful than any of this world; they are seen dancing on the rocks; they are often seen playing at the hurling, hitting balls towards the goal. In each one of their households there is a queen, and she has more power than the rest; but the greatest power belongs to their fool, the Fool of the Forth, Amadan-na-Briona. He is their strongest, the most wicked, the most deadly; there is no cure for any one he has struck.

When they are friendly to a man they give him help in his work, putting their strength into his body. Or they may tell him where to find treasure, hidden gold; or through certain wise men or women who have learned from them or can ask and get their knowledge they will tell where cattle that have strayed may be found, or they will cure the sick or tell if a sickness is not to be cured. They will sometimes work as if against their own will or intention, giving back to the life of our world one who had received the call to go over to their own. They call many there, summoning them perhaps through the eye of a neighbour, the evil eye, or by a touch, a blow, a fall, a sudden terror. Those who have received their touch waste away from this world, lending their strength to the invisible ones; for the strength of a human body is needed by the shadows, it may be in their fighting, and certainly in their hurling to win the goal. Young men are taken for this, young mothers are taken that they may give the breast to newly born children among the Sidhe, young girls that they may themselves become mothers there.

While these are away a body in their likeness, or the likeness of a body, is left lying in their place. They may be given leave to return to their village after a while, seven years it may be, or twice or three times seven. But some are sent back only at the end of the years allotted them at the time of their birth, old spent men and women, thought to have been dead a long time, given back to die and be buried on the face of the earth.

There are two races among the Sidhe. One is tall and handsome, gay, and given to jesting and to playing pranks, leading us astray in the fields, giving gold that turns to withered leaves or to dust. These ride on horses through the night-time in large companies and troops, or ride in coaches, laughing and decked with flowers and fine clothes. The people of the other race are small, malicious, wide-bellied, carrying before them a bag. When a man or woman is about to die, a woman of the Sidhe will sometimes cry for a warning, keening and making lamentation. At the hour of death fighting may be heard in the air or about the house—that is, when the man in danger has friends among the shadows, who are fighting on his behalf.

The dead are often seen among them, and will give help in danger to comrade or brother or friend. Sometimes they have a penance to work out, and will come and ask the living for help, for prayers, for the payment of a debt. They may wander in some strange shape, or be bound in the one place, or go through the air as birds. When the Sidhe pass by in a blast of wind we should say some words of blessing, for there may be among them some of our own dead. The dead are of the nature of the Saints, mortals who have put on immortality, who have known the

10

troubles of the world. The Sidhe have been, like the Angels, from before the making of the earth. In the old times in Ireland they were called gods or the children of gods; now it is laid down they are those Angels who were cast out of heaven, being proud.

This is the news I have been given of the people of the Sidhe by many who have seen them and some who have known their power.

A. G.

Coole, February, 1916.

CONTENTS

I

SEA-STORIES

"The Celtic Twilight" *was the first book of Mr. Yeats's that I* *read, and even before I met him, a little time later, I had begun* *looking for news of the invisible world; for his stories were of* *Sligo and I felt jealous for Galway. This beginning of know-* *ledge was a great excitement to me, for though I had heard all* *my life some talk of the faeries and the banshee (have indeed* *reason to believe in this last), I had never thought of giving* *heed to what I, in common with my class, looked on as fancy or* *superstition. It was certainly because of this unbelief that I had* *been told so little about them. Even when I began to gather* *these stories, I cared less for the evidence given in them than for* *the beautiful rhythmic sentences in which they were told. I had* *no theories, no case to prove, I but "held up a clean mirror to* *tradition."*

It is hard to tell sometimes what has been a real vision and what is tradition, a legend hanging in the air, a "vanity" as our people call it, made use of by a story-teller here and there, or impressing itself as a real experience on some sensitive and imaginative mind. For tradition has a large place in "the Book of the People" showing a sowing and re-sowing, a continuity and rebirth as in nature. "Those," "The Others," "The Fallen Angels" have some of the attributes of the gods of ancient Ireland; we may even go back yet farther to the early days of the world when the Sons of God mated with the Daughters of Men. I believe that if Christianity could be blotted out and forgotten tomorrow, our people would not be moved at all from the belief in a spiritual world and an unending life; it has been with them since the Druids taught what Lucan called "the happy error of the immortality of the soul." I think we found nothing so trivial in our search but it may have been worth the lifting; a clue, a thread, leading through the maze to that mountain top where things visible and invisible meet.

To gather folk-lore one needs, I think, leisure, patience, reverence, and a good memory. I tried not to change or alter anything, but to write down the very words in which the story had been told. Sometimes Mr. Yeats was with me at the telling;

or I would take him to hear for himself something I had been told, that he might be sure I had missed or added nothing. I filled many copybooks, and came to have a very faithful memory for all sides of folk-lore, stories of saints, of heroes, of giants and enchanters, as well as for these visions. For this I have had to "pay the penalty" by losing in some measure that useful and practical side of memory that is concerned with names and dates and the multiplication table, and the numbers on friends' houses in a street.

It was on the coast I began to gather these stories, and I went after a while to the islands Inishmor, Inishmaan, Inisheer, and so I give the sea-stories first.

I was told by:

A Man on the Height near Dun Conor:

It's said there's everything in the sea the same as on the land, and we know there's horses in it. This boy here saw a horse one time out in the sea, a grey one, swimming about. And there were three men from the north island caught a horse in their nets one night when they were fishing for mackerel, but they let it go; it would have broke the boat to bits if they had brought it in, and anyhow they thought it was best to leave it. One year at Kinvara, the people were missing their oats that was eaten in the fields, and they watched one night and it was five or six of the sea-horses they saw eating the oats, but they could not take them, they made off to the sea.

And there was a man on the north island fishing on the rocks one time, and a mermaid came up before him, and was partly like a fish and the rest like a woman. But he called to her in the name of God to be off, and she went and left him.

There was a boy was sent over here one morning early by a friend of mine on the other side of the island, to bring over some cattle that were in a field he had here, and it was before daylight, and he came to the door crying, and said he heard thirty horses or more galloping over the roads there, where you'd think no horse could go.

Surely those things are on the sea as well as on the land. My father was out fishing one night off Tyrone and something came beside the boat, that had eyes shining like candles. And then a wave came in, and a storm rose of a moment, and whatever was in the wave, the weight of it had like to sink the boat. And then they saw that it was a woman in the sea that had the shining eyes. So my father went to the priest, and he bid him always to take a drop of holy water and a pinch of salt out in the boat with him, and nothing would harm him.

A Galway Bay Lobster-Seller:
They are on the sea as well as on the land, and their boats are often to be seen on the bay sailing boats and others. They look like our own, but when you come near them they are gone in an instant.[1]

My mother one time thought she saw our own boat come in to the pier with my father and two other men in it, and she got the supper ready, but when she went down to the pier and called them there was nothing there, and the boat didn't come in till two hours after.

There were three or four men went out one day to fish, and it was a dead calm; but all of a sudden they heard a blast and they looked, and within about three mile of the boat they saw twelve men from the waist, the rest of them was under water. And they had sticks in their hands and were striking one another. And where they were, and the blast, it was rough, but smooth and calm on each side.

There's a sort of a light on the sea sometimes; some call it a "Jack O'Lantern" and some say it is sent by *them* to mislead them.[2]

There's many of them out in the sea, and often they pull the boats down.[3] It's about two years since four fishermen went out from Aran, two fathers and two sons, where they saw a big ship coming in and flying the flag for a pilot, and they thought she wanted to be brought in to Galway. And when they got near the ship, it faded away to nothing and the boat turned over and they were all four drowned.

There were two brothers of my own went to fish for the herrings, and what they brought up was like the print of a cat, and it turned with the inside of the skin outside, and no hair. So they pulled up the nets, and fished no more that day. There was one of *them* lying on the strand here, and some of the men of the village came down of a sudden and surprised him. And when he saw he was taken he began a great crying. But they only lifted him down to the sea and put him back into it. Just

like a man they said he was. And a little way out there was
another just like him, and when he saw that they treated
the one on shore so kindly, he bowed his head as if to thank
them.

Whatever's on the land, there's the same in the sea, and between the islands of Aran they can often see the horses galloping about at the bottom.[4]

There was a sort of a big eel used to be in Tully churchyard,
used to come and to root up the bodies, but I didn't hear of him
of late—he may be done away with now.

There was one Curran told me one night he went down to
the strand where he used to be watching for timber thrown up
and the like. And on the strand, on the dry sands, he saw a boat,
a grand one with sails spread and all, and it up farther than any
tide had ever reached. And he saw a great many people round
about it, and it was all lighted up with lights. And he got afraid
and went away. And four hours after, after sunrise, he went
there again to look at it, and there was no sign of it, or of any
fire, or of any other thing. The Mara-warra (mermaid) was seen
on the shore not long ago, combing out her hair. She had no
fish's tail, but was like another woman.

John Corley:

There is no luck if you meet a mermaid and you out at sea,
but storms will come, or some ill will happen.

There was a ship on the way to America, and a mermaid was
seen following it, and the bad weather began to come. And the
captain said, "It must be some man in the ship she's following,
and if we knew which one it was, we'd put him out to her and
save ourselves." So they drew lots, and the lot fell on one man,
and then the captain was sorry for him, and said he'd give him
a chance till tomorrow. And the next day she was following them
still, and they drew lots again, and the lot fell on the same man.
But the captain said he'd give him a third chance, but the third
day the lot fell on him again. And when they were going to
throw him out he said, "Let me alone for a while." And he went
to the end of the ship and he began to sing a song in Irish, and
when he sang, the mermaid began to be quiet and to rock like
as if she was asleep. So he went on singing till they came to
America, and just as they got to the land the ship was thrown
up into the air, and came down on the water again. There's a
man told me that was surely true.

And there was a boy saw a mermaid down by Spiddal not long ago, but he saw her before she saw him, so she did him no harm. But if she'd seen him first, she'd have brought him away and drowned him.

Sometimes a light will come on the sea before the boats to guide them to the land. And my own brother told me one day he was out and a storm came on of a sudden, and the sail of the boat was let down as quick and as well as if two men were in it. Some neighbour or friend it must have been that did that for him. Those that go down to the sea after the tide going out, to cut the weed, often hear under the sand the sound of the milk being churned. There's some didn't believe that till they heard it themselves.

A Man from Roundstone:

One night I was out on the boat with another man, and we saw a big ship near us with about twenty lights. She was as close to us as that rock (about thirty yards), but we saw no one on board. And she was like some of the French ships that sometimes come to Galway. She went on near us for a while, and then she turned towards the shore and then we knew that she was not a right ship. And she went straight on to the land, and when she touched it, the lights went out and we saw her no more.

There was a comrade of mine was out one night, and a ship came after him, with lights, and she full of people. And as they drew near the land, he heard them shouting at him and he got afraid, and he went down and got a coal of fire and threw it at the ship, and in a minute it was gone.

A Schoolmaster:

A boy told me last night of two men that went with poteen to the Island of Aran. And when they were on the shore they saw a ship coming as if to land, and they said, "We'll have the bottle ready for those that are coming." But when the ship came close to the land, it vanished. And presently they got their boat ready and put to sea. And a sudden blast came and swept one of them off. And the other saw him come up again, and put out the oar across his breast for him to take hold of it. But he would not take it but said, "I'm all right again now," and sank down again and was never seen no more.

19

John Nagle:

For one there's on the land there's ten on the sea. When I lived at Ardfry there was never a night but there was a voice heard crying and roaring, by them that were out in the bay. A baker he was from Loughrea, used to give short weight and measure, and so he was put there for a punishment.

I saw a ship that was having a race with another go suddenly down into the sea, and no one could tell why. And afterwards one of the Government divers was sent down to look for her, and he told me he'd never as long as he'd live go down again, for there at the bottom he found her, and the captain and the saloon passengers, and all sitting at the table and eating their dinner, just as they did before.

A Little Girl:

One time a woman followed a boat from Galway twenty miles out, and when they saw that she was some bad thing, wanting some of them, they drowned her.

Mrs. Casey:

I was at home and I got some stories from a man I had suspected of having newses. And he told me that when he was a youngster he was at a height where there used to be a great many of them. And all of a sudden he saw them fly out to where a boat was coming from Duras with seaweed. And they went in two flights, and so fast that they swept the water away from each side the boat, and it was left on the sand, and this they did over and over, just to be humbugging the man in the boat, and he was kept there a long time. When they first rose up, they were like clouds of dust, but with all sorts of colours, and then he saw their faces turned, but they kept changing colour every minute.[5] Laughing and humbugging they seemed to be.

My uncle that used to go out fishing for mackerel told me that one night some sort of a monster came under the boat and it wasn't a fish, and it had them near upset.

At an evening gathering in Inishmaan, by a Son of the House:

There was a man on this island was down on the beach one evening with his dog, and some black thing came up out of the sea, and the dog made for it and began to fight it. And the man began to run home and he called the dog, and it followed him, but every now and again it would stop and begin to fight again. And when he got to the house he called the dog in and shut the door, and whatever was outside began hitting against the door but it didn't get in. But the dog went in under the bed in the room, and before morning it was dead.

The Man of the House:

A horse I've seen myself on the sea and on the rocks—a brown one, just like another. And I threw a stone at it, and it was gone in a minute. We often heard there was fighting amongst *these*. And one morning before daybreak I went down to the strand with some others, and the whole of the strand, and it low tide, was covered with blood.

Colman Kane:

I knew a woman on this island and she and her daughter went down to the strand one morning to pick weed, and a wave came and took the daughter away. And a week after that, the mother saw her coming to the house, but she didn't speak to her.

There was a man coming from Galway here and he had no boatman. And on the way he saw a man that was behind him in the boat, that was putting up the sail and taking the management of everything, and he spoke no word. And he was with him all the way, but when the boat came to land, he was gone, and the man isn't sure, but he thinks it was his brother.

You see that sand below on the south side. When the men are out with the mackerel boats at early morning, they often see those sands covered with boys and girls.

There were some men out fishing in the bay one time, and a man came and held on to the boat, and wanted them to make room for him to get in, and after a time he left them. He was one of *those*. And there was another of them came up on the rocks one day, and called out to Martin Flaherty that was going out and asked what was his name.

There's said to be another island out there that's enchanted, and there are some that see it. And it's said that a fisherman landed on it one time, and he saw a little house, and he went in, and a very nice-looking young woman came out and said, "What will you say to me?" and he said, "You are a very nice lady." And a second came and asked him the same thing and a third, and he made the same answer. And after that they said, "You'd

best run of your life," and so he did, and his curragh was floating along and he had but just time to get into it, and the island
was gone. But if he had said "God bless you," the island would
have been saved.

A Fisherman on Kilronan Pier:

I don't give in to these things myself, but they'd make you
believe them in the middle island. Mangan, that I lodged with
there, told me of seeing a ship when he was out with two other
men, that followed them and vanished. And he said one of the
men took to his bed from that time and died. And Doran told
me about the horse he saw, that was in every way like a horse
you'd see on land. And a man on the south island told me how
he saw a calf one morning on the strand, and he thought it belonged to a neighbour, and was going to drive it up to his field,
when its mother appeared on the sea, and it went off to
her.

They are in the sea as well as on the land. That is well known
by those that are out fishing by the coast. When the weather is
calm, they can look down sometimes and see cattle and pigs and
all such things as we have ourselves. And at nights their boats
come out and they can be seen fishing, but they never last out
after one o'clock.

The cock always crows on the first of March every year at
one o'clock. And there was a man brought a cock out with him
in his boat to try them. And the first time when it crowed they
all vanished. That is how they were detected.

There are more of them in the sea than on the land, and they
sometimes try to come over the side of the boat in the form of
fishes, for they can take their choice shape.

Pat O'Hagan:

There was two fine young women—red-haired women—died
in my village about six months ago. And I believe they're living
yet. And there are some have seen them appear. All I ever saw
myself was one day I was out fishing with two others, and we
saw a canoe coming near us, and we were afraid it would come
near enough to take away our fish. And as we looked it turned
into a three-masted ship, and people in it. I could see them well,
dark-coloured and dressed like sailors. But it went away and did
us no harm.

One night I was going down to the curragh, and it was a night

22

in harvest, and the stars shining, and I saw a ship fully rigged going towards the coast of Clare where no ship could go. And when I looked again, she was gone.

And one morning early, I and other men that were with me, and one of them a friend of the man here, saw a ship coming to the island, and he thought she wanted a pilot, and put out in the curragh. But when we got to where she was, there was no sign of her, but where she was the water was covered with black gulls, and I never saw a black gull before, thousands and crowds of them, and not one white bird among them. And one of the boys that was with me took a tarpin and threw it at one of the gulls and hit it on the head, and when he did, the curragh went down to the rowlocks in the water—up to that—and it's nothing but a miracle she ever came up again, but we got back to land. I never went to a ship again, for the people said it was on account of me helping in the Preventive Service it happened, and that if I'd hit at one of the gulls myself, there would have been a bad chance for us. But those were no right gulls, and the ship was no living ship.

The Old Man in the Kitchen:

It's in the middle island the most of them are, and I'll tell you a thing that I know of myself that happened not long ago. There was a young girl, and one evening she was missing, and they made search for her everywhere and they thought that she was drowned or that she had gone away with some man. And in the evening of the next day there was a boy out in a curragh, and as he passed by a rock that is out in the sea there was the girl on it, and he brought her off. And surely she could not go there by herself. I suppose she wasn't able to give much account of it, and now she's after going to America.[6]

And in Aran there were three boys and their uncle went out to a ship they saw coming, to pilot her into the bay. But when they got to where she was, there was no ship, and a sea broke over the canoe, and they were drowned, all fine strong men. But a man they had with them that was no use or of no account, he came safe to land. And I know a man in this island saw curraghs and curraghs full of people about the island of a Sunday morning early, but I never saw them myself. And one Sunday morning in my time there were scores and scores lying their length by the sea on the sand below, and they saw a woman in the sea, up to her waist, and she racking her hair and settling

23

herself and as clean and as nice as if she was on land. Scores of them saw that.

There's a house up there where the family have to leave a plate of potatoes ready every night, and all's gone in the morning.[7]

They are said to have all things the same as ourselves under the sea, and one day a cow was seen swimming as if for the headland, but before she got to it she turned another way and went down. And one time I got a small muc-warra (porpoise) and I went to cut it up to get what was good of it, for it had about two inches of fat, and when I cut it open the heart and the liver and every bit of it were for all the world like a pig you would cut up on land.

There's a house in the village close by this that's haunted. My sister was sitting near it one day, and it empty and locked, and some other little girls, and they heard a noise in it, and at the same time the flags they were sitting on grew red-hot, that they had to leave them. And another time the woman of the house was sick, and a little girl that was sitting by the fire in the kitchen saw standing in the door the sister of the woman that was sick, and she a good while dead, and she put up her arm, as if to tell her not to notice her. And the poor woman of that house, she had no luck, nothing but miscarriages or dead babies. And one child lived to be nine months old, and there was less flesh on it at the end of the nine months than there was the day it was born. She has a little girl now that's near a year old, but her arm isn't the size of that, and she's crabbed and not like a child as she should be. Many a one that's long married without having a child goes to the fortune-teller in Galway, and those that think anything of themselves go to Roundstone.

A Man near Loughmore:
I know a woman was washed and laid out, and it went so far that two half-penny candles were burned over her. And then she sat up, came back again, and spoke to her husband, and told him how to divide his property, and to manage the children well. And her step-son began to question her, and he might have got a lot out of her but her own son stopped him and said to let her alone. And then she turned over on her side and died. She was not to say an old woman. It's not often the old are taken. What use would there be for them? But a woman to be taken young, you know there's demand for her. It's the people in the middle

island know about these things. There were three boys from there lost in a curragh at the point near the lighthouse, and for long after their friends were tormented when they came there fishing, and they would see ships there when the people of this island that were out at the same time couldn't see them. There were three or four out in a curragh near the lighthouse, and a conger-eel came and upset it, and they were all saved but one, but he was brought down and for the whole day they could hear him crying and screeching under the sea. And they were not the only ones, but a fisherman that was there from Galway had to go away and leave it, because of the screeching.

There was a coast-guard's wife there was all but gone, but she was saved after. And there's a boy here now was for a long time that they'd give the world he was gone altogether, with the state he was in, and now he's as strong as any boy in the island; and if ever any one was away and came back again, it was him. Children used often to be taken, but there's a great many charms in use in these days that saves them. A big sewing-needle you'll see the woman looking for to put back again into the world before they die in the place of some young person. And even a beast of any consequence if anything happens to it, no one in the island would taste it; there might be something in it, some old woman or the like.

There were a few young men from here were kept in Galway for a day, and they went to a woman there that works the cards. And she told them of deaths that would come in certain families. And it wasn't a fortnight after that five boys were out there, just where you see the curragh now, and they were upset and every one drowned, and they were of the families that she had named on the cards.

My uncle told me that one night they were all up at that house up the road, making a match for his sister, and they stopped till near morning, and when they went out, they all had a drop taken. And he was going along home with two or three others and one of them, Michael Flaherty, said he saw people on the shore. And another of them said that there were not, and my uncle said, "If Flaherty said that and it not true, we have a right to bite the ear off him, and it would be no harm." And then they parted, and my uncle had to pass by the beach, and then he saw whole companies of people coming up from the sea, that he didn't know how he'd get through them, but they opened before him and let him pass.

There were men going to Galway with cattle one morning from the beach down there, and they saw a man up to his middle in the sea—all of them saw it.

There was a man was down early for lobsters on the shore at the middle island, and he saw a horse up to its middle in the sea, and bowing its head down as if to drink. And after he had watched it awhile it disappeared.

There was a woman walking over by the north shore—God have mercy on her—she's dead since–and she looked out and saw an island in the sea, and she was a long time looking at it. It's known to be there, and to be enchanted, but only few can see it.

There was a man had his horse drawing seaweed up there on the rocks, the way you see them drawing it every day, in a basket on the mare's back. And on this day every time he put the load on, the mare would let its leg slip and it would come down again, and he was vexed and he had a stick in his hand and he gave the mare a heavy blow. And that night she had a foal that was dead, not come to its full growth, and it had spots over it, and every spot was of a different colour. And there was no sire on the island at that time, so whatever was the sire must have come up from the sea.[8]

A Man Watching the Weed-gatherers:
There's no doubt at all about the sea-horses. There was a man out at the other side of the island, and he saw one standing on the rocks and he threw a stone at it and it went off in the sea. He said it was grand to see it swimming, and the mane and the tail floating on the top of the water.

A Woman from the Connemara Side:
I was told there was a mare that had a foal, and it had never had a horse. And one day the mare and foal were down by the sea, and a horse put up its head and neighed, and away went the foal to it and came back no more.

And there was a man on this island watched his field one night where he thought the neighbours' cattle were eating his grass, and what he saw was horses and foals coming up from the sea. And he caught a foal and kept it, and set it racing, and no horse or no pony could ever come near it, till one day the race was on the strand, and away with it into the sea, and the jockey along with it, and they never were seen again.

26

Mrs. O'Dea and Mrs. Daly:

There was a cow seen come up out of the sea one day and it walked across the strand, and its udder like as if it had been lately milked. And Tommy Donohue was running up to tell his father to come down and see it, and when he looked back it was gone out to sea again.

There was a man here was going to build a new house, and he brought a wise woman to see would it be in the right place. And she made five heaps of stones in five places, and said, "Whatever heap isn't knocked in the night, build it there." And in the morning all the heaps were knocked but one, and so he built it there.[9]

One time I was out over by that island with another man, and we saw three women standing by the shore, beating clothes with a beetle. And while we looked, they vanished, and then we heard the cry of a child passing over our heads twenty feet in the air.

I know they go out fishing like ourselves, for Father Mahony told me so; and one night I was out myself with my brother, beyond where that ship is, and we heard talk going on, so we knew that a boat was near, and we called out to let them know we heard them, and then we saw the boat and it was just like any other one, and the talk went on, but we couldn't understand what they were saying. And then I turned to light my pipe, and while I lighted it, the boat and all in it were gone.

Mrs. Casey:

I got a story from an old man down by the sea at Tyrone. He says there was a man went down one night to move his boat from the shore where it was to the pier. And when he had put out, he found it was going out to sea, instead of to touch the pier, and he felt it very heavy in the water, and he looked behind him and there on the back of the boat were six men in shiny black clothes like sailors, and there was one like a harvest-man dressed in white flannel with a belt round his waist. And he asked what they were doing, and the man in white said he had brought the others out to make away with them there, and he took and cut their bodies in two and threw them one by one over the boat, and then he threw himself after them into the sea. And the boat went under water too, and the poor man himself lost his wits, but it came up again and he said he had never seen as many people as he did in that minute under the water. And then he got home

27

and left the boat, and in the morning he came down to it, and there was blood in it; and first he washed it and then he painted it, but for all he could do, he couldn't get rid of the blood.

Peter Donohue:
There was a woman, a friend of this man's, living out in the middle island, and one day she came down to where a man of this island was putting out his curragh to come back, and she said, "I just saw a great crowd of them—that's the Sheogue—going over to your island like a cloud." And when he got home he went up to a house there beyond, where the old woman used to be selling poteen on the sly. And while he was there her little boy came running in and cried, "Hide away the poteen, for the police are on the island! Such a man called to me from his curragh to give warning, for he saw the road full of them with the crowd of them and they with their guns and cutlasses and all the rest." But the man was in the house first knew well what it was, after what he heard from the woman on the other island, and that they were no right police, and sure enough no other one ever saw them. And that same day, my mother had put out wool to dry in front of where that house is with the three chimneys, near the Chapel. And I was there talking to some man, one on each side of the yard, and the wall between us. And the day was as fine as this day is and finer, and not a breath of air stirring. And a woman that lived near by had her wool out drying too. And the wool that was in my mother's yard began to rise up, as if something was under it, and I called to the other man to help me to hold it down, but for all we could do it went up in the air, a hundred feet and more, till we could see it no more. And after a couple of hours it began to drop again, like snow, some on the thatch and some on the rocks and some in the gardens. And I think it was a fortnight before my mother had done gathering it. And one day she was spinning it, I don't know what put it in my mind, but I asked her did she lose much of that wool. And what she said was, "If I didn't get more than my own, I didn't get less." That's true and no lie, for I never told a lie in my life—I think. But the wool belonging to the neighbouring woman was never stirred at all.

And the woman that had the wool that wasn't stirred, she is the woman I married after, and that's now my wife.

There was a man, one Power, died in this island, and one night that was bright there was a friend of his going out for mackerel, and he saw these sands full of people hurling, and he well knew Power's voice that he heard among them.

There was a cousin of my own built a new house, and when they were first in it and sitting round the fire, the woman of the house that was singing for them saw a great blot of blood come down the chimney on to the floor, and they thought there would be no luck in the house and that it was a wrong place. But they had nothing but good luck ever after.

Peter Dolan:
There was a man that died in the middle island, that had two wives. And one day he was out in the curragh he saw the first wife appear. And after that one time the son of the second wife was sick, and the little girl, the first wife's daughter, was out tending cattle, and a can of water with her and she had a waist-coat of her father's put about her body, where it was cold. And her mother appeared to her in the form of a sheep, and spoke to her, and told her what herbs to find, to cure the step-brother, and sure enough they cured him. And she bid her leave the waistcoat there and the can, and she did. And in the morning the waistcoat was folded there, and the can standing on it. And she appeared to her in her own shape another time, after that. Why she came like a sheep the first time was that she wouldn't be frightened. The girl is in America now, and so is the step-brother got well.[10]

A Galway Woman:
One time myself, I was up at the well beyond, and looking into it, a very fine day, and no breath of air stirring, and the stooks were ripe standing about me. And all in a minute a noise began in them, and they were like as if knocking at each other and fighting like soldiers all about me.

Mary Moran:
There was a girl here that had been to America and came back, and one day she was coming over from Liscannor in a curragh, and she looked back and there behind the curragh was the "Gan ceann" the headless one. And he followed the boat a great way, but she said nothing. But a gold pin that was in her hair fell out, and into the sea, that she had brought from America, and then it disappeared. And her sister was always asking her where was the pin she brought from America, and she was

afraid to say. But at last she told her, and the sister said, "It's well for you it fell out, for what was following you would never have left you, till you threw it a ring or something made of gold." It was the sister herself that told me this.

Up in the village beyond they think a great deal of these things and they won't part with a drop of milk on May Eve, and last Saturday week that was May Eve there was a poor woman dying up there, and she had no milk of her own, and as is the custom, she went out to get a drop from one or other of the neighbours. But not one would give it because it was May Eve. I declare I cried when I heard it, for the poor woman died on the second day after.

And when my sister was going to America she went on the first of May and we had a farewell party the night before, and in the night a little girl that was there saw a woman from that village go out, and she watched her, and saw her walk round a neighbour's house, and pick some straw from the roof.

And she told of it, and it happened a child had died in that house and the father said the woman must have had a hand in it, and there was no good feeling to her for a long while. Her own husband is lying sick now, so I hear.

II

SEERS AND HEALERS

BIDDY EARLY

In talking to the people I often heard the name of Biddy Early,
and I began to gather many stories of her, some calling her a
healer and some a witch. Some said she had died a long time
ago, and some that she was still living. I was sure after a while
that she was dead, but was told that her house was still stand-
ing, and was on the other side of Slieve Echtge, between Feakle
and Tulla. So one day I set out and drove Shamrock, my pony,
to a shooting lodge built by my grandfather in a fold of the
mountains, and where I had sometimes, when a young girl,
stayed with my brothers when they were shooting the wild deer
that came and sheltered in the woods. It had like other places
on our estate a border name brought over from Northumber-
land, but though we called it Chevy Chase the people spoke of
its woods and outskirts as Daire-caol, the Narrow Oak Wood,
and Daroda, the Two Roads, and Druim-da-Rod, their Ridge.
I stayed the night in the low thatched house, setting out next
day for Feakle "eight strong miles over the mountain." It was
a wild road, and the pony had to splash his way through two
unbridged rivers, swollen with the summer rains. The red mud
of the road, the purple heather and foxglove, the brown bogs
were a contrast to the grey rocks and walls of Burren and
Aidhne, and there were many low hills, brown when near, misty
blue in the distance; then the Golden Mountain, Slieve nan-Or,
"where the last great battle will be fought before the end of the
world." Then I was out of Connacht into Clare, the brown turn-
ing to green pasture as I drove by Raftery's Lough Greine.
  I put up my pony at a little inn. There were portraits of John
Dillon and Michael Davitt hanging in the parlour, and the land-
lady told me Parnell's likeness had been with them, until the
priest had told her he didn't think well of her hanging it there.
There was also on the wall, in a frame, a warrant for the arrest
of one of her sons, signed by, I think, Lord Cowper, in the
days of the Land War. "He got half a year in gaol the same year

31

Parnell did. *He got sick there, and though he lived for some years the doctor said when he died the illness he got in gaol had to do with his death."*

I had been told how to find Biddy Early's house "beyond the little humpy bridge," and I walked on till I came to it, a poor cottage enough, high up on a mass of rock by the roadside. There was only a little girl in the house, but her mother came in afterwards and told me that Biddy Early had died about twenty years before, and that after they had come to live in the house they had been "annoyed for a while" by people coming to look for her. She had sent them away, telling them Biddy Early was dead, though a friendly priest had said to her, "Why didn't you let on you were her and make something out of them?" She told me some of the stories I give below, and showed me the shed where the healer had consulted with her invisible friends. I had already been given by an old patient of hers a "bottle" prepared for the cure, but which she had been afraid to use. It lies still unopened on a shelf in my storeroom. When I got back at nightfall to the lodge in the woods I found many of the neighbours gathered there, wanting to hear news of "the Tulla Woman" and to know for certain if she was dead. I think as time goes on her fame will grow and some of the myths that always hang in the air will gather round her, for I think the first thing I was told of her was, "There used surely to be enchanters in the old time, magicians and freemasons. Old Biddy Early's power came from the same thing."[11]

An Old Woman in the Lodge Kitchen says:
Do you remember the time John Kevin beyond went to see Biddy Early, for his wife, she was sick at the time. And Biddy Early knew everything, and that there was a forth behind her house, and she said, "Your wife is too fond of going out late at night."

I was told by a Gate-keeper:
There was a man at Cranagh had one of his sheep shorn in the night, and all the wool taken. And he got on his horse and went to Feakle and Biddy Early, and she told him the name of the man that did it, and where it was hidden, and so he got it back again.

There was a man went to Biddy Early, and she told him that the woman he'd marry would have had her husband killed by his brother. And so it happened, for the woman he married was sitting by the fire with her husband, and the brother came in, having a drop of drink taken, and threw a pint pot at him that hit him on the head and killed him. It was the man that married her that told me this.

Mrs. Kearns:
Did I know any one that was taken by them? Well, I never knew one that was brought back again. Himself went one time to Biddy Early for his uncle, Donohue, that was sick, and he found her there and her fingers all covered with big gold rings, and she gave him a bottle, and she said: "Go in no house on your way home, or stop nowhere, or you'll lose it." But going home he had a thirst on him and he came to a public-house, and he wouldn't go in, but he stopped and bid the boy bring him out a drink. But a little farther on the road the horse got a fall, and the bottle was broke.

Mrs. Cregan:
It's I was with this woman here to Biddy Early. And when she saw me, she knew it was for my husband I came, and she looked in her bottle and she said, "It's nothing put upon him by my people that's wrong with him." And she bid me give him cold oranges and some other things—herbs. He got better after.

Daniel Curtin:
Did I ever hear of Biddy Early? There's not a man in this countryside over forty year old that hasn't been with her some time or other. There's a man living in that house over there was sick one time, and he went to her, and she cured him, but says she, "You'll have to lose something, and don't fret after it." So he had a grey mare and she was going to foal, and one morning when he went out he saw that the foal was born, and was lying dead by the side of the wall. So he remembered what she said to him and he didn't fret.
There was one Dillane in Kinvara, Sir William knew him well, and he went to her one time for a cure. And Father Andrew came to the house and was mad with him for going, and says he, "You take the cure out of the hands of God." And Mrs. Dillane said, "Your Reverence, none of us can do that." "Well," says

c   33

Father Andrew, "then I'll see what the devil can do and I'll send my horse tomorrow, that has a sore in his leg this long time, and try will she be able to cure him."

So next day he sent a man with his horse, and when he got to Biddy Early's house she came out, and she told him every word that Father Andrew had said, and she cured the sore. So after that, he left the people alone; but before it, he'd be dressed in a frieze coat and a riding whip in his hand, driving away the people from going to her.

She had four or five husbands, and they all died of drink one after another. Maybe twenty or thirty people would be there in the day looking for cures, and every one of them would bring a bottle of whiskey. Wild cards they all were, or they wouldn't have married her. She'd help too to bring the butter back. Always on the first of May, it used to be taken, and maybe what would be taken from one man would be conveyed to another.

Mr. McCabe:

Biddy Early? Not far from this she lived, above at Feakle. I got cured by her myself one time. Look at this thumb—I got it hurted one time, and I went out into the field after and was ploughing all the day, I was that greedy for work. And when I went in I had to lie on the bed with the pain of it, and it swelled and the arm with it, to the size of a horse's thigh. I stopped two or three days in the bed with the pain of it, and then my wife went to see Biddy Early and told her about it, and she came home and the next day it burst, and you never seen anything like all the stuff that came away from it. A good bit after I went to her myself, where it wasn't quite healed, and she said, "You'd have lost it altogether if your wife hadn't been so quick to come." She brought me into a small room, and said holy words and sprinkled holy water and told me to believe. The priests were against her, but they were wrong. How could that be evil doing that was all charity and kindness and healing?

She was a decent looking woman, no different from any other woman of the country. The boy she was married to at the time was lying drunk in the bed. There were side-cars and common cars and gentry and country people at the door, just like Gort market, and dinner for all that came, and everyone would bring her something, but she didn't care what it was. Rich farmers would bring her the whole side of a pig. Myself, I brought a bottle of whiskey and a shilling's worth of bread, and a quarter of sugar and a quarter pound of tea. She was very rich, for there wasn't a farmer but would give her the grass of a couple of bullocks or a filly. She had the full of a field of fillies if they'd all been gathered together. She left no children, and there's no doubt at all that the reason of her being able to do cures was that she was *away* seven years. She didn't tell me about it but she spoke of it to others.

When I was coming away I met a party of country people on a cart from Limerick, and they asked where was her house, and I told them: "Go on to the cross, and turn to the left, and follow the straight road till you come to the little humpy bridge, and soon after that you'll come to the house."

But the priests would be mad if they knew that I told anyone the way.

She died about twelve year ago; I didn't go to the wake myself, or the funeral, but I heard that her death was natural.

No, Mrs. Early is no relation to Biddy Early—the nuns asked her the same thing when she was married. A cousin of hers had her hand cut with a jug that was broke, and she went up to her and when she got there, Biddy Early said: "It's a thing you never should do, to beat a child that breaks a cup or a jug." And sure enough it was a child that broke it, and she beat her for doing it. But cures she did sure enough.

Bartley Coen:

There was a neighbour of my own, Andrew Dennehy:

I was knocked up by him one night to go to the house, because he said *they* were calling to him. But when they got there, there was nothing to be found. But some see these things, and some can't. It's against our creed to believe in them. And the priests won't let on that they believe in them themselves, but they are more in dread of going about at night than any of us. They were against Biddy Early too. There was a man I knew living near the sea, and he set out to go to her one time. And on his way he went into his brother-in-law's house, and the priest came in there, and bid him not to go on. "Well, Father," says he, "cure me yourself if you won't let me go to her to be cured." And when the priest wouldn't do that (for the priests can do many cures if they like to), he went on to her. And the minute he came in, "Well," says she, "you made a great fight for me on the way." For though it's against our creed to believe it, she could hear any earthly thing that was said in every part, miles

35

off. But she had two red eyes, and some used to say, "If she can cure so much, why can't she cure her own eyes?"

No, she wasn't *away* herself. It is said it was from a son of her own she got the knowledge, a little chap that was astray. And one day when he was lying sick in the bed he said: "There's such and such a woman has a hen down in the pot, and if I had the soup of the hen, I think it would cure me." So the mother went to the house, and when she got there, sure enough, there was a hen in the pot on the fire. But she was ashamed to tell what she came for, and she let on to have only come for a visit, and so she sat down. But presently in the heat of the talking she told what the little chap had said. "Well," says the woman, "take the soup and welcome, and the hen too if it will do him any good." So she brought them with her, and when the boy saw the soup, "It can't cure me," says he, "for no earthly thing can do that. But since I see how kind and how willing you are, and did your best for me, I'll leave you a way of living." And so he did, and taught her all she knew. That's what's said at any rate.

Mr. Fahy:
Well, that's what's believed, that it's from her son Biddy Early got it. After his death always lamenting for him she was, till he came back, and gave her the gift of curing.

She had no red eyes, but was a fresh clean-looking woman; sure any one might have red eyes when they'd got a cold.

She wouldn't refuse even a person that would come from the very bottom of the black North.

I was with Biddy Early myself one time, and got a cure from her for my little girl that was sick. A bottle of whiskey I brought her, and the first thing she did was to open it and to give me a glass out of it. "For," says she, "you'll maybe want it my poor man." But I had plenty of courage in those days.

The priests were against her; often Father Boyle would speak of her in his sermons. They can all do those cures themselves, but that's a thing it's not right to be talking about.

The Little Girl of Biddy Early's House:
The people do be full of stories of all the cures she did. Once after we came to live here a carload of people came, and asked was Biddy Early here, and my mother said she was dead. When she told the priest he said she had a right to shake a bottle and

36

say she was her, and get something from them. It was by the bottle she did all, to shake it, and she'd see everything when she looked in it. Sometimes she'd give a bottle of some cure to people that came, but if she'd say to them, "You'll never bring it home," break it they should on the way home, with all the care they'd take of it.

She was as good, and better, to the poor as to the rich. Any poor person passing the road, she'd call in and give a cup of tea or a glass of whiskey to, and bread and what they wanted.

She had a big chest within in that room, and it full of pounds of tea and bottles of wine and of whiskey and of claret, and all things in the world. One time she called in a man that was passing and gave him a glass of whiskey, and then she said to him, "The road you were going home by, don't go by it." So he asked why not, and she took the bottle—a long shaped bottle it was—and looked into it, holding it up, and then she bid him look through it, and he'd see what would happen him. But her husband said, "Don't show it to him, it might give him a fright he wouldn't get over." So she only said, "Well, go home by another road." And so he did and got home safe, for in the bottle she had seen a party of men that wouldn't have let him pass alive. She got the rites of the Church when she died, but first she had to break the bottle.

It was from her brother that she got the power, when she had to go to the workhouse, and he came back, and gave her the way of doing the cures.

The Blacksmith I met near Tulla:
I know you to be a respectable lady and an honourable one because I know your brothers, meeting them as I do at the fair of Scariff. No fair it would be if they weren't there. I knew Biddy Early well, a nice fresh-looking woman she was. It's to her the people used to be flocking, to the door and even to the window, and if they'd come late in the day, they'd have no chance of getting to her, they'd have to take lodgings for the night in the town. She was a great woman. If any of the men that came into the house had a drop too much drink taken, she'd turn them out if they said an unruly word. And if any of them were fighting or disputing or going to law, she'd say, "Be at one, and ye can rule the world." The priests were against her and used to be taking the cloaks and the baskets from the country people to keep them back from going to her.

I never went to her myself—for you should know that no ill or harm ever comes to a blacksmith.

An Old Midwife:
Tell me now is there anything wrong about you or your son that you went to that house? I went there but once myself, when my little girl that was married was bad, after her second baby being born. I went to the house and told her about it, and she took the bottle and shook it and looked in it, and then she turned and said something to himself [her husband] that I didn't hear —and she just waved her hand to me like that, and bid me go home, for she would take nothing from me. But himself came out and told that what she was after seeing in the bottle was my little girl, and the coffin standing beside her. So I went home, and sure enough on the tenth day after, she was dead.

The lodge people came rushing out to see the picture of Biddy Early's house and ask, "Did she leave the power to any one else?" and I told of the broken bottle. But Mr. McCabe said, "She only had the power for her own term, and no one else could get it from her."

I asked old Mr. McCabe if he had lost anything when she cured him, and he said: "Not at that time, but sometimes I thought afterwards it came on my family when I lost so many of my children. A grand stout girl went from me, stout and broad, what would ail her to go?"

I was told by Mat King:
Biddy Early surely did thousands of cures. Out in the stable she used to go, where her *friends* met her, and they told her all things. There was a little priest long ago used to do cures— Soggarthin Mina, they used to call him—and once he came in this house he looked up and said, "There—it's full of them— there they are."

There was a man, one Flaherty, came to his brother-in-law's house one day to borrow a horse. And the next day the horse was sent back, but he didn't come himself. And after a few days more they went to ask for him, but he had never come back at all. So the brother-in-law went to Biddy Early's and she and some others were drinking whiskey, and they were sorry that they were near at the bottom of the bottle. And she said: "That's no matter, there's a man on his way now, there'll soon be more." And sure enough there was, for he brought a bottle with him. So when he came in, he told her about Flaherty having disappeared. And she described to him a corner of a garden at the back of a house and she said, "Go look and you'll find him there," and so they did, dead and buried.

Another time a man's cattle was dying, and he went to her and she said, "Is there such a place as Benburb, having a forth up on the hill beyond there? for it's there they're gone." And sure enough, it was towards that forth they were straying before they died.

An Old Man on the Beach:
The priests were greatly against Biddy Early. And there's no doubt it was from the faeries she got the knowledge. But who wouldn't go to hell for a cure if one of his own was sick? And the priests don't like to be doing cures themselves. Father Flynn said to me (rather incoherent in the high wind), if I do them, I let the devil into me. But there was Father Carey used to do them, but he went wrong, with the people bringing too much whiskey to pay him—and Father Mahony has him stopped now.

Maher of Slieve Echtge:
I knew a man went to Biddy Early, and while she was in the other room he made the tongs red hot and laid them down, and when she came back she took them up and burned herself. And he said, if she had known anything she'd have known not to touch it, that it was red hot. So he walked off and asked for no cure.

The Spinning-Woman:
Biddy Early was a witch, wherever she got it. There was a priest at Feakle spoke against her one time, and soon after he was passing near her house and she put something on the horse so that he made a bolt into the river and stopped there in the middle, and wouldn't go back or forward. Some people from the neighbourhood went to her, and she told them all about the whole place, and that one time there was a great battle about the castle, and that there is a passage going from here to the forth beyond on Dromore Hill, and to another place that's near Maher's house. And she said that there is a cure for all sicknesses

hidden between the two wheels of Ballylee mill. And how did she know that there was a mill here at all? Witchcraft wherever she got it; away she may have been in a trance. She had a son, and one time he went to the hurling beyond at some place in Tipperary, and none could stand against him; he was like a deer.

I went to Biddy Early one time myself, about my little boy that's now in America that was lying sick in the house. But on the way to her I met a sergeant of police and he asked where was I going, and when I told him, he said, to joke with me, "Biddy Early's dead." "May the devil die with her," says I. Well, when I got to the house, what do you think, if she didn't know that, and what I said. And she was vexed and at the first, she would do nothing for me. I had a pound for her here in my bosom. But when I held it out she wouldn't take it, but she turned the rings on her fingers, for she had a ring for every one, and she said, "A shilling for this one, sixpence for another one." But all she told me was that the boy was nervous, and so he was, she was right in that, and that he'd get well, and so he did.

There was a man beyond in Cloon, was walking near the gate the same day and his little boy with him, and he turned his foot and hurt it, and she knew that. She told me she slept in Ballylee mill last night, and that there was a cure for all things in the world between the two wheels there. Surely she was *away* herself, and as to her son, she brought him back with her, and for eight or nine year he lay in the bed in the house. And he'd never stir so long as she was in it, but no sooner was she gone away anywhere than he'd be out down the village among the people, and then back again before she'd get to the house.

She had three husbands, I saw one of them when I was there, but I knew by the look of him he wouldn't live long. One man I know went to her and she sent him on to a woman at Kilrush— one of her own sort, and they helped one another. She said to some woman I knew: "If you have a bowl broke or a plate throw it out of the door, and don't make any attempt to mend it, it vexes *them*."

Mrs. McDonagh:
Our religion doesn't allow us to go to fortune tellers. They don't get the knowledge from God, and so it must be from demons.

The priests took the bottle from Biddy Early before she died, and they found black things in it.

I never went to Biddy Early myself. I think there was a good deal of devilment in the things she did. The priests can do cures as well as she did, but they don't like to do them, unless they're curates that like to get the money.

There was a man in Cloughareeva and his wife was that bad she would go out in her shift at night into the field. And he went to Biddy Early and she said, "Within three days a disgraced priest will come to you and will cure her."

And after three days the disgraced priest that had been put out for drink came bowling into the house, and they reached down from the shelf a bottle of whiskey. Father Boyle was mad when he heard of it, but he cured her all the same.

There was a man on this estate, and he sixty years, and he took to the bed, and his wife went to Biddy Early and she said, "It can't be by *them* he's taken, what use would it be to them, he being so old." And Biddy Early is the one that should surely know. I went to her myself one time, to get a cure for myself when I fell coming down that hill up there, and got a hurt on my knee. And she gave me one and she told me all about the whole place, and that there was a bowl broken in the house, and so there was. The priests can do cures by the same power that she had, but those that have much stock don't like to be doing them, for they're sure to lose all.

I knew one went to Biddy Early about his wife, and as soon as she saw him, she said, "On the fourth day a discarded priest will call in and cure your wife"; and so he did—one Father James.

Mrs. Nelly:
The old man here that lost his hair went to Biddy Early but he didn't want to go, and we forced him and persuaded him. And when he got to the house she said, "It wasn't of your own free will you came here," and she wouldn't do anything for him.

She didn't like either for you to go too late. Dolan's sister was sick a long time, and when the brother went at the last to

41

Biddy Early she gave him a bottle with a cure. But on the way home the bottle was broke, and the car, and the horse got a fright and ran away. She said to him then, "Why did you go to cut down the bush of white thorn you see out of the window?" And then she told him an old woman in the village had overlooked him—Murphy's sister—and she gave him a bottle to sprinkle about her house. I suppose she didn't like that bush being interfered with, she had too much charms.

And when Doctor Folan was sent for to see her he was led astray, and it is beyond Ballylee he found himself. And surely she was *taken* if ever any one was.

An Old Woman:

I went up to Biddy Early's one time with another woman. A fine stout woman she was, sitting straight up on her chair. She looked at me and she told me that my son was worse than what I was, and for myself she bid me to take what I was taking before, and that's dandelions. Five leaves she bid me pick and lay them out on the table with three pinches of salt on the three middle ones. As to my son, she gave me a bottle for him but he wouldn't take it and he got better without.

The priests were against her, but there was one of them passed near her house one day, and his horse fell forward. And he sent his boy to her and she said, "Tell him to spit on the horse and to say, 'God bless it,'" and he did and it rose again. He had looked at it proud-like without saying "God bless it" in his heart.

Daniel Shea:

It was all you could do to get to Biddy Early with your skin whole, the priests were so set against her. I went to her one time myself, and it was hard when you got near to know the way, for all the people were afraid to tell it.

It was about a little chap of my own I went, that some strange thing had been put upon. When I got to her house there were about fifty to be attended to before me, and when my turn came she looked in the bottle, a sort of a common greenish one that seemed to have nothing in it. And she told me where I came from, and the shape of the house and the appearance of it, and of the lake you see there, and everything round about. And she told me of a lime-kiln that was near, and then she said, "The harm that came to him came from the forth beyond that." And I

42

never knew of there being a forth there, but after I came home I went to look, and there sure enough it was.

And she told me how it had come on him, and bid me remember a day that a certain gentleman stopped and spoke to me when I was out working in the hayfield, and the child with me playing about. And I remembered it well, it was old James Hill of Creen, that was riding past, and stopped and talked and was praising the child. And it was close by that forth beyond that James Hill was born.

It was soon after that day that the mother and I went to Loughrea, and when we came back, the child had slipped on the threshold of the house and got a fall, and he was screeching and calling out that his knee was hurt, and from that time he did no good, and pined away and had the pain in the knee always.

And Biddy Early said, "While you're talking to me now the child lies dying," and that was at twelve o'clock in the day. And she made up a bottle for me, herbs I believe it was made of, and she said, "Take care of it going home, and whatever may happen, don't drop it"; and she wrapped it in all the folds of my handkerchief. So when I was coming home and got near Tillyra I heard voices over the wall talking, and when I got to the Roxborough gate there were many people talking and coming to where we were. I could hear them and see them, and the man that was with me. But when I heard them I remembered what she said, and I took the bottle in my two hands and held it, and so I brought it home safely. And when I got home they told me the child was worse, and that at twelve o'clock the day before he lay as they thought dying. And when I brought the bottle to him, he pulled the bed-clothes up over his head, and we had the work of the world to make him taste it. But from the time he took it, the pain in the knee left him and he began to get better, and Biddy Early had told me not to let many days pass without coming to her again, when she gave me the bottle. But seeing him so well, I thought it no use to go again, and it was not on May Day, but it was during the month of May he died. He took to the bed before that, and he'd be always calling to me to come inside the bed where he was and if I went in, he'd hardly let me go. But I got afraid, and I didn't like to be too much with him.

He was but eight years old when he died, but Ned Cahel that used to live beyond there then told me privately that when I'd

43

be out of the house and he'd come in, the little chap would ask for the pipe, and take it and smoke it, but he'd never let me see him doing it. And he was old-fashioned in all his ways.

Another thing Biddy Early told me to do was to go out before sunrise to where there'd be a boundary wall between two or three estates, and to bring a bottle, and lay it in the grass and gather the dew into it. But there were hundreds of people she turned away, because she'd say, "What's wrong with you has nothing to do with my business."

There was a Clare woman with me when I went there, and she told me there was a boy from a village near her was brought tied in a cart to Biddy Early, and she said, "If I cure you, will you be willing to marry me?" And he said he would. So she cured him and married him. I saw him there at her house. It might be that she had the illness put upon him first.

The priests don't do cures by the same means, and they don't like to do them at all. It was in my house that you see that Father Gregan did one on Mr. Phayre. And he cured a girl up in the mountains after, and where is he now but in a madhouse. They are afraid of the power they do them by, that it will be too strong for them. Some say the bishops don't like them to do cures because the whiskey they drink to give them courage before they do them is very apt to make drunkards of them. It's not out of the prayer-book they read, but out of the Roman ritual, and that's a book you can read evil out of as well as good.

There was a boy of the Saggartons in the house went to Biddy Early and she told him the house of his bachelor [the girl he would marry] and he did marry her after. And she cured him of a weakness he had and cured many, but it was seldom the bottle she'd give could be brought home without being spilled. I wonder did she go to *them* when she died. She got the cure among them anyway.

Mrs. Dillon:

My mother got crippled in her bed one night—God save the hearers—and it was a long time before she could walk again with the pain in her back. And my father was always telling her to go to Biddy Early, and so at last she went. But she could do nothing for her, for she said, "What ails you has nothing to do with my business." And she said, "You have lost three, and one was a grand little fair-haired one, and if you'd like to see her again, I'll show her to you." And when she said that, my mother had no courage to look and to see the child she lost, but fainted then and there. And then she said, "There's a field of corn beyond your house and a field with hay, and it's not long since that the little fellow that wears a Llanberis cap fell asleep there on a cock of hay. And before the stooks of corn are in stacks he'll be taken from you, but I'll save him if I can." And it was true enough what she said, my little brother that was wearing a Llanberis cap had gone to the field, and had fallen asleep on the hay a few days before. But no harm happened him, and he's all the brother I have living now. Out in the stable she used to go to meet her *people.*

Mrs. Locke:

It was my son was thatching Heniff's house when he got the touch, and he came back with a pain in his back and in his shoulders, and took to the bed. And a few nights after that I was asleep, and the little girl came and woke me and said, "There's none of us can sleep, with all the cars and carriages rattling round the house." But though I woke and heard her say that, I fell into a sound sleep again and never woke till morning. And one night there came two taps at the window, one after another, and we all heard it and no one there. And at last I sent the eldest boy to Biddy Early and he found her in the house. She was then married to her fourth man. And she said he came a day too soon and would do nothing for him. And he had to walk away in the rain. And the next day he went back and she said, "Three days later and you'd have been too late." And she gave him two bottles, the one he was to bring to a boundary water and to fill it up, and that was to be rubbed to the back, and the other was to drink. And the minute he got them he began to get well, and he left the bed and could walk, but he was always delicate. When we rubbed his back we saw a black mark, like the bite of a dog, and as to his face, it was as white as a sheet.

I have the bottle here yet, though it's thirty year ago I got it. She bid the boy to bring whatever was left of it to a river, and to pour it away with the running water. But when he got well I did nothing with it, and said nothing about it—and here it is now for you to see. I never let on to Father Folan that I went to her, but one time the Bishop came, MacInerny. I knew he was a rough man, and I went to him and made my confession, and I said, "Do what you like with me, but I'd walk the world for my son when he was sick." And all he said was, "It would have been no wonder if the two feet had been cut off from the messenger." And he said no more and put nothing on me.

There was a boy I saw went to Biddy Early, and she gave him a bottle and told him to mind he did not lose it in the crossing of some road. And when he came to the place it was broke.

Often I heard of Biddy Early, and I knew of a little girl was sick and the brother went to Biddy Early to ask would she get well. And she said, "They have a place ready for her, room for her they have." So he knew she would die, and so she did.

The priests can do things too, the same way as she could, for there was one Mr. Lyne was dying, a Protestant, and the priest went in and baptized him a Catholic before he died, and he said to the people after, "He's all right now, in another world." And it was more than the baptizing made him sure of that.

Mrs. Brennan, in the house beyond, went one time to Biddy Early, where the old man was losing his health. And all she told him was to bid him give over drinking so much whiskey. So after she said that, he used only to be drinking gin.

There was a boy went to Biddy Early for his father, and she said, "It's not any of my business that's on him, but it's good for yourself that you came to me. Weren't you sowing potatoes in such a field one day and didn't you find a bottle of whiskey, and bring it away and drink what was in it?" And that was true and it must have been a bottle *they* brought out of some cellar and dropped there, for they can bring everything away, and put in its place what will look like it.

There was a boy near Feakle got the touch in three places, and he got a great desire to go out night-walking, and he got sick. And they asked Biddy Early and she said, "Watch the hens when they come in to roost at night, and catch a hold of the last one that comes." So the mother caught it, and then she thought she'd like to see what would Biddy Early do with it. So she brought it up to her house and laid it on the floor, and it began to rustle its wings, and it lay over and died. It was from her brother Biddy Early got the cure. He was sick a long time, and there was a whitethorn tree out in the field, and he'd go and lie under it for shade from the sun. And after he died, every day for a year she'd go to the whitethorn tree, and it is there she'd cry her fill. And then he brought her under and gave her the cure. It was after that she was in service beyond Kinvara. She did her first cure on a boy, after the doctors giving him up.

An Old Man from Kinvara:

My wife is paralysed these thirty-six years, and the neighbours said she'd get well if the child died, for she got it after her confinement, all in a minute. But the child died in a year and eleven months, and she got no better. And then they said she'd get taken after twenty-one years, but that passed, and she's just the same way. And she's as good a Christian as any all the time.

I went to Biddy Early one time about her. She was a very old woman, all shaky, and the crankiest woman I ever saw. And the husband was a fine young man, and he lying in the bed. It was a man from Kinvara half-paralysed I brought with me, and she would do nothing for him at first, and then the husband bid her do what she could. So she took the bottle and shook it and looked in it, and she said what was in him was none of her business. And I had work to get him a lodging that night in Feakle, for the priests had all the people warned against letting any one in that had been to her. She wouldn't take the whiskey I brought, but the husband and myself, we opened it and drank it between us.

She gave me a bottle for my wife, but when I got to the workhouse, where I had to put her in the hospital, they wouldn't let me through the gate for they heard where I had been. So I had to hide the bottle for a night by a wall, on the grass, and I sent my brother's wife to find it, and to bring it to her in the morning into the workhouse. But it did her no good, and Biddy Early told her after it was because I didn't bring it straight to her, but had left it on the ground for the night.

Biddy Early beat all women. No one could touch her. I knew a girl, a friend of my own, at Burren and she was sick a long while and the doctors could do nothing for her, and the priests read over her but they could do nothing. And at last the husband went to Biddy Early and she said, "I can't cure her, and the woman that can cure her lives in the village with her." So he went home and told this and the women of the village came

into the house and said, "God bless her," all except one, and
nothing would make her come into the house. But they watched
her, and one night when a lot of them were sitting round the fire
smoking, she let a spit fall on the floor. So they gathered that
up (with respects to you), and brought it in to the sick woman
and rubbed it to her, and she got well. It might have done as
well if they brought a bit of her petticoat and burned it and
rubbed the ashes on her. But there's something strange about
spits, and if you spit on a child or a beast it's as good as if you'd
say, "God bless it."

John Curtin:
I was with Biddy Early one time for my brother. She was
out away in Ennis when we got to the house, and her husband
that she called Tommy. And the kitchen was full of people
waiting for her to come in. So then she came, and the day was
rainy, and she was wet, and she went over to the fire, and began to take off her clothes, and to dry them, and then she said to
her husband: "Tommy, get the bottle and give them all a
drop." So he got the bottle and gave a drink to everyone. But
my brother was in behind the door, and he missed him and
when he came back to the fire she said: "You have missed out
the man that has the best heart of them all, and there he is
behind the door." And when my brother came out she said,
"Give us a verse of a song," and he said, "I'm no songster,"
but she said, "I know well that you are, and a good dancer as
well." She cured him and his wife after.
There was a neighbour of mine went to her too, and she said:
"The first time you got the touch was the day you had brought
a cart of turf from that bog at Ballinabucky to Scahanagh. And
when you were in the road you got it, and you had to lie down
on the creel of turf till you got to the public road." And she
told him that he had a pane of glass broke in his window and
that was true enough. She must have been away walking with the
faeries every night or how did she know that, or where the village
of Scahanagh was?

Mrs. Kenny has been twice to Biddy Early. Once for her
brother who was ill, and light-headed and sent to Galway.
And Biddy Early shook the bottle twice, and she said, "It is none
of my business, and it's a heavy cold that settled in his head."
And she would not take the shilling. A red, red woman she was.

48

Mary Glyn:

I am a Clare woman, but the last fifty years I spent in Connacht. Near Feakle I lived, but I only saw Biddy Early once, the time she was brought to the committee and to the courthouse. She lived in a little house near Feakle that time, and her landlord was Dr. Murphy in Limerick, and he sent men to evict her and to pull the house down, and she held them in the door and said: "Whoever will be the first to put a bar to the house, he'll remember it." And then a man put his bar in between two stones, and if he did, he turned and got a fall someway and he broke the thigh. After that Dr. Murphy brought her to the court, "Faeries and all," he said, for he brought the bottle along with her. So she was put out, but Murphy had cause to remember it, for he was living in a house by himself, and one night it caught fire and was burned down, and all that was left of him was one foot that was found in a corner of the walls. She had four husbands, and the priest wouldn't marry her to the last one, and it was by the teacher that she was married. She was a good-looking woman, but like another, the day I saw her. My husband went to her the time Johnny, my little boy, was dying. He had a great pain in his temple, and she said: "He has enough in him to kill a hundred; but if he lives till Monday, come and tell me." But he was dead before that. And she said, "If you came to me before this, I'd not have let you stop in that house you're in." But Johnny died; and there was a blush over his face when he was going, and after that I couldn't look at him, but those that saw him said that *he* wasn't in it. I never saw him since, but often and often the father would go out thinking he might see him. But I know well he wouldn't like to come back and to see me fretting for him.

We left the house after that and came here. A travelling woman that came in to see me one time in that house said, "This is a fine airy house," and she said that three times, and then she said, "But in that corner of it you'll lose your son," and so it happened, and I wish now that I had minded what she said. A man and his family went into that house after, and the first summer they were in it, he and his sons were putting up a stack of hay in the field with pitchforks, and the pitchfork in his hand turned some way into his stomach and he died.

It is Biddy Early had the great name, but the priests were against her. There went a priest one time to stop her, and when he came near the door the horse fell that was in his car. Biddy Early came out then and bid him to give three spits on the horse, and he did that, and it rose up then and there. It was himself had put the evil eye on it. "It was yourself did it, you bodach," she said to the priest. And he said, "You may do what you like from this out, and I will not meddle with you again."

Mrs. Crone:

I was myself digging potatoes out in that field beyond, and a woman passed by the road, but I heard her say nothing, but a pain came on my head and I fell down, and I had to go to my bed for three weeks. My mother went then to Biddy Early. Did you ever hear of her? And she looked in the blue bottle she had, and she said my name. And she saw me standing before her, and knew all about me and said, "Your daughter was digging potatoes with her husband in the field, and a woman passed by and she said, 'It is as good herself is with a spade as the man,'" for I was a young woman at the time. She gave my mother a bottle for me, and I took three drinks of it in the bed, and then I got up as well as I was before.

Peter Feeney:

Biddy Early said to a man that I met in America and that went to her one time, that this place between Finevara and Aughanish is the most haunted place in all Ireland.

Surely Biddy Early was *away* herself. That's what I always heard. And I hear that at a hurling near Feakle the other day there was a small little man, and they say he was a friend of hers and has got her gift.

MRS. SHERIDAN

MRS. SHERIDAN, as I call her, was wrinkled and half blind, and had gone barefoot through her lifetime. She was old, for she had once met Raftery, the Gaelic poet, at a dance, and he died before the famine of '47. She must have been comely then, for he had said to her: "Well planed you are; the carpenter that planed you knew his trade"; and she was ready of reply and answered him back, "Better than you know yours," for his fiddle had two or three broken strings. And then he had spoken of a neighbour in some way that vexed her father, and he would let him speak no more with her. And she had carried a regret for this through her long life, for she said: "If it wasn't for him speaking as he did, and my father getting vexed, he might have made words about me like he did for Mary Hynes and for Mary Brown." She had never been to school she told me, because her father could not pay the penny a week it would have cost. She had never travelled many miles from the parish of her birth, and I am sure had never seen pictures except the sacred ones on chapel walls; and yet she could tell of a Cromwellian castle built up and of a drawbridge and of long-faced, fair-haired women, and of the yet earlier round house and saffron dress of the heroic times, I do not know whether by direct vision, or whether as Myers wrote: "It may even be that a World-soul is personally conscious of all its past, and that individual souls, as they enter into deeper consciousness enter into something which is at once reminiscence and actuality. . . . Past facts were known to men on earth, not from memory only but by written record; and these may be records, of what kind we know not, which persist in the spiritual world. Our retrocognitions seem often a recovery of isolated fragments of thought and feeling, pebbles still hard and rounded amid the indecipherable sands over which the mighty waters are 'rolling evermore.'"

She had never heard of the great mystic Jacob Behman, and yet when an unearthly visitor told her the country of youth is not far from the place where we live, she had come near to his root idea that "the world standeth in Heaven and Heaven in the World, and are in one another as day and night."

I was told by Mrs. Sheridan:
There was a woman, Mrs. Keevan, killed near the big tree at Raheen, and her husband was after that with Biddy Early, and she said it was not the woman that had died at all, but a cow that died and was put in her place. All my life I've seen *them* and enough of them. One day I was with Tom Mannion by the big hole near his house, and we saw a man and a woman come from it, and a great troop of children, little boys they seemed to be, and they went through the gate into Coole, and

there we could see them running and running along the wall. And I said to Tom Mannion, "It may be a call for one of us." And he said, "Maybe it's for some other one it is." But on that day week he was dead.

One time I saw the old Colonel standing near the road, I know well it was him. But while I was looking at him, he was changed into the likeness of an ass.

I was led astray myself one day in Coole when I went to gather sticks for the fire. I was making a bundle of them, and I saw a boy beside me, and a little grey dogeen with him, and at first I thought it was William Hanlon, and then I saw it was not. And he walked along with me, and I asked him did he want any of the sticks and he said he did not, and he seemed as we were walking to grow bigger and bigger. And when he came to where the caves go underground he stopped, and I asked him his name, and he said, "You should know me, for you've seen me often enough." And then he was gone, and I know that he was no living thing.

There was a child I had, and he a year and a half old, and he got a quinsy and a choking in the throat and I was holding him in my arms beside the fire, and all in a minute he died. And the men were working down by the river, washing sheep, and they heard the crying of a child from over there in the air, and they said, "That's Sheridan's child." So I knew sure enough that he was *taken*.

Come here close and I'll tell you what I saw at the old castle there below (Ballinamantane). I was passing there in the evening and I saw a great house and a grand one with screens (clumps of trees) at the ends of it, and the windows open— Coole house is nothing like what it was for size or grandeur. And there were people inside and ladies walking about, and a bridge across the river. For they can build up such things all in a minute. And two coaches came driving up and across the bridge to the castle, and in one of them I saw two gentlemen, and I knew them well and both of them had died long before. As to the coaches and the horses I didn't take much notice of them for I was too much taken up with looking at the two gentlemen. And a man came and called out and asked me would I come across the bridge, and I said I would not. And he said, "It would be better for you if you did, you'd go back heavier than you came." I suppose they would have given me some good thing. And then two men took up the bridge and laid it

against the wall. Twice I've seen that same thing, the house and
the coaches and the bridge, and I know well I'll see it a third
time before I die.[12]

One time when I was living at Ballymacduff there was two
little boys drowned in the river there, one was eight years old
and the other eleven years. And I was out in the fields, and the
people looking in the river for their bodies, and I saw a man
coming away from it, and the two boys with him, he holding a
hand of each and leading them away. And he saw me stop and
look at them and he said, "Take care would you bring them
from me, for you have only one in your own house, and if you
take these from me, she'll never come home to you again."
And one of the little chaps broke from his hand and ran to me,
and the other cried out to him, "Oh, Pat, would you leave me!"
So then he went back and the man led them away. And then I
saw another man, very tall he was, and crooked, and watching
me like this with his head down and he was leading two dogs
the other way, and I knew well where he was going and what he
was going to do with them.

And when I heard the bodies were laid out, I went to the
house to have a look at them, and those were never the two boys
that were lying there, but the two dogs that were put in their
places. I knew this by a sort of stripes on the bodies such as
you'd see in the covering of a mattress; and I knew the boys
couldn't be in it, after me seeing them led away.

And it was at that time I lost my eye, something came on it,
and I never got the sight again. All my life I've seen *them* and
enough of them. One time I saw one of the fields below full of
them, some were picking up stones and some were ploughing
it up. But the next time I went by there was no sign of it being
ploughed at all. They can do nothing without some live person
is looking at them, that's why they were always so much after
me. Even when I was a child I could see them, and once they
took my walk from me, and gave me a bad foot, and my father
cured me, and if he did, in five days after he died.

But there's no harm at all in them, not much harm.

There was a woman lived near me at Ballymacduff, and she
used to go about to attend women; Sarah Redington was her
name. And she was brought *away* one time by a man that came
for her into a hill, through a door, but she didn't know where
the hill was. And there were people in it, and cradles and a

53

woman in labour, and she helped her and the baby was born, and the woman told her it was only that night she was brought away. And the man led her out again and put her in the road near her home and he gave her something rolled in a bag, and he bid her not to look at it till she'd get home, and to throw the first handful of it away from her. But she wouldn't wait to get home to look at it, and she took it off her back and opened it, and there was nothing in it but cowdung. And the man came to her and said, "You have us near destroyed looking in that, and we'll never bring you in again among us."

There was a man I know well was away with them, often and often, and he was passing one day by the big tree and they came about him and he had a new pair of breeches on, and one of them came and made a slit in them, and another tore a little bit out, and they all came running and tearing little bits till he hadn't a rag left. Just to be humbugging him they did that. And they gave him good help, for he had but an acre of land, and he had as much on it as another would have on a big farm. But his wife didn't like him to be going and some one told her of a cure for him, and she said she'd try it and if she did, within two hours after she was dead; killed they had her before she'd try it. He used to say that where he was brought was into a round very big house, and Cairns that went with them told me the same.[13]

Three times when I went for water to the well, the water spilled over me, and I told Bridget after that they must bring the water themselves, I'd go for it no more. And the third time it was done there was a boy, one of the Heniffs, was near, and when he heard what happened me he said, "It must have been the woman that was at the well along with you that did that." And I said there was no woman at the well along with me. "There was," said he; "I saw her there beside you, and the two little tins in her hand."

One day after I came to live here at Coole, a strange woman came into the house, and I asked what was her name and she said, "I was in it before ever you were in it," and she went into the room inside and I saw her no more.

But Bridget and Peter saw her coming in, and they asked me who she was, for they never saw her before. And in the night when I was sleeping at the foot of the bed, she came and threw me out on the floor, that the joint of my arm has a mark in it yet. And every night she came, and she'd spite me or annoy

me in some way. And at last we got Father Nolan to come and
to drive her out. And as soon as he began to read, there went
out of the house a great blast, and there was a sound as loud as
thunder. And Father Nolan said, "It's well for you she didn't
have you killed before she went."

There's something that's not right about an old cat and it's
well not to annoy them. I was in the house one night, and one
came in, and he tried to bring away the candle that was lighted
in the candlestick, and it standing on the table. And I had a
little rod beside me, and I made a hit at him with it, and with
that he dropped the candle and made at me as if to tear me.
And I went on my knees and asked his pardon three times, and
when I asked it the third time he got quiet all of a minute, and
went out at the door.

And as to hares—bid Master Robert never to shoot a hare, for
you wouldn't know what might be in it. There were two women
I knew, mother and daughter, and they died. And one day I was
out by the wood, and I saw two hares sitting by the wall, and
the minute I saw them I knew well who they were. And the
mother made as though she'd kill me, but the daughter stopped
her. Bad they must have been to have been put into that shape,
and indeed I know that they weren't too good. I saw the mother
another time come up near the door as if to see me, and when
she got near, she turned herself into a red hare.

The priests can do cures out of their book, and the time the
cure is done is when they turn the second leaf. There was a boy
near Kinvara got a hurt and he was brought into a house and
Father Grogan was got to do a cure on him. And he did it, and
within two days the priest's brother was made a fool of, and
is locked up in a madhouse ever since, and it near seven years
ago.[14]

There was a boy of the Nally's died near a year ago; and
when I heard he was dead I went down to the house, and there
I saw him outside and two men bringing him away, and one of
them said to me, "We couldn't do this but for you being there
watching us." That's the last time I saw any of them.

There was a boy got a fall from a cart near the house beyond,
and he was brought in to Mrs. Raynor's and laid in the bed and
I went in to see him. And he said what he saw was a little boy
run across the road before the cart, and the horse took fright

and ran away and threw him from it. And he asked to be brought to my house, for he wouldn't stop where he was; "for" says he, "the woman of this house gave me no drink and showed me no kindness, and she'll be repaid for that." And sure enough within the year she got the dropsy and died. And he was carried out of the door backwards, but the mother brought him to her own house and wouldn't let him come to mine, and 'twas as well, for I wouldn't refuse him, but I don't want to be annoyed with *them* any more than I am.

Did you know Mrs. Byrne that lived in Doolin? Swept she was after her child was born. And near a year after I saw her coming down the road near the old castle. "Is that you, Mary?" I said to her, "and is it to see me you are coming?" But she went on. It was in May when *they* are all changing.[15] There was a priest, Father Waters, told me one time that he was after burying a boy, one Fahy, in Kilbecanty churchyard. And he was passing by the place again in the evening, and there he saw a great fire burning, but whether it was of turf or of sticks he couldn't tell, and there was the boy he had buried sitting in the middle of it.

I know that I used to be away among them myself, but how they brought me I don't know, but when I'd come back, I'd be cross with the husband and with all. I believe when I was with them I was cross that they wouldn't let me go, and that's why they didn't keep me altogether, they didn't like cross people to be with them. The husband would ask me where I was, and why I stopped so long away, but I think he knew I was *taken* and it fretted him, but he never spoke much about it. But my mother knew it well, but she'd try to hide it. The neighbours would come in and ask where was I, and she'd say I was sick in the bed—for whatever was put there in place of me would have the head in under the bed-clothes. And when a neighbour would bring me in a drink of milk, my mother would put it by and say, "Leave her now, maybe she'll drink it tomorrow." And maybe in a day or two I'd meet someone and he'd say, "Why wouldn't you speak to me when I went into the house to see you?" And I was a young fresh woman at that time. Where they brought me to I don't know, or how I got there, but I'd be in a very big house, and it round, the walls far away that you'd hardly see them, and a great many people all round about. I saw there neighbours and friends that I knew, and they in their own clothing and with their own appearance, but they wouldn't speak to me nor I to them, and when I'd met them again I'd never say to them that I saw them there. But the others had striped clothes of all colours, and long faces, and they'd be talking and laughing and moving about. What language had they? Irish of course, what else would they talk?

And there was one woman of them, very tall and with a long face, standing in the middle, taller than any one you ever saw in this world, and a tall stick in her hand; she was the mistress. She had a high yellow thing on her head, not hair, her hair was turned back under it, and she had a long yellow cloak down to her feet and hanging down behind. Had she anything like that in the picture in her hand? [a crown of gold balls or apples.] It was not on her head, it was lower down here about the body, and shining, and a thing [a brooch] like that in the picture, but down hanging low like the other. And that picture you have there in your hand, I saw no one like it, but I saw a picture like it hanging on the wall.[16] It was a very big place and very grand, and a long table set out, but I didn't want to stop there and I began crying to go home. And she touched me here in the breast with her stick, she was vexed to see me wanting to go away. They never brought me away since. Grand food they'd offer me and wine, but I never would touch it, and sometimes I'd have to give the breast to a child.

Himself died, but it was *they* took him from me. It was in the night and he lying beside me, and I woke and heard him move, and I thought I heard some one with him. And I put out my hand and what I touched was an iron hand, like knitting needles it felt. And I heard the bones of his neck crack, and he gave a sort of a choked laugh, and I got out of the bed and struck a light and I saw nothing, but I thought I saw some one go through the door. And I called to Bridget and she didn't come, and I called again and she came and she said she struck a light when she heard the noise and was coming, and someone came and struck the light from her hand. And when we looked in the bed, himself was lying dead and not a mark on him.

There was a woman, Mrs. Leary, had something wrong with her, and she went to Biddy Early. And nothing would do her but to bring my son along with her, and I was vexed. What call had she to bring him with her? And when Biddy Early saw him she said, "You'll travel far, but wherever you go you'll not escape them." The woman he went up with died about six

57

months after, but he went to America, and he wasn't long there when what was said came true, and he died. They followed him as far as he went.

And one day since then I was on the road to Gort, and Madden said to me, "Your son's on the road before you." And I said, "How could that be, and he dead?" But still I hurried on. And at Coole gate I met a little boy and I asked did he see any one and he said, "You know well who I saw." But I got no sight of him at all myself.

I saw the coach one night near Kiltartan Chapel. Long it was and black, and I saw no one in it. But I saw who was sitting up driving it, and I knew it to be one of the Miskells that was taken before that.[17]

One day I was following the goat to get a sup of milk from her, and she turned into the field and up into the castle of Lydican and went up from step to step up the stairs to the top, and I followed and on the stairs a woman passed me, and I knew her to be Colum's wife. And when we got to the room at the top, I looked up, and there standing on the wall was a woman looking down at me, long-faced and tall and with grand clothes, and on her head something yellow and slippery, not hair but like marble.[18] And I called out to ask her wasn't she afraid to be up there, and she said she was not. And a shepherd that used to live below in the castle saw the same woman one night he went up to the top, and a room and a fire and she sitting by it, but when he went there again there was no sign of her nor of the room, nothing but the stones as before.

I never saw them on horses; but when I came to live at Peter Mahony's he used to bring in those red flowers [ragweed] that grow by the railway, when their stalks were withered, to make the fire. And one day I was out in the road, and two men came over to me and one was wearing a long grey dress. And he said to me, "We have no horses to ride on and have to go on foot, because you have too much fire." So then I knew it was their horses we were burning.[19]

I know the cure for anything they can do to you, but it's few I'd tell it to. It was a strange woman came in and told it to me, and I never saw her again. She bid me spit and use the spittle, or to take a graineen of dust from the navel, and that's what you should do if any one you care for gets a cold or a shivering, or *they* put anything upon him.

One time I went up to a forth beyond Raheen to pick up a few sticks, and I was beating one of the sticks on the ground to break it, and a voice said from below, "Is it to break down the house you want?" And a thing appeared that was like a cat, but bigger than any cat ever was. And another time in a forth a man said, "Here's gold for you, but don't look at it till you go home." And I looked and I saw horse-dung and I said, "Keep it yourself, much good may it do you." They never gave me anything did me good, but a good deal of torment I had from them. And they're often walking the road, and if you met them you wouldn't know them from any other person; but I'd know them well enough, but I'd say nothing—and that's a grand bush we're passing by—whether it belongs to them I don't know, but wherever they get shelter, there they might be—but anyway it's a very fine bush—God bless it.

And when you speak of them you should always say the day of the week. Maybe you didn't notice that I said, "This is Friday" just when we were hardly in at the gate.

It's very weak I am, and took to my bed since yesterday. *They've* changed now out of where they were near the castle, and it's inside Coole demesne they are. It was an old man told me that, I met him on the road there below. First I thought he was a young man, and then I saw he was not, and he grew very nice-looking after, and he had plaid clothes. "We're moved out of that now," he said, "and it's strangers will be coming in it. And you ought to know me," he said. And when I looked at him I thought I did.

And one day I was down in Coole I saw their house, more like a big dairy, with red tiles and a high chimney and a lot of smoke out of it, and there was a woman at the door and two or three outside. But they'll do you no harm, for the man told me so. "They needn't be afraid," he said, "we're good neighbours, but let them not say too much if the milk might go from the cows now and again."

I was over beyond Raheen one time, and I saw a woman milking and she at the wrong side of the cow. And when she saw me she got up, and she had a bucket that was like a plate, and it full of milk and she gave it to a man that was waiting there, that

I thought first was one of the O'Heas, and they went away. And the cow was a grand fine one, but who it belonged to I didn't know—maybe to themselves.

It's about a week ago one night some one came into the room in the dark, and I saw it was my son that I lost—he that went to America—James. He didn't die, he was whipped away—I knew he wasn't dead, for I saw him one day on the road to Gort on a coach, and he looked down and he said, "That's my poor mother." And when he came in here, I couldn't see him, but I knew him by his talk. And he said, "It's asleep she is," and he put his two hands on my face and I never stirred. And he said, "I'm not far from you now." For he is with the others inside Coole near where the river goes down the swallow hole. To see me he came, and I think he'll be apt to come again before long. And last night there was a light about my head all the night and no candle in the room at all.

Yes, the Sidhe sing, and they have pipers among them, a bag on each side and a pipe to the mouth, I think I never told you of one I saw.

I was passing a field near Kiltartan one time when I was a girl, where there was a little lisheen, and a field of wheat, and when I was passing I heard a piper beginning to play, and I couldn't but begin to dance, it was such a good tune; and there was a boy standing there, and he began to dance too. And then my father came by, and he asked why were we dancing, and no one playing for us. And I said there was, and I began to search through the wheat for the piper, but I couldn't find him, and I heard a voice saying, "You'll see me yet, and it will be in a town." Well, one Christmas eve I was in Gort and my husband with me, and that night at Gort I heard the same tune beginning again— the grandest I ever heard—and I couldn't but begin to dance. And Glynn the chair-maker heard it too, and he began to dance with me in the street, and my man thought I had gone mad, and the people gathered round us, for they could see or hear nothing. But I saw the piper well, and he had plaid clothes, blue and white, and he said, "Didn't I tell you that when I saw you again it would be in a town?"

I never saw fire go up in the air, but in the wood beyond the tree at Raheen I used often to see like a door open at night, and the light shining through it, just as it might shine through the house door, with the candle and the fire inside, if it would be left open.

Many of *them* I have seen—they are like ourselves only wearing bracket clothes,²⁰ and their bodies are not so strong or so thick as ours, and their eyes are more shining than our eyes. I don't see many of them here, but Coole is alive with them, as plenty as grass; I often go awhile and sit inside the gate there. I saw them make up a house one time near the natural bridge, and I saw them coming over the gap twice near the chapel, a lot of little boys, and two men and a woman, and they had old talk and young talk. One of them came in here twice, and I gave him a bit of bread, but he said, "There's salt in it" and he put it away.²¹

When Annie Rivers died the other day, there were two funerals in it, a big funeral with a new coffin and another that was in front of them, men walking, the handsomest I ever saw, and they with black clothes about their body. I was out there looking at them, and there was a cow in the road, and I said, "Take care would you drive away the cow." And one of them said, "No fear of that, we have plenty of cows *on the other side of the wall.*" But no one could see them but myself. I often saw them and it was they took the sight of my eyes from me. And Annie Rivers was not in the grand coffin, she was with *them* a good while before the funeral.

That time I saw the two funerals at Rivers's that I was telling you about, I heard Annie call to those that were with her, "You might as well let me have Bartley; it would be better for the two castles to meet." And since then the mother is uneasy about Bartley, and he fell on the floor one day and I know well he is *gone* since the day Annie was buried. And I saw others at the funeral, and some that you knew well among them. And look now, you should send a coat to some poor person, and your own friends among the dead will be covered, for you could see the skin here. [*She made a gesture passing her hand down each arm, exactly the same gesture as old Mary Glynn of Slieve Echtge had made yesterday when she said, "Have you a coat you could send me, for my arms are bare?" and I had promised her one.*]

*　　*　　*

Would I have gone among them if I had died last month? I think not. I think that I have lived my time out, since my father was taken.

He was a young man at that time, and one time I was out in the field, and I got a knock on the foot, and a lump rose; there is the mark of it yet. It was after that I was on the road with my father, near Kinvara, and a man came and began to beat him. And I thought that he was going to beat me, and I got in near the wall and my father said, "Spare the girl!" "I will do that, I will spare her," said the man. He went away then, and within a week my father was dead.

And my mother told me that before the burying, she saw the corpse on the bed, sitting on the side of the bed, and his feet hanging down. I saw my father often since then, but not this good while now. He had always a young appearance when I saw him.

A big woman came to the window and looked in at me, the time I was on the bed lately. "Rise up out of that," she said. I saw her another time on the road, and the wind blew her dress open, and I could see that she had nothing at all on underneath it.

In May they are as thick everywhere as the grass, but there's no fear at all for you or for Master Robert. I know that, for *one* told it to me.

"Tir-nan-og" that is not far from us. One time I was in the chapel at Labane, and there was a tall man sitting next me, and he dressed in grey, and after the Mass I asked him where he came from. "From Tir-nan-og," says he. "And where is that?" I asked him. "It's not far from you," he said; "it's near the place where you live." I remember well the look of him and him telling me that. The priest was looking at us while we were talking together.[22]

She died some years ago and I am told:
"There is a ghost in Mrs. Sheridan's house. They got a priest to say Mass there, but with all that there is not one in it has leave to lay a head on the pillow till such time as the cock crows."

62

MR. SAGGARTON

I WAS told one day by our doctor, a good fowler and physician, now, alas, passed away, of an old man in Clare who had knowledge of "the Others," and I took Mr. Yeats to see him.

We found him in his hayfield, and he took us to his thatched lime-white house and told us many things. A little later we went there again to verify what I had put down. I remember him as very gentle and courteous, and that a cloth was spread and tea made for us by his daughters, he himself sitting at the head of the table.

Mr. Yeats at that time wore black clothes and a soft black hat, but gave them up later, because he was so often saluted as a priest. But this time another view was taken, and I was told after a while that the curate of the Clare parish had written to the curate of a Connacht parish that Lady Gregory had come over the border with "a Scripture Reader" to try and buy children for proselytizing purposes. But the Connacht curate had written back to the Clare curate that he had always thought him a fool, and now he was sure of it.

The old man I have called Mr. Saggarton said:
Our family diminished very much till at last there were but three brothers left, and they separated. One went to Ennis and another came here and the other to your own place beyond. It was a long time before they could make one another out again. It was my uncle used to go away among *them.* When I was a young chap, I'd go out in the field working with him, and he'd bid me go away on some message, and when I'd come back it might be in a faint I'd find him. It was he himself was taken; it was but his shadow or some thing in his likeness was left behind. He was a very strong man. You might remember Ger Kelly what a strong man he was, and stout, and six feet two inches in height. Well, he and my uncle had a dispute one time, and he made as if to strike at him, and my uncle, without so much as taking off his coat, gave one blow that stretched him on the floor. And at the barn at Bunahowe he and my father could throw a hundred weight over the collar beam, what no other could do.[23] My father had no notion at all of managing things. He lived to be eighty years, and all his life he looked as innocent

63

as that little chap turning the hay. My uncle had the same innocent look; I think they died quite happy.

One time the wife got a touch, and she got it again, and the third time she got up in the morning and went out of the house and never said where she was going. But I had her watched, and I told the boy to follow her and never to lose sight of her, and I gave him the sign to make if he'd meet any bad thing. So he followed her, and she kept before him, and while he was going along the road something was up on top of the wall with one leap—a red-haired man it was, with no legs and with a thin face.[24] But the boy made the sign and got hold of him and carried him till he got to the bridge. At the first he could not lift the man, but after he made the sign he was quite light. And the woman turned home again, and never had a touch after. It's a good job the boy had been taught the sign. Make that sign with your thumbs if ever when you're walking out you feel a sort of a shivering in the skin, for that shows there's some bad thing near, but if you hold your hands like that, if you went into a forth itself, it couldn't harm you. And if you should any time feel a sort of a pain in your little finger, the surest thing is to touch it with human dung. Don't neglect that, for if they're glad to get one of us, they'd be seven times better pleased to get the like of you.

Youngsters they take mostly to do work for them, and they are death on handsome people, for they are handsome themselves. To all sorts of work they put them, and digging potatoes and the like, and they have wine from foreign parts, and cargoes of gold coming in to them. Their houses are ten times more beautiful and ten times grander than any house in this world. And they could build one of them up in that field in ten minutes. Clothes of all colours they wear, and crowns like that one in the picture, and of other shapes.[25] They have different queens, not always the same. The people they bring away must die some day; as to themselves, they were living from past ages, and they can never die till the time when God has His mind made up to redeem them.

And those they bring away are always glad to be brought back again. If you were to bring a heifer from those mountains beyond and to put it into a meadow, it would be glad to get back again to the mountain, because it is the place it knows.

Coaches they make up when they want to go driving, with wheels and all, but they want no horses. There might be twenty of them going out together sometimes, and all full of them.

They are everywhere around us, and may be within a yard of us now in the grass. But if I ask you, "What day is tomorrow," and you said, "Thursday," they wouldn't be able to overhear us. They have the power to go in every place, even on to the book the priest is using.

There was one John Curran lived over there towards Bunahowe, and he had a cow that died, and they were striving to rear the calf—boiled hay they were giving it, the juice the hay was boiled in. And you never saw anything to thrive as it did. And one day some man was looking at it and he said, "You may be sure the mother comes back and gives it milk." And John Curran said, "How can that be, and she dead?" But the man said, "She's not dead, she's in the forth beyond. And if you go towards it half an hour before sunrise you'll find her, and you should catch a hold of her and bring her home and milk her, and when she makes to go away again, take a hold of her tail and follow her." So he went out next morning, half an hour before sunrise, up toward the forth, and brought her home and milked her, and when the milking was done she started to go away and he caught a hold of the tail and was carried along with her. And she brought him into the forth, through a door. And behind the door stood a barrel, and what was in the barrel is what they put their finger in, and touch their forehead with when they go out, for if they didn't do that all people would be able to see them. And as soon as he got in, there were voices from all sides. "Welcome, John Curran, welcome, John Curran." And he said: "The devil take you, how well you know my name; it's not a welcome I want, it's my cow to bring home again." So in the end he got the cow and brought her home. And he saw there a woman that had died out of the village about ten years before, and she suckling a child.[26]

Surely I knew Biddy Early, and my uncle was a friend of hers. It was from the same power they got the cures. My uncle left me the power, and I was well able to do them and did many, but my stock was all dying and what could I do? So I gave a part of the power to Mrs. Tobin that lives in Gort, and she can cure a good many things. Biddy Early told me herself that where she got it was when she was a servant girl in a house, there was a baby lying in the cradle, and he went on living for a few years. But he was friendly to her and used to play tunes for her and when he went away he gave her the bottle and the power.

She had but to look in it and she'd see all that had happened and all that was going to happen. But he made her make a promise never to take more than a shilling for any cure she did, and she would not have taken fifty pounds if you offered it to her, though she might take presents of bread and wine and such things.

The cure for all things in the world? Surely she had it and knew where it was. And I knew it myself too—but I could not tell you of it. Seven parts I used to make it with, and one of them is a thing that's in every house.

There's a lake beyond there, and my uncle one day told us by name of a man that would be drowned there at twelve o'clock that day. And so it happened.

One time I was walking on the road to Galway, near the sea, and another man along with me. And I saw in a field beside the road a very small woman walking down towards us, and she smiling and carrying a can of water in her hand, and she was dressed in a blue spencer. So I asked the other man did he see her, and he said he did not, and when I came up to the wall she was gone.

One time myself when I went to look for a wife, I went to the house, and there was a hen and some chickens before the door. Well, after I went home one of the chickens died. And what do you think they said, but that it was I overlooked it.

They hate me because I do cures, and they hated Biddy Early too. The priests do them but not in the same way—they do them by the power of Almighty God.

My wife got a touch from them, and they have a watch on her ever since. It was the day after I married and I went to the fair at Clarenbridge. And when I came back the house was full of smoke, but there was nothing on the hearth but cinders, and the smoke was more like the smoke of a forge. And she was within lying on the bed, and her brother was sitting outside the door crying. So I went to the mother and asked her to come in, and she was crying too. And she knew well what had happened, but she didn't tell me, but she sent for the priest. And when he came he sent me for Geoghegan and that was only an excuse to get me away, and what he and the mother tried to bring her to do was to face death, and they knew I wouldn't allow that if I was there. But the wife was very stout and she wouldn't give in to them. So the priest read more, and he asked would I be willing to lose something, and I said, so far as a cow or a calf I wouldn't mind losing that. Well, she partly recovered, but from that day, no year went by but I lost ten lambs maybe or other things. And twice they took my children out of the bed, two of them I have lost. And the others they gave a touch to. That girl there—see the way she is, and can't walk. In one minute it came on her out in the field, with the fall of a wall.[27]

It was one among *them* that wanted the wife. A woman and a boy we often saw come to the door, and she was the matchmaker. And when we would go out, they would have vanished.

Biddy Early's cure that you heard of, it was the moss on the water of the mill-stream between the two wheels of Ballylee. It can cure all things brought about by *them*, but not any common ailment. But there is no cure for the stroke given by a queen or a fool. There is a queen in every house or regiment of them. It is of those they steal away they make queens for as long as they live or that they are satisfied with them.

There were two women fighting at a spring of water, and one hit the other on the head with a can and killed her. And after that her children began to die. And the husband went to Biddy Early and as soon as she saw him she said, "There's nothing I can do for you, your wife was a wicked woman, and the one she hit is a queen among them, and she is taking your children one by one and you must suffer till twenty-one years are up." And so he did.

The stroke of a fool, there's no cure for either. There are many fools among them dressed in strange clothes like one of the mummers that used to be going through the country. But it might be the fools are the wisest after all. There are two classes, the Dundonians that are like ourselves, and another race, more wicked and more spiteful. Very small they are and wide, and their belly sticks out in front, so that what they carry they don't carry it on the back, but in front, on the belly in a bag.[28]

They were fighting when Johnny Casey died; that's what often happens. Everyone has friends among them, and the friends would be trying to save you when the others would be trying to bring you away. Youngsters they pick up here and there, to help them in their fights and in their work. They have cattle and horses, but all of them have only three legs.

They don't have children themselves, only the women that are brought away among them, they have children, but they don't live for ever, like the Dundonians.

The handsome they like, and the good dancers. And if they get a boy amongst them, the first to touch him, he belongs to her.

There was a boy was a splendid dancer, and straight and firm, for they don't like those that go to right or left as they walk. Well, one night he was going to a house where there was a dance, and when he was about half-way to it, he came to another house, where there was music and dancing going on. So he turned in, and there was a room all done up with curtains and with screens, and a room inside where the people were sitting, and it was only those that were dancing sets that came to the outside room.

As to their treasure, it's best to be without it. There was a man living by a forth, and where his house touched the forth, he built a little room and left it for them, clean and in good order, the way they'd like it. And whenever he'd want money, for a fair or the like, he'd find it laid on the table in the morning. And when he had it again, he'd leave it there, and it would be taken away in the night. But after that going on for a time he lost his son.

There was a room at Crags where things used to be thrown about, and everyone could hear the noises there. They had a right to clear it out and settle it the way they'd like it. You should do that in your own big house. Set a little room for them —with spring water in it always—and wine you might leave— no, not flowers—they wouldn't want so much as that—but just what would show your good will.

Now I have told you more than I told my wife.

"A GREAT WARRIOR IN THE BUSINESS"

IT was on the bounds of Connemara I heard of this healer, and went to see his wife in her little rockbuilt cabin among the boulders, to ask if a cure could be done for Mr. Yeats, who was staying at a friend's house near, and who was at that time troubled by uncertain eyesight.

One evening later we walked beside the sea to the cottage where we were to meet the healer; a storm was blowing and we were glad when the door was opened and we found a bright turf fire.

He was short and broad, with regular features, and his hair was thick and dark, though he was an old man. He wore a flannel-sleeved waistcoat, and his trousers were much patched on the knees. He sat on a low bench in the wide chimney nook, holding a soft hat in his hands which kept nervously moving. The woman of the house came over now and then to look at the iron tripod on the hearth. She, like the healer, spoke only Irish. The man of the house sat between us and interpreted, holding a dip candle in his hands. A dog growled without ceasing at one side of the hearth, a reddish cat sat at the other. The woman seemed frightened and angry at times as the old man spoke, and clutched the baby to her breast.

I was told by the man of the house, Coneely:

There's a man beyond is a great warrior in this business, and no man within miles of the place will build a house or a cabin or any other thing without him going there to say if it's in a right place.

It was Fagan cured me of a pain I had in my arm, I couldn't get rid of. He gave me a something to drink, and he bid me go to a quarry and to touch some of the stones that were lying outside it and not to touch others of them. Anyway I got well.

And one time down by the hill we were gathering in the red seaweed, and there was a boy there that was leading a young horse, the same way he'd been leading him a year or more. But this day of a sudden he made a snap to bite him, and secondly he reared as if to jump on top of him, and thirdly turned around and made at him with the hoofs. And the boy threw himself to one side and escaped, but with the fright he got he went into his

69

bed and stopped there. And the next day Fagan came and told him everything that had happened, and he said, "I saw thousands on the strand near where it was last night."

Fagan's wife said to me in her house:
Are you *right?* You are? Then you're my friend. Come here close and tell me is there anything himself can do for you?

I do the fortunes no more since I got great abuse from the priest for it. Himself got great abuse from the priest too—Father Haverty—and he gave him plaster of Paris—I mean by that he spoke soft and blathered him, but he does them all the same, and Father Kilroy gave him leave when he was here.

It was from his sister he got the cure. Taken she was when her baby was born. She died in the morning and the baby at night. We didn't tell John of it for a month after, where he was away, caring horses. But he knew of it before he came home, for she followed him there one day he was out in the field, and when he didn't know her she said, "I'm your sister Kate." And she said, "I bring you a cure that you may cure both yourself and others." And she told him of the herb and the field he'd find it growing, and that he must choose a plant with seven branches, the half of them above the clay and the half of them covered up. And she told him how to use it.

Twenty years she's gone, but she's not dead yet, but the last time he saw her he said that she was getting grey. Every May and November he sees her, he'll be seeing her soon now. When her time comes to die, she'll be put in the place of some other one that's taken, and so she'll get absolution.[29]

He has cured many. But sometimes they are vexed with him, for some cure he has done, when he interferes with some person they're meaning to bring away. And many's the good beating they gave him out in the fields for doing that.

Myself they gave a touch to, here in the thigh, so that I lost my walk; vexed with me they are for giving up the throwing of the cup.

A nurse she's been all the time among them. And don't believe those that say they have no children. A boy among them is as clever as any boy here, but he must be matched with a woman from earth. And the same way with their women, they must get a husband here. And they never can give the breast to a child, but must get a nurse from here.

One time I saw them myself, in a field and they hurling.

70

Bracket caps they wore and bracket clothes that were of all colours.

Some were the same size as ourselves and some looked like gossoons that didn't grow well. But himself has the second sight and can see them in every place.

There's as many of them in the sea as on the land, and sometimes they fly like birds across the bay.

The first time he did a cure it was on some poor person like ourselves, and he took nothing for it, and in the night the sister came and bid him not to do it any more without a fee. And that time we lost a fine boy.

They'll all be watching round when a person is dying; and suppose it was myself, there'd be my own friends crying, crying, and themselves would be laughing and jesting, and glad I'd go.[30]

There is always a mistress among them. When one of us goes among them they would all be laughing and jesting, but when that tall mistress you heard of would tip her stick on the ground, they'd all draw to silence.

Tell me the Christian name of your friend you want the cure for. "William Butler," I'll keep that.[31] And when himself gathers the herb, if it's for a man, he must call on the name of some other man, and call him a king—Righ—and if it's for a woman he must call on the name of some other woman and call her a queen that is calling on the king or the queen of the plant.

Fagan said to W. B. Yeats and to me:

It's not from *them* the harm came to your eyes. I see them in all places—and there's no man mowing a meadow that doesn't see them at some time or other. As to what they look like, they'll change colour and shape and clothes while you look round. Bracket caps they always wear. There is a king and a queen and a fool in each house of them, that is true enough—but they would do you no harm. The king and the queen are kind and gentle, and whatever you'll ask them for they'll give it. They'll do no harm at all if you don't injure them. You might speak to them if you'd meet them on the road, and they'd answer you, if you'd speak civil and quiet and show respect, and not be laughing or humbugging—they wouldn't like that. One night I was in bed with the wife beside me, and the child near me, near the fire. And I turned and saw a woman sitting by the fire, and she made a snap at the child, and I was too quick for her and

71

got hold of it, and she was at the door and out of it in one minute, before I could get to her.

Another time in the field a woman came beside me, and I went on to a gap in the wall and she was in it before me. And then she stopped me and she said: "I'm your sister that was taken; and don't you remember how I got the fever first and you tended me, and then you got it yourself, and one had to be taken and I was the one." And she taught me the cure, and the way to use it. And she told me that she was in the best of places, and told me many things that she bound me not to tell. And I asked was it here she was kept ever since, and she said it was, but she said, "In six months I'll have to move to another place, and others will come where I am now, and it would be better for you if we stopped here, for the most of us here now are your neighbours and your friends." And it was she gave me the second sight.[32]

Last year I was digging potatoes and a man came by, one of *them*, and one that I knew well before. And he said, "You have them this year, and we'll have them the next two years." And you know the potatoes were good last year and you see that they are bad now, and have been made away with.[33] And the sister told me that half the food in Ireland goes to them, but that if they like they can make out of cow-dung all they want, and they can come into a house and use what they like and it will never be missed in the morning.

The old man suddenly stooped and took a handful of hot ashes in his hand, and put them in his pocket. And presently he said he'd be afraid tonight going home the road. When we asked him why, he said he'd have to tell what errand he had been on.

He said one eye of W. B. Y.'s was worse than the other, and asked if he had ever slept out at nights. We asked if he goes to enquire of them (the Others) what is wrong with those who came to him and he said, "Yes, when it has to do with their business—but in this case it has nothing to do with it."[34]

Coneely said next day:
I walked home with the old man last night, he was afraid to go by himself. He pointed out to me on the way a graveyard where he had got a great beating from *them* one night. He had a drop too much taken after being at a funeral, and he went there and gathered the plant wrong. And they came and

punished him, that his head is not the better of it ever since.

He told me the way he knows in the gathering of the plant what is wrong with the person that is looking for a cure. He has to go on his knees and say a prayer to the king and the queen and the gentle and the simple among them, and then he gathers it, and if there are black leaves about it, or white ones, but chiefly a black leaf folded down, he knows the illness is some of their business; but for this young man the plant came fresh and green and clean. He has been among them and has seen the king and the queen, and he says that they are no bigger than the others, but the queen wears a wide cap, and the others have bracket caps.

He never would allow me to build a shed there beside the house, though I never saw anything there myself.

OLD DERUANE

OLD DERUANE lived in the middle island of Aran, Inish-maan, where I have stayed more than once. He was one of the evening visitors to the cottage I stayed in, when the fishers had come home and had eaten, and the fire was stirred and flashed on the dried mackerel and conger eels hanging over the wide hearth, and the little vessel of cod oil had a fresh wick put in it and lighted. The men would sit in a half-circle on the floor, passing the lighted pipe from one to another; the women would find some work with yarn or wheel. The talk often turned on the fallen angels or the dead, for the dwellers in those islands have not been moulded in that dogma which while making belief in the after-life an essential, makes belief in the shadow-visit of a spirit yearning after those it loved a vanity, a failing of the great essential, common sense, and sets down one who believes in such things as what Burton calls in his Anatomy "a melancholy dizzard."

I was told by Old Deruane:
I was born and bred in the North Island, and ten old fathers of mine are buried there.

I can speak English, because I went to earn in England in

the hard times, and I was for five quarters in a country town called Manchester; and I have threescore and fifteen years.

I knew two fine young women were brought away after childbirth, and they were seen after in the North Island going about with *them*. One of them I saw myself there, one time I was out late at night going to the east village. I saw her pattern walking on the north side of the wall, on the road near me, but she said nothing. And my body began to shake, and I was going to get to the south side of the wall, to put it between us; but then I said, "Where is God?" and I walked on and passed her, and she looked aside at me but she didn't speak. And I heard her after me for a good while, but I never looked back, for it's best not to look back at them.

And there was another woman had died, and one evening late I was coming from the schoolmaster, for he and I are up to one another, and he often gives me charity. And then I saw her or her pattern walking along that field of rock you passed by just now. But I stopped and I didn't speak to her, and she went on down the road, and when she was about forty fathoms below me I could hear her abusing some one, but no one there. I thought maybe it was that she was vexed at me that I didn't question her. She was a young woman too. I'll go bail they never take an old man or woman—what would they do with them? If by chance they'd come among them they'd throw them out again.

Another night I was out and the moon shining, I knew by the look of it the night was near wore away. And when I came to the corner of the road beyond, my flesh began to shake and my hair rose up, and every hair was as stiff as that stick. So I knew that some evil thing was near, and I got home again. This island is as thick as grass with them, or as sand; but good neighbours make good neighbours, and no woman minding a house but should put a couple of the first of the potatoes aside on the dresser, for there's no house but they'll visit it some time or other. Myself, I always brush out my little tent clean of a night before I lie down, and the night I'd do it most would be a rough night. How do we know what poor soul might want to come in?

I saw them playing ball one day when the slip you landed at was being made, and I went down to watch the work. There were hundreds of them in the field at the top of it, about three feet tall, and little caps on them; but the men that were working there, they couldn't see them.[35] And one morning I went down to the well to leave my pampooties in it to soak—it was a Sabbath morning and I was going to Mass—and the pampooties were hard and wore away my feet, and I left them there. And when I came back in a few minutes they were gone, and I looked in every cleft, but I couldn't find them. And when I was going away, I felt *them* about me, and coming between my two sticks that I was walking with. And I stopped and looked down and said, "I know you're there," and then I said, "*Gentlemen,* I know you're here about me," and when I said that word they went away. Was it they took my pampooties? Not at all—what would they want with such a thing as pampooties? It was some children must have taken them, and I never saw them since.

One time I wanted to settle myself clean, and I brought down my waistcoat and a few little things I have, to give them a rinse in the sea-water, and I laid them out on a stone to dry, and I left one of my sticks on them. And when I came back after leaving them for a little time, the stick was gone. And I was vexed at first to be without it, but I knew that they had taken it to be humbugging me, or maybe for their own use in fighting. For there is nothing there is more fighting among than them. So I said, "Welcome to it, *Gentlemen,* may it bring you luck; maybe you'll make more use of it than ever I did myself."

One night when I was sleeping in my little tent, I heard a great noise of fighting, and I thought it was down at Mrs. Jordan's house, and that maybe the children were troublesome in the bed, she having a great many of them. And in the morning as I passed the house I said to her, "What was on you in the night?" And she said there was nothing happened there, and that she heard no noise. So I said nothing but went on; and when I came to the flag-stones beyond her house, they were covered with great splashes and drops of blood. So I said nothing of that either, but went on. What time of the year? Wait till I think, it was this very same time of the year, the month of May.

One time I was out putting seed in the ground, and the ridges all ready and the seaweed spread in them; and it was a fine day, but I heard a storm in the air, and then I knew by signs that it was they were coming. And they came into the field and tossed the seaweed and the seed about, and I spoke to them civil and then they went into a neighbour's field, and from that down to the sea, and there they turned into a ship, the grandest that ever I saw.

There was a man was passing by that Sheoguey place below, fishing in his curragh, and when they were about a mile out they saw a ship coming towards them, and when they looked again, instead of having three masts she had none, and just when they were going to take up the curragh to bring it ashore, a great wave came and turned it upside down. And the man that owned her got such a fright that he couldn't walk, and the other two had to hold him under the arms to bring him home. And he went to his bed, and within a week after, he was dead.

One night I heard a crying down the road, and the next day, there was a child of Tom Regan's dead. And it was a few months after that, that I heard a crying again. And the next day another of his children was gone.

There was a fine young man was buried in the graveyard below, and a good time after that, there was work being done in it, and they came on his coffin, and the mother made them open it, and there was nothing in it at all but a broom, and it tied up with a bit of a rope.

There was a man was passing by that Sheoguey place below, "Breagh" we call it. And he saw a man come riding out of it on a white horse. And when he got home that night there was nothing for him or for any of them to eat, for the potatoes were not in yet. And in the morning he asked the wife was there anything to eat, and she said a neighbour had sent in a pan of meal. So she made that into stirabout, and he took but a small bit of it out of her hand to leave more for the rest. And then he took a sheet, and bid her make a bag of it, and he got a horse and rode to the place where he saw the man ride out, for he knew he was the master of *them*. And he asked for the full of the bag of meal, and said he'd bring it back again, when he had it. And the man brought the bag in, and filled it for him and brought it out again. And when the oats were ripe, the first he cut, he got ground at the mill and brought it to the place and gave it in. And the man came out and took it, and said whatever he'd want at any time, to come to him and he'd get it.

In a bad year they say they bring away the potatoes and that may be so. They want provision, and they must get them at one place or another.

Mr. McArdle joins in and says:
This I can tell you and be certain of, and I remember well that the man in the third house to this died after being sick a

long time. And the wife died after, and she was to be buried in the same place, and when they came to the husband's coffin they opened it, and there was nothing in it at all, neither brooms nor anything else.

There's a boy, I know him well, that was up at that forth above the house one day, and a blast of wind came and blew the hat off him. And when he saw it going off in the air he cried out, "Do whatever is pleasing to you, but give me back my cap!" And in the moment it was settled back again on to his head.

Old Deruane goes on:

There are many can do cures, because they have something walking with them, what one may call a ghost from among the Sheogue. A few cures I can do myself, and this is how I got them. I told you that I was for five quarters in Manchester, and where I lodged were two old women in the house, from the farthest end of Mayo, for they were running from Mayo at the time because of the hunger. And I knew that they were likely to have a cure, for St. Patrick blessed the places he was not in more than the places he was in, and with the cure he left and the fallen angels, there are many in Mayo can do them.

Now it's the custom in England never to clean the table but once in the week and that on a Saturday night. And on that night all is set out clean, and all the crutches of bread and bits of meat and the like are gathered together in a tin can, and thrown out in the street, and women that have no other way of living come round then with a bag that would hold two stone, and they pick up all that's thrown out in the street, and live on it for a week. And often I didn't eat the half of what was before me, and I wouldn't throw it out, but I'd bring it to the two old women that were in the house, so they grew very fond of me.

Well, when the time came that I thought to draw towards home, I brought them one day to a public-house and made a drop of punch for them, and then I picked the cure out of them, for I was wise in those days.

Those that get a touch I could save from being brought away, but I couldn't bring back a man that's away, for it's only those that have been living among them for a while that can do that. There was a neighbour's child was sick, and I got word of it, and I went to the house, for the woman there had showed me kindness. And I went in to the cradle and I lifted the quilt off the child's face and you could see by it, and I knew the sign, that there was some of their work there. And I said, "You are not likely to have the child long with you, Ma'am." And she said, "Indeed I know I won't have him long." So I said nothing but I went out, and whatever I did, and whatever I got there, I brought it again and gave it to the child, and he began to get better. And the next day I brought the same thing again, and gave it the child, and I looked at it and I said to the mother, "He'll live to comb his hair grey." And from that time he got better, and now there's no stronger child in the island, and he the youngest in the house.

After that the husband got sick, and the woman said to me one day, "If there's anything you can do to cure him, have pity on me and on my children, and I'll give you what you'll wish." But I said, "I'll do what I can for you, but I'll take nothing from you except maybe a grain of tea or a glass of porter, for I wouldn't take money for this, and I refused £2 one time for a cure I did." So I went and I brought back the cure, and I mixed it with flour and made it into three little pills that it couldn't be lost, and gave them to him, and from that time he got well.

There's a woman lived down the road there, and one day I went in to the house, when she was after coming from Galway town, and I asked charity of her. And it was in the month of August when the bream fishing was going on, and she said, "There's no one need be in want now, with fresh fish in the sea and potatoes in the gardens"; and gave me nothing. But when I was out the door she said, "Well, come back here." And I said, "If you were to offer me all you brought from Galway, I wouldn't take it from you now."

And from that time she began to pine and to wear away and to lose her health, and at the end of three years, she walked outside her house one day, and when she was two yards from her own threshold she fell on the ground, and the neighbours came and lifted her up on a door and brought her into the house, and she died.

I think I could have saved her then— I think I could, when I saw her lying there. But I remembered that day, and I didn't stretch out a hand and I spoke no word.

I'm going to rise out of the cures and not to do much more of them, for *they* have given me a touch here in the right leg, so that it's the same as dead. And a woman of my village that does cures, she is after being struck with a pain in the hand.

Down by the path at the top of the slip from there to the hill, that's the way they go most nights, hundreds and thousands of them. There are two old men in the island got a beating from them; one of them told me himself and brought me out on the ground, that I'd see where it was. He was out in a small field, and was after binding up the grass, and the sky got very black over him and very dark. And he was thrown down on the ground, and got a great beating, but he could see nothing at all. He had done nothing to vex them, just minding his business in the field.

And the other was an old man too, and he was out on the roads, and they threw him there and beat him that he was out of his mind for a time.

One night sleeping in that little cabin of mine, I heard them ride past, and I could hear by the feet of the horses that there was a long line of them.

This is a story was going about twenty years ago. There was a curate in the island, and one day he got a call to the other island for the next day. And in the evening he told the servant maid that attended him to clean his boots good and very good, for he'd be meeting good people where he was going. And she said, "I will, Holy Father, and if you'll give me your hand and word to marry me for nothing, I'll clean them grand." And he said "I will; whenever you get a comrade I'll marry you for nothing, I give you my hand and word." So she had the boots grand for him in the morning. Well, she got a sickness after, and after seven months going by, she was buried. And six months after that, the curate was in his parlour one night and the moon shining, and he saw a boy and a girl outside the house, and they came to the window, and he knew it was the servant girl that was buried. And she said, "I have a comrade now, and I came for you to marry us as you gave your word." And he said, "I'll hold to my word since I gave it," and he married them then and there, and they went away again.[36]

79

III

THE EVIL EYE—THE TOUCH—THE PENALTY

"SOME friendly Teyâmena, sorry to see my suffering plight, said to me: 'This is because thou hast been eye-struck—what! you do not understand 'eye-struck'? Certainly they have looked in your eyes, Khalîl. We have lookers (God cut them off!) among us, that with their only (malignant) eye-glances may strike down a fowl flying; and you shall see the bird tumble in the air with loud shrieking kâk-kâ-kâ-kâ-kâ. Wellah their looking can blast a palm-tree so that you shall see it wither away. These are things well ascertained by many faithful witnesses.'"
—DOUGHTY'S *Travels in the Arabian Desert.*

There is one visit I have always been a little remorseful about. It was in Mayo where I had gone to see the broken walls and grass-grown hearthstone that remain of the house where Raftery the poet was born. I was taken to see an old woman near, and the friend who was with me asked her about "Those." I could see she was unwilling to speak, and I would not press her, for there are some who fear to vex invisible hearers; so we talked of America where she had lived for a little while. But presently she said, "All I ever saw of them myself was one night when I was going home, and they were behind in the field watching me. I couldn't see them but I saw the lights they carried, two lights on the top of a sort of dark oak pole. So I watched them and they watched me, and when we were tired watching one another the lights all went into one blaze, and then they went away and it went out." She told also one or two of the traditional stories, of the man who had a hump put on him, and the woman "taken" and rescued by her husband, who she had directed to seize the horse she was riding with his left hand.

Then she gave a cry and took up her walking stick from the hearth, burned through, and in two pieces, though the fire had seemed to be but a smouldering heap of ashes. We were very sorry, but she said "Don't be sorry. It is well it was into it the harm went." I passed the house two or three hours afterwards; shutters and door were closed, and I felt that she was fretting

80

*for the stick that had been "America and back with me, and
had walked every part of the world," and through the loss of
which, it may be, she had "paid the penalty."*

*I told a neighbour about the doctor having attended a man
on the mountains—and how after some time, he found that one
of the children was sick also, but this had been hidden from him,
because if one had to die they wanted it to be the child.*

*"That's natural," he said. "Let the child pay the penalty if it
has to be paid. That's a thing that might happen easy enough."*

I was told by M. McGarity:

There was a boy of the Cloonans I knew was at Killinane
thatching Henniff's house. And a woman passed by, and she
looked up at him, but she never said, "God bless the work."
And Cloonan's mother was in the road to Gort and the woman
met her and said, "Where did your son learn thatching?" And
that day he had a great fall and was brought home hurt, and the
mother went to Biddy Early. And she said, "Didn't a red-haired
woman meet you one day going into Gort and ask where did
your son learn thatching? And didn't she look up at him as she
passed? It was then it was done." And she gave a bottle and
he got well after a while.[37]

Some say the evil eye is in those who were baptized wrong,
but I believe it's not that, but if, when a woman is carrying,
some one that meets her says, "So you're in that way," and she
says, "The devil a fear of me," as even a married woman might
say for sport or not to let on, the devil gets possession of the
child at that moment, and when it is born it has the evil eye.

Margaret Bartly:

There was a woman below in that village where I lived to my
grief and my sorrow, and she used to be throwing the evil eye,
but she is in the poorhouse now—Mrs. Boylan her name is.
Four she threw it on, not children but big men, and they lost the
walk and all, and died. Maybe she didn't know she had it, but
it is no load to any one to say "God bless you." I faced her one
time and told her it would be no load to her when she would
see the man in the field, and the horses ploughing to say "God
bless them," and she was vexed and she asked did I think she

had the evil eye, and I said I did. So she began to scold and I left her. That was five years ago, and it is in the poor-house in Ballyvaughan she is this two years; but she can do no harm there because she has lost her sight.

Mrs. Nelly of Knockmogue:

There was a girl lived there near the gate got sick. And after waiting a long time and she getting no better the mother brought in a woman that lived in the bog beyond, that used to do cures. And when she saw the girl, she knew what it was, and that she had been overlooked. And she said, "Did you meet three men on the road one day, and didn't one of them, a dark one, speak to you and give no blessing?" And she said that was so. And she would have done a cure on her, but we had a very good priest at that time, Father Hayden, a curate, and he used to take a drop of liquor and so he had courage to do cures. And he said this was a business for him, and he cured her, and the mother gave him money for it.

It was by herbs that woman used to do cures, and whatever power she got in the gathering of them, she was able to tell what would happen. But she was in great danger all her life from gathering the herbs, for *they* don't like any one to be cured that they have put a touch on.

Mrs. Clerey:

I can tell you what happened to two sons of mine. A woman that passed by them said, "You've often threatened me by night, and my curse is on you now." And the one answered her back but the other didn't. And after that they both took sick, but the one that didn't answer her was the worst. And they pined a long time. And I brought the one that was so bad over to Kilronan to the priest and he read over him. It was a lump in his mouth he had, that you could hardly put down a spoonful of milk, and there was a good doctor there and he sliced it, and he got well. But the priest often told me that but for what he did for him he would never have got well. For there's no doubt there's *some* in the world it's not well to talk with.

The time my son got the pain, he came in roaring and said he got a stab in the knee. It was surely some evil thing that put it on him. There are some that have the evil eye, and that don't know it themselves. Father McEvilly told me that. He said a woman that was carrying, and that was not married, but that got married while she was carrying, she might put the evil eye on you, and not know it at all. And he said anyway it would be no great load to say "God bless you" to any one you might meet.

The priests can do cures if they like, but those that have stock don't like to be doing it, Father Folan won't do it, but Father McEvilly would.

One time my brother got a great pain, and my father sent me to Father Gallagher, to ask could he cure and read the Mass of the Holy Ghost over him. But when I asked him he called out, "I won't do that, I won't read for any one." He was afraid to go as far as that for fear it might fall on his stock, that he had a great deal of.

James Fahey:
Do you think the *drohuil* is not in other places besides Aran? My mother told me herself that she was out at a dance one evening, and there was a fine young man there and he dancing till he had them all tired; and a woman that was sitting there said "He can do what he likes with his legs," and at that instant he fell dead. My mother told me that herself, and she heard the woman say it, and so did many others that were there.

Frank McDaragh:
There's none can do cures well in this island like Biddy Early used to do. I want to know of some good man or woman in that line to go to, for that little girl of my own got a touch last week. Coming home from Mass she was, and she felt a pain in her knee, and it ran down to the foot and up again, and since then the feet are swelled, you might see them.

Mrs. Meade:
And about here they all believe in the faeries—and I hear them say—but I don't give much heed to it—that Mrs. Hehir the butcher's sister that died last week—but I don't know much about it. But anyhow she was married three years, and had a child every year, and this time she died. And when the coffin was leaving the house, the young baby began to scream, and to go into convulsions, for all the world as if it was put on the fire.

Another says about this same woman, Mrs. Hehir:
It's overlooked she was when she went out for a walk with a

83

scholar from the seminary that is going to be a priest, and she without a shawl over her head. It's then she was overlooked; they seeing what a fine handsome woman she was, she was took away to be nurse to *themselves*.

Mrs. Quade:

A great pity it was about Mrs. Hehir and she leaving three young orphans. But sure they do be saying a great big black bird flew into the house and around about the kitchen—and it was the next day the sickness took her.

The Doctor:

Mrs. Hehirs was a difficult case to diagnose, and I could not give it a name. At the end she was flushed and delirious; and when one of the women attending her said, "She looks so well you wouldn't think it was herself that was in it at all," I knew what was in their minds. Afterwards I was told that the day the illness began she had been churning, and a strange woman came in and said, "Give me a hold of the staff and I'll do a bit of the churning for you." But she refused and the woman said, "It's the last time you'll have the chance of refusing anyone that asks you" and went out, and she was not see again, then or afterwards.

J. Madden:

There's one thing should never be done, and that's to say "That's a fine woman," or such a thing and not to say "God bless her." I never believed that till a man that lives in the next holding to my own told me what happened to a springer he had. She was as fine a creature as ever you seen, and one day a friend of his came in to see him, and when he was going away, "That's a grand cow," says he, but he didn't say "God bless it." Well, the owner of the cow went into the house and he sat down by the fire and lit a pipe, and when he had the pipe smoked out he came out again, and there she was lying down and not able to stir. So he remembered what happened and he went after his friend, and found him in a neighbour's house. And he brought him back with him, and made him go into the field and say, "God bless it," and spit on the cow. And with that she got up and walked away as well as before.

John McManus:

They can only take a child or a horse or such things through the eye of a sinner. If his eye falls on it, and he speaks to praise it and doesn't say "God bless it," they can bring it away then. But if you say it yourself in your heart, it will do as well.

There was a man lived about a mile beyond Spiddal, and he was one day at a play, and he was the best at the hurling and the throwing and every game. And a woman of the crowd called out to him, "You're the straightest man that's in it." And twice after that a man that was beside him and that heard that said, saw him pass by with his coat on before sunrise. And on the fifth day after that he was dead.

He left four or five sons and some of them went to America and the eldest of them married and was living in the place with his wife. And he was going to Galway for a fair, and his wife was away with her father and mother on the road to Galway and she bid him to come early, that she'd have some commands for him to do. So it was before sunrise when he set out, and he was going over a little side road through the fields, and he came on the biggest fair he ever saw, and the most people in it. And they made a way for him to pass through and a man with a big coat and a tall hat came out from them and said, "Do you know me?" And he said, "Are you my father?" And the man said, "I am, and but for me you'd be sorry for coming here, but I saved you, but don't be coming out so early in the morning again." And he said, "It was a year ago that Jimmy went to America. And that was time enough." And then he said, "And it was you that drove your sister away, and gave her no fortune." And that was true enough.

One time there was two brothers standing in a gap in that field you're looking at. And a woman passed by, I wouldn't like to tell you her name, for we should speak no evil of her and she's dead now,—the Lord have mercy on her. And when she passed they heard her say in Irish, "The devil take you," but whether she knew they were there or not, I don't know. And the elder of the brothers called out, "The devil take yourself as well." But the younger one said nothing. And that night the younger one took sick, and through the night he was calling out and talking as if to people in the room. And the next day the mother went to a woman that gathered herbs, the mother of the woman that does cures by them now, and told her all that happened.

And she took a rag of an old red coat, and went down to the

last village, and into the house of the woman that had put it, the evil eye, on him. And she sat there and was talking with her, and watched until she made a spit on the floor, and then she gathered it up on the rag and came to the sick man in the bed and rubbed him with it, and he got well on the minute.

It was hardly ever that woman would say "God bless the work" as she passed, and there were some would leave the work and come out on the road and hold her by the shoulder till she'd say it.

A Man on the Boat:

There are many can put on the *drohuil*. I knew a child in our village and a neighbour came in and said, "That's a fine child"; and no sooner was he gone than the child got a fit. So they brought him back and made him spit on the child and it got well after. Those that have that power, I believe it's born with them, and it's said they can do it on their own children as well as on ours.

There was a boy called Faherty, nephew to Faherty that keeps the licensed house, and he was a great one for all games, and at every pattern, and whenever anything was going on. And one time he went over to Kilronan where they had some sports, and it the 24th of June. And they were throwing the weight, and he took it up and he threw it farther than the police or any that were there; and the second time he did the same thing. And when he was going to throw it the third time, his uncle came to him and said "It's best for you to leave it now; you have enough done." But he wouldn't mind him, and threw it the third time, and farther than they all.

And the next year at that time on the 24th of June, he was stretched on his bed, and he died. And some one was talking about the day he did so much at Kilronan, and the father said: "I remember him coming into the house after that, and he put up his arm on the dresser as if there was something ailed him." And the boy spoke from his bed and said, "You ought to have said 'God bless you' then. If my mother had been living then she'd have said it, and I wouldn't be lying here now."

There were two other fine young men died in the same year, and one night after, the three of them appeared to a sick man, Jamsie Power, on the south island, and talked with him. But they didn't stay long because, they said, they had to go on to the coast of Clare.

My own first-born child wasn't spared. He was born in February and all the neighbours said they never saw so fine a child. And one night towards the end of March, I was in the bed, and the child on my arm between me and the wall, sleeping warm and well, and the wife was settling things about the house. And when she got into bed, she wanted to take the child, and I said, "Don't stir him, where he's so warm and so well"; but she took him in her own arm. And in the morning he was dead. And up to the time he was buried, you'd say he wasn't dead at all, so fresh and so full in the face he looked.

There was a neighbour about the same time had a child and it was in the bed with them, but it was sick. And one night he was sure he heard some one say outside the house, "It's time he should be stretched out to me." So he got up and opened the window, and he threw a vessel of dirty water over whatever was outside, and he heard no more, and his child got well and grew up strong.

An Island Woman:

And there's some people the fishermen wouldn't pass when they are going to the boats, but would turn back again if they'd meet them. One day two boys of mine, Michael and Danny, were down on the rocks, bream-fishing with lines, and I had a job of washing with the wife of the head coastguard. But when it came to one o'clock something came over me, and I thought the boys might have got the hunger, and I went to Mrs. Patterson and said I must leave work for that day, and I went and bought a three-halfpenny loaf and brought it down to where they were fishing, and when I got there I saw that Michael the younger one was limping, and I said, "It must be from the hunger you're not able to walk." "Oh, no," he said, "but it's a pain I got in my heel, and I can't put it to the ground." And when we got home he went into his bed, and he didn't leave it for three months. And one day I said to him, "What was it happened you, did you meet any one on the road that day that said anything to you?" And he said, "I did, I met a woman of the village and she said, 'It's good to be you and to have a fine basket of bream,' and she said no more than that, and that very minute the pain came on my heel. But I won't tell you her name,

87

for fear there'd be a row." But I made him tell me, and I promised never to say a word to her and I never did; but he's not the first she did that to.

An Old Man with a Basket:
They can put the *drohuil* here and I suppose in all parts, and you should watch not to let any one meet you unless they would say, "God bless you," and spit.

There was a woman in this island lost her walk for a year and a half, till they went to Galway to a woman that throws the cups, and she bid them go into the next house where there was a black man living, and give him tobacco to be smoking, and take up the spit and rub his leg. And she got well after that.

There was another man in that island besides that neighbour of mine that would give the *drohuil*—the evil eye. Tom Griffith his name was. There was one Flanagan came back from Clare one day with three bonifs he bought there. And Griffith came out as he passed and said, "No better bonifs than those ever came into the island." And when Flanagan came home, there was a little hill in the front of his house and two of them fell down against it on their side. And when Mrs. Flanagan came out to see the bonifs, there was only one of them living before her.

There's a man in this island now puts the evil eye—the *drohuil*. It's about four years since I heard of him doing it last. There was a nice young woman he passed and he said, "You're the best walker in Aran." And that day she got a pain in her leg and she took to her bed, and there she lay for six months, and then she sent for him, and he was made—with respects to you—to throw a spit on her. And after that she got well and got up again. And there was a child died about the same time, and the friends said it was he did it. Ned Buckley is his name. Devil a foot he ever goes to a wedding or such like; they wouldn't ask him, they'd be afraid of him. But he goes to Mass—at least he did in his bloom—but he's an old man now. Does the priest know about him? It's not likely he does. There's no one would like to go and make an attack on him like that. And anyway the priests don't like any one to speak to them of such things, they'd sooner not hear about them.

88

Mrs. Folan:

There was one of my brothers overlooked, no doubt at all about that. He was the best rower of a canoe that ever was, and there was a match at Kinvara today and he won it, and there was a match at Ballyvaughan tomorrow and he was in it, and the foam was as high as mountains, that the hooker could hardly stand, and he won there. And when he was come to the pier and the people all running to carry him in their arms, the way the jockey is carried after a race, he was ruz up his own height off the ground, and no one could see what did it.

He was wrong in the head after that, and he would sit by the hearth without speaking. My mother that would be out binding the wheat would say to me now and again "There he is coming across to us," and she put it on me to think it, but I could see nothing, for it is not everyone can see those things. Then she would ask the father when we went in, did he stir from the fireside, and when he said he never stirred she knew it was his shadow she saw and that he had not long to live, and it was not long till he was gone.

Mr. Stephens:

There was a man coming along the road from Gort to Garryland one night, and he had a drop taken, and before him on the road he saw a pig walking. And having a drop in, he gave a shout and made a kick at it and bid it get out of that.

And from the time he got home, his arm had swelled from the shoulder to be as big as a bag, and he couldn't use his hand with the pain in it. And his wife brought him after a few days to a woman that used to do cures at Rahasane.

And on the road all she could do would hardly keep him from lying down to sleep on the grass. And when they got to the woman, she knew all that happened, and says she: "It's well for you that your wife didn't let you fall asleep on the grass, for if you had done that but for an instant, you'd be a gone man."

Mrs. Casey:

There was a woman lived near Ballinasloe and she had two children, and they both died, one after the other. And when the third was born, she consulted an old woman, and she said to watch the cradle all day where it was standing by the side of the fire. And so she did, and she saw a sort of a shadow come into it, and give the child a touch. And she came in, and drove

89

it away. And the second day the same thing happened, and she was afraid that the third time the child would go, the same as the others. So she went to the old woman again, and she bid her take down the hanger from the chimney, and the tongs and the waistcoat of the child's father and to lay them across the cradle, with a few drops of water from a blessed well. So she did all this and laid these three things in the cradle, but she saw the shadow or whatever it was come again, and she ran in and drove it away.

But when she told the old woman she said "You need trouble yourself no more about it being touched or not, for no harm will come to it if you keep those three things on it for twelve days." So she did that, and reared eight children after, and never lost one.

An Old Woman from Kinvara:

Did I know any one was taken? My own brother was, and no mistake about it. It was one day he was out following two horses with the plough, and it was about five o'clock, for a gentleman was passing when he got the touch, and one of his tenants asked him the time, and he said five o'clock. And what way it came I don't know, but he fell twice on the stones—God bless the hearers and the place I'm telling it in. And at ten o'clock the next morning he was dead in his bed. Young he was, not twenty year, and nothing ailed him when he went out, but the place he was ploughing in that day was a bad pass. Sure and certain I am it's by *them* he was taken. I used often to hear crying in the field after, but I never saw him again.

A Connemara Woman:

There was a boy going to America, and when he was going he said to the girl next door "Wherever I am, when you are married I'll come back to the wedding"; and not long after he went to America he died. And when the girl was married and all the friends and neighbours in the house, he appeared in the room, but no one saw him but his comrade he used to have here, and the girl's brother saw him too, but no one else. And the comrade followed him and went close to him and said, "Is it you indeed?" And he said, "It is, and from America I came tonight." And he asked, "How long did that journey take?" and he said, "Three-quarters of an hour," and then he went away. And the comrade was never the better of it, or he got the touch or the other called him, very true friends as they were, and he soon died. But the girl is now middle-aged and is living in that house we are just after passing and is married to one Kelly.

Whether all that die go among them I can't say, but it is said they can take no one without the touch of a Christian hand, or the want of a blessing from a Christian that would be noticing them.

A North Galway Woman:
There are many young women taken in childbirth. I lost a sister of my own in that way.

There's a place in the river at Newtown where there's stepping-stones in the middle you can get over by, and one day she was crossing, and there in the middle of the river, and she standing on a stone, she felt a blow on the face. And she looked round to see who gave it and there was no one there, so then she knew what had happened, and she came to the mother's house, and she carrying at the time. I was a little slip at that time, with my books in my hand coming from school, and I ran in and said to my mother, "Here's Biddy coming," and she said, "What would bring her at this time of day?" But she came in and sat down on a chair and she opened the whole story, and my mother said to quiet her, "It was only a pain in the ear you got, and you thought it was a blow." And she said, "I never got a blow that hurted me like that." And the next day, and every day after that, the ear would swell a little in the afternoon, and then she began to eat nothing, and five minutes after her baby was born she died. And my mother used to watch for her for three or four years after, thinking she'd come back, but she never did.

There was a forth near our house in Meath, and when I was a baby a woman was carrying me in her arms, and she walked down the four steps that led into it, and there was a nice garden around it, and she slipped and fell, and my cheek struck against one of the steps—you can see the mark yet that I got there. And the woman told my mother and said, "It's a wonder the child wasn't taken altogether then and there."

One day I was out digging in the field for my brothers, and there was a sort of a half-ditch between the oats and the potatoes, and I was digging it down, and of a sudden a sleep came on me and I lay down. And I suppose I had been asleep about twenty minutes when I was waked with a hard clout on the face. And I thought it was one of my brothers and I called out, "You have no right to give me a clout like that." But my brother was away down the field, and came when he heard me calling. And I felt a pain in my side as well, and I went into the house and didn't leave it for two months after with pleurisy, and the pain never left me till after I was married. I suppose I must have been on some way of theirs, or some place that belonged to them and that was known to be an enchanted place, and my father used often to see it lighted up with candles.

A Man Herding Sheep:
I'll tell you now what happened to a little one of my own. She was just five years. And the day I'm speaking of she was running to school down the path before me, as strong and as funny as the day she was born, and laughing and looking back at me. And that night she went to bed as well as ever she was. And at about eleven o'clock in the night she awoke and gave a great cry, and she said there was a great pain in her knee, and it was in no other part of her. And in the morning she had it yet, and her walk had gone, and I lifted her and brought her out into the street, and she couldn't walk one step if you were to give her the three isles of Aran. And she lived for two nights after that.

When the doctor came and I told him, he said it was the strangest case he ever heard of, and the schoolmistress said, "I thought if I'd brought that child to the hill beyond and threw her down into the sea it would do her no harm, she was that strong."

But if such things happen, it happened to her, and touched she was. It was not death, it was being took away.

An Old Woman in an Aran village:
I'll tell you what happened a son of my own that was so strong and so handsome and so good a dancer, he was mostly the pride of the island. And he was that educated that when he was twenty-six years, he could write a letter to the Queen. And one day a pain came in the thigh, and a little lump came inside it, and a hole in it that you could hardly put the point of a pin in, and it was always drawing. And he took to his bed and was there for eleven months. And every night when it would be twelve o'clock, he would begin to be singing and laughing and going on. And what the neighbours said was, that it was at that hour there was some other left in his place. I never went to

any one or any witchcraft, for my husband wouldn't let me but left it to the will of God; and anyway at the end of the eleven months he died.

And his sister was in America, and the same thing came to her there, a little lump by the side of the face, and she came home to die. But she died quiet and was like any other in the night.

And a daughter-in-law of mine died after the second birth, and even the priest said it was not *dead* she was, he that was curate then. I was surprised the priest to say that, for they mostly won't give in to it, unless it's one that takes a drop of drink.

An Old Man in the Kitchen:

I had a son that it was mostly given in to in Aran to be the best singer to give out a couple of verses, so that he'd hardly go out of the house but some one would want to be bringing him into theirs. And he took sick of a sudden, with a pain in his shoulder. I went to the doctor and he says, "Does your wife take tea?" "She does when she can get it," says I, and he told me then to put the spout of the kettle to where the pain was. And after that he went to Galway Hospital, but he got no better there and a Sister of Mercy said to him at last, "I'm thinking by the look of you, your family at home is poor." "That's true enough," says he. Then says she: "It's best for you to stop here, and they'll be free from the cost of burying you." But he said he'd sooner go die at home, if he had but two days to live there. So he came back and he didn't last long. It's always the like of him that's taken, that are good for singing or dancing, or for any good thing at all. And young women are often taken in that way, both in the middle island and in this.

Patrick Madden:

I'll tell you how I lost the first son I had. He was just three years old and as fine and as strong as any child you'd see. And one day my wife said she'd bring the child to her mother's house to stop the evening with her, for I was going out. And there was a neighbour of ours, a man that lived near us, and no one was the better of being spoken to by him. And as they were passing his house he came out, and he said, "That's the finest child that's in the island." And a woman that was passing at the same time stopped and said, "It was the smallest that ever

I saw the day it was born, God bless it." And the mother knew what she meant, and she wanted to say "God bless him," but it was like as if a hand took and held her throat, and choked her that she couldn't say the words. And when I came to the mother's house, and began to make fun with the child, I saw a round mark on the side of his head, the size of a crown piece. And I said to the wife, "Why would you beat the child in the head, why don't you get a little rod to beat him if he wants it?" And she said that she had never touched him at all.

And at that time I was very much given to playing cards, and that night I went out to a friend's house to play. And the wife before she went to bed broiled a bit of fish and put it on a plate with potatoes, and put it in a box in the room, for fear it might be touched by a cat or a rat or such like. But I was late coming in and didn't mind to eat it. And the next night I was out again. And when we were playing cards we'd play first with tobacco and we'd go on to tea, and we'd end up with whiskey. And the next morning when the wife opened the box she laughed and she said "You didn't drink your tea when you were out last night, for I see you have your dinner eaten." And I said, "Why should you say that? I never touched it." And she held up the plate and showed me that the potatoes were taken off it; but the fish wasn't touched, for it was a bit of a herring and salty.

Well, the child was getting sick all the day, and I didn't go out that evening. And in the night we could hear the noise as if of scores of rats, going about the room. And every now and again I struck a light, but soon as the light was in it we'd hear nothing. But the noise would begin again as soon as it was dark, and sometimes it would seem as if they came up on the bed, and I could feel the weight of them on my chest as if they would smother me.

And in the morning I chanced to open the box where the dinner used to be put, and it as big a box as any in Aran, and when I opened it I saw it was all full of blood, up the sides and to the top, that you couldn't put your hand in without it getting bloody. I said nothing but shut the lid down again. But after, when I came into the house, I saw the wife rubbing at it with a thing they call flannel they got at Killinny, and I asked her what was she doing, and she said, "I'm cleaning the box, where it's full of blood." And after that I gave up the child and I had no more hope for its life. But if they had told me that about the

94

neighbour speaking to him, I'd have gone over, and I'd have killed him with my stick, but I'd have made him come and spit on him. After that we didn't hear the noise the same again, but we heard like the sound of a clock all through the night and every night. And the child got a swelling under the feet, and he couldn't put a foot to the ground. But that made little difference to him, for he didn't hold out a week.

I lost another son after – but he died natural, there was nothing of that sort. And I have one son remaining now, and one day he went to sleep out in a field and that's a bad thing to do. And the sister found him there, and when she woke him he couldn't get up hardly, or move his hand, and she had to help him to the house.

Pat Doherty:
I know a gentleman too got the touch, one of the Butlers. It was on a day he made a great leap he got it. And he went to the bed and for three or four days he couldn't stir, and red marks came out over him shaped like a bow. And then I went for the priest and brought him to see him, and when he heard of the marks, "I'm as bad as that myself," he said, making fun; "for I'm after making a journey in a curragh." But when the clothes were stripped back and he saw his skin, "Oh, murder!" he said, and he put on his stole and got out a book. And he said, "Did you hear what I did to the man at Iona? He went to the well with a tin can for water, and when he got to the well, a few yards away from it, it was spilled. And he went back and filled it again, and the second time at the well it was spilled, and he fell along with it, and he got a little cut in the fall, and he began to bleed, and all the people said as much blood as would be in three men came away from him. And they sent for me, and the minute I came the bleeding stopped, and he was all right again and the cut closed up."
And then he put his head down and what he read I don't know, but he hardly got to the turn of the road outside the house, when the boy stood up from the bed and asked for something to eat.

Another time I was drawing turf that came in the boats from Connemara to Kilronan pier. And of a sudden there came a swelling in my arm, and it was next day the size of an egg, and it turned black. And I couldn't lift the arm, and Healy the coastguard said to me to go to Doctor Lydon. And I said I would, but in the way I met with Father Jordan and I showed it to him. And he said; "What do you want with your Healy and your Lydons? Let me see it." And he pressed his hand on it two or three times like that, and the swelling began to go, and when I got home they were clearing weed on the shore, and I was able to go down and to give them a hand with it.

A Piper:

There was a cousin of my own used to feel some heavy thing coming on him in the bed in the night time. And he went to the friars at Esker to take it off of him, and they took it off. But Father Williams said, "If this is gone from you some other thing will be put on you." And sure enough it wasn't a twelvemonth after, he was carting planks and the horse fell, and the planks fell on his foot and broke it in two pieces. And after that again he got a fall, over some stones, and he died with throwing off blood.

I had a fall myself in Galway the other day that I couldn't move my arm to play the pipes if you gave me Ireland. And a man said to me—and they are very smart people in Galway—that two or three got a fall and a hurt in that same place. "There is places in the sea where there is drowning," he said, "and places on the land as well where there do be accidents, and no man can save himself from them, for it is the Will of God."

Mrs. Scanlon:

Some people call Mrs. Tobin "Biddy Early." She has done a good many cures. Her brother was *away* for a while and it was from him she got the knowledge. I believe that it's before sunrise that she gathers the herbs, anyway no one ever saw her gathering them.[38] She has saved many a woman from being brought away when their child was born, by whatever she does. She told me herself that one night when she was going to the lodge gate to attend the woman there, three magpies came before her and began roaring into her mouth, to try to drive her back. Father Folan must know about her, but he is a dark man and says nothing, and anyway the priests know as much, and are as much in dread as any one else.

I wish I had sent for her for my own little boy. It's often he asked me to bring him to the friars at Loughrea. But he never would tell how or where he got the touch. It came like a lump in the back, and he got weaker and smaller till you could put him into a tin can, and he twenty years. Often I asked him about it, but he'd say nothing. I believe that they are afraid to tell or they would be worse treated. I asked him was it at the jumping, for they used to be jumping over a pole, and he said it was not, and that he never took a jump that was too much for him.

But some that saw his back said he had been beat. And when the Doctor came in to see him, he was lying on the bed, and he turned him over and looked at him and said, "If he had all Lady Gregory's estate he couldn't live a week." And sure enough within five days he died. And many of the neighbours said they never heard such a storm of wind as rose about the house that night. I never saw him since, and I went late and early, in the mill and down by the river. But it's maybe a hundred or two hundred miles he was brought away.

Tom Flatley:
There is a priest now, a curate down in Cloughmore, is doing great cures. There is often silence between him and the parish priest, Father Rock, for he wouldn't like him to be doing them. There was a little chap went to bed one night as well as yourself, and in the morning he rose up with one of his ears as deaf as that he wouldn't hear you if he died. And the mother brought him to Father Dolan and he came out as well as ever he was. It was but a fortnight ago that happened, and I didn't hear did the misfortune fall on any of the stock.

But wherever there is a cure something will go, and what would a sheep or a heifer be beside a misfortune on a child?

There was a priest near Ennis, a woman I knew went to for a cure, and he wouldn't do it. *"Tha me bocht,"* he said, "I am poor, but I will not do it." "I will pay you well," said the woman. "I will not do it," said he, "for my heart was killed two years ago with one I did. And it isn't money I'd ask of you if I did it," he said, "but to offer you my blessing and the blessing of God."

Mrs. Casey:
There was a woman down by the sea that had a very severe time when her baby was born, and they did not think she or the baby would live after. So the husband went and brought Father Rivers and he said, "Which would you sooner lose—the wife or

the child—for one must go?" And the husband said, "If the wife is taken I might as well close the door." And then Father Rivers said, "She's going up and down like the swinging of a clock, but for all that I'll strive to keep her for you, but maybe you must lose two or more." So he read some prayers over her, and the next day the baby died, and a fine cow out in the field, but the woman recovered and is living still. But Father Rivers died within two years. They never live long when they do these cures, because that they say prayers that they ought not to say.

There's Father Heseltine of Killinan has lost his health and no person knows where he is. They say he's gone abroad because he did a cure on one of his sisters.

Mrs. Cassilis:
A young mare I lost. It was on the 15th August, something came on it in the field, and it did no good, and the son was tending it. And on St. Colman's Day he was taken with a weakness in the chapel that they had to bring him home, and he did not go fasting to the chapel. He got well, but the mare died. I didn't mind that, I knew something must go, and it was better the mare to go than the son.

There were many said, the mare not to have died there would be no chance for him. So I am well content, for whatever way we'll struggle we might get another mare. But a person to go, there is no one for you to get in his place.

A County Galway Magistrate:
That time I was laid up at Luke Manning's they sent for Father Heseltine to "read a gospel" over me. He said when he came in, "You'll lose something tonight." I heard him say this, but what he read over me I don't know, it seemed a sort of muttering. At all events I got well after it, and the next morning, a sheep was found dead.

Pat Hayden:
My father was gardener here at Coole in the time of Mrs. Robert's grandfather. He was sick one time, and he thought to go to the friars at Esker for a cure, and he asked Mr. Gregory for the loan of a horse, and he bade him to take it. So he saddled and bridled the horse, and he set out one morning and went to

98

the friars, and whatever they did they cured him, and he came back again. But in the morning the horse was found dead in the stable. I suppose whatever they took off him they put upon the horse. And when Mr. Gregory came out in the morning, "How is Pat?" he says to one of the men. "Pat is well," says he, "but the horse he brought with him is dead in the stable." "So long as Pat is well," said Mr. Gregory, "I wouldn't mind if five horses in the stable were dead."

Mrs. Manning:

There was a friar in Esker could do cures. Many I've seen brought to him tied in a cart, and able to walk home after. Father Callaghan he was. There was one man brought to him, wrong in his head he was, and he cured him and he gave him some sort of a Gospel rolled up, and bid him to put it about his neck, and never to take it off. Well, he went to America after that and was as well as another and got work, and sent home £10 one time to Father Callaghan he was that grateful to him.

But one day in America he was shaving, and whether he cut the string or that he took it off I don't know, but he laid the charm down on a table. And when he looked for it again, if he was to burn the house down he couldn't find it. And it all came back on him again, and he was as bad as he was before.

So the wife wrote home to Father Callaghan, and he sent out another thing of the same sort; and bid him wear it, and from the time he put it on, he got well again. A priest has the power to do cures, but if he does he can keep nothing, one thing will die after another.

Biddy Early could do the same thing, she had to cast the sickness on some other thing—it might be a dog or a goat or a bird.

Priests can do cures if they will, but they are afraid to do them because their stock will die, and because they are afraid of loss in the other world as well as in this. There's a neighbour of your own lost his milch cow the other day for a small one he did—Father Mulhall that is.

There was Father Rivers was called in to a woman that was bad, between Roxborough and Dunsandle. And he said to the father, "Which would you sooner keep, the wife or the child?" And he said, "Sure I'd sooner have the wife than all the children of the world." So Father Rivers went in and cured her so that she got well, but he put whatever she had on the son, so that he grew up an idiot. Harmless he used to be, not doing much. Well, when he came to twenty years, the mother said, "Come outside into the field, and cut the eyes of a few stone of potatoes for me." But he took up the graip that was at the door and made at her to kill her. And she ran in and shut the door, and then he made for the window and broke it. And at that time Mr. Singleton from Ceramina was passing by, and he stopped and called some men and they took him and took the graip from him, and he was brought away to Ballinasloe Asylum, but he didn't live more than six months after. Waiting all that time he was to do his revenge, but hadn't the power to do it till the twenty years were up.

There is a man that is living strong and well in the village of Lochlan and that has sixteen or seventeen children, and one time something came on him and he wore away till there was no more strength in him than in that thraneen. And there was an old woman used to be doing cures with herbs, and he sent for her, and she went out into the field and she picked two or three leaves of a plant she knew of. And as she was carrying it through the fields to the house she fell dead.

And his strength came back to him when the death fell on her and he was as well and as strong as ever he was. I will bring you three of those leaves if I have to walk two miles—three-cornered leaves they are (penny royal). No harm will come upon me, for I am nothing but an old hag. Before sunrise they must be picked, and the best day to do it is a Friday.

An Old Army Man:
I knew a man had charms for headache and for toothache and other things, and he did a great many cures, but all his own children began to die. So then he put away the charms, and made a promise not to do cures for others again; and after that he lost no more children.

Priests can do cures as well as Biddy Early did, and there was a man of the neighbours digging potatoes in that field beyond, and a woman passed by, and she never said anything. And presently the top of his fingers got burned off, and he called out with the pain, a blast he got from her as she passed. Often he'd come into this house, and crying out with the hurt of the pain. And at last he went to the priests at Esker, and they cured him, but they said, "Your own priests could have done the same for you." And when he came back there were two cows dead.

And the same thing when Carey's wife—that is a tenant of your own— was sick, they called in Father Gardiner and he cured her, and he told them to watch by her for two or three days. And then the priest went out to see the stabling, and Carey with him, for Carey had always a pair of good horses. And when they went into the stable, the horses were dead before them.

It was Flaherty gave his life for my sister that was his wife. When she fell sick he brought her to Biddy Early in the mountains beyond. And she cured her the first time. But she said, "If you bring her again, you'll pay the penalty." But when she fell sick again he brought her, but he stopped a mile from the house. But she knew it well, and told the wife where he was, and that time the horse died. But the third time she fell sick he went again, knowing full well he'd pay the penalty; and so he did and died. But she was cured; and married one O'Dea afterwards.

The priests know well about these things, but they won't let on to have seen them, and the people don't much like to be telling them about them. But there was Father Gallagher that did cures by means of them, and at last he got a touch himself, and was sent for a while to an asylum, and now he has promised to leave them alone. Fallen angels some say they are. I know a man that saw them hurling up there in Hanlon's field. Red caps they wore and looked very diminutive, but they were hurling away like Old Boots.

The way the bad luck came on Tom Hurley was when a cow fell sick on him and lay like dead. He had a right to leave it or to kill it; but the father-in-law cut a bit off the leg of it and it rose again, and they sold it for seven pounds at the fair of Tubber. But he had no luck since then, but lost four or five head of cattle, near all that he owned.

There was a man did a cure on his son that came from America sick. He didn't like to see him ailing, and one night he

101

did the cure. But before sunrise the sight of one of his eyes was gone.

A Mountainy Man:
There's some people living about three miles from here on Slieve-Mor, and they came from the North at the time of the famine, and they can do cures, but they don't like to say much about it—for the people of the North all have it. Their names are natural, McManus, and Irwin and Taylor. There's one of them gave a cure for a man that was sick, and he grew better, but a calf died. And the son was going to him again, but the mother said: "Let him alone, let him die, or we'll lose all the stock"; for she'd sooner have the husband die than any other beast. So the son was out and he met the man, and he said, "It is to me you're coming?" And the son said it was, for he didn't like to tell about what his mother said or about the death of the calf. So the man got him a bottle, and said he'd come home with him, but when they were on the road they met some one that spoke of the death of the calf. So when the man heard that, he was angry and he said, "If I knew that I wouldn't have helped you," and he broke the bottle against the wall. So the father died, and the wife kept the stock—a very unkind woman she was.

There was a woman of my village never put a shoe on her feet from the time of her birth till the time of her death. Doing a penance she said she was. And she never married and would never eat meat.

As to cures, there's none can do them like the priests can, if they will. There was a woman I knew, and her little boy was sick and couldn't move. And she got the priest to come and do a cure on him, but no one knew what he did. And often he said to the woman: "You have a horse and a pony, and which do you value the most?" And she said she valued the pony the most. And next day the horse had died, but the little boy got well.

A Man of the Islands:
There's an old woman here now—there she is passing the road—that does cures with herbs. But last year she got a sore hand and she had to go to the hospital, and before she came

back they took two fingers off her. And there's no luck about bone-setters either. There's one here on the island and a good many go to him. But he had but one son and he never did any good, and now he's gone away from him.

John Curtis:
When Father Callan was a curate he did a cure for me one time for my cattle, and I gave him half a sovereign in his hand for it, in this road. It was the time I had so much trouble, and my brothers trying to rob me, and but for our landlord I wouldn't have kept the farm. And all my stock began to die. There was hardly a day I'd come out but I'd see maybe two or three sheep lying there in the field with froth at their mouths, and they turning black. The same thing was happening Tommy Hare's stock, and he went to Father Callan and he came to the house and read some sort of a Mass and took the sickness off them. So then I went to him myself, and he said he'd read a Mass in the chapel for me, and so he did. And the stock were all right from that time, and the day he came to see them and that I gave him the money, there ran a dog out of Roche's house and came behind the priest and gave him a bite in the leg, that he had to go to Dublin to cut it out. Why did the dog do it? He did it because he was mad when he saw the stock getting well. And weren't the Roches queer people that they wouldn't kill the dog when the priest wanted it, the way he'd be in no danger if the dog would go mad after?

IV

AWAY

*PWYLL, Prince of Dyved ... let loose the dogs in the wood
and sounded the horn and began the chase. And as he followed
the dogs he lost his companions; and while he listened to the
hounds he heard the cry of other hounds, a cry different from
his own, and coming in the opposite direction ... And he saw
a horseman coming towards him on a large light-grey steed with
a hunting horn round his neck, and clad in garments of grey
woollen in the fashion of a hunting garb, and the horseman drew
near and spoke to him thus: ... "A crowned King I am in the
land whence I come ... There is a man whose dominions are
opposite to mine, who is ever warring against me, and by ridding
me of this oppression which thou can'st easily do, shalt thou
gain my friendship." "Gladly will I do this," said he. "Show
me how I may." "I will show thee. Behold, thus it is thou
mayest. I will send thee to Annwvn in my stead, and I will
give thee the fairest lady thou didst ever behold to be thy companion, and I will put my form and semblance upon thee, so
that not a page of the chamber nor an officer nor any other man
that has always followed me shall know that it is not I. And this
shall be for the space of a year from tomorrow and then we will
meet in this place." ... "Verily," said Pwyll, "what shall I do
concerning my kingdom?" Said Arawn: "I will cause that no
one in all thy dominions, neither man nor woman, shall know
that I am not thou, and I will go there in thy stead."*
—"The Mabinogion."

I was told by a Man of Slieve Echtge:
That girl of the Cohens that was away seven year, she was
bid tell nothing of what she saw, but she told her mother some
things and told of some she met there. There was a woman—
a cousin of my own—asked was her son over there, and she
had to press her a long time, but at last she said he was. And he
was taken too with little provocation, fifty years ago. We were

working together, myself and him and a lot of others, making that trench you see beyond, to drain the wood. And it was contract work, and he was doing the work of two men and was near ready to take another piece. And some of them began to say to him, "It's a shame for you to be working like that, and taking the bread out of the hands of another," and I standing there. And he said he didn't care, and he took the spade and sent the scraws out flying, to the right and to the left. And he never put a spade into the ground again, for that night he was taken ill, and died shortly after. Watched he was, and taken by *them*.

As to the woman brought back again, it was told me by a boy going to school there at the time, so I know there's no lie in it. It was one of the Taylors, a rich family in Scariff. His wife was sick and pining away for seven years, and at the end of that time one day he came in he had a drop of drink taken, and he began to be a bit rough with her. And she said, "Don't be rough with me now, after bearing so well with me all these seven years. But because you were so good and so kind to me all that time," says she, "I'll go away from you now and I'll let your own wife come back to you." And so she did, for it was some old hag she was, and the wife came back again and reared a family. And before she went away, she had a son that was reared a priest, and after she came back, she had another son that was reared a priest, so that shows a blessing came on them.[39]

A Man on the Beach:
I remember when a great many young girls were taken, it is likely by *them*. And two year ago two fine young women were brought away from Aranmor one in a month and one in a week after the birth. And lately I heard that her own little girl and another little girl that was with her saw one of them appear in a cabin outside when she came to have a look at the child she left, but she didn't want to appear herself.

John Flatley:
There was a man I knew, Andy White, had a little chap, a little *summach* of four years. And one day Andy was away to sell a pig in the market at Mount Bellew, and the mother was away some place with the dinner for the men in the field, and the little chap was in the house with the grandmother, and he sitting by the fire. And he said to the grandmother: "Put down

105

a skillet of potatoes for me, and an egg." And she said: "I will not; what do you want with them, sure you're not long after eating." And he said, "Take care but I'll throw you over the roof of the house." And then he said, "Andy"—that was his father—"is after selling the pig to a jobber, and the jobber has it given back to him again, and he'll be at no loss by that, for he'll get a half-a-crown more at the end." So when the grandmother heard that she wouldn't stop in the house with him but ran out, and he only four years old.

When the mother came back and was told about it she went out and she got some of the leaves of the Lus-Mor, and she brought them in and put them on him; and he went, and her own child came back again. They didn't see him going or the other coming, but they knew it by him. But if her child had died among them, and they can die there as well as in this world, then he wouldn't come back, but that shape in his place would take the appearance of death.

Mrs. Cooke:

There's a man in Kildare that lost his wife. And every night at twelve o'clock she came back, to look at her child. And it was told the husband that if he had twelve men with him with forks when she came in, they would be able to stop her from going out again.

So the next night he was there, and with him his twelve friends with forks. And when she came in they shut the door, and when she could not get out she sat down and was quiet.

And one night she was sitting by the hearth with them all, she said to her husband, "It's a strange thing that Lenchar would be sitting there so quiet, with the bottom after knocked out of his churn."

So the husband went to Lenchar's house, and he found it was true what she had said, and the bottom was after being knocked out of his churn. But after that he left her, and lived in the village and wouldn't go near her any more.

Myself, I saw when I was but a child a woman come to the door that had been seven years with the good people, but do you think that could be true? And she had two strong girls with her. My brother was ill at the time, where he had his hip hurt with the shaft of a cart he was backing into the shed, and my

106

father asked her could she cure him. And she said, "I will, if you will give me the reward I ask for." "What is that?" said he. And she stooped down and pointed at a little kettle that stood below the dresser, and it was the last thing my mother had bought in this world before she died. So he was vexed because she cast her eye on that, and he bid her go out of the house for she wouldn't get it, and so she went away.

But I remember well her being there and telling us that while the seven years were going by, she was often glad to come outside the houses in the night-time, and pick a bit of what was in the pigs' troughs. And she bid us always to leave a bit somewhere about the house for them that couldn't come in and ask for it. And though my father was a cross man and didn't believe in such things, to the day of his death he never dared to go up to bed without leaving a bit of food outside the door.[40]

A Herd:
The McGarritys in the house beyond, they have plenty of money. It was money they got *out,* buried money, and *they* are after them.

There is one of them—Ned—is rather silly; I meet him often on the farm stretched by the side of the wall. He met with something one night and he is not the same since then.

There is another of them was walking one evening by the brink of the bushes and he met with two fillies—he thought them to be fillies—and one of them called out, "How are you, John?" and he legged it home as fast as he could. It is likely it was the father or the uncle.

Sure leaving town one time he was brought away to the railway station, and some of the people brought him hither again and set him towards home and he was brought back to the very same place. They had a right to have got the priest to say a few Masses in that house before they went to live in it at all.

It was the time their uncle was dying there was a whistle heard outside and the man in the bed answered it, and it was that very night he died. To keep money you would get *out* like, that is not right unless you might give the first of it in a few Masses. It was the man the money was took from gave that whistle.

Mrs. Donnely:
My mother told me that when she was a young girl, and before the time of side-cars, a man that was living in Duras married a

107

girl from Ardrahan side. And it was the custom in those days for a newly married girl to ride home on a horse, behind her next-of-kin.

And she was sitting behind her uncle on the horse, and when they were passing by Ardrahan churchyard he felt her to shiver and nearly to slip off the horse, and he put his hand behind for to support her, and all he could feel in his hand was for all the world like a piece of tow. So he asked her what ailed her, and she said that she thought of her mother when she was passing by the churchyard. A year after that when her baby was born, then she died. But everyone said the night she was taken was on her wedding-night.

And sure a sister-in-law of my own was taken the same way that poor Mrs. Hehir was. It was a couple of days after her baby was born, and I went to see her, and she Fardy's daughter and niece to Johnson that has the demesne land. And she was sitting up on the bed and so well and so strong that her mother says to me, "Catherine, try could you get a chicken any place; I think she'll be able to eat it tomorrow." Chickens is scarce, ma'am," says I, "but anyway I'll do my best and someway or other I'll find one."

Well, after that we left, and her husband being tired with the nights he'd been sitting up came with us to sleep at the house of his uncle, Johnson. And hardly had he got to the house when bad news followed him. And when he got home his wife was dead before him. Hardly were we out of the house when she said to her mother "Take off my boots." "Sure, you have no boots on," said the mother. "Well," says she, "lay me at the foot of the bed." And presently she says, "Send in to the McInerneys and ask them if the coffin they have is a better one than mine." And the mother saw she was going, and sent for the husband, but she was gone before he could come. And she so well and sitting up in the bed. But Hehir's wife was out of bed altogether, and brought her husband his tea in the hayfield before she was took.

And now I'll tell your ladyship a story that's all truth and no lie. There was an uncle of my own living near Kinvara, and one night his wife was coming home from Kinvara town, and she passed three men that were lying by the roadside. And the first of them said to her in Irish, "Go home, my poor woman." And the second said, "Go home if you can." And when she got home and told the story, she said the voice of the second was like the voice of her brother that was dead.

And from that day she began to waste away, and was wasting for seven year, until she died. And at the last some person said to her husband, "It's time for you to ask her what way she's been spending these seven years."

So he went into the room where she was on the bed, and said, "I believe it's time to ask you now what way have you been spending these seven years." And she said, "I'll tell you presently when you come in again, but leave me now for a while." And he went back into the kitchen and took his pipe for to have a smoke before he'd go back and ask her again. And the servant girl that was in the house was the first to go into the room, and found her cold and dead before her.

They had her took away before she had the time to tell what she had been doing all those seven years.

J. Kenny:
I was in a house one night with a man used to go away with the faeries. He got up in the night and opened the house door and went out. About four hours he was away, and when he came back he seemed to be very angry. I saw him putting off his clothes.

Nora Whelan:
Indeed Moneen has a great name for things that do be going on there beside that big forth. Sure there's many can hear them galloping, galloping all the night. You know Stephen's house at the meadow? Well, his daughter got a touch from them one night when she heard them going past with horses and with carriages, and she the only one in the house that felt them. She got silly like for a bit, but she's getting better now.

An old woman from Loughrea told me that a woman, I believe it was from Shragwalla close to the town, was taken away one time for fourteen years when she went out into the field at night with nothing on but her shift. And she was swept there and then, and an old hag put into the bed in her place, and she suckling her young son at the time.

It was a great many years after that, there was a pedlar used to be going about, and in his travels he went to England. And up in the north of England he saw a rich house and went into the kitchen of it, and there he saw that same woman, in a corner working. And he went up to her and said, "I know where you come from." "Where's that?" says she, and he gave her the name of her own village. Well, she laughed and she went out of the kitchen, and I don't know did she buy anything from him. But anyhow not long after that she came back and walked into her own house.

The husband never knew her, but the boy that was then fourteen year come up and touched her, and the father cried out, "Leave off putting your hand on that fine dress," for she had very rich clothes on. But she stood up and said, "I'm no other than your wife come back again, and the first thing you have to do is to bring in all you can carry of turf, and to make a big fire here in the middle of the floor."

Well, the old hag was in the room within, in the bed where she'd been lying a long time, and they thinking she was dying. And when the smoke of the fire went in at the door she jumps up and away with her out of the house, and tale or tidings of her they never had again.

My mother often told me about her sister's child—my cousin—that used to spend the nights in the big forth at Moneen. Every night she went there, and she got thin and tired like. She used to say that she saw grand things there, and the horses galloping and the riding. But then she'd say, "I must tell no more than that, or I'll get a great beating." She wasted away, but one night they were so sure that she was dead they had the pot boiling full of water to wash her. But she recovered again and lived five years after that.

Sure there was a faery in the house out beyond fourteen years. Katie Morgan she was called. She never kept the bed, but she'd sit in the corner of the kitchen on a mat, and from a good stout lump of a girl that she was she wasted to nothing, and her teeth grew as long as your fingers and then they dropped out. And she'd eat nothing at all only crabs and sour things. And she'd never leave the house in the day-time, but in the night she'd go out and pick things out of the fields she could eat. And the hurt she got or whatever it was touched her, it was one day that she was swinging on the corner gate just there by the forth. She died as quiet as another. But you wouldn't like to be looking at her after the teeth fell out.

Martin Rabitt:

There's some people it's lucky to meet and others it's unlucky, and if you set off to go to America or around the world,
and one of the unlucky ones comes and speaks to you on the
boat, you might as well turn back and come home again.

My own sister was taken away, she and her husband within
twenty-four hours, and not a thing upon them, and she with a
baby a week old. Well, the care of that child fell on me, and sick
or sorry it never was but thriving always.

And a friend of mine told me the same thing. His wife was
taken away in childbirth—and the five children she left that
did be always ailing and sickly—from that day there never was
a ha'porth ailed them.

Did the mother come back to care them? Sure and certain
she did, and I'm the one can tell that. For I slept in the room
with my sister's child after she dying; and as sure as I stand
here talking to you, she was back in the room that night.

Walking towards nightfall myself, I've seen the shadows
dancing before me, but I wasn't afeared, no more than I am of
you. And I've felt them other times crying and groaning about
the house.

As to the faeries, up beyond Ballymore there's a woman that
was said to be with them for seven years. But she came back after
that and had an impediment in her speech ever since.

Martin King:

There's a little forth on this side of Clough behind Glyn's
house, and there was a boy in Clough was said to have passed
a night and a day in it. I often saw him, and he was dull looking,
but for cleverness there was no one could touch him. I saw a
picture of a train he drew one time, with not a bolt nor a ha'porth
left out; and whatever he put his hand to he could do it, and he
with no more teaching than any other poor boy in the town. I
believe that he went to America afterwards.

And I remember a boy was about my own age over at Annagh
at the other side of the water, and it's said that he was away for
two years. Anyway for all that time he was sick in bed, and no
one ever saw bite or sup cross his lips in all that time, though
the food that was left in the room would disappear, whatever
happened it. He recovered after and went to America.

*   *   *

111

There was a girl near taken, in the Prestons' house. I saw her myself in the bed, near gone. But of a sudden she sat up and looked on the floor and began to curse, and then they left her for they can't bear curses. They have the hope of Heaven or they wouldn't leave one on the face of the earth, and they are afraid of God. They'll not do you much harm if you leave them alone; it's best not to speak to them at all if you should meet them. If they bring any one away they'll leave some old good-for-nothing thing in its place, and the same way with a cow or a calf or such things. But a sheep or a lamb it's beyond their power to touch, because of our Lord.

An Old Butcher:

I was born myself by daylight, and my mother often told me that I'd never see anything worse than myself. There's some can see those things and some that can't.

But one time I went up by the parish of Killisheen to look for half-beef, I having at the time a contract for the workhouse. And I went astray on the mountains, and near Killifin I came to a weaver's house and went in. And there was sitting in the corner such a creature as I never saw before, with nothing on him but a shirt, and eyes that would go through you. And I wouldn't stop in the house but went out again. And the weaver followed me and says he, "Is it afraid of him you are?" "It is," says I. "I thought you would be," says he, "and would you believe that he's my own son, and as fine a young chap as ever you seen until seven year ago when I sent him to Clough on a message, and he fell going over a wall, and it's then he got the touch, and it's like this he's been ever since." "Does he ask to eat much?" says I. "He'd eat the whole world," says he. "Then it's not your son that's in it, you may be sure of that," says I, and I turned and went away and never went back there again.

And it's not many year ago that such a lot of fine women were taken from Clough, very sudden, after childbirth—fine women—I knew them all myself. And I'll tell you a thing I heard of in the country. There was a woman died, and left her child. And every night at twelve o'clock she'd come back, and brought it out of the bed to the fire, and she'd comb it and wash it. And at last six men came and watched and stopped her at the door, and she went very near to tear them all asunder. But they got the priest, and he took it off her. Well, the husband had got another wife, and the priest came and asked him would he put her away, and take the first again. And so he did, and he brought her to the chapel to be married to her again, and the whole congregation saw her there. That was rather hard on the second wife? Well, but wasn't it a great thing for the first poor creature to be brought back? Sure there's many of those poor souls wandering about.

Sure enough, some are brought away and kept for years, but sometimes they come back again. There was a woman beyond at Cahirmacun was away for a year, and came back and reared a family after. They knew well what happened then, but they don't speak of it. There was a young fellow got a touch there near Ballytown, and a little chap met him wandering in the field. And he bid him put out food for him every night, for he had none of their food ate yet, and so they hadn't got full power over him. So food was left for him, and after a time he came back as well as another.

A Connemara man:
There are many that die and don't go out of the world at all. The priests know that. There was a boy dying in a house up the road, and the priest came to him and he was lying as if dead, that he could not speak nor hear, and the priest said, *"The boys have a hand in this."* He meant by that, the faeries. I was outside the house myself at the time, for the boy was a friend of mine, and I didn't like him to die. And you never saw such a storm as arose when the priest was coming to the house, a storm of wind, and a cloud over the moon. But after a while the boy died, and the storm went down and the moon shone out as bright as before.

There was a man was said to go away of nights with *them.* When he got the call, away he must go if he liked it or not.

And one day he was out in the bay with some others, and all of a sudden he said, "Let me go home, my horse is like to die." And they wouldn't mind him for a time, but at last they turned and rowed home, and they found his horse that was well when he went out, stretched on the field.

Another time he was with a man that had a grand three-year-old filly and was showing it to him. And he said, "You won't have her long"; and it wasn't long after that she died.

Mrs. Feeney:
There was a man died and his wife died, and an uncle took charge of the children. The man had a shop but the uncle lived

H   113

a little way from the shop, and he would leave the children alone through the night. There were two men making a journey, and a storm rose up, and they asked could they have a part of the night in the house where the shop was, and the uncle said they could, and he went to his own house.

The men were sitting up by the fire and the children were sleeping at the other side of the room. And one of the men said to the other "God rest the soul of the man that died here. He was a good man." And the other said, "The wife wasn't so good." And just then they heard a noise below, and they saw the wife that had died coming into the room and she went across and lay down on the bed where the baby was. And the baby that was crying before got quiet then and made no sound at all.

But as to the two men, bad as the storm was outside, they thought better to be out in it than to stop in the room where the woman was, so they went away. It was to quiet the baby she used to come back.

There was an old woman I remember, Mrs. Sheridan, and she had to go with them for two or three hours every night for a while, and she'd make great complaints of the hardship she'd meet with, and how she'd have to spend the night going through little boreens or in the churchyard at Kinvara, or they'd bring her down to the seashore. They often meet with hardships like that, those they bring with them, so it's no wonder they're glad to get back. This world's the best.

There was a woman living over there near Aughsulis, and a few years ago she lost a fine young milch cow, with its first calf. And she and the three boys in the house salted it down and they ate the half of it and they couldn't eat the other half, it was too hard or too tough, and they put it under the dung that was in the yard, the way it would melt into it. And when the spring-time came, they turned up the dung, and in the place it was buried they found nothing but three planks of the wood that's cut in Connemara—deal they call it. So the cow never died, but was brought away with *themselves*. For many a young boy and young woman goes like that, and there's no doubt at all that Mary Hynes was taken. There's some living yet can remember her coming to the pattern was there beyond, and she was said to be the handsomest girl in Ireland.[41]

*　　*　　*

114

There's a man now living between this place and Kinvara,
Fannen his name is, and he goes away with them, and he's got
delicate and silly like. One night he was in that bad place that's
near the chapel of Kinvara, and he found a great crowd of them
about him and a man on a white horse was with them, and tried
to keep him, and he cried and struggled and they let him go at
last. But now the neighbours all say he does be going with them,
and he told me himself he does. I wouldn't be afraid of him
when I'd meet him on the road, but many of the neighbours
would be afraid.

And two of his sons have got silly. They found a bar of gold
one time out playing in the field, and the money they got for it
they put it in the bank. But I believe it's getting less now, and
what good did it do them when they went like that? One of the
boys was to be a priest, but they had to give that up when he got
silly. It was no right money. And they'd best not have touched it.

Mrs. Finnegan:
Dreams, we should not pay too much attention to, and we
should judge them well, that is, if a dream is bad or good, we
should say "It's a good dream"; and we should never tell a
dream to anyone fasting; and it's said if you tell your dream to
a tree fasting, it will wither up. And it's better to dream of a
person's downfall than of him being up. When the good people
take a cow or the like, you'll know if they did it by there being
no fat on what's left in its place and no eyes in it. When my
own springer died so sudden this year, I was afraid to use it.
But Pat Hevenor said, "It's a fool you are, and it might save
you the price of a bag of meal to feed the bonifs with a bit of it."
And he brought the cart and brought it home to me. So I put
down a bit to boil for the bonifs to try it, for I heard that if it
was *their* work, it would go to water. But there was fat rising
to the top, that I have enough in the shed to grease the cart
wheels for a year. So then I salted a bit of it down.

If they take any one with them, yourself or myself it might be,
they'll put some old spent man in his place, that they had with
them a long time, and the father and the mother and the children
will think it is the child or the father or the mother that is in it.
And so it may be he'd get absolution. But as for the old faeries
that were there from the beginning, I don't know about
them.[42]

It's said that if we know how to be neighbourly with them,

they'd be neighbourly and friendly with us. It's said it was they brought away the potatoes in the bad time, when all the potatoes turned black. But it wasn't for spite, it was because they wanted them themselves.

Mrs. Casey:

There was a woman in Ballinamore died after the baby being born. And the husband took another wife and she very young, that everyone wondered she'd like to go into the house. And every night the first wife came to the loft, and looked down at her baby, and they couldn't see her; but they'd know she was there by the child looking up and smiling at her.

So at last some one said that if they'd go up in the loft after the cock crowing three times they'd see her. And so they did, and there she was, with her own dress on, a plaid shawl she had brought from America, and a cotton skirt with some edging at the bottom.

So they went to the priest, and he said Mass in the house, and they didn't see so much of her after that. But after a year, the new wife had a baby. And one day she bid the first child to rock the cradle. But when she sat down to it, a sort of a sickness came over her, and she could do nothing, and the same thing always happened, for her mother didn't like to see her caring the second wife's baby.

And one day the wife herself fell in the fire and got a great many burns, and they said that it was *she* did it.

So they went to the blessed well Tubbermacduagh near Kinvara, and they were told to go there every Friday for twelve weeks, and they said seven prayers and gathered seven stones every time. And since then she doesn't come to the house, but the little girl goes out and meets her mother at a faery bush. And sometimes she speaks to her there, and sometimes in her dreams. But no one else but her own little girl has seen her of late.

There was one time a tailor, and he was a wild card, always going to sprees. And one night he was passing by a house, and he heard a voice saying, "Who'll take the child?" And he saw a little baby held out, and the hands that were holding it, but he could see no more than that. So he took it, and he brought it to the next house, and asked the woman there to take it in for the night.

116

Well, in the morning the woman in the first house found a dead child in the bed beside her. And she was crying and wailing and called all the people. And when the woman from the neighbouring house came, there in her arms was the child she thought was dead. But if it wasn't for the tailor that chanced to be passing by and to take it, we know very well what would have happened it.

That's a thing happens to many, to have faery children put upon them.

A Man at Corcomroe:
There was one Delvin, that lies under a slab yonder, and for seven years he was brought away every night, and into this abbey. And he was beat and pinched, and when he'd come home he'd faint; but he used to say that the place that he went to was grander than any city. One night he was with a lot of others at a wake, and they knew the time was coming for him to go, and they all took hold of him. But he was drawn out of the door, and the arms of those that were holding him were near pulled out of their sockets.

Mischievous they are, but they don't do much harm. Some say they are fallen angels, and hope yet to be saved.

A Slieve Echtge Woman:
I knew another was away for seven years—and it was in the next townland to this she lived. Bridget Clonkelly her name was. There was a large family of them, and she was the youngest, and a very fine-looking fair-haired girl she was. I knew her well, she was the one age with myself.

It was in the night she used to go to them, and if the door was shut, she'd come in by the key-hole. The first time they came for her, she was in bed between her two sisters, and she didn't want to go. And they beat her and pinched her, till her brother called out to know what was the matter.

She often told me about them, and how she was badly treated because she wouldn't eat their food. She got no more than about three cold potatoes she could eat all the time she was with them.

All the old people about here put out food every night, the first of the food before they have any of it tasted themselves. And she said there was a red-haired girl among them, that would throw her into the river she got so mad with her. But if she'd had their food ate, she'd never have got away from them at all.

She married a serving-man after, and they went to Sydney, and if nothing happened in the last two years they're doing well there now.

Mrs. Casey:

Near my own house by the sea there was a girl went out one day to get nuts near the wood, and she heard music inside the wood. And when she went home she told her mother. But the next day she went again, and the next, and she stopped so long that the mother sent the other little girl to look for her, but she could see no one. But she came in after a time, and she went inside into the room, and while she was there the mother heard music from the room; but when the girl came out she said she heard nothing. But the next day after that she died.

The neighbours all came in to the wake, and there was tobacco and snuff there, but not much, for it's the custom not to have so much when a young person dies. But when they looked at the bed, it was no young person they saw in it, but an old woman with long teeth that you'd be frightened, and the face wrinkled, and the hands. So they didn't stop but went away, and she was buried the next day. And in the night the mother would hear music all about the house, and lights of all colours flashing about the windows.

She was never seen again except by a boy that was working about the place. He met her one evening at the end of the house, dressed in her own clothes. But he could not question her where she was, for it's only when you meet them by a bush you can question them there.

A Man of Slieve Echtge:

There was a man, and he a cousin of my own, lost his wife. And one night he heard her come into the room, where he was in bed with the child beside him, and he let on to be asleep, and she took the child and brought her out to the kitchen fire and sat down beside it and suckled it.

And then she put it back into the bed again, and he lay still and said nothing. The second night she came again, and he had more courage and he said, "Why have you got no boots on?" For he saw that her feet were bare. And she said, "Because

118

there's iron nails in them." So he said, "Give them to me," and he got up and drew all the nails out of them, and she brought them away.

The third night she came again, and when she was suckling the child he saw that she was still barefoot, and he asked why didn't she wear the boots. "Because," says she, "you left one sprig in them, between the upper and the lower sole. But if you have courage," says she, "you can do more than that for me. Come tomorrow night to the gap up there beyond the hill, and you'll see the riders going through, and the one you'll see on the last horse will be me. And bring with you some fowl droppings and urine, and throw them at me as I pass, and you'll get me again." Well he got so far as to go to the gap, and to bring what she told him, and when they came riding through the gap, he saw her on the last horse, but his courage failed him, and he let it drop, and he never got the chance to see her again.

Why she wanted the nails out of her boots? Because it's well known *they* will have nothing to do with iron. And I remember when every child would have an old horse nail hung round its neck with a bit of straw, but I don't see it done now.

There was another man though, one of the family of the Coneys beyond there, and his wife was away from him four years. And after that he put out the old hag was in her place, and got his wife back and reared children after that, and one of them was trained a priest.

There was a drunken man in Scariff, and one night he had drink taken he couldn't get home, and fell asleep by the road-side near the bridge. And in the night he awoke and heard *them* at work with cars and horses. And one said to another, "This work is too heavy, we'll take the white horse belonging to so and so"—giving the name of a rich man in the town. So as soon as it was light he went to this man, and told him what he had heard them say. But he would only laugh at him and say, "I'll pay no attention to what a drunkard dreams." But when he went out after to the stable, his white horse was gone.

That's easy understood. They are shadows, and how could a shadow move anything? But they have power over mankind that they can bring them away to do their work.

*   *   *

There was a woman used to go out among them at night, and she said to her sister, "I'll be out on a white horse and I'll stop and knock at your door," and so she would do sometimes.

And one day there was a man asked her for a debt she owed, and she said, "I have no money now." But then she put her hand behind her and brought it back filled with gold. And then she rubbed it in her hand, and when she opened the hand there was nothing in it but dried cow-dung. And she said, "I could give you that but it would be no use to you."

An Old Woman Talking of Cruachmaa:

I remember my father being there, and telling me of a girl that was away for seven years, and all thought she was dead. And at the end of the seven years she walked back one day into her father's house, and she all black-looking. And she said she was married there and had two children, but they died and then she was driven away. And she stopped on at her father's house, but the neighbours used to say there was never a day but she'd go up the hill and be there crying for one or two hours.

An Old Woman who only Speaks Irish:

I remember a young man coming to the island fourteen years ago that had never been in it before and that knew everything that was in it, and could tell you as much as to the stones of the chimney in every house. And after a few days he was gone and never came again, for they brought him about to every part. But I saw him and spoke to him myself.

Mr. Sullivan:

There was a man had buried his wife, and she left three children. And then he took a second wife, and she did away with the children, hurried them off to America, and the like. But the first wife used to be seen up in the loft, and she making a plan of revenge against the other wife.

The second one had one son and three daughters; and one day the son was out digging the field, and presently he went into what is called a faery hole. And there was a woman came before him, and, says she, "what are you doing here trespassing on my ground?" And with that she took a stone and hit him in the head, and he died with the blow of the stone she gave him. And all the people said it was by the faeries he was taken.

Peter Henderson:

There was a first cousin of mine used sometimes to go out the house, that none would see him going. And one night his brother followed him, and he went down a path to the sea, and then he went into a hole in the rocks, that the smallest dog wouldn't go into. And the brother took hold of his feet and drew him out again. He went to America after that, and is living there now; and sometimes in his room they'll see him kicking and laughing as if *some* were with him.

One night when some of the neighbours from these islands were with him, he told them he'd been back to Inishmaan, and told all that was going on. And some would not believe him. And he said, "You'll believe me next time." So the next night he told them again he had been there, and he brought out of his pocket a couple of boiled potatoes and a bit of fish and showed them, so then they all believed it.

An Old Man from the State of Maine says, hearing this:

I knew him in America, and he used often to visit this island, and would know about all of them were living, and would bring us word of them, and all he'd tell us would turn out right. He's living yet in America.

An Aran Woman:

There was a woman in Killinny was dying, and it was she used to be minding the Lodge over there, and when she was near death her own little girl went out, and she saw her standing, and a black-haired woman with her. And she came back and said to her father "Don't be fretting, my mother's not there in the bed, I saw her up by the Lodge and a black woman with her, that took her in with her." And there was a man from Arklow there, and he said, "That's not your wife at all that's in the bed—that's not Maggie Mulkair. That is a black woman and Maggie Mulkair is red-haired." And the husband looked in the bed, and so it wasn't Maggie Mulkair that was in it, but at that minute she died. It's well known they bring back the old to put in the place of the young.

There was a girl in the County Clare, and she went to get married, and she and the husband were riding back on the one horse and it slipped and fell. And when she got to the house, she sat quiet and not a word out of her. And everybody said she used to be a pleasant, jolly girl, but this was like an old woman.

And she sat there by the hob for three days and she didn't turn her face to the people. But the husband said, "Let her alone, maybe she's shy yet." But his mother got angry at last and she said, "I'd sooner be rubbing stones on the clothes than watching an idle woman." And she went out to the flax and she said to the girl, "You'd best get the dinner ready before the men come in." But when she came in there was nothing done; and she gave her a blow with some pieces of the flax that were in her hand, and said, "Get out of this for a good-for-nothing woman!" And with that she went up the chimney and was gone. And the mother got the dinner ready, and then she went out, not knowing in the world how to tell the husband what she had done. But when she got to the field where they were working, there was the girl walking down the hill, and she took the two hands of the mother and said, "It's well for me you hadn't patience to last two days more or I'd never have got back, but I never touched any of the food while I was with them."

Mrs. Casey:
There was a girl one time, and a boy wanted to marry her, but the father and mother wouldn't let her have him, for he had no money. And he died, and they made a match for her with another. And one day she was out going to her cousins' house, and he came before her and put out his hand and said, "You promised yourself to me, and come with me now." And she ran, and when she got to the house she fell on the floor. And the cousins thought she had taken a drop of drink, and they began to scold her.

Another day after that she was walking with her husband and her brother, and a little white dog with them, and they came to a little lake. And he appeared to her again, and the husband and the brother didn't see him, but the dog flew at him, and began barking at him and he was hitting at the dog with a stick, and all the time trying to get hold of the girl's hand. And the husband and the brother wondered what the dog was barking at and why it drew down to the lake in the end, and out into the water. For it was into it that he was wanting to draw the girl.

It's a strange thing that you'll see a man in his coffin and buried; and maybe a fortnight after, the neighbours will tell you they saw him walking about. There was one Flaherty lived up at Johnny Reed's and he died. And a few days later Johnny Reed's sister and another woman went out with baskets of turnips to the field where the sheep were, to throw them out for them. And when they got to the field they could see Flaherty walking, just in the same clothes he had before he died, long skirts and a jacket, and frieze trousers. So they left the turnips and came away.

There was a man up there near Loughrea, one of the Mahers, was away for seven years. In the night he'd be taken, and sometimes in the daytime when he was in the bed sick, that's the time he'd be along with them; riding out and going out across the bay, going as fast as the wind in the sky. Did he like to be with them? Not at all, he'd sooner be at home; and it is bad for the health too to be going out these rough nights. There were three men near him that had horses, Daniel O'Dea and Farragher and Flynn, and he told them they should sell their horses. And Daniel O'Dea and Farragher sold theirs, but the other man wouldn't mind him. And after a few days his horse died. Of course they had been with him at night riding their own horses, and that's how he knew what would happen and gave the warning.

The Spinning Woman:
There was a man got married, and he began to pine away, and after a few weeks the mother asked him what ailed him. And he opened his coat and showed her his breast inside, that it was all torn and bloody. And he said: "That's the way I am; and that's what she does to me in the nights." So the mother brought her out and bid her to pick the green flax, and she was against touching it, but the mother made her. And no sooner had she touched three blades of it but she said, "I'm gone now," and away with her. And when they went back to the room they found the daughter lying in a deep sleep, where she had just been put back.

An Old Woman at Kinvara:
There was a woman put in her coffin for dead, but a man that was passing by knew that she wasn't dead, and he brought her away and married her and lived with her for seven years, and had seven children by her. And one day he brought her to

123

a fair near the place she came from, and the people that saw her said: "If that woman that died ever had a sister, that would be her sister." So he let it out to them then about her. But his mother always minded her, that she wouldn't wet her hands. But one day the mother was hurried, and the woman made a cake. And after making it she washed her hands, and with that they had her again and she went from the husband and from her children.

A Herd:

One time I was tending this farm for Flaherty, and I came in late one evening after being out with cattle, and I sent my wife for an ounce of tobacco, and I stopped in the house with the child. And after a time I heard the rattle of the door, and the wife came in half out of her mind. She said she was walking the road and she met four men, and she knew that they were not of this world, and she fell on the road with the fright she got, but she thought one of them was her brother, and he put his hand under her head when she fell, so that she got no hurt. And for a long time after she wasn't in her right mind, and she'd bring the child out in the field, to see her brother. And at last I brought her to the priest, and when we were on the way there she called out that those fields of stones were full of them, and they all dressed in tall hats and black coats. But the priest read something over her and she's been free from them since then.

There were three women died within a year, one here, John Harragher's wife, and two at Inishmaan. And the year after they were all seen together, riding on white horses at the other side of the island.

There were two young women lived over in that village you see there, and they were not good friends, for they were in two public houses. And one of them died in January, after her baby being born. Some said it was because of her mother or the nurse giving her strong tea, but it wasn't that, it was because her time had come. And when the other woman heard it she said to her husband, "Give me the concertina, and I'll play till you dance for joy that Mrs. Considine is gone." But in April her own child was born, and though the doctor tried to save her he couldn't and she died.

And since then they're often seen to appear walking together.

People wonder to see them together, and they not friends while they lived. But it's bad to give way to temper, and who is nearer to us than a neighbour ?

A Young Woman:
I know a girl that lost her mother soon after she was born. And surely the mother came back to her every night and suckled her, for she'd lie as quiet as could be, without a bottle or a hap'orth and they'd hear her sucking. And one night the grandmother felt her daughter that was gone lying in the clothes, and made a grab at her, but she was gone. Maybe she'd have kept her if she'd taken her time, for there's charms to bring such back. But the little girl grew, that she was never the same in the morning that she was the night before, and there's no finer girl in the island now. I call to my own mother sometimes when things go wrong with me, and I think I'm always the better of it. And I often say those that are gone are troubled with those they leave behind. But God have mercy on all the mothers of the world!

Mrs. Maher:
There was a woman with her husband passing by Esserkelly, and she had left her child at home. And a man came and called her in, and promised to leave her on the road where she was before. So she went, and there was a baby in the place she was brought to, and they asked her to suckle it. And when she had come out again she said, "One question I'll ask. What were those two old women sitting by the fire?" And the man said, "We took the child today, and we'll have the mother tonight and one of them will be put in her place, and the other in the place of some other person." And then he left her where she was before.
But there's no harm in them, no harm at all.

Tom Hislop:
Scully told me he was by the hedge up there by Ballinamantane one evening and a blast came, and as it passed he heard something crying, crying, and he knew by the sound that it was a child that they were carrying away.

And a woman brought in at Esserkelly heard a baby crying and a woman singing to it not to fret, for such a woman would die that night or the next and would come to mind her. And the

125

very next night the woman she heard the name of died in child-birth.

At Aughanish there were two couples came to the shore to be married, and one of the new-married women was in the boat with the priest, and they going back to the island. And a sudden blast of wind came, and the priest said some blessed Aves that were able to save himself, but the girl was swept.

Peter Hanrahan:
No, I never went to Biddy Early. What would they want with the like of me? It's the good and the pious they come for.

I remember fourteen years ago how eleven women were taken in childbirth from this parish. But as to the old, what business would they have with them? They'd be nothing but a bother to them. There was a woman living by the road that goes to Scahanagh, and one day a carriage stopped at her door, and a grand lady came out of it, and asked would she come and give the breast to her child, and she said she couldn't leave her own children. But the lady said no harm would happen her, and brought her away to a big house, but when she got there she wouldn't stop, but went home again. And in the morning the woman's cow was dead. And the husband that had a card for carding flax looked through it; and in the place of the cow, there was nothing but an old man.

And there was a man and a girl that gave one another a hard promise he never to marry any other woman, and she never to marry any other man. But he broke his promise and married another. And the girl died, and one night he saw a sort of a shadow coming across the grass, and she spoke to him, and it was the girl he had promised to marry, and she kept him in talk till midnight. And she came every night after that, and would stop till midnight, and he began to waste away and to get thin, and his wife asked him what was on him, and she picked out of him what it was. And after that the girl asked him to come and save her, and she would be on the second horse going through a gap. And he went, and when he got there his courage failed, and he did nothing to save her, but after that he never saw her again.

Mrs. Roche:
There was a woman used to go away with them, and they'd leave her at the doorstep in the morning, and she wouldn't be

the better for a long time of all she'd gone through. She got out of it after, and was a fine woman when I knew her.

My mother told me of a woman that used to go with them, and one night they were passing by a house, and there was no clean water in it, and it was readied up. And they said, "We'll have the blood of the man of the house." And there was a big pot of broth on the fire for the morning, for the poor people had no tea in those days; and the woman said, "Won't broth do you?" And they took the broth. And in the morning early, the woman after she was left back went to the house, and there was the woman of the house getting ready the broth, for it looked just like it did before. And she said, "Throw it out before you lose your husband." For she knew that the first that would taste it would die, and that it's to the man of the house that the first share is always given.

My mother was always wanting to call one of her children Pat, the name of her own father, but my father always made her give them some different name. But when one of the youngest was born he said, "Give him what name you like." So they gave him the name of her father; and he was like the apple of her eye, she was so fond of him. But a sickness came on him and he wasted away, and she went to a strange forge and brought forge water away, for she wouldn't take it from our own forge, and gave him a drink of it. And I saw her and I said to her, "I'll tell my father you're giving forge water to Paddy." And she said, "If you do I'll kill you," so I said nothing. And she gave him a second drink of it and not a third, for he was gone before he could get it. If it had been her own child, it would have saved him, but she told me after she knew it was another, his kneecaps were so big and other parts of his body.

There was another little one she lost. She was sitting one time nursing it outside the door, and a lady and a gentleman came up the road, and the lady said, "Who are you nursing the child for?" And she said, "For no one in the world but God and myself." And then the lady and the gentleman were gone and no sign of them, though it was a straight road, you know that long straight road in Galway that goes by Prospect, and it wasn't many days after that when the child got ill, and in a few days it was dead. And when it was lying there stretched out on two chairs, the lady came in again and looked at it and said,

"What a pity!" And then she said, "It's gone to a better place." "I hope it may be so," said my mother, stiff like that; and she went away.

I was delicate one time myself, and I lost my walk, and one of the neighbours told my mother it wasn't myself that was there. But my mother said she'd soon find that out, for she'd tell me that she was going to get a herb that would cure me, and if it was myself I'd want it, but if I was another I'd be against it. So she came in and she said to me, "I'm going to Dangan to look for the *lus-mor*, that will soon cure you." And from that day I gave her no peace till she'd go to Dangan and get it; so she knew that I was all right. She told me all this afterwards.

M. Cushin:

It is about the forths they are, not about the churchyards. The Amadán is the worst of them all.

They say people are brought away by them. I knew a girl one time near Ballyvaughan was said to be with them for nine months. She never eat anything all that time, but the food used to go all the same.

There was a man called Hession died at that time and after the funeral she began to laugh, and they asked her what was she laughing at, and she said, "You would all be laughing yourselves if you could open the coffin and see what it is you were carrying in it." The priest heard of her saying that and he was vexed.

Did they open the coffin? They did not, where would be the use, for whatever was in it would be in the shape of some person, young or old. They would see nothing by looking at that.

There was a woman near Feakle, Mrs. Colman, brought away for seven years; she was the priest's sister. But she came back to her husband after, and she cured till the day of her death came every kind of sores, just putting her hand on them and saying, "In the Name of the Father, of the Son, and the Holy Ghost."

There was a man in Gort was brought for a time to Tir-nan-og, that is a part of heaven.

A North Galway Woman:

There was a woman died near this after her baby being born, and there was only the father to mind it. And a girl of the neighbours that came in to watch it one night said that surely she saw the mother come back to it, and stoop down to the cradle and give it the breast. And anyway she grew and throve better than any other child around. And there was a woman died near Monivea, and sometimes in the daytime they'd see her in the garden combing the children's hair.

There was a Connemara man digging potatoes in that field beyond, and he told us that back in Connemara there was a woman died, and a few nights after she came back and the husband saw her. And she said, "Let you not put a hand on me *yourself*, but I'll come back tomorrow night and others with me, and let me not cross the threshold when we are going out, but let your brother be there that has the strength of six men in him, and let him hold me." And so they did, and she reared four children after.

There was a woman died two houses from this, and it wasn't many days after she being buried the woman in the next house, Sibby her name is, came in here in the morning, and she told me she saw her coming in here the night before. And the sweat was on Sibby's face and she said, "God knows I am speaking the truth. Why would I put a lie on that poor woman?" And why would she indeed?

And she said that in the night when she was in her bed, and two or three children along with her, the woman that had died came beside the bed and called her, and then she went out and said, "I'll come again and I'll bring my company with me."

And so she did, for she came back and her company with her, and they with umbrellas and hats in their hands, dressed grand, just now like the servants at Newtown. And she stooped over the bed again, and she said, "It was through Thomas I was lost." For there was one of her sons was called Thomas, and coming home one day he got a little turn of his foot, that the mother was doing what she could for with herbs and the like for a long time, so that he got well all but a little limp. So that's why she said that it was through Thomas she was lost. And she said, "There'll be a station at Athenry on such a day, and send three of the children"—and she named the three—"to do it for me." And so they did, and she was seen no more. And I'm sure it was no lie Sibby was telling. And she told the priest about what she saw and all he said was, "Well, if you saw that you're happy."

There was a woman died, and every night she'd come back and bring the baby to the fire, and dress it and suckle it. And the brother got to speak with her one night, and she said, "Oh why wasn't I put in the coffin with my own dress on that I was wearing? It's ashamed I was to go into such a crowd and such a congregation with nothing about me but a white sheet. And if it wasn't that I saw a boy of the neighbours among them that I knew before, I would have been very lonely."

There were two boys that were comrades, and if you'd see Dermot you'd say, "Where is Pat?" And if you'd see Pat you'd say, "Where is Dermot?" And one of them died, and everybody wondered at the comrade not being all the day to the corpse-house. And when he came in the evening he took a pinch of snuff, and he held it to the nose of the boy that was laid out on the table and he saw it sniff a little. So he made up the fire and he called another boy, and they laid the body down behind the fire; and if they did away with it, the boy himself came walking in at the door.

There was a girl I heard of brought away among *them*— and there was the finest of eating to be had. But there's always a friend in such places, and she got warning not to eat a bit of the food without she'd get salt with it. So when they put her down to eat, she asked a grain of salt, but not a grain was to be had. So she would eat nothing. But I believe they did away with her after.

John Phelan:
Mike Folan was here the other day telling us newses, and he told the strangest thing ever I heard—that happened to his own first cousin. She died and was buried, and a year after, her husband was sitting by the fire, and she came back and walked in. He gave a start, but she said, "Have no fear of me, I was never in the coffin and never buried, but I was kept away for the year." So he took her again and they reared four children after that. She was Mike Folan's own first cousin and he saw the four children himself.

An Old Army Man:
My family were of the Glynns of Athenry. I had an aunt
that married a man of the name of Roche, and their child was
taken. So they brought it to the Lady Well near Athenry, where
there's patterns every fifteenth of August, to duck it. And such a
ducking they gave it that it walked away on crutches, and it
swearing. And their own child they got back again, but he didn't
live long after that.

There was a man I know, that was my comrade often, used
to be taken away for nights, and he'd speak of the journeys he
had with them. And he got severe treatment and didn't want to
go, but they'd bring him by force. He recovered after, and joined
the army, and I was never so surprised as I was the day he
walked in when I was in India.

Mrs. Brown:
There was a woman in Tuam, Mrs. Shannon knew her well,
was said to be away for seven years. And she was always sitting
in the corner by the fire, not speaking, but a kind of a sound
like moaning she'd make to herself; and they'd always bring
her her dinner over in the corner, and if any one came in to see
her—and many came hearing she was away—she'd draw the
shawl over her face. And at the end of the seventh year she
began to get a little life and strength coming in to her, and within a week she was strong and well, and lived a good many years
after. And it's not long since some one that had a falling out
with her daughters said to them, "It's well known your mother
was away in Cruachmaa." And the poor girls when they heard
that said cried a great deal.

Mrs. Casey:
Some people from Lismara I was talking to told me there was
a girl the mother thought to be away, and she'd go out in the
evening. And the mother followed her one time, and after she
went a bit into the fields she saw her with an old woman very
strangely dressed, with a white cap with an edging, and a green
shawl and a black apron and a red petticoat. And the woman
was smoking, and she gave the girl a smoke of the pipe. And
the mother went home, and by and by the girl came in, and she
smelling of tobacco. And the mother asked where was she? And
she said, in some neighbour's house; and the mother knew she

wasn't there, but that she was going with the faeries. And two or three days after that, they had her taken altogether; and the clergy that attended her said it was some old hag that was put in her place.

Mrs. Oliver:

There was Fardy Folan's wife going, going, and all the night they thought that she was at the last puff. But the minute the cock crew, she sat up straight and strong. "I had a hard fight for it," she said, "but care me well now ye have me back again." And she lived a bit, but not long, after that.

That child of the Latteys that is silly, she was walking about today shaking hands with everyone that would come into the house. And the reason she's like that is, when she was born the breath had left her and the mother began to cry and to scream and to roar, and then the breath came back. She had a right to have let her go and not to have brought her back.

There's a girl of Fardy Folan's is said to be away. Anyway she's a fool, and a blow from her would kill you, it is always like that with a fool. And it was her mother I told you of that was as they thought gone, and that sat up again and said, "Take care of me now, I had a hard fight for it." But indeed she didn't live long after that.

Mrs. Feeney:

When one is taken, the body is taken as well as the spirit, and some good-for-nothing thing left in its place. What they take them for is to work for them, and to do things they can't do themselves. You might notice it's always the good they take. That's why when we see a child good for nothing we say, "Ah, you little faery."

There was a man lost his wife and a hag was put in her place, and she came back and told him to come out at night where she'd be riding with the rest, and to throw something belonging to her after her—he'd know her by her being on a white horse. And so he did and got her back again. And when they were going home he said, "I'll have the life of that old hag that was put in your place." But when they got to the house, she was out of it before him, and was never heard of again.

There was a man telling me it was in a house where the woman was after a youngster, and she died, that is, we'll call it died, but she was *taken,* that the husband saw her coming back to give the breast to the child and to wash it. And the second night he got hold of her and held her until morning, and when the cock crowed she sat down again and stayed; they had no more power over her.

Surely some go among them for seven years. There was Kitty Hayes lived at Kilcloud, for seven years she had everything she could want, and music and dancing could be heard around her house every night, and all she did prospered; but she ate no food all that time, only she took a drink of the milk after the butter being churned. But at the end of the seven years all left her, and she was glad at the last to get Indian meal.

There was a man driving cattle from Craughwell to Athenry for a fair. And it was before sunrise and dark, and presently he saw a light by the side of the road, and he was glad of it, for he had no matches and he wanted to light his pipe to smoke it. So he turned aside, and there were some people sitting there, and they brought him in, through a sort of a door and asked him to sit down. And so he did, and he saw that they were all strangers, not one he knew among them. And there was a fire and they put food and drink on the table, and asked him what would he have. And there opposite him he saw his own cows that were brought in too, and he knew that he was in a faery place. But in all these places there's always one well-wisher, so while he was sitting there, an old woman came to him and whispered in his ear, "Don't for your life eat a bit or drink a drop of what they give you, or you'll never go away again." So he would take nothing. If it hadn't been for the old woman, he might have taken something, just not to vex them. And at sunrise they let him out, and he was on the road again and his cattle before him.

Well, when he was coming back from the fair, there were two men with him, and he pointed them out the place where all this happened, for when three persons are together, there's no fear of anything and they can say what they like. And the others told him it was a faery place and many strange things had happened there. And they told him how there was a woman had a baby lived close by there, and before it was a week old her husband had to leave her because of his brother having died. And no sooner was she left alone than she was *taken,* and they sent for the priest to say Mass in the house, but she was calling out every sort of thing they couldn't understand, and within a few days she was dead.

And after death the corpse began to change, and first it looked like an old woman, and then like an old man, and they had to bury it the next day. And before a week was over she began to appear. They always appear when they leave a child like that. And surely she was taken to nurse the faery children, just like poor Mrs. Raynor was last year.

There's a well near Kinvara, Tubbermacduagh it's called, and it's all hung with rags, and piles of seven stones about it, for it's a great place to bring children to, to get them back when they've been changed by the faeries. Nine days they should be going to it, and saying prayers each day. And you'll see the child that's coming back will be like itself one day and like an old person another day and sometimes it will feel a picking, picking at it and it in its mother's arms. McCullagh's daughter that was *taken* is often to be seen there.

When any one is taken something is put in their place—even when a cow or the like goes. There was one of the Simons used to be going about the country skinning cattle and killing them, even for the country people if they were sick. One day he was skinning a cow that was after dying by the roadside, and another man with him. And Simon said, "It's a pity he can't sell this meat to some butcher, he might get something for it." But the other man made a ring of his fingers like this, and looked through it and then bade Simon to look, and what he saw was an old piper; and when he thought he was skinning the cow, what he was doing was cutting off his leather breeches. So it's very dangerous to eat beef you buy from any of those sort of common butchers. You don't know what might have been put in its place.

A Man at Corcomroe:
There was Shane Rua that was away every night for seven years. He told his brother-in-law that told me that in that hill behind the abbey there is the most splendid town that was ever seen. Often he was in it, and ought not to have been talking about it, but he said he wouldn't give them the satisfaction of it, he didn't care what they did to him. But he fainted that night

they took him from the wake, and you know what a strong man Peter Nestor was, and *he* couldn't hold him.

Buried he is now beside that wall.

Cloran the plumber's mother was taken away, it's always said. The way it's known is, it was not long after her baby was born but she was doing well. And one morning very early a man and his wife were going in a cart to Loughrea one Thursday for the market, and they met some of *those people* and they asked the woman that had her own child with her, would she give a drink to their child that was with them, and while she was doing it they said, "We won't be in want of a nurse tonight, we'll have Mrs. Cloran of Cloon." And when they got back in the evening, Mrs. Cloran was dead before them.

They said it of Glynn's wife last year. And anyway, her mother was taken in the same way before her.

There was a boy I know lived between our house and Clough, and his hand was lame all his life from a burn he got when he was a child. And one evening in winter he walked out of the house and was never heard of or seen again, or any account of him. And it was not the time of year to go look for work, and anyway, he could never make a living with his lame hand.

Mrs. Casey:
My sister told me that near Tyrone or Cloughballymore there was a man walking home one night late, and he had to pass by a smith's forge where one Kinealy used to work. And when he came near, he heard the noise of the anvil, and he wondered Kinealy would be working so late in the night. But when he went in he saw that they were strange men that were in it. So he asked them the time, and they told him, and he said, "I won't be home this long time yet." And one of the men said, "You'll be home sooner than what you think." And another said, "There's a man on a grey horse gone the road, you'll get a lift from him." And he wondered that they'd know the road he was going to his home. But sure enough as he was walking he came up with a man on a grey horse, and he gave him a lift. But when he got home his wife saw that he looked strange-like, and she asked what ailed him, and he told her all that happened. And when she looked at him she saw that he was taken. So he went into the bed, and the next evening he was dead. And all the people that came in knew by the appearance of the corpse

that it was an old man had been put in his place, and that he was taken when he got on the grey horse. For there's something not right about a grey horse or a white horse, or about a red-haired woman.

There was a girl buried in Kilisheen, one of the Shaws, and when she was laid out on the bed a woman that went in to look at her saw that she opened her eyes, and made a sort of a face at her. But she said nothing, but sat down by the hearth. But another woman came in after that and the same thing happened, and she told the mother, and she began to cry and to roar that they'd say such a thing of her poor little girl. But it wasn't the little girl that was in it all but some old person. And the man that nailed down the coffin left the nails loose, and when they came to Kilisheen churchyard he looked in, and not one thing was inside it but the sheet and a bundle of shavings.

There was a man lived beyond on the Kinvara road, and his child died and he buried it. But he was passing the place after, and he asked a light for his pipe in some house, and after lighting it he threw the sod, and it glowing, just where he buried the child, and what do you think but it came back then in a trance. She went to America after, but didn't live long.

Mrs. Hayden of Slieve Echtge:
There was a woman one time travelling here with my sister from Loughrea, and she had her child in the cart with her. And as they went along the road, a man came out of a sort of a hollow with bushes beside the road, and he asked the woman to come along with him for a minute. And she reddened, but my sister bid her go, and so she went. And the man brought her into a house, and there lying on a bed was a baby, and she understood she was to give suck to it and so she did, and came away; and when she was away out, she saw that the man that brought her was her brother that was dead, and that is the reason she was chosen.

There was another woman, my husband knew here, was taken and an old hag put in her place, that keeps to her bed all the time. And when the seven years were at an end, she got restless like, for they must change every seven years.

So she told the husband the way he should redeem his wife, and where he'd see her with the riders if he'd go out to some place at night. And so he did, and threw what he had at her and she sitting on a horse behind a young man. And when they came home, the old hag was gone. She said the young man was very kind to her and had never done anything to offend her. And she had two or three children and left them behind. But for all that she was glad to come back to her own house. When children are left like that, the mother being brought back again, it's then they want a nurse for them, to give them milk and to attend them.

I know a man was away among them. Every night he would be taken and his wife got used to it after some time; at first she didn't like him to be taken out of the bed beside her. And in harvest, to see that man reap —he'd reap three times as much as any other help he had—of course that's well known.

One Dempsey:
There was a girl at Inniskill in the east of the country, of the same name as my own, was lying on a mat for eight years. When she first got the touch the mother was sick, and there was no room in the bed, so they laid a mat on the floor for her, and she never left it for the eight years; but the mother died soon after.

She never got off the mat for any one to see. But one night there was a working-man came to the house, and they gave him lodging for the night, and he watched from the other room, and in the night he saw the outer door open, and three or four boys come in, and a piper with them or a fiddler—I'm not sure which —and he played to them and they danced, and the girl got up off the mat and joined them. And in the morning when he was sitting at breakfast he looked over to her where she was lying and said, "You were the best dancer among them last night."

There was a priest came when she had been about two years lying there and said something should be done for her, and he came to the house and read Masses, and then he took her by the hand and bid her stand up. But she snatched the hand away and said, "Get away you devil." At last Father Lahiff came to Inniskill, and he came and whatever he did, he drove away what was there, and brought the girl back again, and since then she walks and does the work of the house as well as another. And Father Lahiff said in the Chapel it was a shame for no priest to have done that for her before.

(*Later.*)

Sibby Dempsey of my own name that lives in the next house to me is away still. Every time I go back she can tell me if anything happened me, and where I was or what I did. And more than that, she can tell the future and what will happen you. But there's not many like to go to her, for the priest is against her, and if he'd hear you went to her house he'd be speaking against you at the altar on Sundays. But she has a good many cured. Some she cured that were going to be brought to the asylum in Ballinasloe. By charms she does it, wherever she gathers herbs, she that never left the bed these ten years. Twenty years she was when she got the touch, and it's on her ten years now.

There was a woman had a little girl, and her side got paralysed that she couldn't stir, and she went to the priest, Father Dwyer—he's dead since. For the priests can do all cures, but they wouldn't like to be doing them, to bring themselves into danger. And she asked him to do a cure on the little girl, but what he said was, "Do you ask me to take God's own mercy from Himself?" So when she heard that, she went away, and she went to Sibby Dempsey. And she is the best writer that ever you saw, and she got a pen and wrote some words on a bit of paper, and gave them to the old woman to put on the little girl's arm, and so she did, and on the moment she was cured.

We don't talk much to her now, we don't care to meddle much with those that have been brought back, so we keep out of her way. She'll most likely go to America.

To bring any one back from being in the faeries you should get the leaves of the *lus-mor* and give them to him to drink. And if he only got a little touch from them and had some complaint in him at the same time, that makes him sick-like, that will bring him back. But if he is altogether in the faeries, then it won't bring him back, for he'll know what it is and he'll refuse to drink it.

In a trance the soul goes from the body, but to be among the Sheogue the body is taken and something left in its place.

(*Later.*)

That girl I was telling you about in my own village, Sibby Dempsey, I had a letter about her the other day when I was in Cashel, and she that had been in her bed seventeen years is walking out and going to Mass, a nice respectable woman. They told me no more than that in the letter, but Tom Carden the policeman that had been there for his holiday told that there had come a wandering woman— one of her own sort, it's likely —to the house one night, and asked a lodging in the name of God. Sibby called out, and asked Maggie, the girl, who was that? And the woman stopped the night, and whatever they did was between themselves, and in the morning the wandering woman went away, and Sibby got up out of the bed, that she never had left for seventeen years. Now she never was there all that time in my belief, for if it was an oak stick was lying there through all those years wouldn't it be rotten? It is in the faeries she was, and it not herself used to be in it in the night-time.[43]

(*Later.*) Sibby Dempsey is getting ready now for her wedding. She is all right now; she has gone through her years.

But what do you say to what happened her father shortly after she being brought back? His horse fell with him coming home one evening and both his legs were broke, and the horse was killed. That is the revenge they took for the girl being taken away from them.

One Lanigan:
My own mother was away for twenty-one years, and at the end of every seven years she thought it would be off her, but she never could leave the bed. She could not sit up and make a little shirt or such a thing for us. It was of the fever she died at last.

The way she got the touch was one day after we left the place we used to be in. And we got our choice place in the estate, and my father chose Cahirbohil, but a great number of the neighbours went to Moneen. And one day a woman that had been our neighbour came over from Moneen, and my mother showed her everything and told her of her way of living. And she walked a bit of the way with her, and when they were parting the woman said, "You'll soon be the same as such a one," and as she turned away she felt a pain in her hand. And from that day she lost her health. My father went to Biddy Early, but she said it was too late, she could do nothing, but she would take nothing from him.

There was a man out at Roxborough, Colevin was his name, was known to be away with them. And one day there were a lot of the people footing turf, and a blast of wind came and passed by. And after it passed a joking fellow that was among them called out, "Is Colevin with you?" And the blast turned and knocked an eye out of him, that he never had the sight of it again.

J. Joyce:
There was a little chap I used to go to school with was away. He was in bed for three or four years, and then he could only walk on two sticks, till one day his father was going into Clough and he wanted to go, and the father said, "They'll be laughing at you going on your two sticks." So then he said, "Well, I'll go on one," and threw one away and after that he got rid of the other as well—and got all right. He never would tell anything about where he was, but if any one asked him he'd begin to cry. He was very smart at his books, and very handy, so that when he got well he got a good offer of work and went to America.

An Islander:
There was a girl on the middle island used to be away every night, and they never missed her, for there was something left in her place, but she got thin in the face and wasted away. She told the priest at last, and he bid her go and live in some other place, and she went to America, and there she is still. And she told them after, it was a comrade she had among them used to call her and to bring her about to every place, and that if she took a bit of potato off the skib in the house, it might be on Black Head she'd be eating it. And to parties the other girl would bring her, and she'd be sitting on her lap at them.

But those that are brought away would be glad to be back. It's a poor thing to go there after this life. Heaven is the best place, Heaven and this world we're in now.

A Man whose Son is Said to be Away:
I don't know what's wrong with my son unless that he's a real regular Pagan. He lies in the bed the most of the day and he won't go out till evening and he won't go to Mass. And he has a memory for everything he ever heard or read. I never knew the like. Most people forget what they read in a book within one year after.

A Travelling Man:
A man I met in America told me that one time before they left this country they were working in a field. And in the next field but one they saw a little funeral, a very little one, and it passed into a forth. And there was a child sick in the house near by; and that evening she died. But they had her taken away in the daytime.

Mr. Feeney:
It's a saying that the Sheogue take away the blackberries in the month of November; anyway we know that when the potatoes are taken it's by the *gentry,* and surely this year they have put their fancy on them.

I know the brothers of a man that was away for seven years, and he was none the better for it and had no riches after. It was in that place beyond—where you'd see nothing but hills and hollows—but when he was brought in, he saw what was like a gentleman's avenue, and it leading to a grand house. He didn't mind being among them, when once he got used to it and was one of the force. Of course they wouldn't like you to touch a bush that would belong to them. They might want it for shelter; or it might only be because it belongs to them that they wouldn't like it touched.

There was one of the Readys, John, was away for seven years lying in the bed, but brought away at nights. And he knew everything. And one Kearney up in the mountains, a cousin of his own, lost two hoggets and came and told him. And he saw the very spot where they were and bid him to bring them back again. But they were vexed at that and took away the power, so that he never knew anything again, no more than another.

Surely I believe that any woman taken in childbirth is taken among them. For I knew of a woman that died some years ago and left her young child. And the woman that was put to look after it neglected it. And one night the two doors were blown open, and a blast of wind came in and struck her, and she never was the better of it after.

A Herd:
There was a house I stopped in one night near Tallaght where I was going for a fair, and there was a sick girl in the house, and she lying in a corner near the fire.

141

And some time after, I was told that no one could do anything for her, but that one evening a labouring man that was passing came in and asked a night's lodging. And he was sitting by the fire on a stool and the girl behind him.

And every now and again when no one was looking he'd take a coal of fire and throw it under the stool on to where she was lying till he had her tormented. And in the morning there was the girl lying, and her face all torn and scarred. And he said, "It's not you that was in it these last few months." And she said, "No, but I wouldn't be in it now but for you. And see how the old hag that was in it treated me, she was so mad with the treatment that you gave her last night."

There was one Cronan on the road to Galway, I knew him well, was away with them seven years. It was at night he used to be brought away, and when they called him, go he should. They'd leave some sort of a likeness of him in his place. He had a wart on his back, and his wife would rub her hand down to feel was the wart there, before she'd know was it himself was in it or not. He told some of the way he used to be brought riding about at night, and that he was often in that castle below at Ballinamantane. And he saw then a great many of his friends that were dead.

And Mrs. Kelly asked him did ever he see her son Jimmy that died amongst them. And he told her he did, and that mostly all the people that he knew, that had died out of the village, were amongst them now.

Himself and his pony would go up to the sky.

And if his wife had a clutch of geese, they'd be ten times better than any other one, and the wheat and the stock and all they had was better and more plentiful than what any one else had. Help he got from them of course. And at last the wife got the priest in to read a Mass and to take it off him. But after that all that they had went to flitters.

A Hillside Woman:
Surely there are many taken; my own sister that lived in the house beyond, and her husband and her three children, all in one year. Strong they were and handsome and good—the best —and that's the sort that are taken. They got in the priest when first it came on the husband, and soon after a fine cow died and a calf. But he didn't begrudge that if he'd get his

142

health, but it didn't save him after. Sure Father Andrews in Kilbrennan said not long ago in the chapel that no one had gone to *heaven* for the last ten years.

But whatever life God has granted them, when it's at an end go they must, whether they're among them or not. And they'd sooner be among them than to go to Purgatory.

There was a little one of my own taken. Till he was a year old he was the stoutest and the best and the finest of all my children, and then he began to pine till he wasn't thicker than that straw; but he lived for about four years.

How did it come on him? I know that well. He was the grandest ever you saw, and I proud of him, and I brought him to a ball in his house and he was able to drink punch. And I was stopped one day at a house beyond, and a neighbouring woman came in with her child and she says, "If he's not the stoutest he's the longest," and she took off her apron and the string to measure them both. I had no right to let her do that but I thought no harm at the time. But it was from that night he began to screech and from that time he did no good. He'd get stronger through the winter, and about the Pentecost, in the month of May, he'd always fall back again, for that's the time they're at the worst.

I didn't have the priest in. It does them no good, but harm, to have a priest take notice of them when they're like that.

It was in the month of May at the Pentecost he went at last. He was always pining, but I didn't think he'd go so soon. At the end of the bed he was lying with the others, and he called to me and put up his arms. But I didn't want to take too much notice of him or to have him always after me, so I only put down my foot to where he was. And he began to pick straws out of the bed and to throw them over the little sister beside him, till he had thrown as much as would thatch a goose. And when I got up, there he was dead, and the little sister asleep beside him all covered with straws.

Mrs. Madden:
There were three women living at Ballinakill—Mary Grady, the mother, and Mary Flanagan the daughter, and Ellen Lydon that was a bychild of her's; and they had a little dog called Floss that was like a child to them. And the grandmother went first and then the little dog, and then Mary Flanagan within a half year. And there was a boy wanted to marry Ellen Lydon that

was left alone. But his father and mother wouldn't have her, because of her being a by-child. And the priest wouldn't marry them not to give offence. So it wasn't long before she was taken too, and those that saw her after death knew that it was the mother that was there in place of her. And when the priest was called the day before she died he said, "She's gone since twelve o'clock this morning, and she'll die between the two Masses tomorrow," for it was Father Hubert, that had understanding of these things. And so she did.

There was a man had a son, and he was lying in the bed a long time. And one day, the day of the races, he asked the father and mother were they going to them, and they said they were not. "Well," says he, "I'll show you as good sport as if you went."

And he had a dog, and he called to it and said something to it, and it began to make a run and to gallop and to jump backwards and forwards over the half-door, for there was a very high half-door to the house. "So now," says he, "didn't you see a good sport as if you were in the Newtown racecourse?"

There was my own uncle that lived where the shoemaker's shop is now, and two of his children were brought away from him. And the third he was determined he'd keep, and he put it to sleep between the wife and himself in the bed. And one night a hand came at the window and tried to take the child, and he knew who the hand belonged to, and he saw it was a woman of the village that was dead. So he drove her away and held the child, and he was never troubled again after that.

H. Henty:

There was an old man on the road one night near Burren and he heard a cry in the air over his head, the cry of a child that was being carried away. And he called out some words and the child was let down into his arms and he brought it home. And when he got there he was told that it was dead. So he brought in the live child, and you may be sure that it was some sort of a thing that was good for nothing that was put in its place.

It's the good and the handsome they take, and those that are of use, or whose name is up for some good action. Idlers they don't like, but who would like idlers?

*   *   *

There is a forth away in County Clare, and they say it's so long that it has no end. And there was a pensioner, one Gavornan, came back from the army, and a soldier has more courage than another, and he said he'd go try what was in it, and he got two other men to go with him, and they went a long, long way, and saw nothing. And then they came to where there was the sound of a woman beetling. And then they began to meet people they knew before, that had died out of the village, and they all told them to go back, but still they went on.

And then they met the parish priest of Ballyvaughan, Father Cregan that was dead. And he told them to go back and so they turned and went. They were just beginning to come to the grandeur when they were turned away. Those that are brought away among them never come back, or if they do they're not the same as they were before.

Honor Whelan:
There was a woman beyond at Ardrahan died, and she came back one night and her husband saw her at the dresser, looking for something to eat. And she slipped away from him that time, but the next time she came he got hold of her, and she bid him come for her to the fair at some place, and watch for her at the Customs' gap and she'd be on the last horse that would pass through. And then she said, "It's best for you not come yourself but send your brother." So the brother came and she dropped down to him and he brought her to his house. But in a week after he was dead and buried. And she lived a long time, and never would speak three words to any one that would come into the house, but working, working all the day. I wouldn't have liked to live in the house with her after her being away like that. I don't think the old go among them when they die, but believe me, it's not many of the young they spare, but bring them away till such time as God sends for them. It's about fourteen years since so many young women were brought away after their child being born—Peter Roche's wife, and James Shannan's wife, and Clancy's wife of Lisdaragh—hundreds were carried off in that year—they didn't bring so many since then. I suppose they brought enough then to last them a good time.

All go among them when they die except the old people. And it's better to be there than in the pains of Purgatory. As to Purgatory, I don't think it is after being with *them* we have to go there. But I know we're told to give some clothing to the poor, and it will be thrown down afterwards to quench the flames for us.

A Policeman's Wife:

There was a girl in County Clare was away, and the mother used to hear horses coming about the door every night. And one day the mother was picking flax in the house, and of a sudden there came in her hand an herb with the best smell and the sweetest that ever was smelt.[44] And she closed it with her hand, and called to the son that was making up a stack of hay outside "Come in, Denis, for I have the best smelling herb that ever you saw." And when he came in she opened her hand, and the herb was gone clear and clean. She got annoyed at last with the horses coming about the door, and some told her to gather all the fire into the middle of the floor and to lay the little girl upon it, and to see could she come back again. So she did as she was told, and brought the little girl out of the bed and laid her on the coals. And she began to scream and to call out, and the neighbours came running in, and the police heard of it, and they came and arrested the mother and brought her to the Court-house before the magistrate, Mr. MacWalter, and my own husband was one of the police that arrested her. And when the magistrate heard all, he said she was an ignorant woman, and that she did what she thought right, and he would give her no punishment. And the girl got well and was married. It was after she was married I knew her.

An Old Woman at Chiswick:

There was a woman went to live in a house where the faeries were known to be very much about. And the first day she was there one of them came in and asked her for the loan of a pot, and she gave it. And the next day she came in again and asked for the loan of some meal, and when she got it the woman said, "I hope you'll find it to be fine enough." "It is," she said, "and to show you I think it fine and good, I'll mix it here and boil the stirabout and we'll eat it together." And so they did. And she said "We'll always be your friends; and what you may miss in the morning, never grudge it, for you'll have more than what you lost before night." And her tribe was going away, and when she was going out the door, she made a hole with her heel in the stone, and she filled it up with mud and earth, and she said "If

we die or if anything happens to us, blood will come in this hole
and fill it."

There was a girl used to be away with them, you'd never
know when it was she herself that was in it or not till she'd come
back, and then she'd tell she had been away. She didn't like to
go, but she had to go when they called to her. And she told her
mother always to treat kindly whoever was put in her place,
sometimes one would be put, and sometimes another, for she'd
say "If you are unkind to whoever's there, they'll be unkind to
me."

Three of my uncles were taken by them, young men; some
sort of a little cold they got between them, and there wasn't
more than two months before the first of them going and the
last. They were seen after by a man that lived in the house between there and the school, and that used often to see them,
and to bring them in to dinner with him.

V

HERBS, CHARMS AND WISE WOMEN

THERE is a saying in Irish, "An old woman without learning, it is she will be doing charms"; and I have told in "Poets and Dreamers" of old Bridget Ruane who came and gave me my first knowledge of the healing power of certain plants, some it seemed having a natural and some a mysterious power. And I said that she had "died last winter, and we may be sure that among the green herbs that cover her grave there are some that are good for every bone in the body and that are very good for a sore heart."

As to the book she told me of that had come from the unseen and was written in Irish, I think of Mrs. Sheridan's answer when I asked in what language the strange unearthly people she had been among had talked: "Irish of course—what else would they talk?" And I remember also that when Blake told Crabb Robinson of the intercourse he had had with Voltaire and was asked in what tongue Voltaire spoke he said, "To my sensations it was English. It was like the touch of a musical key. He touched it probably in French, but to my ear it became English".

I was told by her:
There is a Saint at the Oratory in London, but I don't know his name, and a girl heard of him in London, and he sent her back to Gort, and he said, "There's a woman there that will cure you," and she came to me, and I cured her in two days. And if you could find out the name of that Saint through the Press, he'd tell me his remedies, and all the world would be cured. For I can't do all cures though there are a great many I can do. I cured Pat Carty when the doctor couldn't do it, and a woman in Gort that was paralysed and her two sons that were stretched. For I can bring back the dead with the same herbs our Lord was brought back with—the *slanlus* and the *garblus*. But there are some things I can't do. I can't help any one that has got a stroke from the Queen or the Fool of the Forth.

I know a woman that saw the Queen one time, and she said

148

she looked like any Christian. I never heard of any that saw the
Fool but one woman that was walking near Gort, and she called
out, "There's the Fool of the Forth coming after me." So her
friends that were with her called out though they could see
nothing, and I suppose he went away at that for she got no
harm. He was like a big strong man, and half-naked—that's all
she said about him.

It was my brother got the knowledge of cures from a book
that was thrown down before him on the road. What language
was it written in? What language would it be but Irish. Maybe it
was God gave it to him, and maybe it was the *other people.*
He was a fine strong man, and he weighed twenty-five stone—
and he went to England, and then he cured all the world, so
that the doctors had no way of living. So one time he got on a
ship to go to America, and the doctors had bad men engaged to
shipwreck him out of the ship; he wasn't drowned but he was
broken to pieces on the rocks, and the book was lost along with
him. But he taught me a good deal out of it. So I know all herbs,
and I do a good many cures, and I have brought a great many
children home, home to the world—and never lost one, or one
of the women that bore them. I was never away myself, but I
am a cousin of Saggarton, and his uncle was away for twenty-
one years.

This is *dwareen* (knapweed) and what you have to do with
this is to put it down, with other herbs, and with a bit of three-
penny sugar, and to boil it and to drink it for pains in the bones,
and don't be afraid but it will cure you. Sure the Lord put it in
the world for curing.

And this is *corn-corn* (small aromatic tansy); it's very good
for the heart—boiled like the others.

This is *atair-talam* (wild camomile), the father of all herbs—
the father of the ground. This is very hard to pull, and when you
go for it, you must have a black-handled knife.

And this is *camal-buide* (loosestrife) that will keep all bad
things away.

This is *fearaban* (water buttercup) and it's good for every
bone of your body.

This is *dub-cosac* (lichen), that's good for the heart, very
good for a sore heart. Here are the *slanlus* (plantain) and the
garblus (dandelion) and these would cure the wide world, and it
was these brought our Lord from the Cross, after the ruffians

149

that was with the Jews did all the harm to Him. And not one could be got to pierce His heart till a dark man came and said, "Give me the spear, and I'll do it," and the blood that sprang out touched his eyes and they got their sight.

And it was after that, His Mother and Mary and Joseph gathered their herbs and cured His wounds. These are the best of the herbs, but they are all good, and there isn't one among them but would cure seven diseases. I'm all the days of my life gathering them, and I know them all, but it isn't easy to make them out. Sunday evening is the best time to get them, and I was never interfered with. Seven "Hail Marys" I say when I'm gathering them, and I pray to our Lord and to St. Joseph and St. Colman. And there may be *some* watching me, but they never meddled with me at all.

Mrs. Quaid:

Monday is a good day for pulling herbs, or Tuesday, not Sunday. A Sunday cure is no cure. The *cosac* (lichen) is good for the heart, there was Mineog in Gort, one time his heart was wore to a silk thread, and it cured him. The *slanugad* (ribgrass) is very good, and it will take away lumps. You must go down when it's growing on the scraws, and pull it with three pulls, and mind would the wind change when you are pulling it or your head will be gone. Warm it on the tongs when you bring it and put it on the lump. The *lus-mor* (mullein) is the only one that's good to bring back children that are away. But what's better than that is to save what's in the craw of a cock you'll kill on St. Martin's Eve and put it by and dry it, and give it to the child that's away.

There's something in green flax I know, for my mother often told me about one night she was spinning flax, before she was married and she was up late. And a man of the faeries came in. She had no right to be sitting up so late, they don't like that. And he told her to go to bed, for he wanted to kill her, and he couldn't touch her while she was handling the flax. And every time he'd tell her to go to bed, she'd give him some answer, and she'd go on pulling a thread of the flax, or mending a broken one, for she was wise, and she knew that at the crowing of the cock he'd have to go. So at last the cock crowed, and he was gone, and she was safe then, for the cock is blessed.

Mrs. Ward:

As to the *lus-mor*, whatever way the wind is blowing when you begin to cut it, if it changes while you're cutting it, you'll lose your mind. And if you're paid for cutting it, you can do it when you like, but if not *they* mightn't like it. I knew a woman was cutting it one time, and a voice, an enchanted voice, called out, "Don't cut that if you're not paid, or you'll be sorry." But if you put a bit of this with every other herb you drink, you'll live for ever. My grandmother used to put a bit with everything she took, and she lived to be over a hundred.

An Old Man on the Beach:

I wouldn't give into those things, but I'll tell you what happened to a son of my own. He was as fine and as stout a boy as ever you saw, and one day he was out with me, and a letter came and told of the death of some one's child that was in America, and all the island gathered to hear it read. And all the people were pressing to each other there. And when we were coming home, he had a bit of a kippeen in his hand, and getting over a wall he fell, and some way the kippeen went in at his throat, where it had a sharp point and hurt the palate of his mouth, and he got paralysed from the waist up.

There was a woman over in Spiddal, and my wife gave me no ease till I went to her, and she gave me some herb for him. He got better after, and there's no man in the island stronger and stouter than what he is but he never got back the use of his left hand, but the strength he has in the other hand is equal to what another man would have in two. Did the woman in Spiddal say what gave him the touch? Oh well, she said all sorts of things. But I wouldn't like to meddle too much with such as her, for it's by witchcraft I believe it's done. There was a woman of the same sort over in Roundstone, and I knew a man went to her about his wife, and first she said the sickness had nothing to do with *her* business, but he said he came too far to bring back an answer like that. So she went into a little room, and he heard her call on the name of all the devils. So he cried out that that was enough, and she came out then and made the sign of the Cross, but he wouldn't stop in it.

But a priest told me that there was a woman in France used to cure all the dumb that came to her, and that it was a great loss and a great pity when she died.

Mrs. Cloonan:

I knew some could cure with herbs; but it's not right for any one that doesn't understand them to be meddling with them. There was a woman I knew one time wanted a certain herb I knew for a cure for her daughter, and the only place that herb was to be had was down in the bottom of a spring well. She was always asking me would I go and get it for her, but I took advice, and I was advised not to do it. So then she went herself and she got it out, a very green herb it was, not watercress, but it had a bunch of green leaves. And so soon as she brought it into the house, she fell as if dead and there she lay for two hours. And not long after that she died, but she cured the daughter, and it's well I didn't go to gather the herb, or it's on me all the harm would have come.

I used to be gathering an herb one time for the Bishop that lived at Loughmore, dandelion it was. There are two sorts, the white that has no harm in it, that's what I used to be gathering, and the red that has a *pishogue* in it, but I left that alone.

Old Heffernan:

The best herb-doctor I ever knew was Conolly up at Ballyturn. He knew every herb that grew in the earth. It was said that he was away with the faeries one time, and when I knew him he had the two thumbs turned in, and it was said that was the sign they left on him. I had a lump on the thigh one time and my father went to him, and he gave him an herb for it but he told him not to come into the house by the door the wind would be blowing in at. They thought it was the evil I had, that is given by *them* by a touch, and that is why he said about the wind, for if it was the evil, there would be a worm in it, and if it smelled the herb that was brought in at the door, it might change to another place. I don't know what the herb was, but I would have been dead if I had it on another hour, it burned so much, and I had to get the lump lanced after, for it wasn't the evil I had.

Conolly cured many a one. Jack Hall that fell into a pot of water they were after boiling potatoes in, had the skin scalded off him and that Doctor Lynch could do nothing for, he cured.

He boiled down herbs with a bit of lard, and after that was rubbed on three times, he was well.

And Pat Cahel that was deaf, he cured with the *rib-mas-seala*, that herb in the potatoes that milk comes out of. His wife was against him doing the cures, she thought that it would fall on herself. And anyway, she died before him. But Connor at Oldtown gave up doing cures, and his stock began to die, and he couldn't keep a pig, and all he had wasted away till he began to do them again; and his son does cures now, but I think it's more with charms than with herbs.

John Phelan:
The *bainne-bo-bliatain* (wood anemone) is good for the headache, if you put the leaves of it on your head. But as for the *lus-mor* it's best not to have anything to do with that.

Mrs. West:
Dandelion is good for the heart, and when Father Prendergast was curate here, he had it rooted up in all the fields about, to drink it, and see what a fine man he is. *Garblus;* how did you hear of that? That is the herb for things that have to do with the faeries. And when you'd drink it for anything of that sort, if it doesn't cure you, it will kill you then and there. There was a fine young man I used to know and he got his death on the head of a pig that came at himself and another man at the gate of Ramore, and that never left them, but was at them all the time till they came to a stream of water. And when he got home, he took to his bed with a headache, and at last he was brought a drink of the *garblus* and no sooner did he drink it than he was dead. I remember him well. Biddy Early didn't use herbs, but let people say what they like, she was a sure woman. There is something in flax, for no priest would anoint you without a bit of tow. And if a woman that was carrying was to put a basket of green flax on her back, the child would go from her, and if a mare that was in foal had a load of flax put on her, the foal would go the same way.

Mrs. Allen:
I don't believe in faeries myself, I really don't. But all the people in Kildare believe in them, and I'll tell you what I saw there one time myself. There was a man had a splendid big white horse, and he was leading him along the road, and a woman, a next-door neighbour, got up on the wall and looked at him. And the horse fell down on his knees and began to shiver, and you'd think buckets of water were poured over him.

And they led him home, but he was fit for nothing, and everyone was sorry for the poor man, and him being worth ninety pounds. And they sent to the Curragh and to every place for vets, but not one could do anything at all. And at last they sent up in to the mountains for a faery doctor, and he went into the stable and shut the door, and whatever he did there no one knows, but when he came out he said that the horse would get up on the ninth day, and be as well as ever. And so he did sure enough, but whether he kept well, I don't know, for the man that owned him sold him the first minute he could. And they say that while the faery doctor was in the stable, the woman came to ask what was he doing, and he called from inside, "Keep her away, keep her away." And a priest had lodgings in the house at the same time, and when the faery doctor saw him coming, "Let me out of this," says he, and away with him as fast as he could. And all this I saw happen, but whether the horse only got a chill or not I don't know.

James Mangan:
My mother learned cures from an Ulster woman, for the Ulster women are the best for cures; but I don't know the half of them, and what I know I wouldn't like to be talking about or doing, unless it might be for my own family. There's a cure she had for the yellow jaundice; and it's a long way from Ennistymon to Creevagh, but I saw a man come all that way to her, and he fainted when he sat down in the chair, he was so far gone. But she gave him a drink of it, and he came in a second time and she gave it again, and he didn't come a third time for he didn't want it. But I don't mind if I tell you the cure and it is this: take a bit of the dirt of a dog that has been eating bones and meat, and put it on top of an oven till it's as fine as powder and as white as flour, and then pound it up, and put it in a glass of whiskey, in a bottle, and if a man is not too far gone with jaundice, that will cure him.

There was one Carthy at Imlough did great cures with charms and his son can do them yet. He uses no herbs, but he'll go down on his knees and he'll say some words into a bit of unsalted butter, and what words he says, no one knows. There was a big man I know had a sore on his leg and the doctor couldn't cure him, and Doctor Moran said a bit of the bone would have to come out. So at last he went to Jim Carthy and he told him to bring him a bit of unsalted butter the next Monday, or Thursday, or Saturday, for there's a difference in days. And he would have to come three time, or if it was a bad case, he'd have to come nine times.

But I think it was after the third time that he got well, and now he is one of the head men in Persse's Distillery in Galway.

A Slieve Echtge Woman:
The wild parsnip is good for gravel, and for heartbeat there's nothing so good as dandelion. There was a woman I knew used to boil it down, and she'd throw out what was left on the grass. And there was a fleet of turkeys about the house and they used to be picking it up. And at Christmas they killed one of them, and when it was cut open they found a new heart growing in it with the dint of the dandelion.

My father went one time to a woman at Ennis, not Biddy Early, but one of her sort, to ask her about three sheep he had lost.

And she told him the very place they were brought to, a long path through the stones near Kinvara. And there he found the skins, and he heard that the man that brought them away had them sold to a butcher in Loughrea. So he followed him there, and brought the police, and they found him—a poor looking little man, but he had £60 within in his box.

There was another man up near Ballylee could tell these things too. When Jack Fahy lost his wool, he went to him, and next morning there were the fleeces at his door.

Those that are *away* know these things. There was a brother of my own took to it for seven years—and we at school. And no one could beat him at the hurling and the games. But I wouldn't like to be mixed with that myself.

There was one Moyra Colum was a great one for doing cures. She was called one time to see some sick person, and the man that came for her put her up behind him, on the horse. And some youngsters began to be humbugging him, and humbugging is always bad. And there was a young horse in the field where the youngsters were and it began to gallop, and it fell over a stump and lay on the ground kicking as if in a fit. And then Moyra Colum said, "Let me get down, for I have pity for the horse." And she got down and went into the field, and she picked a blade of a herb and put it to the horse's mouth and in one minute it got up well.

155

Another time a woman had a sick cow and she sent her little boy to Moyra Colum, and she gave him a bottle and bade him put a drop of what was in it in the cow's ear. And so he did and in a few minutes he began to feel a great pain in his foot. So into the street and broke it, and she said, "It's better to lose the cow than to lose my son." And in the morning the cow was dead.

The herbs they cure with, there's some that's natural, and you could pick them at all times of the day; there's a very good cure for the yellow jaundice I have myself, and I offered it to a woman in Ballygrah the other day, but some people are so taken up with pride and with conceit they won't believe that to cure that sickness you must take what comes from your own nature. She's dead since of it, I hear. But I'll tell you the cure, the way you'll know it. If you are attending a funeral, pick out a few little worms from the earth that's thrown up out of the grave, few or many, twenty or thirty if you like. And when you go home, boil them down in a sup of new milk and let it get cold; and believe me, that will cure the sickness.

There's one woman I knew used to take a bit of tape when you'd go to her, and she'd measure it over her thumb like this; and when she had it measured she'd know what was the matter with you.

For some sicknesses they used herbs that have no natural cure, and those must be gathered in the morning early. Before twelve o'clock? No, but before sunrise. And there's a different charm to be said over each one of them. It is for any sort of pain these are good, such as a pain in the side. There's the *meena madar*, a nice little planteen with a nice little blue flowereen above on it, that's used for a running sore or an evil. And the charm to be said when you're picking it has in it the name of some old curer or magician, and you can say that into a bit of tow three times, and put it on the person to be cured. That is a good charm. You might use that yourself if it was any one close to you was sick, but for a stranger I'd recommend you not do it. *They* know all things and who are using it, and where's the use of putting yourself in danger?

James Mangan:
My mother learned to do a great many cures from a woman
from the North[45] and some I could do myself, but I wouldn't
like to be doing them unless for those that are nearest me; I
don't want to be putting myself in danger.

For a swelling in the throat it's an herb would be used, or for
the evil a poultice you'd make of herbs. But for a pain in the
ribs or in the head, it's a charm you should use, and to whisper
it into a bit of tow, and to put it on the mouth of whoever would
have the pain, and that would take it away. There's a herb
called *rif* in your own garden is good for cures. And this is a
good charm to say in Irish:

A quiet woman.
A rough man.
The Son of God.
The husk of the flax.

The Old Man on the Beach:
In the old times all could do *druith*—like freemasonry—and
the ground was all covered with the likeness of the devil; and
with *druith* they could do anything, and could put the sea between you and the road. There's only a few can do it now, but
all that live in the County Down can do it.

Mrs. Quaid:
There was a girl in a house near this was pining away, and
a travelling woman came to the house and she told the mother
to bring the girl across to the graveyard that's near the house
before sunrise and to pick some of the grass that's growing over
the remains. And so she did, and the girl got well. But the mother
told me that when the woman had told her that, she vanished
away, all in a minute, and was seen no more.

I have a charm myself for the headache, I cured many with
it. I used to put on a ribbon from the back of the head over the
mouth, and another from the top of the head under the chin and
then to press my hand on it, and I'd give them great relief and
I'd say the charm. But one time I read in the Scriptures that the
use of charms is forbidden, so I had it on my conscience, and
the next time I went to confession I asked the priest was it any
harm for me to use it, and I said it to him in Irish. And in

157

English it means "Charm of St. Peter, Charm of St. Paul, an angel brought it from Rome. The similitude of Christ, suffering death, and all suffering goes with Him and into the flax." And the priest didn't say if I might use it or not, so I went on with it, for I didn't like to turn away so many suffering people coming to me.

I know a charm a woman from the North gave to Tom Mangan's mother, she used to cure ulcers with it and cancers. It was with unsalted butter it was used, but I don't know what the words were.

John Phelan:
If you cut a hazel rod and bring it with you, and turn it round about now and again, no bad thing can hurt you. And a cure can be made for bad eyes from the ivy that grows on a white-thorn bush. I know a boy had an ulcer on his eye and it was cured by that.

Mrs. Creevy:
There was Leary's son in Gort had bad eyes and no doctor could cure him. And one night his mother had a dream that she got up and took a half-blanket with her, and went away to a blessed well a little outside Gort, and there she saw a woman dressed all in white, and she gave her some of the water, and when she brought it to her son he got well. So the next day she went there and got the water, and after putting it three times on his eyes, he was as well as ever he was.

There was a woman here used to do cures with herbs—a midwife she was. And if a man went for her in a hurry, and on a horse, and he'd want her to get up behind him, she'd say, "No," that she was never on horseback. But no matter how fast he'd go home, there she'd be close after him.

There was a child was sick and it was known itself wasn't in it. And a woman told the mother to go to a woman she told her of, and not to say anything about the child but to say, "The calf is sick" and to ask for a cure for it. So she did and the woman gave her some herb, and she gave it to the child and it got well.

There was a man from Cuillean was telling me how two women came from the County Down in his father's time,

158

mother and daughter, and they brought two spinning wheels with them, and they used to be in the house spinning. But the milk went from the cow and they watched and saw it was through charms. And then all the people brought turf and made a big fire outside, and stripped the witch and the daughter to burn them. And when they were brought out to be burned the woman said, "Bring me out a bit of flax and I'll show you a pishogue." So they brought out a bit of flax and she made two skeins of it, and twisted it some way like that (interlacing his fingers) and she put the two skeins round herself and the daughter, and began to twist it, and it went up in the air round and round and the two women with it, and the people all saw them going up, but they couldn't stop them. The man's own father saw that himself.

There was a woman from the County Down was living up on that mountain beyond one time, and there was a boy in the house next to mine that had a pain in his heart, and was crying out with the pain of it. And she came down, and I was in the house myself and I saw her fill the bowl with oatenmeal, and she tied a cloth over it, and put it on the hearth. And when she took it off, all the meal was gone out of one side of the bowl, and she made a cake out of what was left on the other side, and ate it. And the boy got well.

There was a woman in Clifden did many cures and knew everything. And I knew two boys were sent to her one time, and they had a bottle of poteen to bring her, but on the road they drank the poteen. But they got her another bottle before they got to the house, but for all that she knew well, and told them what they had done.

There's some families have a charm in them, and a man of those families can do cures, just like King's blood used to cure the evil, but they couldn't teach it to you or to me or another.

There's a very good charm to stop bleeding; it will stop it in a minute when nothing else can, and there's one to take bones from the neck, and one against ulcers.

Kevin Ralph:
I went to Macklin near Loughrea myself one time, when I had an ulcer here in my neck. But when I got to him and asked for the charm, he answered me in Irish, "The Soggarth said to

me, any man that will use charms to do cures with will be damned." I persuaded him to do it after, but I never felt that it did me much good. Because he took no care to do it well after the priest saying that of him. But there's some will only let it be said in an outhouse if there's a cure to be done in the house.

A Woman in County Limerick:

It is twenty year ago I got a pain in my side, that I could not stoop; and I tried Siegel's Syrup and a plaster and a black blister from the doctor, and every sort of thing and they did me no good. And there came in a man one day, a farmer I knew, and he said, "It's a fool you are not to go to a woman living within two miles of you that would cure you—a woman that does charms." So I went to her nine times, three days I should go and three stop away, and she would pass her hand over me, and would make me hold on to the branch of an apple tree up high, that I would hang from it, and she would be swinging me as you would swing a child. And she laid me on the grass and passed her hands over me, and what she said over me I don't know. And at the end of the nine visits I was cured, and the pain left me. At the time she died I wanted to go lay her out but my husband would not let me go. He said if I was seen going in, the neighbours would say she had left me her cures and would be calling me a witch. She said it was from an old man she got the charm that used to be called a wizard. My father knew him, and said he could bring away the wheat and bring it back again, and that he could turn the four winds of heaven to blow upon your house till they would knock it.

A Munster Midwife:

Is it true a part of the pain can be put on the man? It is to be sure, but it would be the most pity in the world to do it; it is a thing I never did, for the man would never be the better of it, and it would not take any of the pain off the woman. And shouldn't we have pity upon men, that have enough troubles of their own to go through?

Mrs. Hollaran:

Did I know the pain could be put on a man? Sure I seen my own mother that was a midwife do it. He was such a Molly of an old man, and he had no compassion at all on his wife. He was as if making out she had no pain at all. So my mother gave her a drink, and with that he was on the floor and around the floor crying and roaring. "The devil take you," says he, and the pain upon him; but while he had it, it went away from his wife. It did him no harm after, and my mother would not have done it but for him being so covetous. He wanted to make out that she wasn't sick.

Mrs. Stephens:

At childbirth there are some of the old women are able to put a part of the pain upon the man, or any man. There was a woman in labour near Oran, and there were two policemen out walking that night, and one of them went into the house to light his pipe. There were two or three women in it, and the sick woman stretched beyond them, and one of them offered him a drink of the tea she had been using, and he didn't want it but he took a drink of it, and then he took a coal off the hearth and put it on his pipe to light it and went out to his comrade. And no sooner was he there than he began to roar and to catch hold of his belly and he fell down by the roadside roaring. But the other knew something of what happened, and he took the pipe, and it having a coal on it, and he put it on top of the wall and fired a shot of the gun at it and broke it; and with that the man got well of the pain and stood up again.

No woman that is carrying should go to the house where another woman is in labour; if she does, that woman's pain will come on her along with her own pain when her time comes.

A child to come with the spring tide, it will have luck.

VI

ASTRAY, AND TREASURE

*MR. YEATS in his dedication of "The Shadowy Waters" says
of some of our woods:*

> *"Dim Pairc-na-tarav where enchanted eyes
> Have seen immortal mild proud shadows walk;
> Dim Inchy wood that hides badger and fox
> And martin-cat, and borders that old wood
> Wise Biddy Early called the wicked wood."*

*I have heard many stories of people led astray in these by
invisible power, though I myself, although born at midnight,
have lived many hours of many years in their shades and shelters,
and as the saying is have "never seen anything worse than
myself."*

*Last May a friend staying with us had gone out early in the
afternoon, and had not come back by eight o'clock dinner-time.
As half-hours passed we grew anxious and sent out messengers
riding and on foot, searching with lanterns here and there in
the woods and on Inchy marsh, towards which he had been seen
going. It was not till long after the fall of darkness that he returned, tired out with so many hours of wandering, and with no
better explanation than "Yeats talks of the seven woods of Coole,
but I say there are seventy times seven." It was in dim Inchy
and the wicked wood it borders he had gone astray; and many
said that was natural, for they have a bad name, and May is a
month of danger. Yet some unbelievers may carry their credulity
so far as to believe that the creator of Father Keegan's dreams
may himself have dreamed the whole adventure.*

*I was told by An Army Man who had been through the
Indian Mutiny:*

It's only yesterday I was talking to a man about *the others*,
and he told me that the castle of Ballinamantane is a great place
for them, for it's there a great stand was made long ago in one

162

of their last fights. And one night he was making his way home, and only a field between him and his house, when he found himself turned around and brought to another field, and then to another—seven in all. And he remembered the saying that you should turn your coat and that they'd have no power over you, and he did so, but it did him no good. For after that he was taken again, and found himself in the field over beyond. And he had never a one drop taken, but was quite sober that night.

What did they do it for? It might be that he had trespassed on one of their ways; but it's most likely that there was some sort of a rogue among them that turned and did it for sport.

Mrs. Cloonan:

The other evening I was milking the cow over in Inchy, and a beggar-woman came by, with a sack of potatoes and such things on her back. She makes her living selling ballads in Gort, and then begging afterwards. So she sat down beside me, and she said "I don't like to go on through the wood." So I asked did she ever see anything there. "I did," says she, "three years ago, one night just where the old house is the Dooleys used to live in. There came out of the end of it a woman all in white, and she led me astray all the night, and drove me that I had no time to turn my clothes—and my feet were black with the blows she gave me, and though it was three years ago, I feel the pain in them yet."

Mrs. Coniffe says:

I was in Inchy the other day late, and I met an old beggar-man, and I asked him was he ever led astray there. And he said, "Not in this wood, but in the wood beyond, Garryland. It was one night I was passing through it, and met a great lot of them —laughing they were and running about and drinking wine and wanting me to drink with them. And they had cars with them, and an old woman sitting on a sort of an ass-car. And I had a scapular round my neck, and I thought that would make me independent, but it did not, for it was on the highroad outside I found myself put at last.

A Mason:

My father was led astray one time, when he was coming home from a neighbour's house, and he was led here and there till he didn't know what way he was going. And then the moon began to shine out and he saw his shadow, and another shadow along with it ten feet in length. So with that he ran, and when he got to the wood of Cloon he fell down in a faint.

And I was led astray one night, going across to a neighbour's house—just the length of a field away, and where I could find my way blindfolded. Into the ditch I was led, and to some other field, and I put my hand to the ground, and it was potato ground, and the drills made, but the seed not put in. And if it wasn't at last that I saw a light from Scalp, it's away I'd have been brought altogether.

John Rivers:
Once I was led astray in that field and went round and round and could find no way out—till at last I thought of the old Irish fashion of turning my waistcoat, and did so. And then I got out the gate in one minute.

And one night I was down at the widow Hayley's—I didn't go much there—she used to have the place full of loafers, and they playing cards. But this night I stopped a bit, and then I went out. And the way I was put I could not say, but I found myself in the field with an eight-foot wall behind me—and there I had to stop till some of the men came and found me and brought me out.

A Girl of the Feeneys:
One time my brother when he was coming home late one evening was put asleep in spite of himself, on the grass, at this corner we're passing. None of the boys like to be coming home late, from card-playing or the like, unless there's two or three of them together. And if they go to a wake, they wouldn't for all the world come home before the cock crows. There were many led astray in that hollow beyond, where you see the haycocks. Old Tom Stafford was led astray there by something like a flock of wool that went rolling before him, and he had no power to turn but should follow it. Michael Barrett saw the coach one time driving across Kiltartan bog, and it was seen to many others besides.

As to Michael Barrett, I believe it's mostly in his own head they are. But I knew this that when he pulled down the chimney where he said that the piper used to be sitting and playing, he lifted out stones, and he an old man, that I could not have lifted myself when I was young and healthy.

A Clare Woman:
As to treasure, there was a man here dreamt of some buried things—of a skeleton and a crock of money. So he went to dig, but whether he dreamed wrong or that he didn't wait for the third dream, I don't know, but he found the skeleton, skull and all, but when he found the crock there was nothing in it, but very large snail-shells. So he threw them out in the grass, and next day when he went to look at them they were all gone. Surely there's something that's watching over that treasure under ground.

But it doesn't do to be always looking for money. There was Whaney the miller, he was always wishing to dream of money like other people. And so he did one night, that it was hid under the millstone. So before it was hardly light he went and began to dig and dig, but he never found the money, but he dug till the mill fell down on himself.

So when any one is covetous the old people say, "Take care would you be like Whaney the miller."

Now I'll tell you a story that's all truth. There was a farmer man living there beyond over the mountains, and one day a strange man came in and asked a night's lodging. "Where do you come from?" says the farmer. "From the county Mayo," says he, and he told how he had a dream of a bush in this part of the world, and gave a description of it, and in his dream he saw treasure buried under it. "Then go home, my poor man," said the farmer, "for there's no such place as that about here." So the man went back again to Mayo. But the bush was all the time just at the back of the house, and when the stranger was gone, the farmer began to dig, and, and there, sure enough, he found the pot of gold, and took it for his own use.

But all the children he had turned silly after that; there was one of them not long ago going about the town with long hair over his shoulders.

And after that, a poor scholar, such as used to be going about in those times, came to the house, and when he had sat down, the lid of the pot the gold was found in was lying by the fire. And he took it up and rubbed it, and there was writing on it, in Irish, that no one had ever been able to read. And the poor scholar made it out, "This side of the bush is no better than the other side." So he went out to dig, and there he found another pot on the other side just the same as the first pot and he brought it away with him, and what became of him after is unknown.

John Phelan:

There was a man in Gort, Anthony Hynes, he and two others dreamed of finding treasure within the church of Kilmacdaugh. But when they got there at night to dig, something kept them back, for there's always something watching over where treasure is buried. I often heard that long ago in the nursery at Coole, at the cross, a man that was digging found a pot of gold. But just as he had the cover took off, he saw old Richard Gregory coming, and he covered it up, and was never able again to find the spot where it was.

But there's dreams and dreams. I heard of a man from Mayo went to Limerick, and walked two or three times across the bridge there. And a cobbler that was sitting on the bridge took notice of him, and knew by the look of him and by the clothes he wore that he was from Mayo, and asked him what was he looking for. And he said he had a dream that under the bridge of Limerick he'd find treasure. "Well," says the cobbler, "I had a dream myself about finding treasure, but in another sort of a place than this." And he described the place where he dreamed it was, and where was that, but in the Mayo man's own garden. So he went home again, and sure enough, there he found a pot of gold with no end of riches in it. But I never heard that the cobbler found anything under the bridge at Limerick.

I met a woman coming out one day from Cloon, and she told me that when she was a young girl, she went out one day with another girl to pick up sticks near a wood. And she chanced to lay hold on a tuft of grass, and it came up in her hand and the sod with it. And there was a hole underneath full of half-crowns, and she began to fill her apron with them, and as soon as she had the full of her apron she called to the other girl, and the minute she came there wasn't one to be seen. But what she had in her apron she kept.

A Travelling Man:

There was a sister of mine, Bridget her name was, dreamed three nights of treasure that was buried under the bush up there, by the chapel, a mile to the east; you can see the bush there, blown slantwise by the wind from the sea. So she got three men to go along with her and they brought shovels to dig for it. But it was the woman should have lifted the first sod and she didn't do it, and they saw, coming down from the mountains of Burren, horses and horses, bearing horse-soldiers on them, and they came around the bush, and the soldiers held up their shovels, and my sister and the men that were with her made away across the field.

The time I was in America, I went out to the country to see Tom Scanlon, my cousin, that is a farmer there and had any amount of land and feeding for the cows, and we went out of the house and sat down on a patch of grass the same as we're sitting on now. And the first word he said to me was, "Did Bridget, your sister, ever tell you of the dream she had, and the way we went digging at the bush, for I was one of the men that was along with her?" "She did often," says I. "Well," says he, "all she told you about it was true."

There were two boys digging for razor fish near Clarenbridge, and one of them saw, as he was digging, a great lot of gold. So he said nothing, the way the other boy would know nothing about it. But when he came back for it it was gone.

There was another boy found gold under a flagstone he lifted. But when he went back next day to get it, all the strength he had wouldn't lift the flag.

The Army Man:
There was a forth sometime or other there inside the gate, and one Kelly told me that he was coming by it one night and saw all the hollow spread with gold, and he had not the sense to take it up, but ran away.

A friend I had near Athenry had more sense. He saw the ground spread with gold and he took up the full of his pockets and paid his rent next day and prospered ever after, as everyone does that gets the faery gold.

Another man I knew of had a dream of a place where there was three crooks of gold. And in the morning he went to dig and found the crocks sure enough, and nothing in them but oyster

167

shells. That was because he went to dig after the first dream. He had a right to wait till he had dreamed of it three times.

A girl the same way dreamt of gold hid in a rock and did not wait for the third dream, but went at once, and all she found was the full of an ass-cart near of sewing needles, and that was a queer thing to find in a rock. No, they don't always hinder you, they help you now and again.

There was a working man used to be digging potatoes for me, and whenever he was in want of money, he found it laid on his window-sill in the night. But one day he had a drop of drink taken, he told about it, and never a penny more did he find after that.

Sure, there's an old castle beyond Gort, Fiddane it's called, and there you'd see the gold out bleaching, but no one would like to go and take it. And my mother told me one time that a woman went up in the field beyond where the liss is, to milk the cow, and there she saw on the grass a crock full of gold. So she left the bit she had for holding the cow beside it, and she ran back to the house for to tell them all to come out and see it. But when they came the gold was nowhere to be seen, but had vanished away. But in every part of the field there was a bit of rope like the one she left beside the crock, so that she couldn't know what spot it was in at all.

She had a right to have taken it, and told no one. They don't like to have such things told.

Mrs. Coniffe:

That bush you took notice of, the boy told me that it is St. Bridget's bush, and there is a great lot of money buried under it; they know this from an old woman that used to be here a long time ago. Three men went one time to dig for it and they dug and dug all the day and found nothing and they went home and to bed. And in the night whatever it was came to them, they never got the better of it, but died within a week. And you'd be sorry to see—as the boy did—the three coffins carried out of the three houses. And since then no other person has ever gone to look for the money.

That's no wonder for you to know a faery bush. It grows a

different shape from a common one, and looks different someway.

As to hidden gold, I knew a man, Patrick Connell, dreamed he found it beneath a bush. But he wasn't willing to go look for it, and his sons and his friends were always at him to tell where it was, but he would tell them nothing. But at last his sons one day persuaded him to go with them and to dig for it. So they took their car, and they set out. But when they came to a part of the road where there's a small little ditch about a foot wide beside it, he was walking and he put his foot in it and they had to bring him home, for his leg was broke. So there was no more digging for treasure after that.

A Neighbour:
There's crocks of gold in all the forths, but there's cats and things guarding them. And if any one does find the gold, he doesn't live long afterwards. But sometimes you might see it and think that it was only a heap of dung. It's best to leave such things alone.

VII

BANSHEES AND WARNINGS

"THEN Cuchulain went on his way, and Cathbad that had followed him went with him. And presently they came to a ford, and there they saw a young girl thin and white-skinned and having yellow hair, washing and ever washing, and wringing out clothing that was stained crimson red, and she crying and keening all the time. 'Little Hound,' said Cathbad, 'Do you see what it is that young girl is doing? It is your red clothes she is washing, and crying as she washes, because she knows you are going to your death against Maeve's great army.' "
—"Cuchulain of Muirthemne."

From Cuchulain's day, or it may be from a yet earlier time, that keening woman of the Sidhe has been heard giving her lamentable warning for those who are about to die. Rachel had not yet been heard mourning for her children when the white-skinned girl whose keening has never ceased in Ireland washed red clothes at the ford. It was she or one of her race who told King Brian he was going to meet his death at Clontarf; though after the defeat of the old gods that warning had often been sent by a more radiant messenger, as when Columcille at the dawn of the feast of Pentecost "lifted his eyes and saw a great brightness and an angel of God waiting there above him." And Patrick himself had his warning through his angel, Victor, who met him on the road at midday and bade him go back to the barn where he had lodged the night before, for it was there he had to die. Such a messenger may have been at hand at the death of that Irish born mystic, William Blake, when he "burst out into singing of the things he saw in Heaven, and made the rafters ring." And a few years ago the woman of a thatched house at the foot of Echtge told me "There were great wonders done in the old times; and when my father that worked in the garden there above was dying, there came of a sudden three flashes of light into the room, the brightest light that ever was seen in the world; and there was an old man in the room, one Ruane, and I leaned back on him for I had like to faint. And people coming the road saw the light, and up at Mick Inerney's house they all

170

called out that our house was in flames. *And when they came and heard of the three flashes of light coming into the room and about the bed they all said it was the angels that were his friends that had come to meet him." When Raftery died, the blind poet who wandered through our townlands a hundred years ago, some say there were flames about the house all through the night, "and those were the angels waking him." Yet his warning had not been sent through these white messengers but through a vision that had come to him once in Galway, when Death himself had appeared "thin, miserable, sad and sorrowful; the shadow of night upon his face, the tracks of the tears down his cheeks" and had told him he had but seven years to live. And though Raftery spoke back to him in scornful verse, there are some who say he spent those last seven years in praying and in making his songs of religion. To some it is a shadow that brings the warning, or a noise of knocking or a dream. At the hour of a violent death nature itself will show sympathy; I have been told on a gloomy day that it had darkened because there was a man being hanged; and a woman who had travelled told me that once at Bundoran she had "seen the waves roaring and turning" and she knew later it was because at that very time two young girls had been drowned.*

I was told by Steve Simon:
I will tell you what I saw the night my wife died. I attended the neighbours up to the road, for they had come to see her, but she said there was no fear of her, and she would not let them stop because she knew that they were up at a wake the night before.

So when I left them I was going back to the house, and I saw the shadow of my wife on the road before me, and it was as white as drifted snow. And when I came into the house, there she was dying.

Mrs. Curran:
My cousin Mary that lives in the village beyond told me that she was coming home yesterday week along the road, and she is a girl would not be afraid to walk the whole world with herself. And it was late, and suddenly there was a man walking beside her, inside the field, on the other side of the wall.

171

And at first she was frightened, but then she felt sure it was her cousin John that was dying, and then she wasn't afraid, for she knew her cousin would do her no harm. And after a while he was gone, and when she got near home and saw the lights she was frightened, and when she got into the house she was in a sort of a faint. And next day, this day week, her cousin was dead.

Old Simon:
I heard the Banshee crying not long ago, and within three days a boy of the Murphy's was killed by his own horse and he bringing his cart to Kinvara. And I heard it again a few nights ago, but I heard of no death since then. What is the Banshee? It is of the nature of the Hyneses. Six families it cries for, the Hyneses and the Fahys and I forget what are the others.

I heard her beside the river at Ballylee one time. I would stand barefooted in the snow listening to the tune she had, so nice and so calm and so mournful.

I would yield to dreams because of some things were dreamed to me in my lifetime and that turned out true. I dreamed one time that I saw my daughter that was in America dead, and stretched and a table laid out with the corpse. She came home after, and at the end of five months she wasted and died. And there I saw her stretched as in the dream, and it was on my own table.

One time I was walking the road and I heard a great crying and keening beside me, a woman that was keening, and she conveyed me three miles of the road. And when I got to the door of the house I looked down and saw a little woman, very broad and broad faced—about the bigness of the seat of that table—and a cloak about her. I called out to her that was my first wife—the Lord be with her—and she lighted a candle and I came in weak and lay upon the floor, and I was till 12 o'clock that night lying in the bed.

A man I was talking to said it was the Banshee, and it cries for three families, the Fahys and the O'Briens and another I forget which. My grandmother was a Fahy, and I suppose, father or mother, it follows the generations. I heard it another time and my daughter from America coming into the house that night. It was the most mournful thing ever you heard, keening about the house for the same term as before, till 12 o'clock of night. And within five months my daughter from America was dead.

John Cloran:

There was a man near us that was ploughing a field, and he found an iron box, and they say there was in it a very old Irish book with all the knowledge of the world in it. Anyway, there's no question you could ask him he couldn't answer. And what he says of the Banshee is, that it's Rachel mourning still for every innocent of the earth that is going to die, like as she did for our Lord when the king had like to kill Him. But it's only for them that's sprung from her own tribe that she'll raise her voice.

Mrs. Smith:

As for the Banshee, where she stops is in the old castle of Esserkelly on the Roxborough estate. Many a one has seen her there and heard her wailing, wailing, and she with a red petticoat put about her head. There was a family of the name of Fox in Moneen, and never one of that family died but she'd be heard keening them.

The Spinning Woman:

The Banshee is all I ever saw myself. It was when I was a slip of a girl picking potatoes along with the other girls, we heard crying, crying, in the graveyard beyond at Ryanrush, so we ran like foals to see who was being buried, and I was the first, and leaped up on the wall. And there she was and gave me a slap on the jaw, and she just like a countrywoman with a red petticoat. Often they hear her crying if any one is going to die in the village.

A Seaside Woman:

One time there was a man in the village was dying and I stood at the door in the evening, and I heard a crying—the grandest cry ever you heard—and I said "Glynn's after dying and they're crying him." And they all came to the door and heard it. But my mother went out after that and found him gasping still.

Sure enough it was the Banshee we heard that evening.

And out there where the turf-boat is lying with its sail down, outside Aughanish, there the Banshee does always be crying, crying, for some that went down there some time.

At Fiddoon that strip of land between Tyrone and Duras something appears and cries for a month before any one dies. A great many are taken away sudden there; and they say that it's because of that thing.

The Banshee cries every time one of the Sionnacs dies. And when the old Captain died, the crows all left the place within two days, and never came back for a year.

A Connemara Woman:
There was a boy from Kylemore I met in America used to be able to tell fortunes. He used to be telling them when the work would be done, and we would be having afternoon tea. He told me one time I would soon be at a burying, and it would be a baby's burying, and I laughed at that. But sure enough, my sister's baby, that was not born at the time, died about a month after, and I went to its burying.

A Herd:
Crying for those that are going to die you'd hear of often enough. And when my own wife was dying, the night she went I was sitting by the fire, and I heard a noise like the blow of a flail on the door outside. And I went to see what it was, but there was nothing there. But I was not in any way frightened and wouldn't be if she came back in a vision, but glad to see her I would be.

A Miller:
There was a man that was out in the field and a flock of stares (starlings) came about his head, and it wasn't long after that he died.

There's many say they saw the Banshee, and that if she heard you singing loud she'd be very apt to bring you away with her.

A Connemara Woman:
One night the clock in my room struck six and it had not struck for years, and two nights after—on Christmas night—it struck six again, and afterwards I heard that my sister in America had died just at that hour. So now I have taken the weights off the clock, that I wouldn't hear it again.

174

Mrs. Huntley:

It was always said that when a Lord —— died, a fox was seen about the house. When the last Lord —— lay dying, his daughter heard a noise outside the house one night, and opened the hall-door, and then she saw a great number of foxes laying on the steps and barking and running about. And the next morning there was a meet at some distant covert—it had been changed there from hard by where it was to have taken place on account of his illness—and there was not a single fox to be found there or in any other covert. And that day he died.

J. Hanlon:

There was one Costello used to be ringing the bell and pumping water and such things at Roxborough, and one day he was at the fair of Loughrea. And as he started home he sent word to my grandfather "Come to the corner of the old castle and you'll find me dead." So he set out, and when he got to the corner of the castle, there was Costello lying dead before him.

And once going to a neighbour's house to see a little girl, I saw her running along the path before me. But when I got to the house she was in bed sick, and died two days after.

Pat. Linskey:

Well, the time my own wife died I had sent her into Cloon to get some things from the market, and I was alone in the house with the dog. And what do you think but he started up and went out to the hill outside the house, and there he stood a while howling, and it was the very next day my wife died.

Another time I had shut the house door at night and fastened it, and in the morning it was standing wide open. And as I knew by the dates afterwards that was the very night my brother died in India.

Sure I told Stephen Green that, when he buried his mother in England, and his father lying in Kilmacdaugh. "You should never separate," says I, "in death a couple that were together in life, for sure as fate, the one'll come to look for the other."

And when there's one of them passing in the air you might get a blast of holy wind you wouldn't be the better of for a long time.

Mrs. Curran:

I was in Galway yesterday, and I was told there that the night before those four poor boys were drowned, there were four women heard crying out on the rocks. Those that saw them say that they were young, and they were out of this world. And one of those boys was out at sea all day, the day before he was drowned. And when he came in to Galway in the evening, some boy said to him "I saw you today standing up on the high bridge." And he was afraid and he told his mother and said "Why did they see me on the high bridge and I out at sea?" And the next day he drowned. And some say there was not much at all to drown them that day.

A Man near Athenry:

There is often crying heard before a death, and in that field beside us the sound of washing clothes with a beetle is sometimes heard before a death.

I heard crying in that field near the forth one night, and not long after the man it belonged to died.

An Aran Man:

I remember one morning, St. Bridget's Eve, my son-in-law came into the house, where he had been up that little road you see above. And the wife asked him did he see any one, and he said "I saw Shamus Meagher driving cattle." And the wife said, "You couldn't see him, for he's out laying spillets since daybreak with two other men." And he said, "But I did see him, and I could have spoke with him." And the next day— St. Bridget's Day—there was confessions in the little chapel below and I was in it, and Shamus Meagher, and it was he that was kneeling next to me at the Communion. But the next morning he and two other men that had set the spillets went on in their canoe to Kilronan for salt, for they had come short of salt and had a good deal of fish taken. And that day the canoe was upset, and the three of them were drowned.

A Piper:

My father and my mother were in the bed one night and they heard a great lowing and a noise of the cattle fighting one another, that they thought they were all killed, and they went out and they were quiet then. But they went onto the next house where they heard a lowing, and all the cattle of that house were fighting one another, and so it was at the next. And in the morning a child, one Gannon, was dead—or taken he was.

An Old Man in Aran:
When I was in the State of Maine, I knew a woman from the County Cork, and she had a little girl sick. And one day she went out behind the house and there she saw the fields full of *those*—full of them. And the little girl died.

And when I was in the same State, I was in the house where there was a child sick. And one night I heard a noise outside, as if of hammering. And I went out and I thought it came from another house that was close by that no one lived in, and I went and tried the door but it was shut up.

And I went back and said to the woman, "This is the last night you'll have to watch the child." And at 12 o'clock the next evening it died.

They took my hat from me one time. One morning just at sunrise I was going down to the sea, and a little storm came, and took my hat off and brought it a good way, and then it brought it back and returned it to me again.

An Old Midwife:
I do be dreaming, dreaming. I dreamt one night I was with my daughter and that she was dead and put in the coffin. And I heard after, the time I dreamt about her was the very time she died.

A Woman near Loughrea:
There are houses in Cloon, and Geary's is one of them, where if the people sit up too late the warning comes; it comes as a knocking at the door. Eleven o'clock, that is the hour. It is likely it is some that lived in the house are wanting it for themselves at the time. And there is a house near the Darcys' where as soon as the potatoes are strained from the pot, they must put a plateful ready and leave it for the night, and milk and the fire on the hearth, and there is not a bit left at morning. Some poor souls that come in, looking for warmth and for food.

There is a woman seen often before a death sitting by the river and racking her hair, and she has a beetle with her and she takes it and beetles clothes in the river. And she cries like any good crier; you would be sorry to be listening to her.

Old King:

I heard the Banshee and saw her. I and six others were card playing in the kitchen at the big house, that is sunk into the ground, and I saw her up outside of the window. She had a white dress and it was as if held over her face. They all looked up and saw it, and they were all afraid and went back but myself. Then I heard a cry that did not seem to come from her but from a good way off, and then it seemed to come from herself. She made no attempt to twist a mournful cry but all she said was, "Oh-oh, Oh-oh," but it was as mournful as the oldest of the old women could make it, that was best at crying the dead.

Old Mr. Sionnac was at Lisdoonvarna at that time, and he came home a few days after and took to the bed and died. It is always the Banshee has followed the Sionnacs and cried them.

Mrs. King:

There was a boy of the Naughtons died not far from this, a fine young man. And I set out to go to the burying, and Mrs. Burke along with me. But when we came to the gate we could hear crying for the dead, and I said "It's as good for us wait where we are, for they have brought the corp out and are crying him." So we waited a while and no one came, and so we went on to the house, and we had two hours to wait before they brought out the corp for the burying, and there had been no crying at all till he was brought out. We knew then who it was crying, for if the boy was a Naughton, it is in a house of the Kearns he died, and the Banshee always cries for the Kearns.

A Doctor:

There's a boy I'm attending now, and the first time I went to him, the mother came out of the house with me and said "It's no use to do anything for him, I'm going to lose him." And I asked her why did she say that, and she said "Because the first night he took ill I heard the sound of a chair drawing over to the fire in the kitchen, and it empty, and it was the faeries were coming for him." The boy wouldn't have had much wrong with him, but his brother had died of phthisis, and when he got a cold he made sure he would die too, and he took to the bed. And

178

every day his mother would go in and cry for an hour over him, and then he'd cry and then the father would cry, and he'd say "Oh, how can I leave my father and my mother! Who will there be to mind them when I'm gone?" One time he was getting a little better they sent him over on a message to Scahanagh, and there's a man there called Shanny that makes coffins for the people. And the boy saw Shanny looking at him, and he left his message undone and ran home and cried out "Oh, I'm done for now! Shanny was looking at me to see what size coffin I'd take!" And he cried and they all cried and all the village came in to see what was the matter.

The Old Army man:
As to the invisible world, I hear enough about it, but I have seen but little myself. One night when I was at Calcutta I heard that one Connor was dead—a man that I had been friendly with—so I went to the house. There was a good many of us there, and when it came to just before midnight, I heard a great silence fall, and I looked from one to another to see the silence. And then there came a knock at the window, just as the clock was striking twelve. And Connor's wife said, "It was just at this hour last night there came a knock like that and immediately afterwards he died." And the strange thing is, it was a barrackroom and on the second story, so that no one could reach it from the street.

In India, before Delhi, there was an officer's servant lodged in the same house as me, and was thrown out of his cot every night. And as sure as midnight came, the dogs couldn't stop outside but would come shrinking and howling into the house. Yes indeed, I believe the faeries are in all countries, all over the world; but the banshee is only in Ireland, though sometimes in India I would think of her when I'd hear the hyenas laughing. Keening, keening, you can hear her, but only for the old Irish families, but she'll follow them even as far as Dublin.

179

VIII

IN THE WAY

AN old Athenry man who had been as a soldier all through the Indian Mutiny and had come back to end his days here as a farmer said to me in speaking of "The Others" and those who may be among them: "There's some places of their own we should never touch such as the forths; and if ever we cross their pathways we're like to know it soon enough, for some ill turn they'll do us, and then we must draw back out of their way ... And we should above all things leave the house clean at night, with nothing about that would offend them. For we must all die some day, but God knows we're not all fit for heaven just on the minute; and what the intermediate state may be, or what friends we may want there, I don't know. No one has come back to tell us that."

I was told by John Donovan:

Before I came here I was for two years in a house outside Cloon. And no one that lived there ever prospered but all they did went to loss. I sowed seeds and put in the crop each year, and if I'd stopped there I wouldn't have had enough to keep trousers to my back. *In the way* the place must be. I had no disturbance in the house, but some nights I could hear the barrel rolling outside the door, back and forwards, with a sort of a warning to me.

I knew another house in Clare where the front door is always shut up and they only use the back door, but when I asked them the reason they said if they opened the front door a sudden blast would come in, that would take the roof off the house. And there's another house in Clare built in a forth, a new one, shut up and the windows closed, for no one can live in it.

Andrew Lee:

In the way? Yes that's a thing that often happens. Sure going into Clough, you might see a house that no man ever yet kept a roof on. Surely it's in the way of their coming and going.

And Doctor Nolan's father began to build a barn one time, and whatever was built in the day, in the night it would be pulled down, so at last they gave over. It was only labour and wages wasted.

Mrs. Cloran:

No, I never heard or felt anything since I came here. The old people used to tell many things, they know more than what the youngsters do. My mother saw many a thing, but they did her no harm. No, I remember none of the stories; since my children died and a weight came on my heart all those things went from me. Yes, it's true Father Boyle banished the dog; and there was a cousin of my own used to live in the house at Garryland, and she could get no sleep for what she used to feel at night. But Father Boyle came and whatever he did, "You'll feel them no more," says he, and she never did, though he was buried before her.

That was a bad, bad place we lived in near the sea. The children never felt anything, but often in the night I could hear music playing and no one else in the house could hear it. But the children died one by one, passing away without pain or ache.

All they saw was twice; the two last little girls I had were beside the door at night talking and laughing and they saw a big dark man pass by, but he never spoke. Some old thing out of the walls he must have been. And soon after that they died.

One time when I was there a strange woman came in, and she knew everything and told me everything. "I'd give you money if I had it," said I. "I know well you haven't much of it," says she; "but take my word and go away out of this house to some other place, for you're *in the way*." She told me to tell no one she came, and that shows there was something not right about her; and I never saw her any more.

But if I'd listened to her then, and if I knew then what she meant by the house being *in the way* I wouldn't have stopped in it, and my seven fine children would be with me now. Took away they were by *them* and without ache or pain. I never had a sign or a vision from them since, but often and often they come across me in my sleep.

Her Husband:

The woman that came to give my wife the warning, I didn't see her, and she knew all that was in the house and all about me and what money I had, and that I would grow very poor. And she said that before I'd die, I'd go to the strand and come back again. And we couldn't know what she meant, and we thought it must mean that I'd go to America. But we knew it at last. For one day I was washing sheep down at Cahirglissane, and there is said to be the deepest water in the world in one part of that lake. And as I was standing by it, a sheep made a run and went between my two legs, and threw me into the water, and I not able to swim. And I was brought on the top of the water safe and sound to land again; and I knew well who it was helped me, and saved my life. She that had come before to give advice that would save my children, it's she that was my friend over there. To say a Mass in the house? No use at all that would have been, living in the place we did.

But they're mostly good neighbours. There was a woman they used to help, one of them used to come and help her to clean the house, but she never came when the husband was there. And one day she came and said they were going to move now, to near Clifden. And she bid the woman follow them, and whenever she'd come to a briar turned down, with a thorn stuck in the earth, to build a house there.

A Travelling Man:
I was sleeping at a house one time and *they* came in—the fallen angels. They were pulling the clothes off me, ten times they did that, and they were laughing like geese—just the very sound of geese—and their boots were too large for their feet and were clapping, clapping on the floor. I suppose they didn't like me to be in it, or that the house was built in one of their passages.

My father was driven out of the little garden house at Castle-boy one time he went to sleep in it. In the way, I suppose it must have been.

And I knew of a herd's house, where five or six herds went one after another and every one of them died, and their dogs and their cow. And the gentleman that owned the place came to ask another one to go in it, and his wife said she wouldn't go, for there was some bad luck about it. But she went after, and she was a very clean woman, not like some of them that do have the house dirty. Well, one day a woman came to the door and asked for a dish of oaten meal, and she took it from the shelf, and gave it to her. "I'll bring it back to you tomorrow," says she, "it'll be easy getting it then when it's market day." "Do not," says the woman of the house, "for if you do I won't take it." "Well," says the stranger, "you'll have luck after this; only one thing I tell you, keep that door at the back shut, and if you want any opening there, let you open the window." Well, so she did, and by minding that rule, and keeping the house so clean, she was never troubled but lived there all her life.

An Island Woman:
There are some houses that never bring luck. There is one over there, out of this village, and two or three died in it, and one night it blazed up and burned down, those that were out in the fishing boats could see it, but it was never known how it happened.

There was a house over in the other village and a woman living in it that had two forths of land. And she had clever children, but the most of them died one after another, boys and girls, and then the husband died. And after that one of the boys that had died came to her and said "You'd best leave this house or you'll be as we are, and we are all now living in the Black Rock at the gable end of the house. And two of the McDaraghs are with us there."

So after that she left the house—you can cut grass now in the place where it was, and it's green all through the summer and the winter—and she went up to the north side and she married a young man up there, for she was counted a rich woman. She had but two daughters left, and one of them was married, and there was a match to be made for the other, but the stepfather wouldn't allow her to give any of the land to her, so she said she'd go to America, and the priest drew up a stamped paper for her, that they'd keep a portion of money for her every year till she'd come back. It wasn't long after that the stepfather was out in one of the fields one day and two men came and knocked him down and gave him a beating. And it was his belief it was the father of the girl and one of the brothers that came to beat him.

And one of the neighbours that went to the house one night saw one of the brothers standing at the window, plump and plain. And a first cousin of theirs—a Donovan—was near the Black Rock one night, and he saw them playing ball there, the whole of them that had gone, and others with them. And when

183

they saw him they whistled to make fun of him, and he went away.

The stepfather died after that, and the woman herself died, and was buried a week yesterday. And she had one son by the second husband and he was always silly-like, and the night she died he went into the room where she was, to the other side of the bed, and he called out, and then he came out walking crooked, and his face drawn up on one side; and so he is since, and a neighbour taking care of him. And you'd hardly mind what a poor silly creature like him would say, but what he says is that it was some of the boys that were gone that were in it. And now there's no one to take up the land that so many were after; the girl in America wouldn't for all the world come back to that place.

IX

THE FIGHTING OF THE FRIENDS

"ONE time on Hy, one Brito of Columcille's brotherhood was
dying, and Columcille gave him his blessing but would not see
him die, and went out into the little court of the house. And he
had hardly gone out when the life went from Brito. And
Columcille was out in the little court, and one of the monks saw
him looking upward, and wonder on him, and he asked what was
it he saw. And Columcille said, 'I have seen just at this moment
the holy angels fighting in the air against the power of the enemy,
and I gave thanks to Christ, the Judge, because the winning
angels have carried to heaven the soul of this stranger that is
the first to have died among us in this island. And do not tell
his secret to any person in my lifetime,' he said."
                                            —"Saints and Wonders."

"With that King Arthur entereth into a great forest
adventurous, and rideth the day long until he cometh about
evensong into the thick of the forest. And he espied a little house
beside a little chapel, and it well seemed to him to be a
hermitage . . . And it seemed to him that there was a strife in
the chapel. The ones were weeping so tenderly and sweetly as
it were angels, and the others spake so harshly as it were fiends.
. . . The voices ceased as soon as he was within. He marvelleth
how it came that this house and hermitage were solitary, and
what had become of the hermit that dwelt therein. He drew
nigh the altar of the chapel, and beheld in front thereof a coffin
all discovered, and he saw the hermit lying therein all clad in
his vestments, and his hands crossed upon his breast, and he
had life in him yet, but he was nigh his end, being at the point
of death . . . The King departed and so returned back into the
little house, and sate him down on a seat whereon the hermit
wont to sit. And he heareth the strife and the noise begin again
within the chapel, and the ones he heareth speaking high and
the others low, and he knoweth well by the voices that the ones
are angels and the others devils. And he heareth that the devils
are distraining on the hermit's soul, and that judgment will
presently be given in their favour, whereof make they great joy.

King Arthur is grieved in his heart when he heareth that the angels' voices are stilled. And while he sitteth thus, stooping his head toward the ground, full of vexation and discontent, he heareth in the chapel the voice of a Lady that spake so sweet and clear that no man in this earthly world, were his grief and heaviness never so sore, but and he had heard the sweet voice of her pleading would again have been in joy ... The devils go their way all discomfit and aggrieved; and the sweet Mother of our Lord God taketh the soul of the hermit ... And the angels take it and begin to sing for joy 'Te Deum Laudamus.' And the Holy Lady leadeth them and goeth her way along with them."
—"The High History of the Holy Grail." Translated by Sebastian Evans.

Before I had read this old story from "The High History of the Holy Grail" I had heard on our own roads of the fighting at the hour of death, and how the friends of the dying among the dead come and use their strength on his side, and I had been shown here and there a house where such a fight had taken place. In the old days it was a king or saint who saw and heard this unearthly battle; but now it is not those who live in palaces who are aware of it, and it is not around the roof of a fair chapel the hosts of good and evil gather in combat for the parting soul, but around the thatched and broken roof of the poor.

I was told by An Islander:
There are more of the Sheogue in America than what there are here, and more of other sort of spirits. There was a man from there told me that one night in America he had brought his wife's niece that was sick back from the hospital, and had put her in an upper room. And in the evening they heard a scream from her and she called out "The room is full of them, and my father is with them, and my aunt." And he drove them away and used the devil's name and cursed them. And she was left quiet that night, but the next day she said "I'll be destroyed altogether tonight with them." And he said he'd keep them out, and he locked the door of the house. And towards midnight he heard them coming to the door and trying to get in, but he kept it locked and he called to them by way of the keyhole to keep away out of that. And there was talking among them, and the girl that was upstairs said that she could hear the laugh of her

father and of her aunt. And they heard the greatest fighting among them that ever was, and after that they went away, and the girl got well. That's what often happens, crying and fighting for one that's sick or going to die.

Mrs. Meagher:
There was an old woman the other day was telling me of a little girl that was put to bake a cake, for her mother was sick in the room. And when she turned away her head for a minute the cake was gone. And that happened the second day and the third, and the mother was vexed when she heard it, thinking some of the neighbours had come and taken it away.

But the next day an old man appeared, and she knew he was the grandfather, and he said "It's by me the cake was taken, for I was watching the house these three nights when I knew there was some one sick in it. And you never heard such a fight as there was for her last night, and they would have brought her away but for me that had my shoulder to the door." And the woman began to recover from that time.

Tom Smith:
There does often be fighting when a person is dying. John Madden's wife that lived in this house before I came to it, the night she died there was a noise heard, that all the village thought that every wall of every garden round about was falling down. But in the morning there was no sign of any of them being fallen.

And Hannay that lived at Cahir, the bonesetter, when I went to him one time told me that one night late he was walking the road near Ardrahan. And they heard a great noise of fighting in the castle he was passing by, and no one living in it and it open to the sky. And he turned in and was going up the stairs, and a lady in a white dress stopped him and wouldn't let him pass up. But the next day he went to look and he found the floor all covered with blood.

And before John Casey's death, John Leeson asked me one day were we fighting down at our place, for he heard a great noise of fighting the night before.

A Farmer:
As to fighting for those that are dying, I'd believe in that. There was a girl died not far from here, and the night of her

death there was heard in the air the sound of an army marching, and the drums beating, and it stopped over the house where she was lying sick. And they could see no one, but could hear the drums and the marching plain enough, and there were like little flames of lightning playing about it.

Did they fight for Johnny Casey? No, believe me it's not among the faeries Johnny Casey is. Too old he is for them to want him among them, and too cranky.

I would hardly believe they'd take the old, but we can't know what they might want of them. And it's well to have a friend among them, and it's always said you have no right to fret if your children die, for it's well to have them there before you. And when a person is dying the friends and the others will often come about the house and will give a great challenge for him. They don't want cross people, and they won't take you if you say so much as one cross word. It's only the good and the pious they want. Now isn't that very good of them?

Another:
There was a young man I knew died, a fine young man, twenty-five years of age. He was seven or eight days ill, and the night he died they could hear fighting around the house, and they heard voices but they couldn't know what they were saying. And in the morning the ground was all covered with blood.

When Connors the young policeman died, sure the mother said she never heard such fighting as went on within the house. And there was blood splashed high up on the walls. They never let on how he got the touch, but I suppose they knew it themselves.

A Gatekeeper:
There was a girl near Westport was *away*, and the way it came on her was, she was on the road one day and two men passed her, and one of them said, "That's a fine girl," and the other said, "She belongs to my town," and there and then she got a pain in her knee, and couldn't walk home but had to be brought in a car. And she used to be away at night, and thorns in her feet in the morning, but she never said where she went. But one time the sister brought her to Kilfenora, and when they

188

were crossing a bog near to there, she pointed out a house in the bog, and she said "It's there I was last night." And the sister asked did she know any one she saw in it, and she said "There was one I know, that is my mother's cousin," and she told her name. And she said "But for her they'd have me ill-treated, but she fought for me and saved me." She was thought to be dying one time and given over, and my mother sent me to see her, and how was she. And she was lying on the bed and her eyes turned back, and she speechless, and I told my mother when I came home she hadn't an hour to live. And the next day she was up and about and not a thing on her. It might be the mother's cousin that fought for her again there. She went to America after.

An Aran Woman:
There's often fighting heard about the house where one is sick, that is what we call "the fighting of the friends" for we believe it is the friends and the enemies of the sick person fighting for him.

I knew a house where there were a good many sleeping one night, and in the morning there was blood on the threshold, and the clothes of those that slept on the floor had blood on them. And it wasn't long after that the woman of the house took sick and died.

One night there was one of the boys very sick within, and in the morning the grandmother said she heard a great noise of fighting in the night about the door. And she said: "If it hadn't been for Michael and John being drowned, you'd have lost Martin last night. For they were there fighting for him; I heard them, and I saw the shadow of Michael, but when I turned to take hold of him he was gone."

X

THE UNQUIET DEAD

A GOOD many years ago when I was but beginning my study of the folk-lore of belief, I wrote somewhere that if by an impossible miracle every trace and memory of Christianity could be swept out of the world, it would not shake or destroy at all the belief of the people of Ireland in the invisible world, the cloud of witnesses, in immortality and the life to come. For them the veil between things seen and unseen has hardly thickened since those early days of the world when the sons of God mated with the daughters of men; when angels spoke with Abraham in Hebron or with Columcille in the oakwoods of Derry, or when as an old man at my own gate told me they came and visited the Fianna, the old heroes of Ireland, "because they were so nice and so respectable." Ireland has through the centuries kept continuity of vision, the vision it is likely all nations possessed in the early days of faith. Here in Connacht there is no doubt as to the continuance of life after death. The spirit wanders for a while in that intermediate region to which mystics and theologians have given various names, and should it return and become visible those who loved it will not be afraid, but will, as I have already told, put a light in the window to guide the mother home to her child, or go out into the barley gardens in the hope of meeting a son. And if the message brought seems hardly worth the hearing, we may call to mind what Frederic Myers wrote of more instructed ghosts:

"If it was absurd to listen to Kepler because he bade the planets move in no perfect circles but in undignified ellipses, because he hastened and slackened from hour to hour what ought to be a heavenly body's ideal and unwavering speed; is it not absurder still to refuse to listen to these voices from afar, because they come stammering and wandering as in a dream confusedly instead of with a trumpet's call? Because spirits that bending to earth may undergo perhaps an earthly bewilderment and suffer unknown limitations, and half remember and half forget?"

And should they give the message more clearly who knows if it would be welcome? For the old Scotch story goes that when

S. Columcille's brother Dobhran rose up from his grave and said, "Hell is not so bad as people say," the Saint cried out, "Clay, clay on Dobhran!" before he could tell any more.

I was told by Mrs. Dennehy:
Those that mind the teaching of the clergy say the dead go to Limbo first and then to Purgatory and then to hell or to heaven. Hell is always burning and if you go there you never get out; but these that mind the old people don't believe, and I don't believe, that there is any hell. I don't believe God Almighty would make Christians to put them into hell afterwards.

It is what the old people say, that after death the shadow goes wandering, and the soul is weak, and the body is taking a rest. The shadow wanders for a while and it pays the debts it had to pay, and when it is free it puts out wings and flies to Heaven.

An Aran Man:
There was an old man died, and after three days he appeared in the cradle as a baby; they knew him by an old look in his face, and his face being long and other things. An old woman that came into the house saw him, and she said, "He won't be with you long, he had three deaths to die, and this is the second," and sure enough he died at the end of six years.

Mrs. Martin:
There was a man beyond when I lived at Ballybron, and it was said of him that he was taken away—up before God Almighty. But the blessed Mother asked for grace for him for a year and a day. So he got it. I seen him myself, and many seen him, and at the end of the year and a day he died. And that man ought to be happy now anyway. When my own poor little girl was drowned in the well, I never could sleep but fretting, fretting, fretting. But one day when one of my little boys was taking his turn to serve the Mass he stopped on his knees without getting up. And Father Boyle asked him what did he see and he looking up. And he told him that he could see his little sister in the presence of God, and she shining like the sun. Sure enough that was a vision He had sent to comfort us. So from that day I never cried nor fretted any more.

191

A Herd:

Do you believe Roland Joyce was seen? Well, he was. A man I know told me he saw him the night of his death, in Esserkelly where he had a farm, and a man along with him going through the stock. And all of a sudden a train came into the field, and brought them both away like a blast of wind.

And as for old Parsons Persse of Castleboy, there's thousands of people has seen him hunting at night with his horses and his hounds and his bugle blowing. There's no mistake at all about him being there.

An Aran Woman:

There was a girl in the middle island had died, and when she was being washed, and a priest in the house, there flew by the window the whitest bird that ever was seen. And the priest said to the father: "Do not lament, unless what you like, your child's happy for ever!"

Mrs. Casey:

Near the strand there were two little girls went out to gather cow-dung. And they sat down beside a bush to rest themselves, and there they heard a groan coming from under the ground. So they ran home as fast as they could. And they were told when they went again to bring a man with them.

So the next time they went they brought a man with them, and they hadn't been sitting there long when they heard the saddest groan that ever you heard. So the man bent down and asked what was it. And a voice from below said, "Let some one shave me and get me out of this, for I was never shaved after dying." So the man went away, and the next day he brought soap and all that was needful and there he found a body lying laid out on the grass. So he shaved it, and with that wings came and carried it up to high heaven.

A Chimney-sweep:

I don't believe in all I hear, or I'd believe in ghosts and faeries, with all the old people telling you stories about them and the priests believing in them too. Surely the priests believe in ghosts, and tell you that they are souls that died in trouble. But I have been about the country night and day, and I remember when I used to have to put my hand out at the top of every chimney in Coole House; and I seen or felt nothing to frighten me, except

192

one night two rats caught in a trap at Roxborough; and the old butler came down and beat me with a belt for the scream I gave at that. But if I believed in any one coming back, it would be in what you often hear, of a mother coming back to care for her child.

And there's many would tell you that every time you see a tree shaking there's a ghost in it.

Old Lambert of Dangan was a terror for telling stories; he told me long ago how he was near the Piper's gap on Ballybrit racecourse, and he saw one riding to meet him, and it was old Michael Lynch of Ballybrista, that was dead long before, and he never would go on the racecourse again. And he had heard the car with headless horses driving through Loughrea. From every part they are said to drive, and the place they are all going to is Benmore, near Loughrea, where there is a ruined dwelling-house and an old forth. And at Mount Mahon a herd told me the other day he often saw old Andrew Mahon riding about at night. But if I was a herd and saw that I'd hold my tongue about it.

Mrs. Casey:
At the graveyard of Drumacoo often spirits do be seen. Old George Fitzgerald is seen by many. And when they go up to the stone he's sitting on, he'll be sitting somewhere else.

There was a man walking in the wood near there, and he met a woman, a stranger, and he said "Is there anything I can do for you?" For he thought she was some country-woman gone astray. "There is," says she. "Then come home with me," says he, "and tell me about it." "I can't do that," says she, "but what you can do is this, go tell my friends I'm in great trouble, for twenty times in my life I missed going to church, and they must say twenty Masses for me now to deliver me, but they seem to have forgotten me. And another thing is," says she, "there's some small debts I left and they're not paid, and those are helping to keep me in trouble." Well, the man went on and he didn't know what in the world to do, for he couldn't know who she was, for they are not permitted to tell their name. But going about visiting at country houses he used to tell the story, and at last it came out she was one of the Shannons. For at a house he was telling it at they remembered that an old woman they had, died a year ago, and that she used to be running up little debts unknown to them. So they made inquiry at Findlater's and at another shop that's done away with now, and they found that sure enough she had left some small debts, not more than ten shillings in each, and when she died no more had been said about it. So they paid these and said the Masses, and shortly after she appeared to the man again. "God bless you now," she said, "for what you did for me, for now I'm at peace."

A Tinker's Daughter:
I heard of what happened to a family in the town. One night a thing that looked like a goose came in. And when they said nothing to it, it went away up the stairs with a noise like lead. Surely if they had questioned it, they'd have found it to be some soul in trouble.

And there was another soul came back that was in trouble because of a ha'porth of salt it owed.

And there was a priest was in trouble and appeared after death, and they had to say Masses for him, because he had done some sort of a crime on a widow.

Mrs. Farley:
One time myself I was at Killinan, at a house of the Clancys' where the father and mother had died, but it was well known they often come to look after the children. I was walking with another girl through the fields there one evening and I looked up and saw a tall woman dressed all in black, with a mantle of some sort, a wide one, over her head, and the waves of the wind were blowing it off her, so that I could hear the noise of it. All her clothes were black, and had the appearance of being new. And I asked the other girl did she see her, and she said she did not. For two that are together can never see such things, but only one of them. So when I heard she saw nothing I ran as if for my life, and the woman seemed to be coming after me, till I crossed a running stream and she had no power to cross that. And one time my brother was stopping in the same house, and one night about twelve o'clock there came a smell in the house like as if all the dead people were there. And one of the girls whose father and mother had died got up out of her bed, and began to put her clothes on, and they had to lock the doors to stop her from going away out of the house.

There was a woman I knew of that after her death was kept for seven years in a tree in Kinadyfe, and for seven years after that she was kept under the arch of the little bridge beyond Kilchriest, with the water running under her. And whether there was frost or snow she had no shelter from it, not so much as the size of a leaf.

At the end of the second seven years she came to her husband, and he passing the bridge on the way home from Loughrea, and when he felt her near him he was afraid, and he didn't stop to question her, but hurried on.

So then she came in the evening to the house of her own little girl. But she was afraid when she saw her, and fell down in a faint. And the woman's sister's child was in the house, and when the little girl told her what she saw, she said "You must surely question her when she comes again." So she came again that night, but the little girl was afraid again when she saw her and said nothing. But the third night when she came the sister's child, seeing her own little girl was afraid, said "God bless you, God bless you." And with that the woman spoke and said "God bless you for saying that." And then she told her all that had happened her and where she had been all the fourteen years. And she took out of her dress a black silk handkerchief and said: "I took that from my husband's neck the day I met him on the road from Loughrea, and this very night I would have killed him, because he hurried away and would not stop to help me, but now that you have helped me I'll not harm him. But bring with you to Kilmacduagh, to the graveyard, three cross sticks with wool on them, and three glasses full of salt, and have three Masses said for me; and I'll appear to you when I am at rest." And so she did; and it was for no great thing she had done that trouble had been put upon her.

John Cloran:
That house with no roof was made a hospital of in the famine, and many died there. And one night my father was passing by and he saw some one standing all in white, and two men beside him, and he thought he knew one of the men and spoke to him and said "Is that you, Martin?" But he never spoke nor moved. And as to the thing in white, he could not say was it man or woman, but my father never went by that place again at night.

The last person buried in a graveyard has the care of all the other souls until another is to be buried, and then the soul can go and shift for itself. It may be a week or a month or a year, but watch the place it must till another soul comes.

There was a man used to be giving short measure, not giving the full yard, and one time after his death there was a man passing the river and the horse he had would not go into it. And he heard the voice of the tailor saying from the river he had a message to send to his wife, and to tell her not to be giving short measure, or she would be sent to the same place as himself. There was a hymn made about that.

There was a woman lived in Rathkane, alone in the house, and she told me that one night something came and lay over the bed and gave three great moans. That was all ever she heard in the house.

The shadows of the dead gather round at Samhain time to see is there any one among their friends saying a few Masses for them.

An Islander:
Down there near the point, on the 6th of March, 1883, there was a curragh upset and five boys were drowned. And a man from County Clare told me that he was on the coast that day, and that he saw them walking towards him on the Atlantic.

There is a house down there near the sea, and one day the woman of it was sitting by the fire, and a little girl came in at the door, and a red cloak about her, and she sat down by the fire. And the woman asked her where did she come from, and she said that she had just come from Connemara. And then she went out, and when she was going out the door she made herself known to her sister that was standing in it, and she called out to the mother. And when the mother knew it was the child she had lost near a year before, she ran out to call her, for she wouldn't for all the world to have not known her when she was there. But she was gone and she never came again.

There was this boy's father took a second wife, and he was walking home one evening, and his wife behind him, and there was a great wind blowing, and he kept his head stooped down because of the seaweed coming blowing into his eyes. And she

196

was about twenty paces behind, and she saw his first wife come and walk close beside him, and he never saw her, having his head down, but she kept with him near all the way. And when they got home, she told the husband who was with him, and with the fright she got she was bad in her bed for two or three days—do you remember that, Martin? She died after, and he has a third wife taken now.

I believe all that die are brought among them, except maybe an odd old person.

A Kildare Woman:
There was a woman I knew sent into the Rotunda Hospital for an operation. And when she was going she cried when she was saying good-bye to her cousin that was a friend of mine, for she felt in her that she would not come back again. And she put her two arms about her going away and said, "If the dead can do any good thing for the living, I'll do it for you." And she never recovered, but died in the hospital. And within a few weeks something came on her cousin, my friend, and they said it was her side that was paralysed, and she died. And many said it was no common illness, but that it was the dead woman that had kept to her word.

A Connemara Man:
There was a boy in New York was killed by rowdies, they killed him standing against a lamp-post and he was frozen to it, and stood there till morning. And it is often since that time he was seen in the room and the passages of the house where he used to be living.
And in the house beyond a woman died, and some other family came to live in it; but every night she came back and stripped the clothes off them, so at last they went away.

When some one goes that owes money, the weight of the soul is more than the weight of the body, and it can't get away and keeps wandering till some one has courage to question it.

Mrs. Casey:
My grandmother told my mother that in her time at Clough-ballymore, there was a woman used to appear in the churchyard of Rathkeale, and that many boys and girls and children died with the fright they got when they saw her.

197

So there was a gentleman living near was very sorry for all the children dying, and he went to an old woman to ask her was there any way to do away with the spirit that appeared. So she said if any one would have courage to go and to question it, he could do away with it. So the gentleman went at midnight and waited at the churchyard, and he on his horse, and had a sword with him. So presently the shape appeared and he called to it and said, "Tell me what you are?" And it came over to him, and when he saw the face he got such a fright that he turned the horse's head and galloped away as hard as he could. But after galloping a long time he looked down and what did he see beside him but the woman running and her hand on the horse. So he took his sword and gave a slash at her, and cut through her arm, so that she gave a groan and vanished, and he went on home.

And when he got to the stable and had the lantern lighted, you may think what a start he got when he saw the hand still holding on to the horse, and no power could lift it off. So he went into the house and said his prayers to Almighty God to take it off. And all night long, he could hear moaning and crying about the house. And in the morning when he went out the hand was gone, but all the stable was splashed with blood. But the woman was never seen in those parts again.

A Seaside Man:

And many see the faeries at Knock and there was a carpenter died, and he could be heard all night in his shed making coffins and carts and all sorts of things, and the people are afraid to go near it. There were four boys from Knock drowned five years ago, and often now they are seen walking on the strand and in the fields and about the village.

There was a man used to go out fowling, and one day his sister said to him, "Whatever you do don't go out tonight and don't shoot any wild-duck or any birds you see flying—for tonight they are all poor souls travelling."

An Old Man in Galway Workhouse:

Burke of Carpark's son died, but he used often to be seen going about afterwards. And one time a herd of his father's met with him and he said, "Come tonight and help us against the hurlers from the north, for they have us beat twice, and if they beat us a third time, it will be a bad year for Ireland."

198

It was in the daytime they had the hurling match through the streets of Galway. No one could see them, and no one could go outside the door while it lasted, for there went such a whirlwind through the town that you could not look through the window.

And he sent a message to his father that he would find some paper he was looking for a few days before, behind a certain desk, between it and the wall, and the father found it there. He would not have believed it was his son the herd met only for that.

A Munster Woman:

I have only seen them myself like dark shadows, but there's many can see them as they are. Surely they bring away the dead among them.

There was a woman in County Limerick that died after her baby being born. And all the people were in the house when the funeral was to be, crying for her. And the cars and the horses were out on the road. And there was seen among them a carriage full of ladies, and with them the woman was sitting that they were crying for, and the baby with her, and it dressed.

And there was another woman I knew of died, and left a family, and often after, the people saw her in their dreams, and always in rich clothes, though all the clothes she had were given away after she died, for the good of her soul, except maybe her shawl. And her husband married a serving girl after that, and she was hard to the children, and one night the woman came back to her, and had like to throw her out of the window in her nightdress, till she gave a promise to treat the children well, and she was afraid not to treat them well after that.

There was a farmer died and he had done some man out of a saddle, and he came back after to a friend, and gave him no rest till he gave a new saddle to the man he had cheated.

Mrs. Casey:

There was a woman my brother told me about and she had a daughter that was red-haired. And the girl got married when she was under twenty, for the mother had no man to tend the land, so she thought best to let her go. And after her baby being born, she never got strong but stopped in the bed, and a great many doctors saw her but did her no good.

And one day the mother was at Mass at the chapel and she got a start, for she thought she saw her daughter come in to the chapel with the same shawl and clothes on her that she had before she took to the bed, but when they came out from the chapel, she wasn't there. So she went to the house, and asked was she after going out, and what they told her was as if she got a blow, for they said the girl hadn't ten minutes to live, and she was dead before ten minutes were out. And she appears now sometimes; they see her drawing water from the well at night and bringing it into the house, but they find nothing there in the morning.

A Connemara Man:

There was a man had come back from Boston, and one day he was out in the bay, going towards Aran with £3 worth of cable he was after getting from McDonagh's store in Galway. And he was steering the boat, and there were two turf-boats along with him, and all in a minute they saw he was gone, swept off the boat with a wave and it a dead calm.

And they saw him come up once, straight up as if he was pushed, and then he was brought down again and rose no more.

And it was some time after that a friend of his in Boston, and that was coming home to this place, was in a crowd of people out there. And he saw him coming to him and he said, "I heard that you were drowned," and the man said, "I am not dead, but I was brought here, and when you go home, bring these three guineas to McDonagh in Galway for it's owned him for the cable I got from him." And he put the three guineas in his hand and vanished away.

An Old Army Man:

I have seen hell myself. I had a sight of it one time in a vision. It had a very high wall around it, all of metal, and an archway in the wall, and a straight walk into it, just like what would be leading into a gentleman's orchard, but the edges were not trimmed with box but with red-hot metal. And inside the wall there were cross walks, and I'm not sure what there was to the right, but to the left there was five great furnaces and they full of souls kept there with great chains. So I turned short and went away; and in turning I looked again at the wall and I could see no end to it.

And another time I saw purgatory. It seemed to be in a level place and no walls around it, but it all one bright blaze, and the souls standing in it. And they suffer near as much as in hell, only there are no devils with them there, and they have the hope of heaven.

And I heard a call to me from there "Help me to come out of this!" And when I looked it was a man I used to know in the army, an Irishman and from this country, and I believe him to be a descendant of King O'Connor of Athenry. So I stretched out my hand first but then I called out "I'd be burned in the flames before I could get within three yards of you." So then he said, "Well, help me with your prayers," and so I do.

XI

APPEARANCES

*WHEN I had begun my search for folk-lore, the first to tell me
he himself had seen the Sidhe was an old, perhaps half-crazed
man I will call Michael Barrett (for I do not give the real names
either of those who are living or who have left living relatives).
I had one day asked an old woman who had been spinning wool
for me, to be made into frieze by our weavers, if she had ever
seen the faery host. She said, "I never saw them myself nor I
don't think much of them; it is God that takes us or leaves us
as He will. But a neighbouring man was standing in my door
last night, and there's no day of the year he doesn't hear them
or feel them.*

*"It's in his head I think it does be, and when he stood in the
door last night I said 'the wind does be always in my ears and
the sound of it never stops,' to make him think it was the same
with him. But he said, 'I hear them singing and making music
all the time, and one of them's after bringing out a little flute,
and it's on it he's playing to them.' Sure he has half his chimney
pulled down, where they used to be sitting and singing to him
day and night. But those that are born in the daytime never have
power to see or hear them all their life."*

*Another neighbour talked to me of him and said, "One night
he was walking across the bog, and a lurcher, a bastard hound,
with him. And something ran across the path in the shape of a
white cat, and the lurcher went after him, and Barrett went home
and to bed and left the door open for the lurcher to come in.
And in the morning they found it there, lying under the table,
and it paralysed and not able to stir. But after a few months it
got better, and one night they were crossing the bog again and
the same thing ran across their path, and this time in the form
of a deer. But the dog wouldn't follow it again, but shrank behind Barrett until such time as it had passed by."*

*My spinning woman, coming another time with chickens to
sell, said, "Barrett is after telling me this morning that they
were never so bad as these last two nights. 'Friday fine-day' is
what they say now, in Irish, and he got no sleep till he threatened
to throw dirty water over them. The poor man, they do say*

they are mostly in his head now, but sure he was a fine fresh man twenty years ago, the night he saw them all linked in two lots, like slips of girls walking together. And it was that very same day that Hession's little girl got a touch from them. She was as fine a little girl as ever you saw, and her mother sent her into Gort to do a message. And on the road she met a red-haired woman, with long wisps of hair as bright as silver, and she said, 'Where are you going and who are you?' 'I'm going to Gort on a message,' says she, 'and I'm Mrs. Hession's daughter of such a place.' Well, she came home, and that very night she got a pain in her thigh, with respects to you, and she and her mother have half the world walked since then, trying to get relief for her; but never a bit better did she ever get. And no doubt at all but that's the very same day Michael Barrett saw them in the field near Hession's house."

I asked Mr. Yeats to come with me to see the old man, and we walked up the long narrow lane, from which we could see Slieve Echtge and the Burren hills, the little cabin with its broken chimney where Michael Barrett told us of those that had disturbed his rest. This was the first time we went together to enquire into the Hierarchy of the Sidhe, of which by degrees we have gathered so much traditional and original knowledge.

As to old Barrett, I saw him from time to time, and he told me he was still "tormented," and that "there is one that sat and sang b-b-b all the night" till a few evenings before he had got a bit of rag and tied it to a long stick, and hit at him when he came, and drove him out with the rest. And in the next spring I heard he was ill, and that "on Saturday he had been told by three he was to die." When I visited him I found him better, and he said that since the warning on Saturday they had left him alone "and the children that used to be playing about with them have gone to some other place; found the house too cold for them maybe." That was the last time I saw him; I am glad I had been able to help him to more warmth and comfort before the end.

I asked the old man's brother, a labourer, what he thought of Michael's visions, but he made little of them. "Old he is, and it's all in the brain the things he does be talking of. If it was a young man told us of them we might believe him, but as to him, we pay no attention to what he says at all. Those things are passed away, and you—I beg your pardon for using that word —a person—hears no more of them.

"*John Casey saw queer things? So he might. Them that travel by night, why wouldn't they see queer things? But they'd see nothing if they went to their bed quiet and regular.*

"*Lydon that had the contract for the schoolhouse, we didn't mind much what he said happened him the night he slept there alone, and in the morning he couldn't stir across the floor from the place where he was. But who knows? Maybe he had too much drink taken before he went to bed. It was no wonder in the old times if there was signs and the like where murder had been. But that's come to an end, and time for it.*

"*There's another man, one Doran, has the same dreams and thoughts as my brother, and he leaves pieces of silver on the wall; and when they're took — it's the faeries! But myself I believe it's the boys do be watching him.*

"*No, these things are gone from the world, and there's not the same dread of death there used to be. When we die we go to judgment, and the places we'll get there, they won't be the same as what we had here. The charitable, the kind-hearted, lady or gentleman, who'd have a chance if they didn't? But the tyrants and schemers, what chance will there be for the like of them?*

"*You will have a good place there, Barrett, you and John Farrell. You have done your work better than most of us through all your life, and it's likely you'll be above us there.*

"*I did my work all my life, fair and honest every day; and now that I'm old, I'll keep on the same track to the last. Like a horse that might be racing at Galway racecourse or another, there might be eight leaps or ten leaps he might be frightened at; but when he's once over the last leap there's no fear of him. Why would he fail then, with the winning post so near at hand?*"

I was told by A Gatekeeper:
There was once a family, the O'Hagans living in Dromore Hill, that now belongs to you, well-to-do people. And one day the son that had been at college was coming back, and there was a great dinner being made in the house. And a girl was sent off to a spring by the forth to get some water, and when she passed by the forth, she heard like the crying of a child and some one said to it "Nothing given to us today, no milk spilled for us, nothing laid out for us, but tonight we'll have what we

want and there will be waste and overflow." And that evening the young man that was coming home got a fall from his horse, and was killed, and all the grand things for the dinner were thrown about and went to loss. So never begrudge the drop of milk you'll spill, or the bit you'll let fall, it might turn all to good in the end.

One night at the house below it was just getting dark, and a man came in the gate and to the door and came in and fell down on a chair. And when I saw him shaking and his face so white, I thought it was the *fear gortha* (the hungry grass) he had walked on, and I called to the wife to give him something to eat. But he would take nothing but a cup of water with salt in it, and when he got better he told us that when he was passing the big tree a man and a woman came out and came along with him. They didn't speak but they walked on each side of him, and then the woman seemed to go away, but the man's step was with him till he came in at the gate.

There was a girl of the Heniffs brought the dinner one day to where the men were working near where the river rises at Coole. And when she had left the dinner she began to gather kippeens, and put them in her shawl, and began to twist a rope of the ends of it to tie them up. And at that moment she was taken up, and where she found herself was in Galway, sitting in the Square. And she had no money, and she began to think of the friends she had there and to say, "If they knew where I was they'd give me money to bring me back." And in those days there was a coach that ran from Galway to Kiltartan, and she found herself in it, and it starting, and it left her safe and sound again at home.

Mrs. Casey:
There was a girl at Tyrone was bringing back some apples out of the garden there. And on the road she met a man, and she thought that he was one of the old St. Georges, and he asked where did she get the apples, and bid her put them down in the road, and when she opened the bundle they were all turned to eggs. So she put them up again and brought them home, and when she and her mother looked at them in the house they were beginning to crack, and the chickens to put their beaks through them; so they put them in the corner of the

205

kitchen for the night, and in the morning when they went to look at them they were all turned to apples again, but they thought best not to eat them.

A Munster Woman:
There was a woman I knew in County Limerick, near Foynes —Mrs. Doolan, a nurse. She was called out of bed one night by a small man with a lamp, and he led her to a place she had never seen before, and into a house, and there was a woman in a bed and the child was born after she came. And I always heard her say it was a faery she attended. And the man led her back and gave her a sovereign, and bid her change it before sunrise.

And I know a boy lived on Lord Dunraven's property, one of a family of large farmers, and he had a settle-bed in the kitchen, and one night he saw the kitchen full of them, and they making up the fire and cooking, and they set out the table and ate at it.

I often heard they'd fight in November at the time of harvest, and my father told me that in the year of the famine there was great fighting heard up in the sky, and they were crying out, "Black potatoes, black potatoes, we'll have them now." I suppose it was one tribe of them fighting against another for them. And the oats in that year were all black as well as the potatoes.

A Clare Man:
I saw them myself one night I was going to Ennis with a load of straw. It was when we came to Bunnahow and the moon was shining, and I was on the top of the load of straw, and I saw them in a field. Just like jockeys they were, and riding horses, red clothes and caps they had like a jockey would have, but they were small. They had a screen of bushes put up in the field and some of the horses would jump over it, and more of them would baulk when they'd be put to it. The men that were with me didn't see them, they were walking in the road, but they heard the sound of the horses.

Another Clare Man:
I heard a churning one time in the hill up by the road beyond. I was coming back from Kinvara, and I heard it plain, no mistake about it. I was sorry after I didn't call down and ask for

a drink. Johnny Moon did so, and got it. If you wish for a drink and they put it out for you, it's no harm to take it, but if you refuse it, some harm might happen to you. Johnny Henderson often told that he heard churning in that spot, but I wouldn't believe the sun rising from him, he had so many lies. But after that, I said, "Well, Johnny Henderson has told the truth for once anyhow."

A Miller:
There was Tom Gantly one evening was going to Coole, and he heard a step behind him and it followed him every bit of the way, till he got to the hall door of Coole House; but he could see nothing.

He saw a gig one night on the road there by the wall and it full of ladies laughing and grandly dressed—the best of hats and feathers they had. And it turned and passed him a second time. And with the fright he got, he never would pass that bit of road by himself again.

There were two men went one night to catch rabbits in that field you have let now to Father Fahy, and the one next it. And when they were standing there they heard a churning below. So they went on a little way, and they heard a tambourine below, music going on and the beating of a drum. So they moved a little farther on and then they heard the sound of a fiddle from below. So they came home and caught no rabbits that night.

J. Creevy:
May is a great time with these strangers, and November is a bad month for them, and this month you're in now. I was trying the other day in the town to get a marriage made up for a girl that was seduced—and the family wouldn't have it this month because of that.

One night on the Kiltartan road I saw a flock of wool by the road side, and I gave a kick at it and it didn't move, and then another kick and it didn't move. So it can have been no natural thing.

And Lee told me that one night he saw red men riding through the country and going over ditches.

*   *   *

207

One time I was sick in the bed and I heard music, and I sat up and said: "Is it music I hear, or is it the squealing of pigs?" And they all said they could hear nothing. But I could hear it for a long time, and it the grandest I ever heard—and like a melodeon. And as to the tune, I couldn't tell what it was but I know that I had heard it before.

A Kerry Piper:
One time in Kerry there was a coach coming after me and it passed beside me, and I saw with it Mrs. Mitchell from the big house. And when it came near the bridge it sank into the earth, and I saw no more of it.

And one time I was at Ennistymon I saw the ass-car and the woman and the man out before me. I had a little ass of my own at that time, and I followed them thinking to overtake them, but when I was in the hollow they were on the hill, and when I was on the hill they were in the hollow. And when they got near to the bridge that is over the big river, they were not to be seen. For they can never cross over a mering (boundary) that is a river.

J. Fagan:
One time I was at a party and I didn't leave the house till 2 o'clock so you may think it was late in the night before I got home. And after a while I looked back and I saw someone coming after me, a little old woman about so high (3 feet) and she wearing a white cap with a frilled border, and a red square and a red flannel petticoat. I set off to run when I saw her, for at that time I had the run of a hare, but when I got near home I looked back and she was after me still. When I got inside the door I fell on my two knees. And it was seven years before I got the better of that fright. And from that time to this I never got the run again that I used to have.

There was a respectable woman, Mrs. Gaynor, living in Cloon, told me that whenever she went out of Cloon in the direction of Fiddane in one part of the road there was a woman sometimes met her, that she saw at no other time, and every time she'd meet her she'd spit in her face.

There is a family at Tirneevan and they were having a wedding there. And when it was going on, the wine ran short, and the spirits ran out and they didn't know what to do to get more, Gort being two miles away. And two or three strange people came in that they had never seen before. And when they found what was wanting they said that they'd go get it. And in a few minutes they were back with the spirits and the wine—and no place to get it nearer than Gort.

There was a herd's house up at Burren that no one could live in. But one Holland from Tirneevan said he'd take the place, and try how would he get on there. So he went with his family, and the first day the daughter made the place clean and swept it, and then she went out for a can of milk. And when she was coming in the door, it was knocked out of her hand and spilled over her. And that evening when they sat down to their supper the door opened and eight or nine people came in, and a red man among them. And they sat down and ate. And then they showed Holland one side of the room, and bid him to keep it always clean, and spring water in it.

A Herd:
There was a man woke about three o'clock one morning and he bade the servant girl go down and make the fire and put on the potatoes, where he had to be going out early. So she went down and there she saw one of *them* sitting by the hearth in the kitchen. So she ran upstairs with the fright she got to where the man was in bed with his wife. So then he went down himself, and he saw one of them sure enough sitting by the fire and he asked "How did you come in?" And he said, "By the lock-hole of the door." And the man said, "There's the pot full of potatoes and you might as well have used a few of them." And he said, "We have them used already; and you think now they are potatoes, but when you put the pot down on the fire you'll see they are no more than horse dung."

Thomas Cloonan:
One night my father was beyond on the other side of the lake, going to watch an otter where the water goes away underground. And he heard voices talking, and he thought one was the voice of Father Nagle the parish priest of Kilbecanty, and the other the voice of Father Hynes from Cloon that does be late out fishing for eels. And when he came to where the voices were, there was no one at all in it. And he went and sat in the cave, where

the water goes under, and there was a great noise like as if planks were being thrown down overhead. And you may think how frightened he was when he never took off his boots to cross the river, but run through it just as he was and never stopped till he got to the house.

Mrs. Cloonan:

Two men I saw one time over in Inchy. I was sitting milking the cow and she let a snore and I looked up and I saw the two men, small men, and their hands and their feet the smallest ever I saw, and hats turned back on their heads, but I did not see their faces. Then the cow rose her foot, and I thought, "it will be worse for me if she'll put her foot down on me," and I looked at her, and when I looked up again they were gone. Mrs. Stafford told me it was not for me they came, but for the cow, Blackberry, that died soon after.

There was a man in Gort was brought for a while to Tir-na-Og, that is a part of heaven.

McGarrity that was coming back one night to the new house beyond the lake saw two children, two little girls they were, standing beside the house. Paddy told me that, and he said they came there to foretell him he was stopping there too late.

John Phelan:

I never saw them nor felt them all my life, and I walking the place night and day, except one time when for twelve nights I slept in the little house beyond, in the kitchen garden where the apples were being robbed that time because there was no one living at home. In the night-time in the loft above my head I used to hear a scratching and a scraping, and one time a plank that was above in it began to move about. But I had no fear but stopped there, but I did not put off my clothes nor stretch myself on the bed for twelve nights. They say that one man that slept in the same house was found in the morning choked in his bed and the door locked that they had to burst it in.

And in old Richard Gregory's time there was one Horan slept there, and one night he ran out of it and out of the Gort gate and got no leave to put his clothes on. But there's some can see those things and more that can't, and I'm one of those that can't. Walking Coole demesne I am these forty years, days and nights, and never met anything worse than myself.

But one night standing by the vinery and the moon shining, on a sudden a wind rose and shook the trees and rattled the glass and the slates, and no wind before, and it stopped as sudden as it came. And there were two bunches of grapes gone, and them that took them by the chimney and no other way.

James Hill:
One night since I lived here I found late at night that a black jennet I had at that time had strayed away. So I took a lantern and went to look for him, and found him near Doherty's house at the bay. And when I took him by the halter, I put the light out and led him home. But surely as I walked there was a footstep behind me all the way home.

I never rightly believed in them till I met a priest about two years ago coming out from the town that asked his way to Mrs. Canan's, the time she was given over, and he told me that one time his horse stopped and wouldn't pass the road, and the man that was driving said, "I can't make him pass." And the priest said, "It will be the worse for you, if I have to come down into the road." For he knew some bad thing was there. And he told me the air is full of them. But Father Dolan wouldn't talk of such things, very proud he is, and he coming of no great stock.

One night I was driving outside Coole gate—close to where the Ballinamantane farm begins. And the mare stopped, and I got off the car to lead her, but she wouldn't go on. Two or three times I made her start and she'd stop again. Something she must have seen that I didn't see.

Beasts will sometimes see more than a man will. There were three young chaps I knew went up by the river to hunt coneens one evening, and they threw the dog over the wall. And when he was in the field he gave a yelp and drew back as if something frightened him.

Another time my father was going early to some place, and my mother had a noggin of turnips boiled for him that night before, to give him something to eat before he'd start. So they got up very early and she lighted the fire and put the oven hanging over it for to warm the turnips, and then she went back to bed again. And my father was in a hurry and he went out and

211

brought in a sheaf of wheaten straw to put under the oven, the way it would make a quick blaze. And when he came in, the oven had been taken off the hook, and was put standing in the hearth, and no mortal had been there. So he was afraid to stop, and he went back to the bed, and till daybreak they could hear something that was knocking against the pot. And the servant girl that was in the house, she awoke and heard quick steps walking to the stable, and the door of it giving a screech as if it was being opened. But in the morning there was no sign there or of any harm being done to the pot.

Then the girl remembered that she had washed her feet the night before, and had never thought to throw out the water. And it's well known to wash the feet and not to throw the water out, brings some harm—except you throw fire into the vessel it stands in.

Simon Niland:

Late one night I was out walking, and a gun in my hand, and I was going down a little avenue of stones, and I heard after me the noise of a horse's steps. So I stopped and sat down on the stile, for I thought, the man that's with the horse, I'll have his company a bit of the way. But the noise got louder like as if it was twenty horses coming, and then I was knocked down, and I put out my foot to save the gun from being broken. But when I got up there was no hurt on me or on the gun, and the noise was all gone, and the place quiet. It was maybe four years after that or six, I was walking the same path with the priest and a few others, for a whale had come ashore, and the jaw-bones of it were wanted to make the piers of a gate. And the priest said to me, "Did you ever hear of the battle of Troy?" "I didn't hear but I read about it," says I. "Well," says he, "there was a man at that time called Simon, and they found that whenever he came out with them to fight there was luck with them, and when he wasn't with them, there'd be no luck. And that's why we put you in front of us, to lead us on the path, you having the same name." So that put it in my head, and I told him about what happened that night, and I said, "Now would you believe that?" "I would," says he. "And what are such things done by?" says I. "The fallen angels," he said, "for they have power to do such things and to raise wind and storm, but yet they have the hope of salvation at the last."

*   *   *

212

One clear night and the moon shining, I was walking home down this road, and I had a strong dog at that time. And just here where you stand he began to bark at something and he made rushes at it, and made as if he was worrying it, but I could see nothing, though if it had been even the size of a rat I must have seen it, the night was so clear. And I had to leave him at last and heard him barking and I was at the house-door before he came up with me.

I know a good many on the island have seen *those*, but they wouldn't say what they are like to look at, for when they see them their tongue gets like a stone.

Mrs. Hynes of Slieve Echtge:
When you see a blast of wind pass, pick a green rush and throw it after them, and say, "God speed you." There they all are, and maybe the *stroke lad* at the end of them.

There was a neighbour of mine in late with me one night, and when he was going home, just as he passed that little road you see, a big man came over the wall in front of him, and was growing bigger as he went, till he nearly fainted with the fright he got.

They can do everything. They can raise the wind, and draw the storm.
And to Drogheda they go for wine, for the best wine is in the cellars there.

An Islander:
One night I and another lad were coming along the road, and the dog began to fight, as if he was fighting another dog, but we could see nothing and we called him off but he wouldn't come. And when we got home he answered us, and he seemed as if tired out.

There was a strange woman came to this island one day and told some of the women down below what would happen to them. And they didn't believe her, she being a stranger, but since that time, it's all been coming true.

213

Mrs. Casey:

I knew a woman that every night after she went to bed used to see some sort of a shadow that used to appear to her. So she went to some old woman, and she told her to sprinkle holy water about and to put a blackthorn stick beside her bed. So she got the stick and put it there and sprinkled the holy water, and it never appeared since then. Three sorts of holy water she got, from the priest and from the friars and from some blessed well. And she has them in three pint bottles in the window, and she'd kill you if you so much as looked at them.

A Fisherman:

I never saw anything myself, but one day I was going over the fields near Killeen, and it the quietest day of summer you ever saw. And all of a sudden I heard a great noise like thunder, and a blast of wind passed by me that laid the thistles low, and then all was quiet again. It might be that they were changing, for they change from place to place.

I would not give in to faeries myself but for one thing. There was a little boy of my own, and there was a wedding going to be here, and there was no bread in the house, and none to be had in Kilcolgan, and I bade him to go to Kinvara for bread. I pulled out the ass-car for him and he set out.

And from that time he was never the same, and now he is in the asylum at Ballinasloe.

Did he tell what happened? He never told me anything, but he told a neighbour that he met awful looking people on the road to Kinvara just about midnight, and that whatever they did to him, he could never recover it.

A Carter:

Often and often I heard things. A great shouting I heard one night inside Coole demesne—a hurling it must have been. Another time I was passing at night-time, near Reed the weaver's, and there were rocks thrown at me all along the road, but they did not touch me, and I could not see any one thing there. But I never went that road again at night-time.

It's said those that die are left in the place where they lived to do their penance. Often and often when I came to that house below, I felt knocks under the bed, and like some one walking over it.

Two men I know were going from Gort one night, and there

214

near the wall of the demesne they saw two men ploughing, and they asked one another what could they be to be ploughing by night. And then they saw that as they ploughed, the land was going away from them, and they were gone themselves, and they saw them no more.

An Old Woman who was Housekeeper to the Donnellans:
I'll tell you how the fortune of the family began.

It was Tully O'Donnellan was riding home from Ballinasloe, or some other place, and it was raining, and he came to a river that was in flood, and there used to be no bridges in those times. And when he was going to ride through the river, he saw the *greasa* leprechaun on the bank, and he offered him a lift, and he stooped down and lifted him up behind him on the horse.

And when he got near where the castle was, he saw it in flames before him. And the leprechaun said, "Don't fret after it but build a new castle in the place I'll show you, about a stone's throw from the old one." "I have no money to do that," said Tully Donnellan. "Never mind that," said the leprechaun, "but do as I bid you, and you'll have plenty." So he did as he bade him, and the morning after he went to live in the new castle, when he went into that room that has the stone with his name on it now, it was full up of gold, and you could be turning it like you'd turn potatoes into a shovel. And when the children would go into the room with their father and mother, the nurses would put bits of wax on their shoes, the way bits of the gold would stick to them. And they had great riches and smothered the world with it, and they used to shoe their horses with silver. It was in racing they ran through it, and keeping hounds and horses and horns.

Old Pegs Kelly:
I seen the Sheogue but once, and that was five or six years ago, and I walking the railway where I was looking after my little hens that do be straying. And I saw them coming along, and in a minute I was in the middle of them. Shavings, and shavings, and shavings going along the road as fast as they could go. And I knew there was no shavings to be seen this many year, since the stakes were made for the railway down at Nolan's, and the carpenter that made them dead, and the shop where he made them picked clean. And I knew well they were the horses the Sheogue did be riding. But some that saw them said they

looked like bits of paper. And I threw three stones after them and I heard them cry out as they went. And that night the roof was swept off Tom Dermot's house in Ryanrush and haystacks blown down. And John Brady's daughter that was daft those many years was taken, and Tom Horan's little girl that was picking potatoes, she and her brothers together. She turned black all of a minute and three days after, she was dead.

That's the only time I seen them, and that I never may again, for believe me that time I had my enough, thinking as I did that I hadn't more than three minutes to live.

A Herd's Wife:

Martin's new wife is a fine big woman, if she is lucky. But it's not a lucky house. That's what happened the last wife that lost her baby and died. William Martin knows well *they* are in it, but he is a dark man and would say nothing. I saw them myself about the house one time, and I met one on the forth going through the fields; he had the appearance of a man in his clothes. And sometimes when I look over at Martin's house there is a very dark look like a dark cloud over it and around it.

The other Army Man:

The faeries are all fallen angels. Father Folan told us from the altar that they're as thick as the sands of the sea all about us, and they tempt poor mortals. But as for carrying away women and the like, there's many that says so, but they have no proof. But you have only to bid them begone and they will go. One night myself I was after walking back from Kinvara, and down by the wood beyond I felt one coming beside me, and I could feel the horse that he was riding on and the way that he lifted his legs, but they didn't make a sound like the hoofs of a horse. So I stopped and turned around and said very loud "Be off!" And he went and never troubled me after. And I knew a man that was dying, and one came up on his bed and he cried out to it, "Get out of that, you unnatural animal!" And it left him. There's a priest I heard of that was looking along the ground like as if he was hunting for something, and a voice said to him "If you want to see them you'll see enough of them," and his eyes were opened and he saw the ground thick with them. Singing they do be sometimes and dancing, but all the time they have the cloven foot.

216

Fallen angels they are, and after they fell God said, "Let there be Hell, and there it was in a moment"—("God save us! It's a pity He said that word and there might have been no Hell today" *murmurs the wife*). And then He asked the devil what would he take for the souls of all the people. And the devil said nothing would satisfy him but the blood of a Virgin's Son. So he got that and then the gates of Hell were opened.

The Wife:
I never seen anything, although one night I was out after a cow till 2 o'clock in the morning and old Gantly told me he wondered at me to be out in this place, by the wood near the white gate where he saw a thing himself one night passing. But it's only them that's living in mortal sin can see such things, that's so Thomas, whatever you may say. But your ladyship's own place is middling free from them, but Ratlin's full of them.

And there's many say they saw the banshee, and that if she heard you singing loud, she'd be very apt to bring you away with her.

A Piper:
There was an old priest I knew—Father McManus—and when he would go walking in the green lawn before the house, his man, Keary, would go with him, and he carrying three sticks. And after a while the priest would say, *"Cur do maide"*— Fire your stick—as far as you can, and he would throw it. And he would say the same thing a second and a third time, and after that he would say, "We have no more to protect us now," and he would go in. And another priest I was talking to the other day was telling me they are between earth and air and the grass is full of them.

Mrs. Casey:
There was a boy I knew at Tyrone was a great card player. And one night about 10 o'clock he was coming home from a party, and he had the cards in his hands and he shuffling them as he went along. And presently he saw a man before him on the road, and the man stopped till he came up, and when he saw the cards, he says "Stop here and I'll have a game with you," for the moon was shining bright. So the boy sat down, and the stranger asked him had he any money, and he said he had five

shillings after the night's play. "Well," says the man, "we'll play the first game for half-a-crown." So they sat down and put out the money on a flagstone that was much like a table, and they began to play, and the first game was won by the stranger. "Well now," says he, "we'll have another." So the boy began to shuffle the cards, but as he did, one card dropped on the ground, and he stooped down for it, and when he did, he saw the man's feet that were partly under the flagstone, and they were like the feet of a cow. So with the fright he got, he jumped up and began to run and never stopped till he got inside his house and had the door shut. And when he had been sitting there a few minutes, a knock came to the door, and he heard the voice of the stranger say, "It's well for you you ran away when you did, or you'd be where I am now." And he heard no more; it was the boy himself told me this.

I hear them in this house ever since the first night I came, in the kitchen, when all are in bed. Footsteps, I wouldn't think so much of, but scraping the potatoes, that's another thing.

A daughter I had that went to America died there, and the brother that came back told me that he was with her, and she going, and surely they all heard the jennet coming to the door, and when they opened it, there was nothing there, and many people standing and waiting about it. I knew a woman died beyond in Boher and left a house full of children and the night she died there was a light seen in the sick house.

To leave a few cold potatoes, the first of them, outside, you should surely do it, and not to leave the house without spring water. I knew a boy that was sleeping up in the loft of a house and one night they had forgotten to leave water within in the kitchen. And about midnight he awoke and he saw through a hole in the loft two women, and one of them just after having a baby. And they said, "What way will we wash the child, and no water here; we must take the pan of milk down from the shelf." So the boy said out loud the way they'd hear him, "I must go for spring water. I forgot to leave it below." So he went and got it and left it there, and let on not to see them. And—for I forget what time after that—there was no morning he put his clothes on but he'd find a half-crown in his boot. To do you harm? No, but the best of neighbours they are, if you don't chance to offend them.

A Schoolmaster:
In Donegal one night some of the people were at a still in the mountains, and on a sudden they heard a shot fired, and they thought it was a signal given to the police, and they made home to the village. And all the night they could hear like the tramp of horses and of police and the noise of cars passing by, but nothing could be seen. And next day the police came in earnest, and searched about the place where they had been at work at the still, but no one was there and they found nothing. So they knew it was a warning they were after being given.

John Madden:
One day old Fogarty of Clough was cutting rods in Coole with a black-handled knife, and he put it in his pocket, and presently he felt for it and it was gone. But when he went home and went into the house, there was the knife lying on the table.

My wife's brother was on a cock of hay in that field beyond one time, and he sat down to rest and he saw them hurling in red caps and blue, and a crowd looking in at them. But he said nothing to the men that were with him. They are mostly in forths and lonesome places.

An old man, Kelleher, living in the Wicklow Mountains, told me and W. B. Yeats and Miss Pollexfen:
I often saw them when I had my eyesight; one time they came about me, shouting and laughing and there were spouts of water all around me. And I thought that I was coming home, but I was not on the right path and couldn't find it and went wandering about, but at last one of them said, "Good-evening, Kelleher," and they went away, and then in a moment I saw where I was by the stile. They were very small, like little boys and girls, and had red caps.
I always saw them like that, but they were bigger at the butt of the river; they go along the course of the rivers. Another time they came about me playing music and I didn't know where I was going, and at last one of them said the same way, "Good evening, Kelleher," and I knew that I was at the gate of the College; it is the sweetest music and the best that can be heard, like melodeons and fifes and whistles and every sort.
Mrs. Kelleher says: I often hear that music too, I hear them playing drums.

219

K: We had one of them in the house for a while, it was when I was living up at Ticnock, and it was just after I married that woman there that was a nice slip of a girl at that time. It was in the winter and there was snow on the ground, and I saw one of them outside, and I brought him in and put him on the dresser, and he stopped in the house for a while, for about a week.

Mrs. K: It was more than that, it was two or three weeks.

K: Ah! maybe it was— I'm not sure. He was about fifteen inches high. He was very friendly. It is likely he slept on the dresser at night. When the boys at the public-house were full of porter, they used to come to the house to look at him, and they would laugh to see him but I never let them hurt him. They said I would be made up, that he would bring me some riches, but I never got them. We had a cage here, I wish I had put him in it, I might have kept him till I was made up.

Mrs. K: It was a cage we had for a thrush. We thought of putting him into it, but he would not have been able to stand in it.

K: I'm sorry I didn't keep him—I thought sometimes to bring him into Dublin to sell him.

Mrs. K: You wouldn't have got him there.

K: One day I saw another of the kind not far from the house, but more like a girl and the clothes greyer than his clothes, that were red. And that evening when I was sitting beside the fire with the Missus I told her about it, and the little lad that was sitting on the dresser called out, "That's Geoffrey-a-wee that's coming for me," and he jumped down and went out of the door and I never saw him again. I thought it was a girl I saw, but Geoffrey wouldn't be the name of a girl, would it?

He had never spoken before that time. Somehow I think that he liked me better than the Missus. I used to feed him with bread and milk.

Mrs. K: I was afraid of him—I was afraid to go near him, I thought he might scratch my eyes out—I used to leave bread and milk for him but I would go away while he was eating it.

K: I used to feed him with a spoon, I would put the spoon to his mouth.

Mrs. K: He was fresh-looking at the first, but after a while he got an old look, a sort of wrinkled look.

K: He was fresh-looking enough, he had a hardy look.

Mrs. K: He was wearing a red cap and a little red cloth skirt.

220

K: Just for the world like a Highlander.

Mrs. K: He had a little short coat above that; it was checked and trousers under the skirt and long stockings all red. And as to his shoes, they were tanned, and you could hardly see the soles of them, the sole of his foot was like a baby's.

K: The time I lost my sight, it was a Thursday evening, and I was walking through the fields. I went to bed that night, and when I rose up in the morning, the sight was gone. The boys said it was likely I had walked on one of their paths. Those small little paths you see through the fields are made by *them.*

They are very often in the quarries; they have great fun up there, and about Peacock Well. The Peacock Well was blessed by a saint, and another well near, that cures the headache.

I saw one time a big grey bird about the cowhouse, and I went to a comrade-boy and asked him to come and to help me to catch it, but when we came back it was gone. It was very strange-looking and I thought that it had a head like a man.

Old Manning:
I never saw them except what I told you, the dog fighting, and I heard the horses, and at that same time I saw smoke coming out of the ground near Foley's house at Corker, by the gate.

My mother lived for twenty years in Coole, and she often told me that when she'd pass Shanwalla hill there would people come out and meet her and—with respects to you—they'd spit in her face.

Faeries of course there are and there's many poor souls doing their penance, and how do we know where they may be doing it?

A Farmer:
I might not believe myself there are such things but for what happened not long after I was married when my first little girl was but a week old. I had gone up to Ballybrit to tie some sheep and put fetters on them, and I was waiting for Haverty to come and help me tie them. The baby was a little unwell that day but I was not uneasy about her. But while I was waiting for Haverty, a blast of wind came through the field and I heard a voice say quite clear out of it "Katie is gone." That was the little one, we had called her Catherine, but though she wasn't a week in the world, we had it shortened already to Kate. And sure

enough, the child got worse, and we attended her through the night, and before daybreak she was gone.

An Army Man:

Two nights ago a travelling man came and knocked at John Hanlon's house at 11 o'clock, where he saw a light in the window and he asked would there be any one out hurling so late as that. For in coming by the field beyond the chapel he saw it full of people, some on horses, and hurling going on, and they were all dressed like soldiers, and you would hear their swords clinking as they ran. And he was not sure were they faeries till he asked John Hanlon was it the custom of people in this country to go hurling so late as that. But that was always a great field for them. From eleven to two, that is the time they have for play, but they must go away before the cock crows. And the cock will crow sometimes as early as 1 o'clock, a right one.

It was in the night that Christ our Saviour rose there were some Jews sitting around the fire, and a cock boiling in the pot. And one of them said, "He'll never rise again until that cock crows." And the cock rose out of the pot and crowed, and he that was speaking got scalded with the water that was splashed about.

A Connemara Man:

One night I was sleeping over there by the dresser and I heard them ("Would you say the day of the week," *says the old woman.* "It's Thursday," said I. "Thank you," *says the old man, and goes on*)—I heard them thick all about the house— but what they were saying I couldn't know.

The Old Woman:

It was my uncle that was away at nights and knew the time his horse fell in the ditch, and he out at sea. And another day he was working at the bridge and he said, "Before this day is over, a man will be killed here." And so it happened, and a man was killed there before 12 o'clock. He was in here one day with me, and I said, "I don't give in to you being away and such things." And he says: "Um, Um, Um," three times, and then he says, "May your own living be long." We had a horse, the grandest from this to Galway, had a foal when in this place— and before long, both horse and foal died. And I often can hear them galloping round the house, both horse and foal. And I not the only one, but many in the village even hear them too.

Young Mrs. Phelan:
Often I saw a light in the wood at Derreen, above Ballyturn. It would rise high over the trees going round and round. I'd see it maybe for fifteen minutes at a time, and then it would fall like a lamp.

In the month of May is their chief time for changing, and it's then there's blowing away of hay and such things and great disturbance.

A Mayo Man:
One time I was led astray in a town, in Golden Hill in Staffordshire. I was in the streets and I didn't know what way to turn all of a sudden, and every street looked like a wood before me, and so I went on until I met some man I knew, and I asked him where I was, and I went in, and stayed drinking with the others till 10 o'clock and I went home sober.

I saw the white rabbit too at Golden Hill. (*One of the other men puts in,* "There is always a white rabbit seen there, that turns into a woman before any misfortune happens, such as an accident.") I was walking along the road, and it ran beside me, and then I saw a woman in white before me on the road, and when I got to her, she was gone. And that evening a woman in a house nearby fell dead on her own doorstep.

Another time near this, I was passing the barn where Johnny Rafferty the carpenter and his son used to be working, but it was shut and locked and no one in it. But when I came near it, I felt as if I was walking on wood, and my hair stood up on my head, and I heard the noise of tools, and hammering and sawing in it.

Pete Heffernan:
Old Doran told me that he was near Castle Hacket one time and saw them having a fair, buying and selling for all the world like ourselves, common people. But you or I or fifty others might have been there like him and not seen them. It's only them that are born at midnight that has the second sight.

Fallen angels, they say they are. And they'd do more harm than what they do but for the hope they have that some day they may get to heaven. Very small they are, and go into one another so that what you see might only be a sort of a little bundle. But to leave a couple of cold potatoes about at night one should always do it, and to sweep the hearth clean. Who knows when they might want to come in and warm themselves.

Not to keep the water you wash your feet in in the house at night, not to throw it out of the door where it might go over them, but to take it a bit away from the house, and if by any means you can, to keep a bit of light burning at night, if you mind these three things you'll never be troubled with them.

That woman of mine was going to Mass one day early and she met a small little man, and him with a book in his hand. "Where are you going?" says he. "To the chapel beyond," says she. "Well," says he, "you'd better take care not to be coming out at this hour and disturbing people," says he. And when she got into the chapel she saw him no more.

An Old Woman with Oysters from Tyrone:

Oh, I wouldn't believe in the faeries, but it's no harm to believe in fallen angels!

Mrs. Day:

My own sons are all for education and read all books and they wouldn't believe now in the stories the old people used to tell. But I know one Finnegan and his wife that went to Esserkelly churchyard to cry over her brother that was dead. And all of a sudden there came a pelt of a stone against the wall of the old church and no one there. And they never went again, and they had no business to be crying him and it not a funeral.

Francis, my son that's away now, he was out one morning before the daybreak to look at a white heifer in the field. And there he saw a little old woman, and she in a red cloak—crying, crying, crying. But he wouldn't have seen that if he had kept to natural hours.

There were three girls near your place, and they went out one time to gather cow-dung for firing. And they were sitting beside a small little hill, and while they were there, they heard a noise of churning, churning, in the ground beneath them. And as they listened, all of a minute, there was a noggin of milk standing beside them. And the girl that saw it first said, "I'll not drink of it lest they might get power over me." But the other girl said,

224

"I'll bring it home and drink it." And she began to ridicule them. And because of she ridiculing them and not believing in them, that night in bed she was severely beaten so that she wasn't the better of it for a long time.

Often they'll upset a cart in the middle of the road, when there's no stone nor anything to upset it. And my father told me that sometimes after he had made the hay up into cocks, and on a day without a breath of wind, they'd find it all in the next field lying in wisps. One time too the cart he was driving went over a leprechaun—and the old woman in the cart had like to faint.

Mr. Hosty of Slieve Echtge:
I never would have believed the shadow of a soul could have power, till that hurling match I saw that I told you about.

It was in the old time it happened, that there was war in heaven. He that was called the brightest of the angels raised himself up against God. And when they were all to be thrown out, St. Michael spoke up for them for he saw that when the heavens were weeded out they'd be left without company. So they were stopped in the falling, in the air and in the earth and in the sea. And they are about us sure enough, and whenever they'll be saved I don't know, but it is not for us to say what God will do in the end.

I often heard that our winter is their summer—sure they must have some time for setting their potatoes and their oats. But I remember a very old man used to say when he saw the potatoes black, that it was to them they were gone. "Sure" he used to say, "the other world must have its way of living as well as ourselves."

Mrs. Casey:
Dolan I was talking to the other day, and I asked him if faeries used not to be there. And he said, "They're in it yet. There where you're standing, they were singing and dancing a few nights ago. And the same evening I saw two women down by the lake, and I thought it was the ladies from the house gone out for a walk, but when I came near, it was two strange women I saw, sitting there by the lake, and their wings came, and they vanished into the air."

P
225

John Phelan:

I was cutting trees in Inchy one time. And at 8 o'clock one morning when I got there, I saw a girl picking nuts with her hair hanging down over her shoulders, brown hair, and she had a good clean face and was tall and nothing on her head, and her dress was no way gaudy, but simple. And when she felt me coming, she gathered herself up and was gone as if the earth had swallowed her up. And I followed her and looked for her, but I never could see her again from that day to this, never again.

Mary Shannon:

There was a herd's house near Loughrea that had a bad name; and a strange woman came in one time and told the woman of the house that she must never throw dirty water out of the back-door. "For," said she, "if you had clean linen hanging there on a line before the fire, how would you like any one to come in and to throw dirty water over it?" And she bid her leave food always on the dresser. "For," said she, "wherever you leave it we'll be able to find it." And she told how they often went into Loughrea to buy things, and provisions, and would look like any other person, and never be known, for they can make themselves visible or invisible as they like. You might be talking to one of them and never know she was different from another. At our place there used to be a good many of these people about, these Ingentry women or women from the North we sometimes call them. There was one came into the house one day and told my mother she didn't get all her butter in the milk. And she told her the servant-girl was stealing and hiding some of it, for in these days servants were cheap and we kept a couple; you'd get them for about five shillings a quarter. And my mother went to look, and then she went out of the house, and went off in a minute in a blast. And the husband that was coming into the house, he never saw her at all, and she going out of the door.

Sunset is a bad hour, and just before sunrise in the morning, and about 12 o'clock in the day, it's best not to be too busy or going about too much.

An Aran Man:

Sometimes they travel like a cloud, or like a storm. One day I was setting out the manure in my own garden and they came and rolled it in a heap and tossed it over the wall, and carried it out to sea beyond the lighthouse.

Mr. Finnerty:
People say two days of the week, they name two days. Some say Thursday, and some say whatever day it is, and the day before it, and then they can't be heard. In the village beyond, there were a good many people in a house one night, and lights in it, and talking, and of a sudden some one opened the door— and there outside and round the house *they* were listening to them—and when the door was open they were all seen, and made off as thick as crows to the forth near the Burren hills.

There was one Ward was walking one night near Castle Taylor, and in that big field that's near the corner where Burke was murdered he saw a big fire, and a lot of people round about it, and among them was a girl he used to know that had died.

Last week in that field beyond there, the hay was all taken up, and turned into the next field in wisps.

You must put the potatoes out for them before they are put on the table, for they would not touch them if they had been touched by common persons.

And I saw Horan that had the orchard here bought run to our house in the middle of the night naked with nothing on but his trousers, where he was after being beat out of the house in the kitchen garden. Every night when he was going to bed there did a knocking come in the loft over his head, but he gave no attention to it. But a great storm came and a great lot of the apples was blown down and he gathered them up and filled the loft with them, thinking when he showed them to get compensation. And that is the night he was beat out of bed. And John Phelan knows well what things used to be in that house.

John Creevy:
My father? Yes indeed he saw many things, and I tell you a thing he told me, and there's no doubt in the earthly world about it. It was when they lived at Inchy they came over here one time for to settle a marriage for Murty Delvin's aunt. And when

they had the business settled, they were going home again at dead of night. And a man was after getting married that day, one Delane from beyond Kilmacduagh, and the drag was after passing the road with him and his party going home. And all of a minute the road was filled with men on horses riding along, so that my father had to take shelter in Delane's big haggard by the roadside. And he heard the horsemen calling on Delane's name. And twenty-one days after, Delane lay dead.

There's no doubt at all about the truth of that, and they were no riders belonging to this world that were on those horses.

Thomas Brown:

There was a woman walking in the road that had a young child at home, and she met a very old man, having a baby in his arms. And he asked would she give it a drop of breast-milk. So she did, and gave it a drink. And the old man said: "It's well for you that you did that, for you saved your cow by it. But tomorrow look over the wall into the fields of the rich man that lives beyond the boundary, and you'll see that one of his was taken in the place of yours." And so it happened.

In the old times there used to be many stories of such things, half the world seemed to be on the *other side.*

I used not to believe in them myself, until one night I heard them hurling. I was coming home from town with Jamsie Flann; we were not drunk but we were hearty. Coming along the road beyond we heard them hurling in the field beside us. We could see nothing but we'd hear them hit the ball, and it fly past us like the lightning, so quick, and when they hit the goal, we heard a moan—"Oh! ah!"—that was all. But after we went a little way we sat down by a little hill to rest, and there we heard a thousand voices talking. What they said, we couldn't understand, or the language, but we knew that it was one side triumphing over the other.

But the nights are queer—surely they are queer by sea or by land. There was a friend of mine told me he was out visiting one night, and coming home across the fields he came into a great crowd of them. They did him no harm, and among them he saw a great many he knew, that were dead, five or six out of our own village. And he was in his bed for two months after that, and he told the priest of it. He said he couldn't understand the talk, it was like the hissing of geese, and there was one very big man, that seemed the master of them, and his talk was like you'll hear in a barrel when it's being rolled.

There's a hill, Cruach-na-Sheogue down by the sea, and many have seen them there dancing in the moonlight.

There was a man told me he was passing near it one night, and the walls on each side of the road were all covered with people sitting on them, and he walked between, and they said nothing to him. And he knew many among them that were dead before that. Is it only the young go there? Ah, how do we know what use they may have for the old as well as for the young?

There are but few in these days that die right. The priests know about this more than we do, but they don't like to be talking of *them* because they might be too big in our minds.

They are just the same in America as they are here, and my sister that came home told me they were, and the women that do cures, just like the woman at Clifden, or that woman you know of.

There was one she went to out there, and when you'd come in to ask a cure she'd be lulled into a sleep, and when she woke she'd give the cure. *Away* she was while the sleep lasted.

The Spinning Woman:

No, I never seen them myself, and I born and bred in the same village as Michael Barrett. But the old woman that lives with me, she does be telling me that before she came to this part she was going home one night, where she was tending a girl that was sick, and she had to cross a hill forth. And when she came to it, she saw a man on a white horse, and he got to the house before her, and the horse stopped at the back-door. And when she got there and went in, sure enough the girl was gone.

I never saw anything myself, but one night I was passing the boreen near Kinvara, and a tall man with a tall hat and a long coat came out of it. He didn't follow me, but he looked at me for a while, and then he went away.

And one time I saw the leprechaun. It's when I was a young woman, and there was black frieze wanting at Ballylee, and in those days they all thought there could no black frieze be spun without sending for me. So I was coming home late in the evening, and there I saw him setting by the side of the road, in a hollow between two ridges. He was very small, about the height

229

of my knee, and wearing a red jacket, and he went out of that so soon as he saw me. I knew nothing about him at that time. The boys say if I'd got a hold of his purse I'd be rich for ever. And they say he should have been making boots; but he was more in dread of me than I of him, and had his instruments gathered up and away with him in one second.

There used to be a lot of things seen, but someway the young people go abroad less at night, and I'm thinking the souls of some of *those* may be delivered by this time.

There was a boy looked out of the door, and he saw a woman milking the cow. But after, when he went to milk her, he found as much milk as ever there was.

Mrs. Phelan:
There was a woman at Kilbecanty was out one evening and she saw a woman dressed in white come after her, and when she looked again she had disappeared into a hole in the wall. Small she must have grown to get into that. And for eleven days after that, she saw the same appearance, and after eleven days she died.

There was another woman lived at Kilbecanty, just beside the churchyard, you can see the house yet. And one day she found a plate of food put in at the door, the best of food, meat and other things. So she ate it and the next day the same thing happened. And she told a neighbouring woman about it, and she left her door open, and a plate of food was left in to her that night. But when she saw it she was afraid to eat it, but took it and threw it out. And the next day she died. But the woman that ate the food, nothing happened to her.

There was one Halloran took that farm on the road beyond one time, but he locked the house up, not meaning to go and live in it yet a while, and he kept the key in his pocket. But one night late he was coming by and he saw a light in the window and looked in, and he saw a woman sitting by a fire she was after lighting. So he ran away and never went to live in the house after.

One night myself coming back from Kelly's I saw a man by

the side of the road, and I knew him to be one Cuniff that had died a year before.

There were two men stealing apples in a garden, and when they tried to get out there was a soldier at the door with a sword in his hand. And at the door there he was still before them; so they had to leave the two bags of apples behind.

W. Sullivan:

One night myself I was driving the jennet I had at that time to Cappagh and I went past a place one Halvey had bought and I saw a man having a white front to his shirt standing by the wall, and I said to myself, "Halvey is minding this place well," and I went on, and I saw the man following me, and the jennet let a roar and kicked at me, and at that time we passed a stile, and I saw him no more.

Mrs. Barrett:

I don't know did old Michael see anything or was it in his head. But James, and brother that died, told me one time that he was crossing the way beyond from Brennan's, where the stones are. And there he saw a hurling going on. He never saw a field so full before. And he stood and watched them and wasn't a big frightened, but the dog that was with him shrank between his legs and stopped there.

And my father told me that one time he was stopping with my uncle up there near Mrs. Quaid's, in a house that's pulled down since. And he woke up and saw the night so bright that he went out. And there he saw a hurling going on, and they had boots like soldiers and were all shining with the brightness of the night.

And Micky Smith, God rest his soul, saw them at midday passing in the air above Cahir, as thick as birds.

A Gate-keeper:

Niland that met the coach that time and saw them other times, he told me that there were two sets among them. The one handsome and tall and like the gentry; the others more like ourselves, he said, and short and wide, and the body starting out in front, and wide belts about their waists. Only the women he saw, and they were wearing white caps with borders, and their hair in curls over the forehead and check aprons and plaid shawls. They are the spiteful ones that would do you a mischief, and others that are like the gentry would do nothing but to laugh and criticize you.

One night myself I was outside Loughrea on the road, about 1 o'clock in the morning and the moon was shining. And I saw a lady, a true lady she was, dressed in a sort of a ball dress, white and short in the skirt, and off the shoulders. And she had long stockings and dancing shoes with short uppers. And she had a long thin face, and a cap on her head with frills, and every one of the frills was the breadth of my six fingers. As to flowers or such things, I didn't notice, for I was more fixed in looking at the cap. I suppose they wore them at balls in some ancient times. I followed her a bit, and then she cross the road to Johnny Flanigan the joiner's house, that had a gate with piers. And I went across after her, to have a better view, and when she got to the pier she shrank into it and there was nothing left.

Johnny Kelly that lives in Loughrea was over here one evening, where he had some cattle on the land at Coole. And where the river goes away, he saw two ladies sitting, ladies he thought them to be, and they had long dresses. And they rose up and went on to that hole where the water is and the trees. And there all of a sudden they rose a storm and went up in it, with a sort of a roar or a cry and passed away through the air.

And I was in the house with my wife and I heard the cry, and I thought it might be some drunken man going home, and it about 10 o'clock in the evening. And I went to the door, and presently Kelly came in and you'd have thought him a drunken man, walking and shaking as he did with the fright he got seeing them going off away in the storm.

Mrs. Casey:

I went over to see Kate Cloran the other day, knowing that she had seen some of these things. And she told me that she was led astray by them one time—a great lot of them, they were dressed in white blouses and black skirts and some of them had crimson mantles, but none of them had any covering on their head, and they had all golden hair and were more beautiful than any one she had ever seen.

And one night she met the coach and four, and it was full of ladies, letting the window up and down and laughing out at her. They had golden hair, or it looked so with the lights. They

232

were dressed in white, and there were bunches of flowers about the horses' heads. Roses, chiefly, some pink and some blue. The coachmen were strange looking, you could not say if they were men or women—and their clothes were more like country clothes. They kept their heads down that she could not see their faces, but those in the carriage had long faces, and thin, and long noses.

Mike Martin:
They are of the same size as we are. People only call them diminutive because they are made so when they're sent on certain errands.

There was a man of Ardrahan used to see many things. But he lost his eyesight after. It often happens that those that see these things lose their earthly sight.

The coach and four is seen by many. It appears in different forms, but there is always the same woman in it. Handsome I believe she is, and white; and there she will always be seen till the end of the world.

It's best to be neighbourly with them anyway—best to be neighbourly.

There was a woman woke one night and she saw two women by the fire, and they came over and tried to take away her baby. But she held him and she nudged her husband with her arm, but he was fast asleep. And they tried him again, and all she could do wouldn't waken the husband, but still she had the baby tight, and she called out a curse in the devil's name. So then they went away, for they don't like cursing.

One night coming home from Madden's where I was making frames with him, I began to tremble and to shake, but I could see nothing. And at night there came a knocking at the window, and the dog I had that would fight any dog in Ireland began to shrink to the wall and wouldn't come out. And I looked out the door and saw him. Little clothes he had on, but on his head a quarter cap, and a sort of a bawneen about him. And I would have followed him, but the rest wouldn't let me.

Another time I was crossing over the stile behind Kiltartan chapel into Coole, and others along with me. And a great blast of wind came, and two trees were bent and broken and fell into the river, and the splash of water out of it went up to the skies.

233

And those that were with me saw many figures, but myself I only saw one, sitting there by the bank where the trees fell, dark clothes he had, and he was headless.

They can take all shapes and it's said a pig is the worst, but I believe if you take no notice of them and bless yourself as they pass, they'll do you no harm at all.

There were two men walking by a forth that's beyond Cloon, and one of them must have been in it at some time, for he told the other to look through his arm, and when he looked he could see thousands of people about walking and driving, and ladies and gentry among them.

There was a man in Cloon and he was very religious and very devout and he didn't believe in anything. But one day he was at the Punch-bowl out on the Ennis road, and there he saw two coaches coming through the thick wood and they full of people and of ladies, and they went in to the bushes on the other side. And since he saw that he'd swear to *them* being there.

There was a woman living over near Tirneevan, and one morning three men came galloping up on three horses, and they stopped at the door and tied up the horses and walked in, and they strangers. And the woman put the tongs over the cradle where the baby was sleeping, for that is a *pishogue*. And when they saw the tongs, they looked at one another and laughed, but they did him no harm, but pulled out the table and sat down and played cards for a while, and went away again.

But if they're well treated, and if you know how to humour them, they're the best of neighbours.

There was a woman seen not long ago, all in white, and she standing in a stream washing her feet. But you need never be afraid of anything that's white.

There was a woman I know was away sometimes and used to go into a forth among them. She told me about it, and she said there was big and small among them as there are here. And they wore caps like hurling caps, all striped with blue and different colours, and their dress striped the same way.

A Seaside Man:

There was a girl below in Spiddal was coming home from Galway with her father, and just at the bridge below she saw the coach and four. Like a van it was, with horses, and full of gentlemen. And she tried to make her father see it, and he couldn't. And it passed along the road, and then turned down into a field, over the stones, and it got to the strand and ran along it for a while, and what became of it then I don't know. My father told me that one night he came from a wake, and in the field beyond, that was all a flag then, but the man that owns it has it covered with earth now, he saw about twelve ladies all in white, and they dancing round and round and a fiddler or a flute-player or whatever he was in the middle. And he thought they were some ladies from Spiddal, and called out to them that it was late to be out dancing. And he turned to open the door of the house, and while he was turning they were gone.

There was a man walking one night and he felt a woman come and walk behind him, and she all in white. And the two of them walked on till sunrise, and then a cock crowed, and the man said, "There's the cock crowing." And she said, "That's only a weak cock of the summer." And soon after another cock crowed, and he asked did she hear it, and she said, "That's but a poor cock of the harvest." And the third time a cock crowed and when the man asked her she said, "That's a cock of March. And you're as wise as the man that doesn't tell Friday's dream on Saturday." For if you dream on a Friday, you must never tell the dream of a Saturday.

Mrs. Swift:

My mother told me, and she wouldn't tell a lie, that one time she went to a wake at Ardrahan. And about 12 o'clock, the night being hot, she and her sister went out to the back of the house. And there they saw a lot of people running as hard as they could to the house, and knocking down the walls as they came to them, for there were a lot of small stones. And she said to her sister, "These must be all the first cousins coming, and there won't be room to sit in the house when they come in." So they hurried back. But no one ever came in or came to the door at all.

They are said to be outside the door there often. And some see them hurling, small they are then, and with grey coats and

235

blue caps. And the car-driver told me—he wouldn't tell a lie—
that he often passed them walking like soldiers through the
hollow beyond.

An Old Man on Slieve Echtge:
One night I was walking on that mountain beyond, and a little
lad with me, Martin Lehane, and we came in sight of the lake
of Dairecaol. And in the middle of the lake I saw what was like
the shadow of a tall fire tree, and while I was looking it grew to
be like the mast of a boat. And then ropes and rigging came at
the sides and I saw that it was a ship; and the boy that was with
me, he began to laugh. Then I could see another boat, and then
more and more till the lake was covered with them, and they
moving from one side to another. So we watched for a while,
and then we went away and left them there.

Mrs. Guinan:
It's only a few days ago, I was coming through the field between this and the boreen, and I saw a man standing, a countryman you'd say he was. And when I got near him, all at once he
was gone, and when I told Mrs. Raftery in the next house, she
said she didn't wonder at that, for it's not very long ago she saw
what seemed to be the same man, and he vanished in the same
way.

There's a woman living up that road beyond, is married to a
man of the Matthews, and last year she told me that a strange
woman came into her house, and asked had she good potatoes.
And she said she had. And the woman said: "You have them
this year, but we'll have them next year." And she said: "When
you go out of the house, it's your enemy you'll see standing
outside," that was her near neighbour and was her worst enemy.

They'll often come in the night, and bring away the food. I
wouldn't touch any food that had been lying about in the night,
you wouldn't know what might have happened it. And my mother
often told me, best not eat it, for the food that's cooked at night
and left till the morning, they will have left none of the strength
in it.

There was a hurling seen in a field near our house, little men
they were in green with red caps, and a sergeant of police and

his men that were going by stopped to look at them, but Johnny
Roland a boy I know, was standing in the middle of them all
the time in the field, and never saw anything at all.

A North Galway Woman:
There was a man living over at Caramina, beyond Moyne,
Dick Regan was his name, and one night he was walking over
a little hill near that place. And when he got to the top of it, he
found it like a fair green with all the people that were in it, and
they buying and selling just like ourselves. And they did him
no harm, but they put a basket of cakes into his hand and kept
him selling them all the night. And when he got home, he told
the story. And the neighbours when they heard it gave him the
name of the cakes and to the day of his death he was called
nothing but Richard Crackers.

There was a smith, and a man called on him late one evening,
and asked him to shoe a horse for him and so he did. And then
he offered him pay but he would take none. And the man took
him out behind the house, and there were three hundred horses
with riders on them, and a hundred without, and he said, "We
want riders for those," and they went on.

An Aran Man:
A man that came over here from Connemara named Costello
told me that one night he was making poteen, and a man on a
white horse came up, and the horse put his head into the place
they were making it, and then they rode away again. So he put
a bottle of the whiskey outside the place, and in a little time he
went and looked and it was empty. And then he put another
bottle out, and in a little time he looked again, and it was empty.
And then he put a third, but when he looked the whiskey in it
had not been stirred. And he told me he never did so much with
it or made so much profit as he did in that year.

They are everywhere. Tom Deruane saw them down under
the rocks hurling and they were all wearing black caps. And
sometimes you'd see them coming on the sea, just like a barrel
on the top of the water, and when they'd get near you, no matter
how calm the day, you'd have a hurricane about you. That is
when they are taking their diversions. And one evening late
I was down with the wife burning kelp on the rocks, where we

had a little kiln made. And we heard a talking and a whispering about us on the rocks, and my wife thought it was the child that the sister was bringing down to her, and she said, "God bless the son!" but no one came, and the talking went on again, and she got uneasy, and at last we left the kelp and came home; and we weren't the first that had to leave it for what they heard in that place.

Fallen angels they are said to be. God threw a third part of them into Hell with Lucifer, and it was Michael that interceded for the rest, and then a third part was cast into the air and a third on the land and the sea. And here they are all about us as thick as grass.

A Needlewoman from North Galway Working at Coole:

Myself and Anne (one of the maids) went up the middle avenue after dark last night and we got a fright, seeing what we thought to be faeries. They were men dressed in black clothes like evening clothes, wearing white ruffles round their necks and high black hats without brims. Two walked in front and one behind, and they seemed to walk or march stiff like as if there was no bend in the leg. They held something in each hand and they stopped before the gate pier where there is a sort of cross in white like paint, then they disappeared and we turned and ran.

(When they were going up to bed, I am told, "Anne suddenly stopped under the picture of Mary Queen of Scots and called out, 'That is like the frill they wore' and sank down on the stairs in a kind of faint.")

One time at home I was out about dusk, and presently I heard a creaking, and a priest walked by reading his prayers. But when he came close I saw it was Father Ryan that was dead some time before. And I ran in and told a woman, who used to help in milking, what I had seen, and she said, "If it's Father Ryan you saw I don't wonder, for I saw him myself at the back of the door there only a week ago."

There was a boy was making a wall near Cruachmaa and a lot of *them* came and helped him, and he saw many neighbours that were dead among them. And when they had the wall near built another troop of them came running and knocked it down. And the boy died not long after.

238

A Young Man:

My father told me that he was down one time at the north shore gathering wrack, and he saw a man before him that was gathering wrack too and stooping down. He had a black waistcoat on him and the rest of his clothes were flannel just like the people of this island. And when my father drew near him, he stooped himself down behind a stone; and when he looked there, there was no sight or mind of him.

One time myself when I was a little chap, about the size of Michael there, I was out in the fields, and I saw a woman standing on the top of a wall, and she having a child in her hand. She had a long black coat about her. And then she got down and crossed over the field, and it seemed to me all the time that she was only about so high (three feet) and that there was only about two feet between her and the ground as she walked, and the child always along with her. And then she passed over another wall and was gone.

The Spinning Woman:

There was a new-married woman, and the husband was going out and he gave her wool to spin and to have ready for him. And she couldn't know what in the world to do, for she never learned to spin. And she was there sitting at it and a little man came in, and when she told him about it he said he'd bring it away and spin it for her and bring it back again. And she asked for his name, but he wouldn't tell that. And soon after there was a ragman going the road and he saw a hole and he looked down and there he saw the little man, and he stirring a pot of stirabout with one hand and spinning with the other hand, and he was singing while he stirred: "—— is my name (that's his name in Irish but I won't tell you the meaning of it) and she doesn't know it, and so I'll bring her along with me." So the ragman went in and came to the young woman's house, and told her what the man was singing. So when he came with the wool she called him by his name, and he threw the wool down and went away; for he had no power over her when she knew his name.

Mary Glynn of Slieve Echtge:

That's it, that's it, *the other class* of people don't like us to be going out late, we might be in their way, unless it's for a case, or a thing that can't be helped. And this is Monday, no, Mrs. Deruane, not Tuesday—we'll say it's Monday. It's at night they're seen, God bless them, and their music is heard, God bless them, the finest music you ever heard, like all the fifers of the world and all the instruments, and all the tunes of the world. There was one of those boys that go about from house to house on the morning of the new year, to get a bit of bread or a cup of tea or anything you'll have ready for him, and he told us that he was coming down the hill near us, and he had the full of his arm of bits of bread, and he heard the music, for it was but dawn, and he was frightened and ran and lost the bread. I heard it sometimes myself and there's no music in the world like it, but it's not all can hear it. Round the hill it comes, and you going in at the door. And they are quiet neighbours if you treat them well. God bless them and bring them all to heaven!

For they were in heaven once, and heaven was the first place there was war, and they were all to be done away with, and it was St. Peter asked the Saviour to help them. So he turned His hand like this, and the sky and the earth were full of them, and they are in every place, and you know that better than I do because you read books.

Mary Glynn and Mary Irwin:

One night there was bonavs in the house—God bless the hearers and the place it's told in—God bless all we see and those we don't see! —And there was a man coming to rise dung in the potato field in the morning, and so, late at night, Mary Glynn was making stirabout and a cake to have ready for breakfast.

Mary Irwin's brother was asleep within on the bed. And there came the sound of the grandest music you ever heard from beyond the stream, and it stopped here. And Micky awoke in the bed, and was afraid and said, "Shut up the door and quench the light," and so we did. It's likely they wanted to come into the house, and they wouldn't when they saw us up and the lights about. But one time when there were potatoes in the loft, Mary Irwin and her brothers were well pelted with them when they sat down to their supper. And Mary Glynn got a blow on the side of her face from them one night in the bed. And they have the hope of Heaven, and God grant it to them. And one day there was a priest and his servant riding along the road, and there was a hurling of *them* going on in the field. And a man of them came and stood on the road and said to the priest, "Tell me this for you know it, have we a chance of Heaven?" "You

240

have not," said the priest (*"God forgive him," says Mary Glynn*—*"a priest to say that"*); and the man that was of them said, "Put your fingers in your ears till you have travelled two miles of the road; for when I go back and tell what you are after telling me to the rest, the crying and bawling and the roaring will be so great that if you hear it you'll never hear a noise again in this world." So they put their fingers then in their ears, but after a while the servant said to the priest, "Let me take out my fingers now." And the priest said, "Do not." And then the servant said again, "I think I might take one finger out." And the priest said, "As you are so persevering you may take it out." So he did, and the noise of the crying and the roaring and the bawling was so great that he never had the use of that ear again.

Callan of Slieve Echtge:
We know they are in it, for Father Hobbs that was our parish priest saw them himself one time there was a station here, and when some said they were not in it, he said, "I saw them in a field myself, more people than ever I saw at twenty fairs." It was St. Peter spoke for them, at the time of the war, when the Saviour was casting them out; he said to Him not to empty the heavens. And every Monday morning they think the Day of Judgment may be coming, and they will see Heaven.

There's never a funeral they are not at, walking after the other people. And you can see them if you know the way, that is to take a green rush and to twist it into a ring, and to look through it. But if you do, you'll never have a stim of sight in the eye again, and that's why we don't like to do it.

Resting they do be in the daytime, and going about in the night.

Old Hayden:
One time I was coming home from a fair and it was late in the night and it was dark and I didn't know was I on the right road. And I saw a cabin in a field with a light in it, and I went and knocked at the door and a man opened the door and let me in, and he said, "Have you any strange news?" and I said, "I have not," and he said, "There is no place for you here," and he put me out again. For that was a faery hill, and when they'll ask have you strange news, and you'll say you have not, they'll

do nothing for you. So I went back in the field, and there were men carrying a coffin, and they said, "Give us a hand with this." And I put my hand to it to help them to lift it. And as we walked on we came to a house and we went in and there was a fire on the hearth, and they took the body out of the coffin and put it before the fire, and they said, "Now let you keep turning it." So I sat there and turned it, and then they took it up and we went on till we came to another house and the same thing happened there, and they put me to turn the body. And when we went out from there they all vanished, and there was the cabin before me again with the light in it. And when the man came to the door and asked me, "Is there any strange news?" I said, "There is indeed," and told him all that had happened. And then I looked round, and I was within a few yards of my own house.

Mrs. Keely:

When you see a blast of wind, and it comes sudden and carries the dust with it, you should say, "God bless them," and throw something after them. How do we know but one of our own may be in it? Half of the world is with them.

We see them often going about up and down the hill, Jack O'Lanthorn we call them. They are not the size of your two hands. They would not do you much harm, but to lead you astray.

The Spinning Woman:

I remember one day a strange woman coming in and sitting down there—very clever looking she was, and she had a good suit of clothes. And I bid her rest herself and I'd give her a cup of tea, and she said, "I travelled far today and you're the first that offered me that." And when she had it taken she said, "If I had a bit of tobacco, and a bit of bacon for my dinner, I'd be all right." And I made a sign to the woman I have, under the table, to give her a bit of tobacco. So she got it for her and she said, "I shouldn't take it, and this the second time today you divided it." And that was true, for a neighbouring boy had come in in the morning and asked for a loan of a bit, and she had cut it for him. And I said, "Go to that house beyond and the woman will give you a bit of bacon"; and she said, "I won't go to that woman, for it was she told you that one of the neighbours was bringing away her butter from her," and so she had, sure enough. And then she said, she must be in Cruachmaa that night, and she went away and I never saw her again.

A Mayo Man:
One time I was working in England near Warrington, and I was walking the road alone at night, and I saw a woman under an umbrella in the mist and I said, "Is it a living thing you are or dead?" And she vanished on the minute. And I sat down by the hedge for a while, and I heard feet walking, walking, up and down inside the hedge, and I am sure they were the same thing. And then two strange men passed me, dressed in working clothes, but talking gibberish that I could not understand, and I know that they were no right men. So I went in towards the town and I met a policeman, and he took up his lamp and made it shine in my face, for they carry a lamp in their belt and they will take the measurement of your face with it, the same as by daylight. And he said, "There never was a worse road for an Irishman to walk than this one." It was maybe because of the land and the rough people of it he said that.

A Gate-keeper:
My sister and her husband were driving on the Kinvara road one day, and they saw a carriage coming behind them, and it with bright lamps about it. And they drew the car to one side to let it pass. And when it passed they saw it had no horses, and the men that were sitting up where the drivers should be were headless.

There's many has seen the coach, in different shapes, and some have seen the riders going over the country. Drumconnor is a great place for these things. The Sheehans that lived in the castle had no peace or rest. Mrs. Sheehan looked up one day she was outside, and there was some person standing at the window, and in a moment it was headless. And they'd see them coming in at the gate, sometimes in the shape of a woman, and a sort of a cape in the old fashion and a handkerchief over the head, and sometimes in the shape of a cow or such things. And noises they'd hear, and things being thrown about in the house and packs of wool thrown down the stairs.

And they had a good many children, and all the best and the best-looking were taken. And at last they got the owner to build them a house outside, and since that they have no trouble and have lost no more children.

Mrs. Madden:

Rivers of Cloonmore one time when he was going to Loughrea, at the fish-pond corner saw the coach. I didn't see it, but I saw him draw aside and say to Leary not to let on they saw it.

Meagher another time saw it, and it full of children all in white.

But Egan beyond, he'd never let on to believe in such things and would make them out to be nothing—he has such a gift of talking.

And one time in the night I and my husband woke and heard the car rattling by, and we thought it was St. George going to Ballylee Castle, till we asked in the morning. Four horses it has and they headless, and sure and certain we heard it pass that night.

Mrs. Casey:

And I knew a boy met the coach and four one time. Drawn by four horses it was, and lights about it and music, and the horses dressed with flowers. And in it were sitting ladies, very clever-looking and wild, and their hair twisted up on their heads, and when they went on a little way they called to some man on the road to come with them, and he refused, and they laughed at that and ridiculed him.

I never saw the coach and four with these two eyes; but one time I heard it pass by, about 11 o'clock at night, when I was sitting up mending the sole of a boot. Surely it passed by, but I would not look out to see what it was like.

For there was a woman I knew was walking with a man one night from Kilcolgan to Oranmore. And as they were sitting by the roadside they heard the coach and four coming. And the man stood up and looked at it, but he had no right to do that, he should have turned his head away. And there were grand people in it, ladies, and flowers about them. But no sooner did he look at it than he was struck blind and never had his eyesight since.

It's best not to look at them if they pass. And when you go along the road and a storm comes in the calm and raises all the dust of the road up in the air, turn your head another way, for it's they that are passing. In the month of May is the most time they do be travelling. And it's best not to go near water then, near a river or a lake.

When my father was dying my mother was sitting with him,

and she heard a car pass the door, going light and quick, but when it passed down the road again it went heavy, and that was the coach and four.

There was Sully had the forge one time, and passing one night down the road towards Nolan's gate, he saw a brake pass full of ladies and gentlemen, as he thought, and he believed it to be St. George's carriage. But at Nolan's gate, it turned and came up again, and whatever he saw, when he got home he took to his bed for some days with the fright he got.

Kelly told me one time he saw the coach and four driving through the field above Dillon's, with four horses. And wasn't that a strange place for it to be driving through all the rocks?

There was boys used to be stealing apples from the orchard at Tyrone, and something in white with a candle used to come after them, and then change to something in red. So they went to a forth, and they went to the side of it where the sun rises and there they made the mark of the cross, but after all they had to leave going after the apples.

There was a woman down at Silver's the other night, and when I was standing to go home she said, "I wonder you not to be afraid to go through these fields." So I asked her did ever she see anything, and she said, "I was with another girl one day near Inchy gate, and we heard a voice, and we saw the coach and four coming and we were afraid, and we went in under the bushes to hide ourselves. It passed by us then, it was big and long, longer than a carriage you could see now, and there were people in it, men and women dressed in all colours, blue and red and pink and black, but I could not say what had they on their heads. And there was a man on the box, not a coachman but just a Christian, and he driving the four horses.

"As to the horses, the two that were in front were grey, but the two that were near the carriage were brown; it gave me a great fright at the time."

There is no light about it in the daytime, but at night it is all shining.

There was a girl saw it one time in the same way, drawn by horses that were without heads. She got a great fright and she

245

ran home. And in the morning when she got up, she that had been a dark-haired girl was as white as snow, and her hair grey. She is living yet and is up to nearly a hundred years.

Mrs. Roche:

My father would never believe in anything till one time he was walking near Seanmor with another smith, and he stopped and said "I can't go on with all the people that's in that field." And my father said "I don't see any people." And the other said "Put your right foot on my right foot, and your hand on my right shoulder." And he did, and he saw a great many in the field, but not so many as the other saw; fine men and all dressed in white shirts, shining they were so white. He told us about it when he came home, and he said he wished he didn't see them. He was dead within the twelvemonth, and the man that was with him was dead before that, not much time between them.

XII

BUTTER

I have been told:
Butter, that's a thing that's very much meddled with. On the first of May before sunrise it's very apt to be all taken away out of the milk. And if ever you lend your churn or your dishes to your neighbour, she'll be able to wish away your butter after that. There was a woman used to lend a drop of milk to the woman that lived next door, and one day she was churning, churning, and no butter came. And at last some person came into the house and said, "It's hard for you to have butter here, and if you want to know where it is, look into the next house." So she went in and there was her neighbour letting on to be churning in a quart bottle, and rolls of butter beside her. So she made as if to choke her, and the woman run out into the garden and picked some mullein leaves, and said, "Put these leaves in under your churn, and you'll find your butter come back again." And so she did. And she found it all in the churn after.

To sprinkle a few drops of holy water about the churn, and to put a coal of fire under it, that you should always do—as was always done in the old time—and the *others* will never touch it.

There was a woman in the town was churning, and when the butter came she went out of the house to bring some water for to wash it and to make it up. And there was a tailor sitting sewing on the table. And the woman from next door came in and asked the loan of a coal of fire, and that's a thing that's never refused from one poor person to another in the morning. So he bid her take it. And presently she came in again and said that the coal of fire had gone out, and asked another, and this she did the third time. But the tailor knew well what she was doing, and that every coal of fire she brought away, there was a roll of butter out of the churn went with it. So whatever prayers he said is not known, but he brought the butter all back again, and into a can on the floor, and no hands ever touched it. So when

247

the woman of the house came back, "There's your butter in the can," said he. And she wondered how it came out of the churn to be in three rolls in the can. And then he told her all that had happened.

There was a man was churning, churning, every day and no butter would come only froth. So some wise woman told him to go before sunrise to a running stream and bring a bottle of the water from it. And so he did before sunrise, and had to go near four miles to it. And from that day he had rolls and rolls of butter coming every time he churned.

There was one Burke, he knew how to bring it back out of some old Irish book that has disappeared since he died. There was a woman, a herd's wife, lived beyond, and one time Burke had his own butter taken, and he said he knew a way to find who had done it, and he brought in the coulter of the plough and put it in the fire. And when it began to get red hot, this woman came running, and fell on her knees, for it was she did it. And after that he never lost his butter again. But she took to her bed and was there for years until her death. And she couldn't turn from one side to another without some person to lift her. Her son is now living in Dublin, and is the President of some Association.

If a woman in Aran is milking a cow and the milk is spilled, she says, "There's some are the better for it," and I think it a very nice thought, that they don't grudge it if there is any one it does good to.

There was a man, one Finnegan, had the knowledge how to bring it back. And one time Lanigan that lives below at Kilgarvan had all his butter taken and the milk nothing but froth rising to the top of the pail like barm. So he went to Finnegan and he bid him get the coulter of the plough, and a shoe of the wickedest horse that could be found and some other thing, I forget what. So he brought in the coulter of the plough, and his brother-in-law chanced to have a horse that was so wicked it took three men to hold him, and no one could get on his back. So he got a shoe off of him. But just at that time, Lanigan's wife went to confession, and what did she do but to tell the priest what they were doing to get back the butter. So the priest was mad with them, and bid them to leave such things alone. And when Finnegan heard it he said, "What call had she to go and confess that? Let her get back her own butter for herself any more, for I'll do nothing to help her."

Grass makes a difference? So it may, but believe me that's not all. I've been myself in the County Limerick, where the grass is that rich you could grease your boots in it, and I heard them say there, one quart of cream ought to bring one pound of butter. And it never does. *And where does the rest go to?*

XIII

THE FOOL OF THE FORTH

WE had, before our quest began, heard of faeries and banshees and the walking dead; but neither Mr. Yeats in Sligo nor I in Galway had ever heard of "the worst of them all," the Fool of Forth, the Amadán-na-Briona, he whose stroke is, as death, incurable. As to the fool in this world, the pity for him is mingled with some awe, for who knows what windows may have been opened to those who are under the moon's spell, who do not give in to our limitations, are not "bound by reason to the wheel." It is so in the East also, and I remember the surprise of the European doctor who had charge of an hospital in one of the Native States of India, because when the ruler of the State came one day to visit it, he and his high officials, while generous and pitiful to the bodily sick, bowed down and saluted a young lad who had lost his wits, as if recognizing an emissary from a greater kingdom.

In one of my little comedies "The Full Moon," the cracked woman comforts her half-witted brother, saying of his commonsense critics, "It is as dull as themselves you would be maybe, and the world to be different and the moon to change its courses with the sun." Those commonsense people of Cloon describe a fool as "one that is laughing and mocking, and that would not have the same habits as yourself, or to have no fear of things you would be in dread of, or to be using a different class of food." May it not be the old story of the deaf man thinking all his fellow guests had suddenly lost their reason when they began to dance, and he alone could not hear the call of the pipes?

There is perhaps sometimes a confusion in the mind between things seen and unseen, for an old woman telling me she had often heard of the Amadán-na-Briona went on "And I knew one too, and he's not dead a twelvemonth. It's at night he used to be away with them, and they used to try to bring people away into the forth where he was.

"Was he a fool in this world too? Well, he was mostly, and I think I know another that's living now."

I was told by:
A Woman Bringing Oysters from the Strand:
There was a boy, one Rivers, got the touch last June, from
the Amadán-na-Briona, the Fool of the Forth, and for that touch
there is no cure. It came to the house in the night-time and
knocked at the door, and he was in bed and he did not rise to
let it in. And it knocked the second time, and even then, if he
had answered it, he might have escaped. But when it knocked
the third time he fell back on the bed, and one side of him as if
dead, and his jaw fell on the pillow.

He knew it was the Amadán-na-Briona did it, but he did not
see him—he only felt him. And he used to be running in every
place after that and trying to drown himself, and he was in
great dread his father would say he was mad, and bring him
away to Ballinasloe. He used to be asking me could his father
do that to him. He was brought to Ballinasloe after and he died
there, and his body was brought back and buried at Drumacoo.

Mrs. Murphy:
Cnoc-na-Briona is full of them, near Cappard. The Amadán-
na-Briona is the master of them all, I heard the priest say that.

There was a man of the MacNeills passing by it one night
coming back from the bog, and they brought him in, and when
he came out next day—God save the mark—his face was turned
to his poll. They sent then to Father Jordan, and he turned it
right again. The man said they beat him while he was with them,
and he saw there a great many of his friends that were dead.

The Spinning Woman:
There are fools among them, and the fools we see like that
Amadán at Ballymore go away with them at night. And so do
the women fools, that we call *lenshees*, that means, an ape.

It's true enough there is no cure for the stroke of the Amadán-
na-Briona. There was an old man I knew long ago, he had a
tape, and he could tell what disease you had with measuring you,
and he knew many things. And he said to me one time "What
month of the year is the worst?" And I said, "The month of
May, of course," "It is not," he said, "but the month of June,
for that's the month that the Amadán gives his stroke." They
say he looks like any other man, but he's *leathan*—wide—and
not smart. I know a boy one time got a great fright, for a lamb
looked over the wall at him, and it with a big beard on it, and he

knew it was the Amadán, for it was the month of June. And they brought him to that man I was telling you about, that had the tape. And when he saw him he said "Send for the priest and get a Mass said over him." And so they did, and what would you say but he's living yet, and has a family.

A Seaside Man:

The stroke of the Fool is what there is no cure for; any one that gets that is gone. The Amadán-na-Briona we call him. It's said they are mostly good neighbours. I suppose the reason of the Amadán being wicked is he not having his wits, he strikes out at all he meets.

A Clare Man:

They, the other sort of people, might be passing you close and they might touch you; but any one that gets the touch of the Amadán-na-Briona is done for. And it's true enough that it's in the month of June he's most likely to give the touch. I knew one that got it, and told me about it himself.

He was a boy I knew well, and he told me that one night a gentleman came to him, that had been his landlord, and that was dead. And he told him to come along with him, for he wanted to fight another man. And when he went he found two great troops of them, and the other troop had a living man with them too, and he was put to fight him. And they had a great fight and at last he got the better of the other man, and then the troop on his side gave a great shout, and he was left home again.

But about three years after that he was cutting bushes in a wood, and he saw the Amadán coming at him. He had a big vessel in his arms, and it shining, so that the boy could see nothing else, but he put it behind his back then, and came running; and he said he looked wide and wild, like the side of a hill.

And the boy ran, and the Amadán threw the vessel after him, and it broke with a great noise, and whatever came out of it, his head was gone then and there. He lived for a while after and used to be telling us many things, but his wits were gone. He thought they mightn't have liked him to beat the other man, and he used to be afraid something would come on him.

Mrs. Staunton:

A friend of mine saw the Amadán one time in Poul-na-shionac, low-sized and very wide, and with a big hat on him, very high, and he'd make shoes for you if you could get a hold of him. But there are some say "No, that is not the Amadán-na-Briona, that is the leprechaun."

An Old Woman:
The Amadán-na-Briona is a bad one to meet. If you don't say, "The Lord be between us and harm," when you meet him, you are gone for ever and always. What does he look like? I suppose like any fool in a house—a sort of a clown.

A Man near Athenry:
Biddy Early could cure nearly all things, but she said that the only thing that she could do no cure for was the touch of the Amadán.

Another:
Biddy Early couldn't do nothing for the touch of the Amadán, because its power was greater than hers.

In the Workhouse:
The Amadán-na-Briona, he changes his shape every two days. Sometimes he comes like a youngster, and then he'll come like the worst of beasts. Trying to give the touch he used to be. I heard it said of late that he was shot, but I think myself it would be hard to shoot him.

Ned Meehan of Killinane:
The Amadán is the worst; I saw him myself one time, and I'd be swept if I didn't make away on the moment. It was on a racecourse at Ballybrit, and no one there but myself, and I sitting with my back to the wall and smoking my pipe. And all at once the Amadán was all around me, in every place, and I ran and got out of the field or I'd be swept. And I saw others of them in the field; it was full of them, red scarfs they had on them.

I came home as quick as I could, and I didn't get over the fright for a long time, but there he was all about me.

Meehan's wife says: I remember you well coming in that night, and you trembling with the fright you got. And you told me the appearance he had, like a jockey he was, on a grey horse.

"That is true indeed," *says Ned, and he goes on:*
And one night I was up in that field beyond, watching sheep that were near their time to drop, and I saw a light moving

through the fields beside me, and down the road and no one with it. It stopped for a while where the water is and went on again.

And there was a woman in Ballygra the same night heard the coach-a-baur passing, and she not hearing at all about the lights I saw.

A Man at Kilcolgan:

Father Callaghan that used to be in Esker was able to do great cures; he could cure even a man that had met the Amadán-na-Briona. But to meet the Amadán is to be in prison for ever.

XIV

FORTHS AND SHEOGUEY PLACES

*WHEN as children we ran up and down the green entrench-
ments of the big round raths, the lisses or forths, of Esserkelly
or Moneen, we knew they had been made at one time for defence,
and that is perhaps as much as is certainly known. Those at my
old home have never been opened, but in some of their like I
have gone down steps to small stonebuilt chambers that look too
low for the habitation of any living race.*

*Had we asked questions of the boys who led our donkeys they
would in all likelihood have given us from tradition or vision,
news of the shadowy inhabitants, the Sidhe, whose name in the
Irish is all one with a blast of wind, and of the treasures they
guard. And the old writings tell us that when blessed Patrick of
the Bells walked Ireland, he did not refuse the promise of heaven
to some among those spirits in prison, the old divine race for
whom Mannanan himself had chosen these hidden dwellings,
after the great defeat in battle by the human invaders, the Gaels,
or to some they had brought among them from the face of the
green earth. It was one of their musicians who played to the holy
Clerks till Patrick himself said, "But for some tang of the music
of the Sidhe that is in it, I never heard anything nearer to the
music of heaven." That music is heard yet from time to time;
and it was into one of those hill dwellings that the father of
McDonough the Galway piper, my friend, was taken till the
Sidhe had taught him all their wild tunes and so bewitched his
pipes that they would play of themselves if he threw them up
among the rafters. There were great treasures there also in Saint
Patrick's time, golden vats and horns, and crystal cups, and silk
of the colour of the foxglove. It may be of these treasures that so
many dreams are told.*

*As to the women of the Sidhe, some who have seen them, as
old Mrs. Sheridan, tell of their white skin and yellow hair, for
age has not come on them through the centuries. When one of
them came claiming the fulfilment of an old promise from Caoilte
of the Fianna, Patrick wondered at her young beauty, while the
man who had been her lover was withered and bent and grey.
But Caoilte said that was no wonder "for she is of the Tuatha de*

Danaan who are unfading and whose life is lasting, while I am of the sons of Milesius who are perishable and fade away." Yet then as now, notwithstanding their beauty and grandeur, those swept away into the hill dwellings would rather have the world they know. One of Finn's men meeting a comely young man who had been his comrade but was now an inhabitant of one of those hidden houses, asked how he fared. And for all his fine clothing and his blue weapons and the hound he held in a silver chain, the young man gave the names of three drudges "who had the worst life of any who were with the Fianna," and then he said, "I would rather be living their life than the life I am leading now."

The name of these tribes of the goddess Dana is often confused with that of the northern invaders who were afterwards a terror to Ireland. And so it was of those unearthly tribes an old basket-maker was thinking when he said, in telling of the defeat of the Irish under James, "The Danes were dancing in the raths around Aughrim the night after the battle. Their ancestors were driven out of Ireland before, and they were glad when they saw those that had put them out put out themselves, and everyone of them skivered."

Many of the stories I have gathered tell how those tribes still protect their own; and even today, March 21, 1916, I have read in the "Irish Times" that "a farmer who was summoned by a road contractor for having failed to cut a portion of a hedge on the roadside, told the magistrates at Granard Petty Sessions that he objected to cutting the hedge as it grew in a fort or rath. He however had no objection to the contractor's men cutting the hedge. The magistrates allowed the case to stand till the next Court."

As to Knockmaa, or Cruachmaa, or, as it is called today, Castle Hacket Hill, that overlooks Lough Corrib and the plain of Moytura, and that we see as a blue cloud from our roads, it was in Saint Patrick's time the habitation of Finnbarr a king among the Sidhe and his seventeen sons, and it is to this day spoken of as "a very Sheoguey place."

It was in these enchanted hills that the ale of Goibniu the Smith kept whoever tasted it from sickness and from death, and there is some memory of this in a story told me by an old farmer. "There was a man one time set out from Ireland to go to America or some place; a common man looking for work he was. And something happened to the ship on the way, and they had

256

to put to land to mend it. And in the country where they landed
he saw a forth, and he went into it, and there he saw the smallest
people he ever saw, and they were the Danes that went out of
Ireland; and it was foxes they had for dogs, and weasels were
their cats.

"Then he went back to get into the ship, but it was gone away,
and he left behind. So he went back into the forth, and a young
man came to meet him, and he told him what had happened. And
the young man said 'Come into the room within where my father
is in the bed, for he is out of his health and you might be able to
serve him.' So they went in and the father was lying in the bed,
and when he heard it was a man from Ireland was in it he said,
'I will give you a great reward if you will go back and bring me
a thing I want out of Castle Hacket Hill. For if I had what is
there,' he said, 'I would be as young as my son.' So the man
consented to go, and they got a sailing ship ready, and it is
what the old man told him, to go back to Ireland. 'And buy a
little pig in Galway,' he said, 'and bring it to the mouth of the
forth of Castle Hacket and roast it there. And inside the forth
is an enchanted cat that is keeping guard there, and it will come
out; and here is a shot-gun and some cross-money that will kill
any faery or any enchanted thing. And within in the forth,' he
said, 'you will find a bottle and a rack-comb, and bring them
back here to me.'

"So the man did as he was told and he bought the pig and
roasted it at the mouth of the forth, and out came the enchanted
cat, and it having hair seven inches long. And he fired the cross-
money out of the shot-gun, and the cat went away and he saw it
no more. And he got the bottle and the rack-comb and brought
them back to the old man. And he drank what was in the bottle
and racked his hair with the rack, and he got young again, as
young as his own son."

It may be some of those faery treasures are still given out;
for of the family who have been for a good while owners of the
hill, one at least had the gift of genius. And I remember being
told in childhood, and I have never known if it were fact or
folk-tale, that her mother having as a bride gone to listen to
some debate or royal speech in the House of Lords at West-
minster, the whole assembly had stood up in homage to her
beauty.

I was told by a Miller:
It was the Danes built these forths. They were a fair-haired race, and they married with the Irish that were dark-haired, just like those linen weavers your own great-grandfather brought up from the North, the Hevenors and the Glosters and others, married with the Roman Catholics. There was a king of the Danes called Trevenher that had a daughter that was a great beauty. And she gave a feast, and the young men of the other race dressed like girls and came to it, and sat at it till midnight, and then they threw off the women's clothes and killed all the generals and the king himself. So the Danes were driven out, that's why we have the fires and the wisps on St. John's Eve. And as for Herself there, she wouldn't for all the world let St. Martin's Day pass without killing of cocks—one for the woman and another for the man.

As to the three lisses at Ryanrush, there must have been a great deal of fighting there in the old time. There are some bushes growing on them and no one, man or woman, will ever put a hand to cut them, no more than they would touch the little bush by the well beyond, that used to have lights shining out of it.

And if any one was to fall asleep within the liss himself, he would be taken away and the spirit of some old warrior would be put in his place, and it's he would know everything in the whole world. There's no doubt at all but that there's the same sort of things in other countries. Sure *these* can go through and appear in Australia in one minute. But you hear more about them in these parts, because the Irish do be more familiar in talking of them.

Enchanters and magicians they were in the old times, and could make the birds sing and the stones and the fishes speak.

It's in the forths they mostly live. The last priest that was here told us a lot about them, but he said not to be anyway afraid of them, for they are but poor souls doing their penance.

Mary Nagle:
That's a fine big liss at Ryanrush, and people say they hear things there, and sometimes a great light is seen—no wonder

these things should be seen there, for it was a great place for fighting in the old centuries, and a great deal of bones have been turned up in the fields. There was an open passage I remember into the liss, and two girls got a candle one time and went in, but they saw nothing but the ashes of the fires the Danes used to make. The passage is closed up now I believe, with big stones no man could lift.

One time a woman from the North came to our house, and she said a great deal of people is kept below there in the lisses; she had been there herself, and in the night-time in one moment they'd all be away at Cruachmaa, wherever that may be, down in the North I believe. And she knew everything that was in the house, and told us about my sister being sick, and that there was a hurling going on, as there was that day at the Isabella wood in Coole. And all about Coole House she knew as if she spent her life in it. I'd have picked a lot of stories out of her but my mother got nervous when she heard the truth coming out, and bid me be quiet. She had a red petticoat on her, the same as any country woman, and she offered to cure me, for it was that time I was delicate and your ladyship sent me to the salt water, but she asked a shilling and my mother said she hadn't got it. "You have," says she, "and heavier metal than that you have in the house." So then my mother gave her the shilling, and she put it in the fire and melted it, and says she, "After two days you'll see your shilling again." But we never did. And the cure she left, I never took it; it's not safe, and the priests forbid us to take their cures—for it must surely be from the devil their knowledge comes. But no doubt at all she was one of the Ingentry, that can take the form of a woman by day and another form at night. After that she went to Mrs. Quaid's house and asked her for a bit of tobacco. "You'll get it again" she said, "and more with it." And sure enough, that very day a bit of meat came into Mrs. Quaid's house.[46]

Maurteen Joyce:
There's a forth near Clough that wanders underneath, but a man couldn't get into it without he'd crawl on his hands and knees. Well, Kennedy's filly was brought in there, and lived there for five days without food but what she got from *them,* and no one knew where she was till a man passing by heard her neighing and then she was dug out.

*　　　*　　　*

259

There's a forth near our house, but it's not the good people that are in it, only the old inhabitants of Ireland shut up there below.

There are a few old forths about, some of them you mightn't notice unless you understood such things; but sometimes passing by you'd feel a cold wind blowing from them, would nearly rend you in two.

When I was a young chap myself I used to see a white woman walking about sometimes at midday—that's the worst hour there is—and she'd always go back into a forth, and forth of Cahir near Cloonmore, and disappear into it.

She was known to be a woman that had died nine years before; and she would sometimes come into the sister's house, and bid her keep it clean. But one time the sister's husband went to burn the inside of the forth, and the next morning his barn where he had all the wheat of the harvest and near a ton of hay and two or three packs of wool, was found to be on fire. And his own little girl, about eight years of age, was in the barn, and a labouring man broke through and brought a wet cloth with him and threw it over her and carried her out. But she was as black as cinders and dead. Vexed they were at him burning the forth.

An Old Miller:
Did *they* get help to make those forths? You may know well that they did. There was an engineer here when that road was being made—a sort of an idolater or a foreigner he was—anyway he made it through the forth, and he didn't last long after. Those other engineers, Edgeworth and Hemans beyond at Ardrahan when the railway was made, I'm told they avoided such things.

A Slieve Echtge Man:
There were two brothers taken away sudden, two O'Briens. They were cutting heath one day and filling the cart with it, and a voice told them to leave off cutting the heath, but they went on, and a blow struck the cart on the axle. And soon after that one of the brothers sat down in his chair and died sudden. And the other was one day going to market, I was going to it that day myself, and he wasn't far beyond the white gate when the

axle of the cart broke in that same place where it had got the blow, and so he had to go home again, and near the river where they're cutting the larch he turned in to talk to a poor man that was cutting a tree, and the tree fell, and top of it struck him and killed him. And it was last March that happened.

There was one Leary in Clough had the land taken that's near Newtown racecourse. And he was out there one day building a wall, and it was time for his dinner, but he had none brought with him. And a man came to him and said "Is it home you'll be going for your dinner?" And he said "It's not worth my while to go back to Clough, I'd have the day lost." And the man said, "Well, come in and eat a bit with me." And he brought him into a forth and there was everything that was grand, and the dinner they gave him of the best, so that he ate near two plates of it. And then he went out again to build the wall. And whether it was with lifting the heavy stones I don't know, but (with respects to you) when he was walking the road home he began to vomit, and what he vomited up was all green grass.

A Man on the Connemara Coast:
This is a faery stream we're passing; there were some used to see them by the side of it, and washing themselves in it. And there used to be heard a faery forge here every night, and the hammering of the iron could be heard, and the blast of the furnace.

There is a faery hill beyond there in the mountain, and some have seen fires in it all through the night. And one time the police were out there still-hunting, and the head of them, one Rogers, was in the middle of that place, and there he died, no one could say how, though some of his men were round about him.

That's a nice flat clean place that rock we're passing—that's the sort of place they'd be seen dancing or having their play.

A Piper:
I knew twin sons, Considines, and one was struck with madness in England, and one at home—Pat in England, Mike in Connacht—at the one time. Both were sent to Ballinasloe Asylum, and got well in eight months, and that was ten year ago, and one of them is married and rearing a family. The

mother used to be doing cures with herbs; it is likely that is the reason but she gave it up after they were struck.

There were three of another family went in to the Asylum, one this year, one next year, and one the year after, and no reason but that their house was close to the side of a forth.

Maurteen Joyce:
When I was in Clare there was a forth, and two or three men went down it one time, and brought rushes and lights with them. And they came to where there was a woman washing at a river and they heard the crying of young lambs, and it November, for when we have winter, there is summer there. So they got afraid, and two of the men came back, but one of them stopped there and was never heard of after. The best of things they have, and no trouble at all but to be eating; but they have no chance of being saved till the Day of Judgment.

I knew another forth that two men watched, and at night there came out of it two troops of horses, and they began to graze. But when the men came near them they made for the forths, and all they got was a foal. And they kept it, and it was a mare-horse, and it had foals, and the breed was the best that was ever seen in the country.

Mrs. Leary:
There did strange things happen in that wood, noises would be heard, and those that went in to steal rods could never get them up on their back to bring them away. But there was one man said whatever happened he'd bring them, and he got them on to his back, and then they were lifted off it over the wood. But they fell again and he got them and carried them away; I suppose they thought well of him having so much courage.

Cruachmaa is the great place for them.

A man who had lost a blood mare met an old man from a forth who said "Put your right foot on my right foot." And he did so, and at once he saw the blood mare and his foal close by.

The Old Man Who Is Making a Well:
There was a man and his wife was brought away at Cruachmaa and he was told to go dig, and he'd get her out. And he began to dig, and when he had a hole made at the side of the hill he saw her coming out, but he couldn't stop the pick that he had lifted for the stroke, and it went through her head.

262

J. Doran:

Whether they are in it or not, there are many tell stories of them. And I often saw the half of Cruachmaa covered—like as if there was a mist on it.

But one side of a wall is luckier than another, all the old people will tell you that. There was a big stone in the yard behind our house and my husband thought to blast it, for it was in the way, and my mother said "I'm in the house longer than you, and take my advice and never touch that stone," and he never did. But there was a man built a house close by and he wanted to close a passage, and one morning he came early and was laying hands on that stone to take it. But I was out when I heard him and drove him away. And the house never throve with him, he lost two or three children, and then he died himself.

A Gate-keeper:

At St. Patrick's well at Burren there used to be a great pattern every year. And every year there was something lost and killed at it, a horse or a man or a woman.

So at last the priest put a stop to it. And there was an old woman with me in the barracks at Burren, and she told me she remembered well when she was a young girl and the time came when the pattern used to be, the first year it was stopped her father put her up on a big high wall near the well, and bid her look down. And there she saw the whole place full of the *gentry*, and they playing and dancing and having their own games, they were in such joy to have done away with the pattern. I suppose the well belonged to them before it got the name of St. Patrick.

There's a small little house not far down the road where they used to be very fond of going. And a woman in the town asked the old woman that lived in it what did they look like. And she said "For all the world like people coming in to Chapel."

There was a girl coming back here one time from Clough, and instead of coming here she went the Esserkelly road and was led astray and a man met her and says he, "Why do you say you're going to Labane and it's to Roxborough you're facing?" and he turned her around. And when she got home she took off the bundle she had on her back, and what jumped out of it but a young hare.

Mrs. Casey:

I have a great little story about a woman—a jobber's wife that lived a mile beyond Ardrahan. She had business one time in Ballyvaughan, and when she was on the road beyond Kinvara a man came to her out of a forth and he asked her to go in and to please a child that was crying. So she went in and she pleased the child, and she saw in a corner an old man that never stopped from crying. And when she went out again she asked the man that brought her in, why was the old man roaring and crying. The man pointed to a milch cow in the meadow and he said, "Before the day is over he will be in the place of that cow, and it will be brought into the forth to give milk to the child." And she can tell herself that was true, for in the evening when she was coming back from Ballyvaughan, she saw in that field a cow dead, and being cut in pieces, and all the poor people bringing away bits of it, that was the old man that had been put in its place. There is poison in that meat, but no poison ever comes off the fire, but you must mind to throw away the top of the pot.

The forth where I heard the talking long ago, and left my can, it's only the other day I was telling Pat Stephens of it that has the land. And he told me he put a trough in it to catch the water about a month ago. And the next day one of his best bullocks died.

Mrs. O'Brien:

It's a bad piece of the road that poor boy fell off his cart at and was killed. There's a forth near it, and it's in that forth my five children are that were swept from me. I went and I told Father Carey I knew they were there, and he said "Say your prayers, my poor woman, that's all you can do." When they were young they were small and thin enough, they grew up like a bunch of rushes, but they got strong and stout and good-looking. Too good they were, so that everyone would remark them and would say, "Oh, look at Ellen O'Brien—look at Catherine—look at Martin! So good to work and so handsome, so loyal to their mother." And they were all taken from me, all gone now but one. Consumption they were said to get, but it never was in my family or in the father's, and how would they get it without some provocation? Four of them died with that, and Martin was drowned. One of the little girls was in America

out, "If it's the Banshee it's for me, and I must die today or tomorrow." And in the middle of the next day, he died.

One time I was passing by a forth down there, and I saw a thick smoke coming out of it, straight up it went and then it spread at the top. And when it was clearing away I saw two rows of birds, one on the one side and one on the other, and I stopped to look at them. They were white, and had shoulders and heads like dogs, and there was a great noise like a rattling, and a man that was passing by looked up and said "God speed you," and they flew away.

A Seaside Man:

There were five boys of the Callinans, and they rich and well-to-do, were out in a boat, and a ship came out from the shore and touched it and it sank, and the ship was seen no more. And one of the boys held on to the boat, and some men came out and brought him to land. But the second time after that he went out, he was swept.

An Old Man in Gort Workhouse:

I knew an old man was in here was greatly given to card-playing. And one night he was up on the hill beyond, towards Slieve Echtge, where there is a big forth, and he went into it, and there he found a lot of *them* playing cards. Like any other card-players they looked, and he sat down and played with them, and they played fair. And when he woke in the morning, he was lying outside on the hill, and nothing under his head but a tuft of rushes.

John Mangan:

Old Hanrahan one time went out to the forth that's in front of his house and cut a bush, and he a fresh man enough. And next morning he hadn't a blade of hair on his head—not a blade. And he had to buy a wig and to wear it for the rest of his life. I remember him and the wig well.

And it was some years after that that Delane, the father of the great cricketer, was passing by that way, and the water had risen and he strayed off the road into it. And as he got farther and farther in, till he was covered to better than his waist, he heard like the voice of his wife crying, "Go on, John, go on farther." And he called out, "These are John Hanrahan's faeries

267

that took the hair off him." "And what did you do then?" they asked him when he got safe to the house, and was telling this. And he said, "I turned my coat inside out, and after that they troubled me no more, and so I got safe to the road again." But no one ever had luck that meddled with a forth, so it's always said.

There's Mrs. Lynch's daughter was coming through the trees about eight months ago and when she came to a thicket of bushes, a short little man came out, about three feet high, dressed all in white, and he white himself or grey, and asked her to come with him, and she ran away as fast as she could. And with the fright she got, she fell into a sickness—what they call the sickness of Peter and Paul—and you'd think she'd tear the house down when it comes on her.

I met a woman some time ago told me more about the forths in this place than ever I knew before, and well she might for she had passed seven years in them, working, working, minding children and the like all the time; no singing or dancing for her.

M. Haverty:
There was one Rock, was brought into a forth. A three-legged horse came for him one night and brought him away; and when he got there they all called him by his name.

There was a man up there cut a tree in one of them, and he was took ill immediately after, and didn't live long.

There's a bad bit of road near Kinvara Chapel, just when you get within sight of the sea. I know a man has to pass there, and he wouldn't go on the driver's side of the car, for it's to the right side those things are to be seen. Sure there was a boy lost his life falling off a car there last Friday week.

One night passing the big tree at Raheen I heard the sound of a handsaw in the air, and I looked up and there in the top of a larch tree that's near to a beech I saw a man sitting and cutting it with the handsaw. So I hurried away home. But the next time I passed that way I took a view of it to see might it have been one of the Dillons that might be stealing timber; and there was no sign of a cut or a touch in it at all.

There was a man on the road between Chevy and Marble Hill, where there is a faery plumb-stone, that stands straight up and it about five feet in height, and the man was building a house and carried it away to put above his door. And from the time he brought it away, all his stock began to die, and whenever he went in or out, night or day, he was severely beaten. So at last he took the stone down and put it back where it was before, and from that time nothing has troubled him.

John Mangan:

Myself and two of my brothers were over at Inchy Weir to catch a horse, and growing close by the water there was a bush the form of an umbrella, very close and thick at the top. So we began fooling as boys do, and I said, "I'll bet a button none of you will make a stone go through the bush." So I took up a pebble of cow-dung and threw it, and they all threw, and no sooner did the pebble hit the bush than there came from it music, like a band playing. So we all ran for our lives, and when we had got about two hundred yards we looked back and we saw something moving round the bush, first it had the clothes of a woman and then of a man. So we stopped to see no more.

Well, it was some years after that when Sir William ordered all the bushes in that part to be cut down. And one Prendergast a boy that used to be a beater here and that went to America after, went to cut them just in the same place where I had seen that sight, and a thorn ran into his eye and blinded him, and he never got the sight of it again.

An Old Woman near Ballinsloe:

There are many forths around, and in that one beyond, there is often music heard. The smith's father heard the music one time he was passing and he could not stop from dancing till he was tired. I heard him tell that myself.

And over there to the left there is a forth had an opening in it, and the steward wanted to get it closed up, and he could get no men to do it. And at last a young man said he would, and he went to work and at the end of the week he was dead.

And there was a girl milking a cow not long after that, and she saw him coming to her, and she ran away, and he called to her to stop and she did not, and he said "That you may never milk another cow!" And within a week, she herself was dead.

There was a woman over there in that house you can see, and

she wanted to root up a forth; covetousness it was, she had plenty and she wanted more. And she tried to get a man to do it and she could not, but at last a man that had been turned out of his holding, and that was in want, said he would do it. And before he went to work he went on his two knees, and he wished that whatever harm might come from it might come on her, and not on himself. And so it did, and her hands got crippled and crappled. And they travelled the world and could get no relief for her, and her cattle began to die, and she died herself in the end. And the daughter and the son-in-law had to leave that house and to build another, for they were losing all the cattle, and they are left alone now, but the daughter lost a finger by it.

A Man near Corcomroe:
I saw a light myself one night in the big forth over there near the sea. Like a bonfire it was, and going up about thirty feet into the air.

Ghosts are to be heard about the forths. They make a heavy noise, and there are creaks in their shoes. Doing a penance I suppose they are. And there's many see the lights in the forths at Newtown.

J. Doheny:
One time I was cutting bushes up there near the river, and I cut a big thorn bush, I thought it no harm to do it when it wasn't standing by itself, but in a thicket, and it old and half-rotten. And when I had it cut, I heard some one talking very loud to my wife, that was gathering kippeens down in the field the other side of the wall. And I went down to know who it was talking to her. And when I asked her she said "No, it's to yourself some one was talking, for I heard his voice where you were, and I saw no one." So I said, "Surely it's one of them mourning for the bush I cut," for the sound of his voice was as if he was mad vexed.

I think it's not in the tree at the corner there's anything, it's something in the place. Not long ago there was one Greeley going to Galway with a load of barley, and when he came to that corner he heard the sound of a train crossing from inside the wall, and the horse stopped. And then he heard it a second time and the horse refused to go on, and at the end he had to turn back home again, for he had no use trying to make the horse go on.

There were ash trees growing around the blessed well at Corker, and one night Deeley, the uncle of Pat Deeley that lives beyond, and two other men went to cut them down, to get the makings of a car-body. And the next day Deeley's lip was drawn down—like this—and water running from it for the rest of his life. I often see him; and as to the two other men, they died soon after.

And big Joyce that was a servant to John O'Hara, he went to cut trees one night near that hole at Raheen, near the corner of the road, and he was prevented, and never could get the hand-saw near a tree, nor the other men that were with him.

And there was another man went and cut a bush not far from the Kinvara road, and with the first stroke he heard a sort of a cough or a groan come from beneath it, that was a token to him to leave it alone. But he wouldn't leave off, and his mouth was drawn to one side all of a sudden and in two days after he was dead. Surely, one should leave such things alone.

A Piper:
I had a fall myself in Galway the other day that I couldn't move my arm to play the pipes if you gave me Ireland. And a man said to me—and they are very smart people in Galway—that two or three got a fall and a hurt in that same place. "There is places in the sea where there is drowning," he said, "and places on the land as well where there do be accidents, and no man can save himself from them, for it is the will of God."

A Man Asking Alms:
It's not safe sometimes to meddle with walls. There was a man beyond Gort knocked some old walls not long ago, and he's dead since.

But it's by the big tree outside Raheen where you take the turn to Kinvara that the most things are seen. There was a boy living with Conor in Gort that was out before daylight with a load of hay in a cart, and he sitting on top of it, and he was found lying dead just beside the tree, where he fell from the top of the cart, and the horse was standing there stock-still. There was a shower of rain fell while he was lying there, and I passed the road two hours later, and saw where the dust was dry where

271

his body had been lying. And it was only yesterday I was hearing a story of that very same place. There was a man coming from Galway with a ton weight of a load on his cart, and when he came to that tree the linching of his wheel came out, and the cart fell down. And presently a little man, about two and a half feet in height, came out from the wall and lifted up the cart, and held it up till he had the linching put up again. And he never said a word but went away as he came, and the man came into Gort. And I remember myself, the black and white dog used to be on the road between Hanlon's gate and Gort. It was there for ten years and no one ever saw it, but one evening Father Boyle's man was going out to look at a few little sheep and lambs belonging to the priest, and when he came to the stile the dog put up its paws on it and looked at him, and he was afraid to go on. So next morning he told Father Boyle about it and he said "I think that you won't see it any more." And sure enough from that day it never was seen again.

Steve Simon:
I don't know did I draw down to you before, your ladyship, the greatest wonder ever I saw in my life?

I was passing by the forth at Corcomroe, coming back from some shopping I had done in Belharbour, and I saw twelve of the finest horses ever I saw, and riders on them racing round the forth. Many a race I saw since I lived in this world, but never a race like that, for tipping and tugging and welting the horses; the jockeys in coloured clothes, striped and blue, and little blue caps on them, and a lady in the front of them on a bayish horse and wearing a scarlet jacket.

I told what I saw the same evening to an old woman living near and she said, "Whatever you saw keep it secret, or some harm will come upon you." There was another thing I saw besides the riders. There were crowds and crowds of people, standing as we would against walls or on a stage, and taking a view. They were shouting, but the men racing on the horses said nothing at all. Never a race like that one, with the swiftness and the welting and fine horses that were in it.

What clothing had these people? They had coats on them, and on their back there were pictures, pictures in the form of people. Shields I think they were. Anyway there were pictures on them. Striped the coats were, and a sort of scollop on them the same as that screen in the window (a blind with Celtic design).

272

They had little blue caps, such as wore them, but some had nothing on the head at all; and they had blue slippers—those I saw of them—but I was afeared to take more than a side view except of the racers.

An Old Army Man:
You know the forth where the old man lost his hair? Well there's another man, Waters, that married Brian's sister, has the second sight, and there's a big bush left in that forth, and when he goes there he sees a woman sitting under it, and she lighting a fire.

Cloran's father was living over at Knockmaa one time and his wife died, and he believed it was taken into the hill she was. So he went one morning and dug a hole in the side of the hill. But the next morning when he went back to dig again, the hole was filled up and the grass growing over it as before. And this he did two or three times. And then some one told him to put his pick and his spade across the hole. And so he did, and it wasn't filled up again. But what happened after I don't know.

An Old Army Man:
That's a bad bit of road near Kinvara where the boy lost his life last week; I know it well. And I knew him, a quiet boy, and married to a widow woman; she wanted the help of a man, and he was young. What would ail him to fall off the side of an ass-car and to be killed?

XV

BLACKSMITHS

I have been told:

Yes, they say blacksmiths have something about them, and if there's a seventh blacksmith in succession, from generation to generation, he can do many things, and if he gave you his curse you wouldn't be the better of it. There was one near the cliffs, Pat Doherty, but he did no harm to any one, but was as quiet as another. He is dead now and his son is a blacksmith too.[46]

There was a man one time that was a blacksmith, and he used to go every night playing cards, and for all his wife could say he wouldn't leave off doing it. So one night she got a boy to stand in the old churchyard he'd have to pass, and to frighten him. So the boy did so, and began to groan and to try to frighten him when he came near. But it's well known that nothing of that kind can do any harm to a blacksmith. So he went in and got hold of the boy, and told him he had a mind to choke him, and went his way.

But no sooner was the boy left alone than there came about him something in the shape of a dog, and then a great troop of cats. And they surrounded him and he tried to get away home, but he had no power to go the way he wanted but had to go with them. And at last they came to an old forth and a faery bush, and he knelt down and made the sign of the cross and said a great many "Our Fathers," and after a time they went into the faery bush and left him. And he was going away and a woman came out of the bush, and called to him three times, to make him look back. And he saw that it was a woman that he knew before, that was dead, and so he knew that she was amongst the faeries.

And she said to him, "It's well for you that I was here, and worked hard for you, or you would have been brought in among them, and be like me." So he got home. And the blacksmith got home too and his wife was surprised to see he was no way frightened. But he said, "You might know that there's nothing of that sort could harm me."

For a blacksmith is safe from all, and when he goes out in the night he keeps always in his pocket a small bit of wire, and they know him by that. So he went on playing, and they grew very poor after.

And I knew a woman from the County Limerick had been *away*, and she could tell you all about the forths in this place and how she was recovered. She met a man she knew on the road, and she out riding with them all on horseback, and told him to bring a bottle of forge-water and to throw it on her, and so he did, and she came back again.

Blacksmiths surely are safe from these things. And if a blacksmith was to turn his anvil upside down and to say malicious words, he could do you great injury.

There was a child that was changed, and my mother brought it a nice bit of potato cake one time, for tradesmen often have nice things on the table. But the child wouldn't touch it, for they don't like the leavings of a smith.

Blacksmiths have power, and if you could steal the water from the trough in the forge, it would cure all things.

And as to forges, there's some can hear working and hammering in them through the night.

XVI

MONSTERS AND SHEOGUEY BEASTS

THE Dragon that was the monster of the early world now appears only in the traditional folktales, where the hero, a new Perseus, fights for the life of the Princess who looks on crying at the brink of the sea, bound to a silver chair, while the Dragon is "put in a way he will eat no more kings' daughters." In the stories of today he has shrunk to eel or worm, for the persons and properties of the folk-lore of all countries keep being transformed or remade in the imagination, so that once in New England on the eve of George Washington's birthday, the decorated shop windows set me wondering whether the cherry tree itself might not be a remaking of the red-berried dragon guarded rowan of the Celtic tales, or it may be of a yet more ancient apple. I ventured to hint at this in a lecture at Philadelphia, and next day one of the audience wrote me that he had looked through all the early biographies of Washington, and either the first three or the first three editions of the earliest —I have mislaid the letter—never mention the cherry tree at all.

The monstrous beasts told of today recall the visions of Maeldune on his strange dream-voyage, where he saw the beast that was like a horse and that had "legs of a hound with rough sharp nails," and the fiery pigs that fed on golden fruit, and the cat that with one flaming leap turned a thief to a heap of ashes; for the folk-tales of the world have long roots, and there is nothing new save their reblossoming.

I have been told by a Car-driver:

I went to serve one Patterson at a place called Grace Dieu between Waterford and Tramore, and there were queer things in it. There was a woman lived at the lodge the other side from the gate, and one day she was looking out and she saw a wool-pack coming riding down the road of itself.

There was a room over the stable I was put to sleep in, and no one near me. One night I felt a great weight on my feet, and there was something very weighty coming up upon my body and

I heard heavy breathing. Every night after that I used to light the fire and bring up coal and make up the fire with it that it would be near as good in the morning as it was at night. And I brought a good terrier up every night to sleep with me on the bed. Well, one night the fire was lighting and the moon was shining in at the window, and the terrier leaped off the bed and he was barking and rushing and fighting and leaping, near to the ceiling and in under the bed. And I could see the shadow of him on the walls and on the ceiling, and I could see the shadow of another thing that was about two foot long and that had a head like a pike, and that was fighting and leaping. They stopped after a while and all was quiet. But from that night the terrier never would come to sleep in the room again.

By Others:

The worst form a monster can take is a cow or a pig. But as to a lamb, you may always be sure a lamb is honest.

A pig is the worst shape they can take. I wouldn't like to meet anything in the shape of a pig in the night.

No, I saw nothing myself, I'm not one of those that can see such things; but I heard of a man that went with the others on rent day, and because he could pay no rent but only made excuses, the landlord didn't ask him in to get a drink with the others. So as he was coming home by himself in the dark, there was something on the road before him, and he gave it a hit with the toe of his boot, and it let a squeal. So then he said to it, "Come in here to my house, for I'm not asked to drink with them; I'll give drink and food to you." So it came in, and the next morning he found by the door a barrel full of wine and another full of gold, and he never knew a day's want after that.

Walking home one night with Jack Costello, there was something before us that gave a roar, and then it rose in the air like a goose, and then it fell again. And Jackeen told me after that it had laid hold on his trousers, and he didn't sleep all night with the fright he got.

There's a monster in Lough Graney, but it's only seen once in seven years.

*　　*　　*

There is a monster of some sort down by Duras, it's called the ghost of Fiddeen. Some say it's only heard every seven years. Some say it was a flannel seller used to live there that had a short fardel. We heard it here one night, like a calf roaring.

One night my grandfather was beyond at Inchy where the lads from Gort used to be stealing rods, and he was sitting by the wall, and the dog beside him. And he heard something come running from Inchy Weir and he could see nothing, but the sound of its feet on the ground was like the sound of the feet of a deer. And when it passed by him the dog got in between him and the wall and scratched at him, but still he could see nothing but only could hear the sound of hoofs. So when it was passed he turned away home.

Another time, my grandfather told me, he was in a boat out on the lake here at Coole with two or three men from Gort. And one of them had an eel-spear and he thrust it into the water and it hit something, and the man fainted, and they had to carry him in out of the boat to land. And when he came to himself he said that what he struck was like a horse or like a calf, but whatever it was, it was no fish.

There is a boy I knew, one Curtin near Ballinderreen, told me that he was going along the road one night and he saw a dog. It had claws like a cur, and a body like a person, and he couldn't see what its head was like. But it was moaning like a soul in pain, and presently it vanished, and there came most beautiful music, and a woman came out and he thought at first it was the Banshee, and she wearing a red petticoat. And a striped jacket she had on, and a white band about her waist. And to hear more beautiful singing and music he never did, but to know or to understand what she was expressing, he couldn't do it. And at last they came to a place by the roadside where there was some bushes. And she went in there and disappeared under them, and the most beautiful lights came shining where she went in. And when he got home, he himself fainted, and his mother put her beads over him, and blessed him and said prayers. So he got quiet at last.

I would easily believe about the dog having a fight with something his owner couldn't see. That often happens in this island,

278

and that's why every man likes to have a black dog with him
at night—a black one is the best for fighting such things.

And a black cock everyone likes to have in their house—a
March cock it should be.

I knew the captain of a ship used to go whale fishing, and he
said he saw them by scores. But by his account they were no
way like the ones McDaragh saw; it was I described them to
him.

We don't give in to such things here as they do in the middle
island; but I wouldn't doubt that about the dog. For they can see
what we can't see. And there was a man here was out one night
and the dog ran on and attacked something that was in front of
him—a faery it was—but he could see nothing. And every now
and again it would do the same thing, and seemed to be fighting
something before him, and when they got home the man got safe
into the house, but at the threshold the dog was killed.

And a horse can see many things, and if ever you're out late,
and the horse to stop as if there was something he wouldn't
pass, make the sign of the cross between his ears, and he'll go
on then. And it's well to have a cock always in the house, if you
can have it from a March clutch, and the next year if you can
have another cock from a March clutch from that one, it's the
best. And if you go late out of the house, and that there is something outside it would be bad to meet, that cock will crow before
you'll go out.

I'm sorry I wasn't in to meet you surely, knowing as much as
I do about the faeries. One night I went with four or five others
down by the mill to hunt rabbits. And when we got to the field
by the river there was the sound of hundreds, some crying and
the other part laughing, that we all heard them. And something
came down to the river, first I thought he was a dog and then I
saw he was too big and strange looking. And you'd think there
wouldn't be a drop of water left in the river with all he drank.
And I bid the others say nothing about it, for Patrick Green was
lying sick at the mill, and it might be taken for a bad sign. And
it wasn't many days after that he died.

My father told me that one night he was crossing this road,
and he turned to the wall to close his shoe. And when he turned

again there was something running through the field that was the size of a yearling calf, and black, and it ran across the road, and there was like the sound of chains in it. And when it came to that rock with the bush on it, it stopped and he could see a red light in its mouth. And then it disappeared. He used often to see a black dog in this road, and it used to be following him, and others saw it too. But one night the brother of the priest, Father Mitchell saw it and he told the priest and he banished it.

The lake down there (Lough Graney) is an enchanted place, and old people told me that one time they were swimming there, and a man had gone out into the middle and they saw something like a great big eel making for him, and they called out, "If ever you were a great swimmer show us now how you can swim to the shore," for they wouldn't frighten him by saying what was behind him. So he swam to the shore, and he only got there when the thing behind him was in the place where he was. For there are queer things in lakes. I never saw anything myself, but one time I was coming home late from Scariff, and I felt my hair standing up on my head, and I began to feel a sort of shy and fearful, and I could feel that there was something walking beside me. But after a while there was a little stream across the road, and after I passed that I was all right again and could feel nothing near.

I never saw anything myself but once, early in the morning and I going to the May fair of Loughrea. It was a little way outside of the town I saw something that had the appearance of a black pig, and it was running in under the cart and under the ass's feet. And the ass would keep backing away from it, that it was hardly I could bring her along, till we got to the bridge of Cloon, and once we were over that we saw it no more, for it couldn't pass the running water. And all the time it was with us I was hitting at it with my stick, and it would run from me then, for it was a hazel stick, and the hazel is blessed, and no wicked thing can stay when it is touched with it. It is likely the nuts are blessed too. Aren't they growing on the same tree?

I was over at Phayre's mill one time to get some boards sawed and they said I must wait an hour or so, where the mill wasn't free. And I had a load of turf to get, and I went along the road. And I heard something coming after me in the gutter, and it stood up over me like an elephant, and I put my hands behind me and I said, "Madad Fior," and he went away. It was just at the bridge he was, near Kilchriest, and when I was coming back after a while, just when I got to the bridge there, he was after me again. But I never saw him since then.

One time I was at the fair at Ballinasloe, and I but a young lad at the time, and a comrade with me that was but a young lad too. We brought in the sheep the Monday evening, and they were sold the Tuesday morning, and the master bid us to go home on the train. "Bad cess," said my comrade, "are we to get no good at all out of the fair? Let us stop," says he, "and get the good of it and go back by the mail train." So we went through the fair together and went to a dance, and the master never knew, and we went home on the mail train together. We got out at Woodlawn and we were going home, and we heard a sort of a groaning and we could see nothing, and the boy that was with me was frightened, for though he was a strong boy, he was a timorous man. We found then the groaning coming from beyond the wall, and I went and put my two fists on the wall and looked over it. There were two trees on the other side of the wall, and I saw walking off and down from one tree to the other, something that was like a soldier or a sentry. The body was a man's body, and there was a black suit on it, but it had the head of a bear, the very head and *puss* of a bear. I asked what was on him. "Don't speak to me, don't speak to me," he said, and he stopped by the tree and was groaning and went away.

That is all that ever I saw, and I herding sheep in the lambing season, and falling asleep as I did sometimes, and walking up and down the field in my sleep.

My father told me that in the bad times, about the year '48, he used to be watching about in the fields, where the people did be stealing the crops. And there was no field in Coole he was afraid to go into by night except one, that is number three in the Lake Farm. For the dog that was about in those times stopped the night in the clump there. And Johnny Callan told me one night passing that field he heard the noise of a cart of stones thrown against the wall. But when he went back there in the morning there was no sign of anything at all. My father never saw the dog himself but he was known to be there and he felt him.

And as for the monster, I never saw it in Coole Lake, but one day I was coming home with my two brothers from Tirneevan school, and there as we passed Dhulough we heard a great splashing, and we saw some creature put up its head, with a head and a mane like a horse. And we didn't stop but ran.

But I think it was not so big as the monster over here in Coole Lake, for Johnny Callan saw it, and he said it was the size of a stack of turf. But there's many could tell about that for there's many saw it, Dougherty from Gort and others.

As to the dog that used to be in the road, a friend of his own was driving Father Boyle from Kinvara late one night and there it was—first on the right side and then on the left of the car. And at last he told Father Boyle, and he said. "Look out now for it, and you'll see it no more," and no more he did, and that was the last of it.

But the driver of the mail-car had often seen a figure of a woman following the car till it came to the churchyard beyond Ardrahan, and there it disappeared.

Father Boyle was a good man indeed—a child might speak to him. They said he had the dog or whatever it may be banished from the road, but of late I heard the driver of the mail-car saying he sees it on one spot on the road every night. And there's a very lonely hollow beyond Doran's house, and I know a man that never passed by that hollow but what he'd fall asleep. But one night he saw a sort of a muffled figure and he cried out three times some good wish—such as "God have mercy on you"—and then it gave a great laugh and vanished and he saw it no more. As to the forths or other old places, how do we know what poor soul may be shut up there, confined in pain?

Sure a man the other day coming back from your own place, Inchy, when he came to the big tree, heard a squealing, and there he saw a sort of a dog, and it white, and it followed as if holding on to him all the way home. And when he got to the house he near fainted, and asked for a glass of water.

There's some sort of a monster at Tyrone, rising and slipping up and down in the sun, and when it cries, some one will be sure to die.

I didn't believe in them myself till one night I was coming home from a wedding, and standing on the road beside me I saw John Kelly's donkey that he always used to call Neddy. So he was standing in my way and I gave a blow at him and said, "Get out of that, Neddy." And he moved off only to come across me again, and to stop me from going in. And so he did all the way, till as I was going by a bit of wood I heard come out of it two of the clearest laughs that ever you heard, and then two sorts of shouts. So I knew that it was having fun with me they were, and that it was not Neddy was there, but his likeness.

I knew a priest was stopped on the road one night by some-thing in the shape of a big dog, and he couldn't make the horse pass it.

One night I saw the dog myself, in the boreen near my house. And that was a bad bit of road, two or three were killed there.

And one night I was between Kiltartan Chapel and Nolan's gate where I had some sheep to look after for the priest. And the dog I had with me ran out into the middle of the road, and there he began to yelp and to fight. I stood and watched him for a while, and surely he was fighting with another dog, but there was nothing to be seen.

And in the same part of the road one night I heard horses galloping, galloping past me. I could hear their hoofs, and they shod, on the stones of the road. But though I stood aside and looked—and it was bright moonlight—there were no horses to be seen. But they were there, and believe me they were not with-out riders.

Well, myself I once slept in a house with some strange thing. I had my aunt then, Mrs. Leary, living near, and I but a small little girl at the time. And one day she came to our house and asked would I go sleep with her, and I said I would if she'd give me a ride on her back, and so she did. And for many a night after that she brought me to sleep with her, and my mother used to be asking why, and she'd give no reason.

Well, the cause of her wanting me was this. Every night so sure as she put the candle out, *it* would come and lie upon her feet and across her body and near smother her, and she could feel it breathing but could see nothing. I never felt anything at all myself, I being sound asleep before she quenched the light. At last she went to Father Smith—God rest his soul!—and he gave her a prayer to say at the moment of the Elevation of the

Mass. So the next time she attended Mass she used it, and that night it was wickeder than ever it had been.

So after that she wrote to her son in America to buy a ticket for her, and she went out to him and remained some years. And it was only after she came back she told me and my mother what used to happen on those nights, and the reason she wanted me to be beside her.

There was never any one saw so many of those things as Johnny Hardiman's father on this estate, and now he's old and got silly, and can't tell about them any more. One time he was walking into Gort along the Kiltartan road, and he saw one of them before him in the form of a tub, and it rolling along.

Another time he was coming home from Kinvara, and a black and white dog came out against him from the wall, but he took no notice of it. But when he got near his own house it came out against him again and bit him in the leg, and he got hold of it and lifted it up and took it by the throat and choked it; and when he was sure it was dead he threw it by the roadside. But in the morning he went out first thing early to look at the body, and there was no sign at all of it there.

So I believe indeed that old Michael Barrett hears them and sees them. But they do him no mischief nor harm at all. They wouldn't, and he such an old resident. But there's many wouldn't believe he sees anything because they never seen them themselves.

I never did but once, when I was a slip of a girl beyond at Lissatiraheely, and one time I went across to the big forth to get a can of water. And when I got near to it I heard voices, and when I came to where the water runs out they were getting louder and louder. And I stopped and looked down, and there in the passage where the water comes I seen a dog within, and there was a great noise—working I suppose they were. And I threw down the can and turned and ran, and never went back for it again. But here since I lived in Coole I never seen anything and never was afeared of anything except one time only in the evening, when I was walking down the little by-lane that leads to Ballinamantane. And there standing in the path before me I seen the very same dog that was in the old forth before. And I believe I leaped the wall to get away into the high-road. And what day was that but the very same day that Sir William—

the Lord be with his soul!—was returned a Member of Parliament, and a great night it was in Kiltartan.

But I'm noways afeared of anything and I give you my word I'd walk in the dead of night in the nut-wood or any other place—except only the cross beyond Inchy, I'd sooner not go by there. There's two or three has their life lost there—Heffernan of Kildesert, one of your ladyship's own tenants, he was one. He was at a fair, and there was a horse another man wanted, but he got inside him and got the horse. And when he was riding home, when he came to that spot it reared back and threw him, and he was taken up dead. And another man—one Gallagher—fell off the top of a creel of turf in the same place and lost his life. And there was a woman hurted some way another time. What's that you're saying, John—that Gallagher had a drop too much taken? That might be so indeed; and what call has a man that has drink taken to go travel upon top of a creel of turf?

That dog I met in the boreen at Ballinamantane, he was the size of a calf, and black, and his paws the size of I don't know what. I was sitting in the house one day, and he came in and sat down by the dresser and looked at me. And I didn't like the look of him when I saw the big eyes of him, and the size of his legs. And just then a man came in that used to make his living by making mats, and he used to lodge with me for a night now and again. And he went out to bring his cart away where he was afraid it'd be knocked about by the people going to the big bonfire at Kiltartan cross-roads. And when he went out I looked out the door, and there was the dog sitting under the cart. So he made a hit at it with a stick, and it was in the stones the stick stuck, and there was the dog sitting at the other side of him. So he came in and gave me abuse and said I must be a strange woman to have such things about me. And he never would come to lodge with me again. But didn't the dog behave well not to do him an injury after he hitting it? It was surely some man that was in that dog, some soul in trouble.

Beasts will sometimes see more than a man will. There were three young chaps I know went up near Ballyturn to hunt coneens (young rabbits) and they threw the dog over the wall. And when he was in the field he gave a yelp and drew back as if something had struck him on the head. And with all they could do, and the rabbits and the coneens running about the field, they couldn't get him to stir from that and they had to come home with no rabbits.

One time I was helping Sully, the butcher in Loughrea, and I had to go to a country house to bring in a measly pig the people had, and that he was to allow them something for. So I got there late and had to stop the night. And in the morning at daylight I looked from the window and saw a cow eating the potatoes, so I went down to drive him off. And in the kitchen there was lying by the hearth a dog, a speckled one, with spots of black and white and yellow. And when he saw me he got up and went over to the door and went out through it. And then I saw that the door was shut and locked. So I went back again and told the people of the house what I saw and they were frightened and made me stop the next night. And in the night the clothes were taken off me and a heavy blow struck me in the chest, and the feel of it was like the feel of ice. So I covered myself up again and put my hand under the bedclothes, and I never came to that house again.

I never seen anything myself, but I remember well that when I was a young chap there was a black dog between Coole gatehouse and Gort for many a year, and many met him there. Tom Miller came running into our house one time when he was after seeing him, and at first sight he thought he was a man, where he was standing with his paws up upon the wall, and then he vanished out of sight. But there never was any common dog the size of him, and it's many a one saw him, and it was Father Boyle that banished him out of it at last.

Except that thing at Inchy Weir, I never saw anything myself. But one evening I parted from Larry Cuniffe in the yard, and he went away through the path in Shanwalla and bid me goodnight. But two hours after, there he was back again in the yard, and bid me light a candle was in the stable. And he told me that when he got into Shanwalla a little chap about as high as his knee, but having a head as big as a man's body, came beside him and led him out of the path and round about, and at last it brought him to the limekiln, and there left him.

There is a dog now at Lismara, black and bigger than a

natural dog, is about the roads at night. He wouldn't be there so long if any one had the courage to question him.

Stephen O'Donnell in Connemara told me that one time he shot a hare, and it turned into a woman, a neighbour of his own. And she had his butter taken for the last two years, but she begged and prayed for life on her knees, so he spared her, and she gave him back his butter after that, a double yield.

There was a woman at Glenlough when I was young could change herself into an eel. It was in Galway Workhouse Hospital she got the knowledge. A woman that had the knowledge of doing it by witchcraft asked her would she like to learn, and she said that she would, for she didn't know what it would bring on her. For every time she did it, she'd be in bed a fortnight after with all she'd go through. Sir Martin O'Neill when he was a young lad heard of it, and he got her into a room, and made her do it for him, and when he saw her change to an eel he got frightened and tried to get away, but she got between him and the door, and showed her teeth at him and growled. She wasn't the better of that for a fortnight after.

Indeed the porter did me great good, a good that I'd hardly like to tell you, not to make a scandal. Did I drink too much of it? Not at all, I have no fancy for it, but the nights seemed to be long. But this long time I am feeling a worm in my side that is as big as an eel, and there's more of them in it than that, and I was told to put sea-grass to it, and I put it to the side the other day, and whether it was that or the porter I don't know, but there's some of them gone out of it, and I think it's the porter.

I knew a woman near Clough was out milking her cow, and when she got up to go away she saw one of those worms coming after her, and it eight feet long, and it made a jump about eight yards after her. And I heard of a man went asleep by a wall one time, and one of them went down his throat and he never could get rid of it till a woman from the North came. And what she bade him do was to get a bit of old crock butter and to make a big fire on the hearth, and to put the butter in a half round on the hearth, and to get two men to hold him over it. And when the worms got the smell of the butter they jumped out of his

287

mouth, seven or eight one after another, and it was in the fire they fell and they were burned, and that was an end of them.

As to hares, there's something queer about them, and there's some that it's dangerous to meddle with, and that can go into any form where they like. Sure, Mrs. Madden is after having a young son, and it has a harelip. But she says that she doesn't remember that ever she met a hare or looked at one. But if she did, she had a right to rip a small bit of the seam of her dress or her petticoat, and then it would have no power to hurt her at all.

Doran the herd says, he wouldn't himself eat the flesh of a hare. There's something unnatural about it. But as to them being unlucky, that may be all talk. But there's no doubt at all that a cow is found sometimes to be run dry, and the hare to be seen coming away from her.

One time when we lived just behind Gort my father was going to a fair. And it was the custom in those days to set out a great deal earlier than what it is now. So it was not much past midnight when he got up and went out the door, and the moon shining bright. And then he saw a hare walk in from the street and turn down by the garden, and another after it, and another and another till he counted twelve. And they all went straight one after another and vanished. And my father came in and shut the door, and never went out again till it was broad daylight.

There was a man watching the fire where two hares were cooking and he heard them whistling in the pot. And when the people of the house came home they were afraid to touch them, but the man that heard the whistling ate a good meal of them and was none the worse.

There was an uncle of my own lived over near Garryland. And one day himself and another man were going through the field, and they saw a hare, and the hound that was with them gave chase, and they followed.

And the hound was gaining on the hare and it made for a house, where the half-door was open. And the hound made a snap at it and touched it as it leaped the half-door. And when my uncle and the others came up, they could find no hare, but only an old woman in the house—and she bleeding. So there's no doubt at all but it was she took the form of a hare. My uncle spent too much money after, and gave up his land and went to America.

As to hares, there was a man out with his greyhound and it gave chase to a hare. And it made for a house, and went in at the window, and the hound just touched the leg. And when the man came up, he found an old woman in the house, and he asked leave to search the house and so he did in every place, but there was no hare to be seen. But when he came in she was putting a pot on the fire, so he said that he must look in the pot, and he took the cover off, and it was full of blood. And before the hound gave chase, he had seen the hare sucking the milk from a cow.

As to hares, there's no doubt at all there's some that's not natural. One night I was making pot-whiskey up in that hill beyond. Yes indeed, for three year, I did little but run to and fro to the still, and one December, I was making it for the Christmas and I was taken and got nine weeks in gaol for it—and £16 worth of whiskey spilled that night. But there's mean people in the world; and he did it for half a sovereign, and had to leave the country after and go to England. Well, one night, I was watching by the fire where it was too fierce, and it would have burned the oats. And over the hill and down the path came two hares and walked on and into the wood. And two more after that, and then by fours they came, and by sixes, and I'd want a slate and a pencil to count all I saw, and it just at sunrise. And some of them were as thin as thin. And there's no doubt at all that those were not *hares* I saw that night.

As to hares, they're the biggest fairies of all. Last year the boys had one caught, and I put it in the pot to wash it and it after being skinned, and I heard a noise come from the pot—grr-grr—and nothing but cold water in it. And I ran to save my life, and I told the boys to have nothing to do with it, but they wouldn't mind me. And when they tried to eat it, and it boiled, they couldn't get their teeth into the flesh of it, and as for the soup, it was no different from potato-water.

The village of Lissavohalane has a great name for such things. And it's certain that once one night every year, in the month of

November, all the cats of the whole country round gather together there and fight. My own two cats were nearly dead for days after it last year, and the neighbours told me the same of theirs.

There was a woman had a cat and she would feed it at the table before any other one; and if it did not get the first meat that was cooked, the hair would rise up as high as that. Well, there were priests came to dinner one day, and when they were helped the first, the hair rose up on the cat's back. And one of them said to the woman it was a queer thing to give in to a cat the way she did, and that it was a foolish thing to be giving it the first of the food. So when it heard that, it walked out of the house, and never came into it again.

There's something not right about cats. Steve Smith says he knew a keeper that shot one, and it went into a sort of a heap, and when he came near, it spoke, and he found it was some person, and it said it had to walk its seven acres. And there's some have heard them together at night talking Irish.

There was a hole over the door of the house that I used to live in, where Murphy's house is now, to let the smoke out, for there was no chimney. And one day a black cat jumped in at the hole, and stopped in the house and never left us for a year. But on the day year he came he jumped out again at the same hole and didn't go out of the door that was standing open. There was no mistake about it, it was the day year.

As to cats, they're a class in themselves. They're good to catch mice and rats, but just let them come in and out of the house for that; they're about their own business all the time. And in the old times they could talk. And it's said that the cats gave a shilling for what they have; fourpence that the housekeeper might be careless and leave the milk about that they'd get at it; and fourpence that they'd tread so light that no one would hear them, and fourpence that they'd be able to see in the dark. And I might as well throw out that drop of tea I left on the dresser to cool, for the cat is after that. There might be a hair in it, and the hair of a cat is poison.

There was a man had a house full of children, and one day he was taking their measure for boots. And the cat that was sitting on the hearth said, "Take my measure for a pair of boots along with the rest." So the man did, and when he went to the shoe-maker he told him of what the cat had said. And there was a man in the shop at the time, and he having two greyhounds with him, and one of them all black without a single white hair. And he said, "Bring the cat here tomorrow. You can tell it that the boots can't be made without it coming for its measure." So the next day he brought the cat in a bag, and when he got to his shop the man was there with his greyhounds, and he let the cat out, and it praying him not to loosen the bag. And it made away through the fields and the hounds after it, and whether it killed one of them I don't know, but anyhow the black hound killed it, the one that had not a white hair on its body.

You should never be too attentive to a cat, but just to be civil and to give it its share.

Cats were serpents, and they were made into cats at the time, I suppose, of some change in the world. That's why they're hard to kill and why it's dangerous to meddle with them. If you annoy a cat it might claw you or bite you in a way that would put poison in you, and that would be the serpent's tooth.

There was an uncle of mine near Galway, and one night his wife was very sick, and he had to go to the village to get some-thing for her. And it's a very lonely road, and as he was going what should he see but a great number of cats, walking along the road, and they were carrying a young cat, and crying it.

And when he was on his way home again from the village he met them again, and one of the cats turned and spoke to him like a person would, and said, "Bid Lady Betty to come to the funeral or she'll be late." So he ran on home in a great fright, and he couldn't speak for some time after getting back to the house, but sat there by the fire in a chair. And at last he began to tell his wife what had happened. And when he said that he had met a cat's funeral, his own cat that was sleeping by the hearth began to stir her tail, and looked up at him, affectionate like. But when he got to where he was bid send Lady Betty to the funeral, she made one dash at his face and scraped it, she was so mad that she wasn't told at once. And then she began to tear at the door, that they had to let her out.

For cats is faeries, and every night they're obliged to travel over seven acres; that's why you hear them crying about the country. It was an old woman at the strand told me that, and she should know, for she lived to a hundred years of age.

I saw three young weasels out in the sea, squealing, squealing, for they couldn't get to land, and I put out a bunch of seaweed and brought them to the land, and they went away after. I did that for them. Weasels are not *right*, no more than cats; and I'm not sure about foxes.

Rats are very bad, because a rat if one got the chance would do his best to bite you, and I wouldn't like at all to get the bite of a rat. But weasels are serpents, and if they would spit at any part of your body it would fester, and you would get blood poisoning within two hours.

I knew an old doctor—Antony Coppinger at Clifden—and he told me that if the weasels had the power of other beasts they would not have a human living in the world. And he said the wild wide wilderness of the sea was full of beasts mostly the same as on earth, like bonavs and like cattle, and they lying at the bottom of the sea as quiet as cows in a field.

It is wrong to insult a weasel, and if you pelt them or shoot them they will watch for you forever to ruin you. For they are enchanted and understand all things.

There is Mrs. Coneely that lives up the road, she had a clutch of young geese on the floor, and a weasel walked in and brought away one of them, but she said nothing to that.

But it came in again, and took a hold of another of the geese and Mrs. Coneely said, "Oh, I'm not begrudging you what you have taken, but leave these to me for it is hard I earned them, and it is great trouble I had rearing them. But go," she said, "to the shoemaker's home beyond, where they have a clutch, and let you spare mine. And that I may never sin," she said, "but it walked out, for they can understand everything, and it did not leave one of the clutch that was at the shoemaker's."

It is why I called to you now when I saw you sitting there so near to the sea; I thought the tide might steal up on you, or a weasel might chance to come up with a fish in its mouth, and to give you a start. It's best if you see one to speak nice to it, and to say, "I wouldn't be begrudging you a pair of boots or of shoes if I had them." If you treat them well they will treat you well.

And to see a weasel passing the road before you, there's nothing in the world like that to bring you all sorts of good luck.

I was out in the field one time tilling potatoes, and two or three more along with me, and a weasel put its head out of the wall—a double stone wall it was—and one of the lads fired a stone at it. Well, within a minute there wasn't a hole of the wall but a weasel had put its head out of it, about a thousand of them, I saw that myself. Very spiteful they are. I wouldn't like them.

The weasels, the poor creatures, they will do nothing at all on you if you behave well to them and let them alone, but if you do not, they will not leave a chicken in the yard. And magpies, let you do nothing on them, or they will suck every egg and leave nothing in the garden; but if you leave them to themselves they will do nothing but to come into the street to pick a bit with the birds.

The granyóg (hedgehog) will do no harm to chickens or the like; but if he will get into an orchard he will stick an apple on every thorn, and away with him to a scalp with them to be eating through the winter.

I met with a granyóg one day on the mountain, and that I may never sin, he was running up the side of it as fast as a race-horse.

There is not much luck in killing a seal. There was a man in these parts was very fond of shooting and killing them. And seals have claws the same as cats, and he had two daughters, and when they were born, they had claws the same as seals. I believe there is one of them living yet.

But the thing it is not right to touch is the *ron* (seal) for they are in the Sheogue. It is often I see them on the strand, sitting there and wiping themselves on the rocks. And they have a hand with five fingers, like any Christian. I seen six of them, coming in a boat one time with a man from Connemara, that is the time I saw they had the five fingers.

There was a man killed one of them over there near the point. And he came to the shore and it was night, and he was near dead with the want of a blast of a pipe, and he saw a light from a house on the side of a mountain, and he went in to ask a coal of fire to kindle the pipe. And when he went in, there was a woman, and she called out to a man that was lying stretched on the bed in the room, and she said, "Look till you see who this man is." And the man that was on the bed says, "I know you, for I have the sign of your hand on me. And let you get out of this now," he said, "as fast as you can, and it will be best for you." And the daughter said to him, "I wonder you to let him go as easy as that." And you may be sure that man made off and made no delay. It was a Sheogue house that was; and the man on the bed was the *ron* he had killed, but he was not dead, being of the Sheogues.

XVII

FRIARS AND PRIEST CURES

AN old woman begging at the door one day spoke of the cures done in her early days by the Friars at Esker to the north of our county. I asked if she had ever been there, and she burst into this praise of it:

"*Esker is a grand place; this house and the house of Lough Cutra and your own house at Roxborough, to put the three together it wouldn't be as big as it; it is as big as the whole town of Gort, in its own way; you wouldn't have it walked in a month.*

"*To go there you would get cured of anything unless it might be the stroke of the Fool that does be going with* them; *it's best not be talking of it. The clout he would give you, there is no cure for it.*

"*Three barrels there are with water, and to see the first barrel boiling it is certain you will get a cure. A big friar will come out to meet us that is as big as three. Fat they do be that they can't hardly get through the door. Water there does be rushing down; you to stoop you would hear it talking; you would be afraid of the water.*

"*One well for the rich and one well for the common; blue blinds to the windows like little bars of timber without. You can see where the friars are buried down dead to the end of the world.*

"*They give out clothes to the poor, bedclothes and day clothes; it is the beautifullest place from heaven out; summer houses and pears; glass in the walls around.*"

I have been told:

The Esker friars used to do great cures—Father Callaghan was the best of them. They used to do it by reading, but what it was they read no one knew, some secret thing.

There was a girl brought from Clare one time, that had lost her wits, and she tied on a cart with ropes. And she was brought to Father Callaghan and he began reading over her, and then he made a second reading, and at the end of that, he bid them unloose the ropes, and when they did she got up quite quiet, but very shy looking and ashamed, and would not wait for the cart but walked away.

Father Callaghan was with a man near this one time, one Tully, and they were talking about the faeries and the man said he didn't believe in them at all. And Father Callaghan called him to the door and put up his fingers and bade him look out through them, and there he saw hundreds and hundreds of the smallest little men he ever saw and they hurling and killing one another.

The friars are gone and there are missioners come in their place and all they would do for you is to bless holy water, and as long as you would keep it, it would never get bad.

My daughter, Mrs. Meehan, that lives there below, was very bad after her first baby being born, and she wasted away and the doctors could do nothing for her. My husband went to Biddy Early for her, but she said, "Mother for daughter, father for son" and she could do nothing for her because I didn't go. But I had promised God and the priest I would never go to her, and so I kept to my word. But Mrs. Meehan was so bad she kept to the bed, and one day one of the neighbours said I had a right to bring her to the friars at Esker. And he said, "It's today you should be in it, Monday, for a Monday gospel is the best, the gospel of the Holy Ghost." So I got the cart after and put her in it, and she lying down, and we had to rest and to take out the horse at Lenane, and we got to Craughwell for the night. And the man of the house where we got lodging for the night said the priest that was doing cures now was Father Blake and he showed us the way to Esker. And when we got there he was in the chapel, and my daughter was brought in and laid on a form, and I went out and waited with the cart, and within half an hour the chapel door opened, and my daughter walked out that was carried in. And she got up on the cart herself. It was a gospel had been read over her. And I said, "I wish you had asked a gospel to bring with you home." And after that we saw a priest on the other side of a dry stone wall, and he learning three children. And she asked a gospel of him, and he said, "What you had today will do you, and I haven't one made up at this time." So she came home well. She went another time there, when she had something and asked for a gospel, and Father Blake said, "We're out of doing it now, but as you were with us before, I'll do it for you." And she wanted to give him £1 but he said, "If I took it I would do nothing for you." So she said, "I'll give it to the other man," and so she did.

I often saw Father Callaghan in Esker and the people brought to him in carts. Many cures he did, but he was prevented often. And I knew another priest did many cures, but he was carried away himself after, to a lunatic asylum. And when he came back, he would do no more.

There was a little chap had but seven years, and he was doing no good, but whistling and twirling, and the father went to Father Callaghan, that was just after coming out of the gaol when he got there, for doing cures; it is a gaol of their own they had. The man asked him to do a cure on his son, and Father Callaghan said, "I wouldn't like him to be brought here, but I will go some day to your house; I will go with my dog and my hound as if fowling, and I will bring no sign of a car or a carriage at all." So he came one day to the house and knocked at the door. And when he came in he said to the father, "Go out and bring me in a bundle of sally rods that will be as thin as rushes, and divide them into six small parts," he said, "and twist every one of the six parts together." And when that was done, he took the little bundle of rods, and he beat the child on the head with them one after another till they were in flitters and the child roaring. Then he laid the child in the father's arms, and no sooner there than it fell asleep, and Father Callaghan said to the father, "What you have now is your own, but it wasn't your own that was in it before."

There used to be swarms of people going to Esker, and Father Callaghan would say in Irish. "Let the people in the Sheogue stand at one side," and he would go over and read over them what he had to read.

There was an uncle of my own was working at Ballycluan the time the Quakers were making a place there, and it was the habit when the summer was hot to put the beds out into the barn. And one night he was sleeping in the barn, and something came and lay on him in the bed; he could not see what it was, but it was about the size of the foal of a horse. And the next night it came again and the next, and lay on him, and he put out his left hand to push it from him, and it went from him quite quiet, but if it did, when he rose in the morning, he was not able to stretch out his hand, and he was a long time like that and then his father brought him to the friars at Esker, and within twelve minutes one of them had him cured, reading over him, but I'm not sure was it Father Blake or Father Callaghan.

But it was not long after that till he fell off his cart as if he was knocked off it, and broke his leg. The coppinger had his leg cured, but he did not live long, for the third thing happened was, he threw up his heart's blood and died.

For if you are cured of one thing that comes on you like that, another thing will come on you in its place, or if not on you, on some other person, maybe some one in your own family. It is very often I noticed that to happen.

The priests in old times used to have the power to cure strokes and madness and the like, but the Pope and the Bishops have that stopped; they said that the people will get out of witchcraft little by little.

Priests can do cures if they will, and it's not out of the Gospel they do them, but out of a book specially for the purpose, so I believe. But something falls on them or on the things belonging to them, if they do it too often.

But Father Keeley for certain did cures. It was he cured Mike Madden's neck, when everyone else had failed—so they had—though Mike has never confessed to it.

The priests can do cures surely, and surely they can put harm on you. But they wouldn't do that unless they'd be sure a man would deserve it. One time at that house you see up there beyond, Roche's, there was a wedding and there was some fighting came out of it, and bad blood. And Father Boyle was priest at that time, and he was vexed and he said he'd come and have stations at the house, and they should all be reconciled.

So he came on the day he appointed and the house was settled like a chapel and some of the poeple there was bad blood between came, but not all of them, and Roche himself was not there. And when the stations were over Father Boyle got his book, and he read the names of those he had told to be there, and they answered, like a schoolmaster would call out the names of his scholars. And when Roche's name was read and he not there to answer, with the dint of madness Father Boyle quenched the candles on the altar, and he said this house and all that belong to it will go away to nothing, like the froth that's going down the river.

And if you look at the house now you'll see the way it is, not a stable or an outhouse left standing, and not one of the whole family left in it but Roche, and he paralysed. So they can do both harm and good.

There was a man out in the mountains used to do cures, and one day on a little road the priest met him, and stopped his car and began to abuse him for the cures he was doing.

And then the priest went on, and when he had gone a bit of the road his horse fell down. And he came back and called to the man and said, "Come help me now, for this is your doing, to make the horse fall." And the man said, "It's none of my doing, but it's the doing of my master, for he was vexed with the way you spoke. But go back now and you'll find the horse as he was before." So he went back and the horse had got up and was standing, and nothing wrong with him at all. And the priest said no more against him from that day.

My son is lame this long time; a fine young man he was, about seventeen years—and a pain came in his knee all of a moment. I tried doctors with him and I brought him to the friars in Loughrea, and one of them read a gospel over him, and the pain went after that, but the knee grew out to be twisted like. The friar said it was surely he had been overheated. A little old maneen he was, very ancient. I knew well it was the *drochuil* that did it; there by the side of the road he was sitting when he got the frost.

There was a needlewoman used to be sewing late on a Saturday night, and sometimes if there was a button or a thread wanting she would put it in, even if it was Sunday morning; and she lived in Loughrea that is near your own home. And one day she went to the loch to get a can of water, and it was in her hand. And in a minute a blast of wind came that rose all the dust and the straws and knocked herself. And more than that, her mouth was twisted around to her poll.

There were some people saw her, and they brought her home, and within a week her mother brought her to the priest. And when he saw her he said, "You are the best mother ever there was, for if you had left her nine days without bringing her to me, all I could do would not have taken off her what is on her." He asked then up to what time did she work on the Saturday night, and she said up to one or two o'clock, and sometimes on a Sunday morning. So he took off what was on her, and bade her do that no more, and she got well, but to the last there was a sort of a twisted turn in her mouth.

That woman now I am telling you of was an aunt of my own.

Father Nolan has a kind heart, and he'd do cures. But it's hard to get them, unless it would be for some they had a great interest in. But Father McConaghy is so high in himself, he wouldn't do anything of that sort. When Johnny Dunne was bad, two years ago, and all but given over, he begged and prayed Father McConaghy to do it for him. And he refused and said, "You must commit yourself to the mercy of Almighty God," and Johnny Dunne, the poor man, said, "It's a hard thing for a man that has a house full of children to be left to the mercy of Almighty God."

But there's *some* that can help. My father told me long ago that my sister was lying sick for a long time, and one night a beggarman came to the door and asked for shelter. And he said, "I can't give you shelter, with my daughter lying sick in the room." "Let me in, it's best for you," says he. And in the morning he went away, and the sick girl rose up, as well as ever she was before.

Father Flaherty, when he was a curate, could open the eyes that were all but closed in death, but he wouldn't have such things spoken of now. Losses they may have, but that's not all. Whatever evil thing they raise, they may not have strength after to put it down again, and so they may be lost themselves in the end.

Surely they can do cures, and they can tell sometimes the hour you'd go. There was a girl I knew was sick, and when the priest came and saw her, he said, "Between the two Masses tomorrow she'll be gone," and so she was. And those that saw her after, said that it was the face of her mother that died before that was on the bed, and that it was her mother had taken her to where she was.

And Mike Barrett surely saw a man brought in a cart to Father Curley's house when he lived in Cloon, and carried upstairs to him, and he walked down out of the house again, sound and well. But they must lose something when they do cures—either their health or something else, though many say no one did so many cures as Father Fitzgerald when he was a curate. Father Airlie one time was called in to Glover's house where he was lying sick, and did a cure on him. And he had a cow at the time that was in calf. And soon after some man said to him "The cow will be apt soon to calve," though it wasn't very near the time. And Father Airlie said "She'll never live to do that." And sure enough in a couple of days after she was dead.

WITCHES AND WIZARDS AND IRISH
FOLK-LORE

I

IRELAND was not separated from general European speculation when much of that was concerned with the supernatural. Dr. Adam Clarke tells in his unfinished autobiography how, when he was at school in Antrim towards the end of the eighteenth century, a schoolfellow told him of Cornelius Agrippa's book on Magic and that it had to be chained or it would fly away of itself. Presently he heard of a farmer who had a copy and after that made friends with a wandering tinker who had another. Lady Gregory and I spoke of a friend's visions to an old countryman. He said "he must belong to a society"; and the people often attribute magical powers to Orangemen and to Freemasons, and I have heard a shepherd at Doneraile speak of a magic wand with Tetragramaton Agla written upon it. The visions and speculations of Ireland differ much from those of England and France, for in Ireland, as in Highland Scotland, we are never far from the old Celtic mythology; but there is more likeness than difference. Lady Gregory's story of the witch who in semblance of a hare, leads the hounds such a dance, is the best remembered of all witch stories. It is told, I should imagine, in every countryside where there is even a fading memory of witchcraft. One finds it in a sworn testimony given at the trial of Julian Cox, an old woman indicted for witchcraft at Taunton in Somersetshire in 1663 and quoted by Joseph Glanvill. "The first witness was a huntsman, who swore that he went out with a pack of hounds to hunt a hare, and not far from Julian Cox her house he at last started a hare: the dogs hunted her very close, and the third ring hunted her in view, till at last the huntsman perceiving the hare almost spent and making towards a great bush, he ran on the other side of the bush to take her up and preserve her from the dogs; but as soon as he laid hands on her, it proved to be Julian Cox, who had her head grovelling on the ground, and her globes (as he expressed it) upward. He knowing her, was so affrighted that his hair on his head stood on end; and yet spake to her, and ask'd her what brought her there; but she was so far out of breath that she could not make him any answer; his dogs also came up full cry

302

to recover the game, and smelled at her and so left off hunting any further. And the huntsman with his dogs went home presently sadly affrighted." Dr. Henry More, the Platonist, who considers the story in a letter to Glanvill, explains that Julian Cox was not turned into a hare, but that "Ludicrous Daemons exhibited to the sight of this huntsman and his dogs, the shape of a hare, one of them turning himself into such a form, another hurrying on the body of Julian near the same place," making her invisible till the right moment had come. "As I have heard of some painters that have drawn the sky in a huge landscape, so lively, that the birds have flown against it, thinking it free air, and so have fallen down. And if painters and jugglers, by the tricks of legerdemain can do such strange feats to the deceiving of the sight, it is no wonder that these aerie invisible spirits have far surpassed them in all such prestigious doings, as the air surpasses the earth for subtlety." Glanvill has given his own explanation of such cases elsewhere. He thinks that the sidereal or airy body is the foundation of the marvel, and Albert de Rochas has found a like foundation for the marvels of spiritism. "The transformation of witches," writes Glanvill, "into the shapes of other animals ... is very conceivable; since then, 'tis easy enough to imagine, that the power of imagination may form those passive and pliable vehicles into those shapes," and then goes on to account for the stories where an injury, say to the witch hare, is found afterwards upon the witch's body precisely as a French hypnotist would account for the stigmata of a saint. "When they feel the hurts in their gross bodies, that they receive in their airy vehicles, they must be supposed to have been really present, at least in these latter; and 'tis no more difficult to apprehend, how the hurts of those should be translated upon their other bodies, than how diseases should be inflicted by the imagination, or how the fancy of the mother should wound the foetus, as several credible relations do attest."

All magical or Platonic writers of the times speak much of the transformation or projection of the sidereal body of witch or wizard. Once the soul escapes from the natural body, though but for a moment, it passes into the body of air and can transform itself as it please or even dream itself into some shape it has not willed.

"Chameleon-like thus they their colour change,
And size contract and then dilate again."

One of their favourite stories is of some famous man, John Haydon says Socrates, falling asleep among his friends, who presently see a mouse running from his mouth and towards a little stream. Somebody lays a sword across the stream that it may pass, and after a little while it returns across the sword and to the sleeper's mouth again. When he awakes he tells them that he has dreamed of himself crossing a wide river by a great iron bridge.

But the witch's wandering and disguised double was not the worst shape one might meet in the fields or roads about a witch's house. She was not a true witch unless there was a compact (or so it seems) between her and an evil spirit who called himself the devil, though Bodin believes that he was often, and Glanvill always, "some human soul forsaken of God," for "the devil is a body politic." The ghost or devil promised revenge on her enemies and that she would never want, and she upon her side let the devil suck her blood nightly or at need.

When Elizabeth Style made a confession of witchcraft before the Justice of Somerset in 1664, the Justice appointed three men, William Thick and William Read and Nicholas Lambert, to watch her, and Glanvill publishes an affidavit of the evidence of Nicholas Lambert. "About three of the clock in the morning there came from her head a glistering bright fly, about an inch in length which pitched at first in the chimney and then vanished." Then two smaller flies came and vanished. "He, looking steadfastly then on Style, perceived her countenance to change, and to become very black and ghastly and the fire also at the same time changing its colour; whereupon the Examinant, Thick and Read, conceiving that her familiar was then about her, looked to her poll, and seeing her hair shake very strangely, took it up and then a fly like a great miller flew out from the place and pitched on the table board and then vanished away. Upon this the Examinant and the other two persons, looking again in Style's poll, found it very red and like raw beef. The Examinant ask'd her what it was that went out of her poll, she said it was a butterfly, and asked them why they had not caught it. Lambert said, they could not. I think so too, answered she. A little while after, the informant and the others, looking again into her poll, found the place to be of its former colour. The Examinant asked again what the fly was, she confessed it was her familiar and that she felt it tickle in her poll, and that was the usual time for her familiar to come to her." These sucking devils alike when at

304

their meal, or when they went here and there to do her will or about their own business, had the shapes of pole-cat or cat or greyhound or of some moth or bird. At the trials of certain witches in Essex in 1645 reported in the English state trials a principal witness was one "Matthew Hopkins, gent." Bishop Hutchinson, writing in 1730, describes him as he appeared to those who laughed at witchcraft and had brought the witch trials to an end. "Hopkins went on searching and swimming poor creatures, till some gentlemen, out of indignation of the barbarity, took him, and tied his own thumbs and toes as he used to tie others, and when he was put into the water he himself swam as they did. That cleared the country of him and it was a great pity that they did not think of the experiment sooner." Floating when thrown into the water was taken for a sign of witchcraft. Matthew Hopkins's testimony, however, is uncommonly like that of the countryman who told Lady Gregory that he had seen his dog and some shadow fighting. A certain Mrs. Edwards of Manintree in Essex had her hogs killed by witchcraft, and "going from the house of the said Mrs. Edwards to his own house, about nine or ten of the clock that night, with his greyhound with him, he saw the greyhound suddenly give a jump, and run as she had been in full course after a hare; and that when this informant made haste to see what his greyhound so eagerly pursued, he espied a white thing, about the bigness of a kitlyn, and the greyhound standing aloof from it; and that by and by the said white imp or kitlyn danced about the greyhound, and by all likelihood bit off a piece of the flesh of the shoulder of the said greyhound; for the greyhound came shrieking and crying to the informant, with a piece of flesh torn from her shoulder. And the informant further saith, that coming into his own yard that night, he espied a black thing proportioned like a cat, only it was thrice as big, sitting on a strawberry bed, and fixing the eyes on this informant, and when he went towards it, it leaped over the pale towards this informant, as he thought, but ran through the yard, with his greyhound after it, to a great gate, which was underset with a pair of tumble strings, and did throw the said gate wide open, and then vanished; and the said greyhound returned again to this informant, shaking and trembling exceedingly." At the same trial Sir Thomas Bowes, Knight, affirmed "that a very honest man of Manintree, whom he knew would not speak an untruth, affirmed unto him, that very early one morning, as he passed by the said Anne

West's door" (this is the witch on trial) "about four o'clock, it being a moonlight night, and perceiving her door to be open so early in the morning, looked into the house and presently there came three or four little things, in the shape of black rabbits, leaping and skipping about him, who, having a good stick in his hand, struck at them, thinking to kill them, but could not; but at last caught one of them in his hand, and holding it by the body of it, he beat the head of it against his stick, intending to beat out the brains of it; but when he could not kill it that way, he took the body of it in one hand and the head of it in another, and endeavoured to wring off the head; and as he wrung and stretched the neck of it, it came out between his hands like a lock of wool; yet he would not give over his intended purpose, but knowing of a spring not far off, he went to drown it; but still as he went he fell down and could not go, but down he fell again, so that he at last crept upon his hands and knees till he came at the water, and holding it fast in his hand, he put his hand down into the water up to the elbow, and held it under water a good space till he conceived it was drowned, and then letting go his hand, it sprung out of the water up into the air, and so vanished away." However, the sucking imps were not always invulnerable for Glanvill tells how one John Monpesson, whose house was haunted by such a familiar, "seeing some wood move that was in the chimney of a room, where he was, as if of itself, discharged a pistol into it after which they found several drops of blood on the hearth and in divers places of the stairs." I remember the old Aran man who heard fighting in the air and found blood in a fish-box and scattered through the room, and I remember the measure of blood Odysseus poured out for the shades.

The English witch trials are like the popular poetry of England, matter-of-fact and unimaginative. The witch desires to kill some one and when she takes the devil for her husband he as likely as not will seem dull and domestic. Rebecca West told Matthew Hopkins that the devil appeared to her as she was going to bed and told her he would marry her. He kissed her but was as cold as clay, and he promised to be "her loving husband till death," although she had, as it seems, but one leg. But the Scotch trials are as wild and passionate as is the Scottish poetry, and we find ourselves in the presence of a mythology that differs little, if at all, from that of Ireland. There are orgies of lust and of hatred and there is a wild shamelessness that

would be fine material for poets and romance writers if the world should come once more to half-believe the tale. They are divided into troops of thirteen, with the youngest witch for leader in every troop, and though they complain that the embraces of the devil are as cold as ice, the young witches prefer him to their husbands. He gives them money, but they must spend it quickly, for it will be but dry cow dung in two circles of the clock. They go often to Elfhame or Faeryland and the mountains open before them and as they go out and in they are terrified by the "rowtling and skoylling" of the great "elf bulls." They sometimes confess to trooping in the shape of cats and to finding upon their terrestrial bodies when they awake in the morning the scratches they had made upon one another in the night's wandering, or should they have wandered in the images of hares the bites of dogs. Isobell Godie who was tried at Lochlay in 1662 confessed that "We put besoms in our beds with our husbands till we return again to them . . . and then we would fly away where we would be, even as straws would fly upon a highway. We will fly like straws when we please; wild straws and corn straws will be horses to us, and we put them betwixt our feet and say horse and hillock in the devil's name. And when any see these straws in a whirlwind and do not sanctify themselves, we may shoot them dead at our pleasure."†
When they kill people, she goes on to say, the souls escape them "but their bodies remain with us and will fly as horses to us all as small as straws." It is plain that it is the "airy body" they take possession of; those "animal spirits" perhaps which Henry More thought to be the link between soul and body and the seat of all vital function. The trials were more unjust than those of England, where there was a continual criticism from sceptics; torture was used again and again to distort confessions, and innocent people certainly suffered; some who had but believed too much in their own dreams and some who had but cured the sick at some vision's prompting. Alison Pearson who was burnt in 1588 might have been Biddy Early or any other knowledge-able woman in Ireland today. She was convicted "for haunting and repairing with the Good Neighbours and queen of Elfhame, these divers years and bypast, as she had confessed in her depositions, declaring that she could not say readily how long she was with them; and that she had friends in that court who

---

† I have modernized the old lowland Scotch in these quotations from *Pitcairn's Criminal Trials*.

were of her own blood and who had great acquaintance of the queen of Elfhame. That when she went to bed she never knew where she would be carried before dawn." When they worked cures they had the same doctrine of the penalty that one finds in Lady Gregory's stories. One who made her confession before James I. was convicted for "taking the sick party's pains and sicknesses upon herself for a time and then translating them to a third person."

II

There are more women than men mediums today; and there have been or seem to have been more witches than wizards. The wizards of the sixteenth and seventeenth centuries relied more upon their conjuring book than the witches whose visions and experiences seem but half voluntary, and when voluntary called up by some childish rhyme:

> Hare, hare, God send thee care;
> I am in a hare's likeness now,
> But I shall be a woman even now;
> Hare, hare, God send thee care.

More often than not the wizards were learned men, alchemists or mystics, and if they dealt with the devil at times, or some spirit they called by that name, they had amongst them ascetics and heretical saints. Our chemistry, our metallurgy, and our medicine are often but accidents that befell in their pursuit of the philosopher's stone, the elixir of life. They were bound together in secret societies and had, it may be, some forgotten practice for liberating the soul from the body and sending it to fetch and carry them divine knowledge. Cornelius Agrippa, in a letter quoted by Beaumont, has hints of such a practice. Yet, like the witches, they worked many wonders by the power of the imagination, perhaps one should say by their power of calling up vivid pictures in the mind's eye. The Arabian philosophers have taught, writes Beaumont, "that the soul by the power of the imagination can perform what it pleases; as penetrate the heavens, force the elements, demolish mountains, raise valleys to mountains, and do with all material forms as it pleases."

He shewed hym, er he wente to sopeer,
Forestes, parkes ful of wilde deer;
Ther saugh he hertes with hir hornes hye,
The gretteste that evere were seyn with ye.

    .   .   .   .   .   .

Tho saugh he knyghtes justing in a playn;
And after this, he dide hym swich plaisaunce,
That he hym shewed his lady on a daunce
On which hymself he daunced, as hym thoughte.
And whan this maister, that this magyk wroughte,
Saugh it was tyme, he clapte his handes two,
And, farewel! al our revel was ago.

One has not as careful a record as one has of the works of witches, for but few English wizards came before the court, the only society for psychical research in those days. The translation, however, of Cornelius Agrippa's *De Occulta Philosophia* in the seventeenth century, with the addition of a spurious fourth book full of conjurations, seems to have filled England and Ireland with whole or half wizards. In 1703, the Reverend Arthur Bedford of Bristol, who is quoted by Sibley in his big book on astrology, wrote to the Bishop of Gloucester telling how a certain Thomas Perks had been to consult him. Thomas Perks lived with his father, a gunsmith, and devoted his leisure to mathematics, astronomy, and the discovery of perpetual motion. One day he asked the clergyman if it was wrong to commune with spirits, and said that he himself held that "there was an innocent society with them which a man might use, if he made no compacts with them, did no harm by their means, and were not curious in prying into hidden things, and he himself had discoursed with them and heard them sing to his great satisfaction." He then told how it was his custom to go to a crossway with lantern and candle consecrated for the purpose, according to the directions in a book he had, and having also consecrated chalk for making a circle. The spirits appeared to him "in the likeness of little maidens about a foot and a half high ... they spoke with a very shrill voice like an ancient woman" and when he begged them to sing, "they went to some distance behind a bush from whence he could hear a perfect concert of such exquisite music as he never before heard; and in the upper part he heard something very harsh and shrill like a reed but as it was managed did give a particular grace to the rest." The Reverend Arthur Bedford refused an introduction to the spirits for himself and a friend and warned him very solemnly. Having some doubt of his sanity, he set him a difficult mathematical problem, but finding that he worked it easily, concluded him sane. A quarter of a year later, the young man came again, but showed by his face and his eyes that he was very ill and lamented that he had not followed the clergyman's advice for his conjurations would bring him to his death. He had decided to get a familiar and had read in his magical book what he should do. He was to make a book of virgin parchment, consecrate it, and bring it to the cross-road, and having called up his spirits, ask the first of them for its name and write that name on the first page of the book and then question another and write that name on the second page and so on till he had enough familiars. He had got the first name easily enough and it was in Hebrew, but after that they came in fearful shapes, lions and bears and the like, or hurled at him balls of fire. He had to stay there among those terrifying visions till the dawn broke and would not be the better of it till he died. I have read in some eighteenth-century book whose name I cannot recall of two men who made a magic circle and who invoked the spirits of the moon and saw them trampling about the circle as great bulls, or rolling about it as flocks of wool. One of Lady Gregory's story-tellers considered a flock of wool one of the worst shapes that a spirit could take.

There must have been many like experimenters in Ireland. An Irish alchemist called Butler was supposed to have made successful transmutations in London early in the eighteenth century, and in the *Life of Dr. Adam Clarke,* published in 1833, are several letters from a Dublin maker of stained glass describing a transmutation and a conjuration into a tumbler of water of large lizards. The alchemist was an unknown man who had called to see him and claimed to do all by the help of the devil "who was the friend of all ingenious gentlemen."

1914   W. B. Y.

SWEDENBORG, MEDIUMS, AND THE DESOLATE PLACES

I

SOME fifteen years ago I was in bad health and could not work, and Lady Gregory brought me from cottage to cottage while she began to collect the stories in this book, and presently when I was at work again she went on with her collection alone till it grew to be, so far as I know, the most considerable book of its kind. Except that I had heard some story of "The Battle of the Friends" at Aran and had divined that it might be the legendary common accompaniment of death, she was not guided by any theory of mine, but recorded what came, writing it out at each day's end and in the country dialect. It was at this time mainly she got the knowledge of words that makes her little comedies of country life so beautiful and so amusing. As that ancient system of belief unfolded before us, with unforeseen probabilities and plausibilities, it was as though we had begun to live in a dream, and one day Lady Gregory said to me when we had passed an old man in the wood: "That old man may know the secret of the ages."

I had noticed many analogies in modern spiritism and began a more careful comparison, going a good deal to séances for the first time and reading all writers of any reputation I could find in English or French. I found much that was moving, when I had climbed to the top story of some house in Soho or Holloway, and, having paid my shilling, awaited, among servant girls, the wisdom of some fat old medium. That is an absorbing drama, though if my readers begin to seek it they will spoil it, for its gravity and simplicity depends on all, or all but all, believing that their dead are near.

I did not go there for evidence of the kind the Society for Psychical Research would value, any more than I would seek it in Galway or in Aran. I was comparing one form of belief with another, and like Paracelsus, who claimed to have collected his knowledge from midwife and hangman, I was discovering a philosophy. Certain things had happened to me when alone in my own room which had convinced me that there are spiritual intelligences which can warn us and advise us, and, as Anatole

France has said, if one believes that the Devil can walk the streets of Lisbon, it is not difficult to believe that he can reach his arm over the river and light Don Juan's cigarette. And yet I do not think I have been easily convinced, for I know we make a false beauty by a denial of ugliness and that if we deny the causes of doubt we make a false faith, and that we must excite the whole being into activity if we would offer to God what is, it may be, the one thing germane to the matter, a consenting of all our faculties. Not but that I doubt at times, with the animal doubt of the Middle Ages that I have found even in pious countrywomen when they have seen some life come to an end like the stopping of a clock, or that all the perceptions of the soul, or the weightiest intellectual deductions, are not at whiles but a feather in the daily show.

I pieced together stray thoughts written out after questioning the familiar of a trance medium or automatic writer, by Allen Cardec, or by some American, or by myself, or arranged the fragments into some pattern, till I believed myself the discoverer of a vast generalization. I lived in excitement, amused to make Holloway interpret Aran, and constantly comparing my discoveries with what I have learned of mediaeval tradition among fellow students, with the reveries of a Neoplatonist, of a seventeenth-century Platonist, of Paracelsus or a Japanese poet. Then one day I opened *The Spiritual Diary* of Swedenborg, which I had not taken down for twenty years, and found all there, even certain thoughts I had not set on paper because they had seemed fantastic from the lack of some traditional foundation. It was strange I should have forgotten so completely a writer I had read with some care before the fascination of Blake and Boehme had led me away.

II

It was indeed Swedenborg who affirmed for the modern world, as against the abstract reasoning of the learned, the doctrine and practice of the desolate places, of shepherds and of midwives, and discovered a world of spirits where there was a scenery like that of earth, human forms, grotesque or beautiful, senses that knew pleasure and pain, marriage and war, all that could be painted upon canvas, or put into stories to make one's hair stand up. He had mastered the science of his time, he had

312

written innumerable scientific works in Latin, had been the first to formulate the nebular hypothesis and wrote a cold abstract style, the result it may be of preoccupation with stones and metals, for he had been assessor of mines to the Swedish Government, and of continual composition in a dead language.

In his fifty-eighth year he was sitting in an inn in London, where he had gone about the publication of a book, when a spirit appeared before him who was, he believed, Christ himself, and told him that henceforth he could commune with spirits and angels. From that moment he was a mysterious man describing distant events as if they were before his eyes, and knowing dead men's secrets, if we are to accept testimony that seemed convincing to Emmanuel Kant. The sailors who carried him upon his many voyages spoke of the charming of the waves and of favouring winds that brought them sooner than ever before to their journey's end, and an ambassador described how a queen, he himself looking on, fainted when Swedenborg whispered in her ear some secret known only to her and to her dead brother. And all this happened to a man without egotism, without drama, without a sense of the picturesque, and who wrote a dry language, lacking fire and emotion, and who to William Blake seemed but an arranger and putter away of the old Church, a Samson shorn by the churches, an author not of a book, but of an index. He considered heaven and hell and God, the angels, the whole destiny of man, as if he were sitting before a large table in a Government office putting little pieces of mineral ore into small square boxes for an assistant to pack away in drawers.

All angels were once men, he says, and it is therefore men who have entered into what he calls the Celestial State and become angels, who attend us immediately after death, and communicate to us their thoughts, not by speaking, but by looking us in the face as they sit beside the head of our body. When they find their thoughts are communicated they know the time has come to separate the spiritual from the physical body. If a man begins to feel that he can endure them no longer, as he doubtless will, for in their presence he can think and feel but sees nothing, lesser angels who belong to truth more than to love take their place and he is in the light again, but in all likelihood these angels also will be too high and he will slip from state to state until he finds himself after a few days "with those who are in accord with his life in the world; with them he finds his life, and, wonderful to relate, he then leads a life similar to that he led in the world." This first state of shifting and readjustment seems to correspond with a state of sleep more modern seers discover to follow upon death. It is characteristic of his whole religious system, the slow drifting of like to like. Then follows a period which may last but a short time or many years, while the soul lives a life so like that of the world that it may not even believe that it has died, for "when what is spiritual touches and sees what is spiritual the effect is the same as when what is natural touches what is natural." It is the other world of the early races, of those whose dead are in the rath or the faery hill, of all who see no place of reward and punishment but a continuance of this life, with cattle and sheep, markets and war. He describes what he has seen, and only partly explains it, for, unlike science which is founded upon past experience, his work, by the very nature of his gift, looks for the clearing away of obscurities to unrecorded experience. He is revealing something and that which is revealed, so long as it remains modest and simple, has the same right with the child in the cradle to put off to the future the testimony of its worth. This earth-resembling life is the creation of the image-making power of the mind, plucked naked from the body, and mainly of the images in the memory. All our work has gone with us, the books we have written can be opened and read or put away for later use, even though their print and paper have been sold to the buttermen; and reading his description one notices, a discovery one had thought peculiar to the last generation, that the "most minute particulars which enter the memory remain there and are never obliterated," and there as here we do not always know all that is in our memory, but at need angelic spirits who act upon us there as here, widening and deepening the consciousness at will, can draw forth all the past, and make us live again all our transgressions and see our victims "as if they were present, together with the place, words, and motives"; and that suddenly, "as when a scene bursts upon the sight" and yet continues "for hours together," and like the transgressions, all the pleasure and pain of sensible life awaken again and again, all our passionate events rush up about us and not as seeming imagination, for imagination is now the world. And yet another impulse comes and goes, flitting through all, a preparation for the spiritual abyss, for out of the celestial world, immediately beyond the world of form, fall certain seeds as it were that exfoliate through us into forms, elaborate scenes,

314

buildings, alterations of form that are related by "correspondence" or "signature" to celestial incomprehensible realities.
Meanwhile those who have loved or fought see one another in
the unfolding of a dream, believing it may be that they wound
one another or kill one another, severing arms or hands, or that
their lips are joined in a kiss, and the countryman has need but
of Swedenborg's keen ears and eagle sight to hear a noise of
swords in the empty valley, or to meet the old master hunting
with all his hounds upon the stroke of midnight among the
moonlit fields. But gradually we begin to change and possess
only those memories we have related to our emotion or our
thought; all that was accidental or habitual dies away and we
begin an active present life, for apart from that calling up of the
past we are not punished or rewarded for our actions when in
the world but only for what we do when out of it. Up till now
we have disguised our real selves and those who have lived well
for fear or favour have walked with holy men and women, and
the wise man and the dunce have been associated in common
learning, but now the ruling love has begun to remake circum-
stance and our body.

Swedenborg had spoken with shades that had been learned
Latinists, or notable Hebrew scholars, and found, because they
had done everything from the memory and nothing from thought
and emotion, they had become but simple men. We have already
met our friends, but if we were to meet them now for the first
time we should not recognize them, for all has been kneaded
up anew, arrayed in order and made one piece. "Every man has
many loves, but still they all have reference to his ruling love
and make one with it or together compose it," and our surrender
to that love, as to supreme good, is no new thought, for Villiers
de l'Isle Adam quotes Thomas Aquinas as having said, "Eternity
is the possession of one's self, as in a single moment." During
the fusing and rending man flits, as it were, from one flock of the
dead to another, seeking always those who are like himself, for
as he puts off disguise he becomes unable to endure what is
unrelated to his love, even becoming insane among things that
are too fine for him.

So heaven and hell are built always anew and in hell or heaven
all do what they please and all are surrounded by scenes and
circumstances which are the expression of their natures and the
creation of their thought. Swedenborg because he belongs to
an eighteenth century not yet touched by the romantic revival

315

feels horror amid rocky uninhabited places, and so believes that
the evil are in such places while the good are amid smooth
grass and garden walks and the clear sunlight of Claude
Lorraine. He describes all in matter-of-fact words, his meeting
with this or that dead man, and the place where he found him,
and yet we are not to understand him literally, for space as we
know it has come to an end and a difference of state has begun
to take its place, and wherever a spirit's thought is, the spirit
cannot help but be. Nor should we think of spirit as divided
from spirit, as men are from each other, for they share each
other's thoughts and life, and those whom he has called celestial
angels, while themselves mediums to those above, commune with
men and lower spirits, through orders of mediatorial spirits, not
by a conveyance of messages, but as though a hand were thrust
with a hundred gloves,† one glove outside another, and so there
is a continual influx from God to man. It flows to us through
the evil angels as through the good, for the dark fire is the
perversion of God's life and the evil angels have their office in
the equilibrium that is our freedom, in the building of that
fabulous bridge made out of the edge of a sword.

To the eyes of those that are in the high heaven "all things
laugh, sport, and live," and not merely because they are
beautiful things but because they arouse by a minute correspondence of form and emotion the heart's activity, and being
founded, as it were, in this changing heart, all things continually
change and shimmer. The garments of all befit minutely their
affections, those that have most wisdom and most love being
the most nobly garmented, in ascending order from shimmering
white, through garments of many colours and garments that
are like flame, to the angels of the highest heaven that are naked.

In the west of Ireland the country people say that after death
every man grows upward or downward to the likeness of thirty
years, perhaps because at that age Christ began his ministry,
and stays always in that likeness; and these angels move always
towards "the springtime of their life" and grow more and more
beautiful, "the more thousand years they live," and women who
have died infirm with age, and yet lived in faith and charity, and
true love towards husband or lover, come "after a succession

† The Japanese *Noh* play *Awoi no Uye* has for its theme the exorcism
of a ghost which is itself obsessed by an evil spirit. This evil spirit, drawn
forth by the exorcism, is represented by a dancer wearing a "terrible mask
with golden eyes."

of years" to an adolescence that was not in Helen's Mirror, "for to grow old in heaven is to grow young."

There went on about Swedenborg an intermittent "Battle of the Friends" and on certain occasions had not the good fought upon his side, the evil troop, by some carriage accident or the like, would have caused his death, for all associations of good spirits have an answering mob, whose members grow more hateful to look on through the centuries. "Their faces in general are horrible, and empty of life like corpses, those of some are black, of some fiery like torches, of some hideous with pimples, boils, and ulcers; with many no face appears, but in its place a something hairy or bony, and in some one can but see the teeth." And yet among themselves they are seeming men and but show their right appearance when the light of heaven, which of all things they most dread, beats upon them; and seem to live in a malignant gaiety, and they burn always in a fire that is God's love and wisdom, changed into their own hunger and misbelief.

III

In Lady Gregory's stories there is a man who heard the newly dropped lambs of faery crying in November, and much evidence to show a topsy-turvydom of seasons, our spring being their autumn, our winter their summer, and Mary Battle, my Uncle George Pollexfen's old servant, was accustomed to say that no dream had a true meaning after the rise of the sap; and Lady Gregory learned somewhere on Sleive Ochta that if one told one's dreams to the trees fasting the trees would wither. Swedenborg saw some like opposition of the worlds, for what hides the spirits from our sight and touch, as he explains, is that their light and heat are darkness and cold to us and our light and heat darkness and cold to them, but they can see the world through our eyes and so make our light their light. He seems however to warn us against a movement whose philosophy he announced or created, when he tells us to seek no conscious intercourse with any that fall short of the celestial rank. At ordinary times they do not see us or know that we are near, but when we speak to them we are in danger of their deceits. "They have a passion for inventing," and do not always know that they invent. "It has been shown me many times that the spirits speaking with me did not know but that they were the men and women I was thinking of; neither did other spirits know the contrary. Thus yesterday and today one known of me in life was personated. The personation was so like him in all respects, so far as known to me, that nothing could be more like. For there are genera and species of spirits of similar faculty (? as the dead whom we seek), and when like things are called up in the memory of men and so are represented to them they think they are the same persons. At other times they enter into the fantasy of other spirits and think that they are them, and sometimes they will even believe themselves to be the Holy Spirit," and as they identify themselves with a man's affection or enthusiasm they may drive him to ruin, and even an angel will join himself so completely to a man that he scarcely knows "that he does not know of himself what the man knows," and when they speak with a man they can but speak in that man's mother tongue, and this they can do without taking thought, for "it is almost as when a man is speaking and thinks nothing about his words." Yet when they leave the man "they are in their own angelical or spiritual language and know nothing of the language of the man." They are not even permitted to talk to a man from their own memory for did they do so the man would not know "but that the things he would then think were his when yet they would belong to the spirit," and it is these sudden memories occurring sometimes by accident, and without God's permission that gave the Greeks the idea they had lived before. They have bodies as plastic as their minds that flow so readily into the mould of ours and he remembers having seen the face of a spirit change continuously and yet keep always a certain generic likeness. It had but run through the features of the individual ghosts of the fleet it belonged to, of those bound into the one mediatorial communion.

He speaks too, again and again, of seeing palaces and mountain ranges and all manner of scenery built up in a moment, and even believes in imponderable troops of magicians that build the like out of some deceit or in malicious sport.

IV

There is in Swedenborg's manner of expression a seeming superficiality. We follow an easy narrative, sometimes incredulous, but always, as we think, understanding, for his moral conceptions are simple, his technical terms continually repeated, and for the most part we need but turn for his "correspondence," his symbolism as we would say, to the index of his *Arcana Celestia*. Presently, however, we discover that he treads upon this surface by an achievement of power almost as full of astonishment as if he should walk upon water charmed to stillness by some halcyon; while his disciple and antagonist Blake is like a man swimming in a tumbling sea, surface giving way to surface and deep showing under broken deep. A later mystic has said of Swedenborg that he but half felt, half saw, half tasted the kingdom of heaven, and his abstraction, his dryness, his habit of seeing but one element in everything, his lack of moral speculation have made him the founder of a church, while William Blake, who grows always more exciting with every year of life, grows also more obscure. An impulse towards what is definite and sensuous, and an indifference towards the abstract and the general, are the lineaments, as I understand the world, of all that comes not from the learned, but out of common antiquity, out of the "folk" as we say, and in certain languages, Irish for instance—and these languages are all poetry—it is not possible to speak an abstract thought. This impulse went out of Swedenborg when he turned from vision. It was inseparable from this primitive faculty, but was not a part of his daily bread, whereas Blake carried it to a passion and made it the foundation of his thought. Blake was put into a rage by all painting where detail is generalized away, and complained that Englishmen after the French Revolution became as like one another as the dots and lozenges in the mechanical engraving of his time, and he hated histories that gave us reasoning and deduction in place of the events, and St. Paul's Cathedral because it came from a mathematical mind, and told Crabb Robinson that he preferred to any others a happy, thoughtless person. Unlike Swedenborg he believed that the antiquities of all peoples were as sacred as those of the Jews, and so rejecting authority and claiming that the same law for the lion and the ox was oppression, he could believe "all that lives is holy," and say that a man if he but cultivated the power of vision would see the truth in a way suited "to his imaginative energy," and with only so much resemblance to the way it showed in for other men, as there is between different human forms. Born when Swedenborg was a new excitement, growing up with a Swedenborgian brother, who annoyed him "with bread and cheese

319

advice," and having, it may be, for nearest friend the Swedenborgian Flaxman with whom he would presently quarrel, he
answered the just translated *Heaven and Hell* with the para-
doxical violence of *The Marriage of Heaven and Hell*. Swedenborg was but "the linen clothes folded up" or the angel sitting
by the tomb, after Christ, the human imagination, had arisen.
His own memory being full of images from painting and from
poetry he discovered more profound "correspondences," yet
always in his boys and girls walking or dancing on smooth grass
and in golden light, as in pastoral scenes cut upon wood or
copper by his disciples Palmer and Calvert one notices the
peaceful Swedenborgian heaven. We come there, however, by
no obedience but by the energy that "is eternal delight," for
"the treasures of heaven are not negations of passion but
realities of intellect from which the passions emanate uncurbed
in their eternal glory." He would have us talk no more "of the
good man and the bad," but only of "the wise man and the
foolish," and he cries, "Go put off holiness and put on intellect."

Higher than all souls that seem to theology to have found a
final state, above good and evil, neither accused, nor yet accusing,
live those, who have come to freedom, their senses sharpened
by eternity, piping or dancing or "like the gay fishes on the
wave when the moon sucks up the dew." Merlin, who in the
verses of Chrétien de Troyes was laid in the one tomb with dead
lovers, is very near and the saints are far away. Believing too
that crucifixion and resurrection were the soul's diary and no
mere historical events, which had been transacted in vain should
a man come again from the womb and forget his salvation, he
could cleave to the heroic doctrine the angel in the crystal
made Sir Thomas Kelly renounce and have a "vague memory"
of having been "with Christ and Socrates"; and stirred as
deeply by hill and tree as by human beauty, he saw all Merlin's
people, spirits "of vegetable nature" and fairies whom we "call
accident and chance." He made possible a religious life to those
who had seen the painters and poets of the romantic movement
succeed to theology, but the shepherd and the midwife had they
known him would have celebrated him in stories, and turned
away from his thought, understanding that he was upon an
errand to their masters. Like Swedenborg he believed that
heaven came from "an improvement of sensual enjoyment," for
sight and hearing, taste and touch grow with the angelic years,
but unlike him he could convey to others "enlarged and

numerous senses," and the mass of men know instinctively they are safer with an abstract and an index.

V

It was, I believe, the Frenchman Allen Cardec and an American shoemaker's clerk called Jackson Davis, who first adapted to the séance room the philosophy of Swedenborg. I find Davis whose style is vague, voluble, and pretentious, almost unreadable, and yet his books have gone to many editions and are full of stories that had been charming or exciting had he lived in Connaught or any place else, where the general mass of the people has an imaginative tongue. His mother was learned in country superstition, and had called in a knowledgeable man when she believed a neighbour had bewitched a cow, but it was not till his fifteenth year that he discovered his faculty, when his native village, Poughkeepsie, was visited by a travelling mesmerist. He was fascinated by the new marvel, and mesmerized by a neighbour he became clairvoyant, describing the diseases of those present and reading watches he could not see with his eyes. One night the neighbour failed to awake him completely from the trance and he stumbled out into the street and went to his bed ill and stupefied. In the middle of the night he heard a voice telling him to get up and dress himself and follow. He wandered for miles, now wondering at what seemed the unusual brightness of the stars and once passing a visionary shepherd and his flock of sheep, and then again stumbling in cold and darkness. He crossed the frozen Hudson and became unconscious. He awoke in a mountain valley to see once more the visionary shepherd and his flock, and a very little, handsome, old man who showed him a scroll and told him to write his name upon it.

A little later he passed, as he believed, from this mesmeric condition and found that he was among the Catskill Mountains and more than forty miles from home. Having crossed the Hudson again he felt the trance coming upon him and began to run. He ran, as he thought, many miles and as he ran became unconscious. When he awoke he was sitting upon a gravestone in a graveyard surrounded by a wood and a high wall. Many of the gravestones were old and broken. After much conversation with two stately phantoms, he went stumbling on his way.

Presently he found himself at home again. It was evening and the mesmerist was questioning him as to where he had been since they lost him the night before. He was very hungry and had a vague memory of his return, of country roads passing before his eyes in brief moments of wakefulness. He now seemed to know that one of the phantoms with whom he had spoken in the graveyard was the physician Galen, and the other, Swedenborg.

From that hour the two phantoms came to him again and again, the one advising him in the diagnosis of disease, and the other in philosophy. He quoted a passage from Swedenborg, and it seemed impossible that any copy of the newly translated book that contained it could have come into his hands, for a Swedenborgian minister in New York traced every copy which had reached America.

Swedenborg himself had gone upon more than one somnambulistic journey, and they occur a number of times in Lady Gregory's stories, one woman saying that when she was among the faeries she was often glad to eat the food from the pigs' troughs.

Once in childhood, Davis, while hurrying home through a wood, heard footsteps behind him and began to run, but the footsteps, though they did not seem to come more quickly and were still the regular pace of a man walking, came nearer. Presently he saw an old, white-haired man beside him who said: "You cannot run away from life," and asked him where he was going. "I'm going home," he said, and the phantom answered, "I also am going home," and then vanished. Twice in later childhood, and a third time when he had grown to be a young man, he was overtaken by the same phantom and the same words were spoken, but the last time he asked why it had vanished so suddenly. It said that it had not, but that he had supposed that "changes of state" in himself were "appearance and disappearance." It then touched him with one finger upon the side of his head, and the place where he was touched remained ever after without feeling, like those places always searched for at the witches' trials. One remembers "the touch" and "the stroke" in the Irish stories.

VI

Allen Cardec, whose books are much more readable than those
of Davis, had himself no mediumistic gifts. He gathered the
opinions, as he believed, of spirits speaking through a great
number of automatists and trance speakers, and all the essential
thought of Swedenborg remains, but like Davis, these spirits do
not believe in an eternal Hell, and like Blake they describe un-
human races, powers of the elements, and declare that the soul
is no creature of the womb, having lived many lives upon the
earth. The sorrow of death, they tell us again and again, is not
so bitter as the sorrow of birth, and had our ears the subtlety
we could listen amid the joy of lovers and the pleasure that
comes with sleep to the wailing of the spirit betrayed into a
cradle. Who was it that wrote: "O Pythagoras, so good, so wise,
so eloquent, upon my last voyage, I taught thee, a soft lad, to
splice a rope"?

This belief, common among continental spiritists, is denied by
those of England and America, and if one question the voices
at a séance they take sides according to the medium's nationality.
I have even heard what professed to be the shade of an old
English naval officer denying it with a fine phrase: "I did not
leave my oars crossed; I left them side by side."

VII

Much as a hashish eater will discover in the folds of a curtain
a figure beautifully drawn and full of delicate detail all built up
out of shadows that show to other eyes, or later to his own, a
different form or none, Swedenborg discovered in the Bible the
personal symbolism of his vision. If the Bible was upon his side,
as it seemed, he had no need of other evidence, but had he lived
when modern criticism had lessened its authority, even had he
been compelled to say that the primitive beliefs of all peoples
were as sacred, he could but have run to his own gift for
evidence. He might even have held of some importance his
powers of discovering the personal secrets of the dead and set
up as medium. Yet it is more likely he had refused, for the
medium has his gift from no heightening of all the emotions
and intellectual faculties till they seem as it were to take fire,
but commonly because they are altogether or in part extinguished

while another mind controls his body. He is greatly subject to trance and awakes to remember nothing, whereas the mystic and the saint plead unbroken consciousness. Indeed the author of *Sidonia the Sorceress,* a really learned authority, considered this lack of memory a certain sign of possession by the devil, though this is too absolute. Only yesterday, while walking in a field, I made up a good sentence with an emotion of triumph, and half a minute after could not even remember what it was about, and several minutes had gone by before I as suddenly found it. For the most part, though not always, it is this unconscious condition of mediumship, a dangerous condition it may be, that seems to make possible "physical phenomena" and that over shadowing of the memory by some spirit memory, which Swedenborg thought an accident and unlawful.

In describing and explaining this mediumship and so making intelligible the stories of Aran and Galway I shall say very seldom, "it is said," or "Mr. So-and-So reports," or "it is claimed by the best authors." I shall write as if what I describe were everywhere established, everywhere accepted, and I had only to remind my reader of what he already knows. Even if incredulous he will give me his fancy for certain minutes, for at the worst I can show him a gorgon or chimera that has never lacked gazers, alleging nothing (and I do not write out of a little knowledge) that is not among the sober beliefs of many men, or obvious inference from those beliefs, and if he wants more— well, he will find it in the best authors.†

VIII

All spirits for some time after death, and the "earth-bound," as they are called, the larvae, as Beaumont, the seventeenth-century Platonist, preferred to call them, those who cannot become disentangled from old habits and desires, for many years, it may be for centuries, keep the shape of their earthly bodies

---

† Besides the well-known books of Atsikof, Myers, Lodge, Flammarion, Flournoy, Maxwell, Albert De Rochas, Lombroso, Madame Bisson, Delanne, etc., I have made considerable use of the researches of D'Ochorowicz published during the last ten or twelve years in *Annales des Science Psychiques* and in the English *Annals of Psychical Science,* and of those of Professor Hyslop published during the last four years in the *Journal* and *Transactions of the American Society for Psychical Research.* I have myself been a somewhat active investigator.

and carry on their old activities, wooing or quarrelling, or totting figures on a table, in a round of dull duties or passionate events. Today while the great battle in Northern France is still undecided, should I climb to the top of that old house in Soho where a medium is sitting among servant girls, some one would, it may be, ask for news of Gordon Highlander of Munster Fusilier, and the fat old woman would tell in Cockney language how the dead do not yet know they are dead, but stumble on amid visionary smoke and noise, and how angelic spirits seem to awaken them but still in vain.

Those who have attained to nobler form, when they appear in the séance room, create temporary bodies, commonly like to those they wore when living, through some unconscious constraint of memory, or deliberately, that they may be recognized. Davis, in his literal way, said the first sixty feet of the atmosphere was a reflector and that in almost every case it was mere images we spoke with in the séance room, the spirit itself being far away. The images are made of a substance drawn from the medium who loses weight, and in a less degree from all present, and for this light must be extinguished or dimmed or shaded with red as in a photographer's room. The image will begin outside the medium's body as a luminous cloud, or in a sort of luminous mud forced from the body, out of the mouth it may be, from the side or from the lower parts of the body.[1] One may see a vague cloud condense and diminish into a head or arm or a whole figure of a man, or to some animal shape.

I remember a story told me by a friend's steward in Galway of the faeries playing at hurley in a field and going in and out of the bodies of two men who stood at either goal. Out of the medium will come perhaps a cripple or a man bent with years and sometimes the apparition will explain that, but for some family portrait, or for what it lit on while rumaging in our memories, it had not remembered its customary clothes or features, or cough or limp or crutch. Sometimes, indeed, there is a strange regularity of feature and we suspect the presence of an image that may never have lived, an artificial beauty that

1. Henry More considered that "the animal spirits" were "the immediate instruments of the soul in all vital and animal functions" and quotes Harpocrates, who was contemporary with Plato, as saying, "that the mind of man is . . . not nourished from meats and drinks from the belly but by a clear and luminous substance that redounds by separation from the blood." Ochorowicz thought that certain small oval lights were perhaps the root of personality itself.

may have shown itself in the Greek mysteries. Has some cast in the Vatican, or at Bloomsbury been the model? Or there may float before our eyes a mask as strange and powerful as the lineaments of the Servian's *Frowning Man* or of Rodin's *Man with the Broken Nose*. And once a rumour ran among the séance rooms to the bewilderment of simple believers, that a heavy middle-aged man who took snuff, and wore the costume of a past time, had appeared while a French medium was in his trance, and somebody had recognized the Tartuffe of the Comédie Française. There will be few complete forms, for the dead are economical, and a head, or just enough of the body for recognition, may show itself above hanging folds of drapery that do not seem to cover solid limbs, or a hand or foot is lacking, or it may be that some *Revenant* has seized the half-made image of another, and a young girl's arm will be thrust from the withered body of an old man. Nor is every form a breathing and pulsing thing, for some may have a distribution of light and shade not that of the séance room, flat pictures whose eyes gleam and move; and sometimes material objects are thrown together (drifted in from some neighbour's wardrobe, it may be, and drifted thither again) and an appearance kneaded up out of these and that luminous mud or vapour almost as vivid as are those pictures of Antonio Mancini which have fragments of his paint tubes embedded for the high lights into the heavy masses of the paint. Sometimes there are animals, bears frequently for some unknown reason, but most often birds and dogs. If an image speak it will seldom seem very able or alert, for they come for recognition only, and their minds are strained and fragmentary; and should the dogs bark, a man who knows the language of our dogs may not be able to say if they are hungry or afraid or glad to meet their master again. All may seem histrionic or a hollow show. We are the spectators of a phantasmagoria that affects the photographic plate or leaves its moulded image in a preparation of paraffin. We have come to understand why the Platonists of the sixteenth and seventeenth centuries, and visionaries like Boehme and Paracelsus confused imagination with magic, and why Boehme will have it that it "creates and substantiates as it goes."

Most commonly, however, especially of recent years, no form will show itself, or but vaguely and faintly and in no way ponderable, and instead there will be voices flitting here and there in darkness, or in the half-light, or it will be the medium himself fallen into trance who will speak, or without a trance write from a knowledge and intelligence not his own. Glanvil, the seventeenth-century Platonist, said that the higher spirits were those least capable of showing material effects, and it seems plain from certain Polish experiments that the intelligence of the communicators increases with their economy of substance and energy. Often now among these faint effects one will seem to speak with the very dead. They will speak or write some tongue that the medium does not know and give correctly their forgotten names, or describe events one only verifies after weeks of labour. Here and there amongst them one discovers a wise and benevolent mind that knows a little of the future and can give good advice. They have made, one imagines, from some finer sustance than a phosphorescent mud, or cobweb vapour that we can see or handle, images not wholly different from themselves, figures in a galanty show not too strained or too extravagant to speak their very thought.

Yet we never long escape the phantasmagoria nor can long forget that we are among the shape-changers. Sometimes our own minds shape that mysterious substance, which may be life itself, according to desire or constrained by memory, and the dead no longer remembering their own names become the characters in the drama we ourselves have invented. John King, who has delighted melodramatic minds for hundreds of séances with his career on earth as Henry Morgan the buccaneer, will tell more scientific visitors that he is merely a force, while some phantom long accustomed to a decent name, questioned by some pious Catholic, will admit very cheerfully that he is the devil. Nor is it only present minds that perplex the shades with phantasy, for friends of Count Albert de Rochas once wrote out names and incidents but to discover that though the surname of the shade that spoke had been historical, Christian name and incidents were from a romance running at the time in some clerical newspaper no one there had ever opened.

All these shadows have drunk from the pool of blood and become delirious. Sometimes they will use the very word and say that we force delirium upon them because we do not still our minds, or that minds not stupefied with the body force them more subtly, for now and again one will withdraw what he has said, saying that he was constrained by the neighbourhood of some more powerful shade.

When I was a boy at Sligo, a stable boy met his late master

327

going round the yard, and having told him to go and haunt the lighthouse, was dismissed by his mistress for sending her husband to haunt so inclement a spot. Ghosts, I was told, must go where they are bid, and all those threatenings by the old *grimoires* to drown some disobedient spirit at the bottom of the Red Sea, and indeed all exorcism and conjuration affirm that our imagination is kind. *Revenants* are, to use the modern term, "suggestable," and may be studied in the "trance personalities" of hypnoses and in our dreams which are but hypnosis turned inside out, a modeller's clay for our suggestions, or, if we follow *The Spiritual Diary,* for those of invisible beings. Swedenborg has written that we are each in the midst of a group of associated spirits who sleep when we sleep and become the *dramatis personae* of our dreams, and are always the other will that wrestles with our thought, shaping it to our despite.

IX

We speak, it may be, of the Proteus of antiquity which has to be held or it will refuse its prophecy, and there are many warnings in our ears. "Stoop not down," says the Chaldaean Oracle, "to the darkly splendid world wherein continually lieth a faithless depth and Hades wrapped in cloud, delighting in unintelligible images," and amid that caprice, among those clouds, there is always legerdemain; we juggle, or lose our money with the same pack of cards that may reveal the future. The magicians who astonished the Middle Ages with power as incalculable as the fall of a meteor were not so numerous as the more amusing jugglers who could do their marvels at will; and in our own day the juggler Houdini, sent to Morocco by the French Government, was able to break the prestige of the dervishes whose fragile wonders were but worked by fasting and prayer.

Sometimes, indeed, a man would be magician, jester, and juggler. In an Irish story a stranger lays three rushes upon the flat of his hand and promises to blow away the inner and leave the others unmoved, and thereupon puts two fingers of his other hand upon the outer ones and blows. However, he will do a more wonderful trick. There are many who can wag both ears, but he can wag one and not the other, and thereafter, when he has everybody's attention, he takes one ear between finger and thumb. But now that the audience are friendly and laughing the moment of miracle has come. He takes out of a bag a skein of silk thread and throws it into the air, until it seems as though one end were made fast to a cloud. Then he takes out of his bag first a hare and then a dog and then a young man and then "a beautiful, well-dressed young woman" and sends them all running up the thread. Nor, the old writers tell us, does the association of juggler and magician cease after death, which only gives to legerdemain greater power and subtlety. Those who would live again in us, becoming a part of our thoughts and passion have, it seems, their sport to keep us in good humour, and a young girl who has astonished herself and her friends in some dark séance may, when we have persuaded her to become entranced in a lighted room, tell us that some shade is touching her face, while we can see her touching it with her own hand, or we may discover her, while her eyes are still closed, in some jugglery that implies an incredible mastery of muscular movement. Perhaps too in the fragmentary middle world there are souls that remain always upon the brink, always children. Dr. Ochorowicz finds his experiments upset by a naked girl, one foot one inch high, who is constantly visible to his medium and who claims never to have lived upon the earth. He has photographed her by leaving a camera in an empty room where she had promised to show herself, but is so doubtful of her honesty that he is not sure she did not hold up a print from an illustrated paper in front of the camera. In one of Lady Gregory's stories a countryman is given by a stranger he meets upon the road what seems wholesome and pleasant food, but a little later his stomach turns and he finds that he has eaten chopped grass, and one remembers Robin Goodfellow and his joint stool, and witches' gold that is but dried cow dung. It is only, one does not doubt, because of our preoccupation with a single problem, our survival of the body, and with the affection that binds us to the dead, that all the gnomes and nymphs of antiquity have not begun their tricks again.

X

Plutarch, in his essay on the daemon, describes how the souls of enlightened men return to be the schoolmasters of the living, whom they influence unseen; and the mediums, should we ask how they escape the illusions of that world, claim the protection of their guides. One will tell you that when she was a little girl she was minding geese upon some American farm and an old man came towards her with a queer coat upon him, and how at first she took him for a living man. He said perhaps a few words of pious commonplace or practical advice and vanished. He had come again and again, and now that she has to earn her living by her gift, he warns her against deceiving spirits, or if she is working too hard, but sometimes she will not listen and gets into trouble. The old witch doctor of Lady Gregory's story learned his cures from his dead sister whom he met from time to time, but especially at Hallowe'en, at the end of the garden, but he had other helpers harsher than she, and once he was beaten for disobedience.

Reginald Scott gives a fine plan for picking a guide. You promise some dying man to pray for the repose of his soul if he will but come to you after death and give what help you need, while stories of mothers who come at night to be among their orphan children are as common among spiritists as in Galway or in Mayo. A French servant girl once said to a friend of mine who helped her in some love affair: "You have your studies, we have only our affections"; and this I think is why the walls are broken less often among us than among the poor. Yet according to the doctrine of Soho and Holloway and in Plutarch, those studies that have lessened in us the sap of the world may bring to us good, learned, masterful men who return to see their own or some like work carried to a finish. "I do think," wrote Sir Thomas Browne, "that many mysteries ascribed to our own invention have been the courteous revelations of spirits; for those noble essences in heaven bear a friendly regard unto their fellow creatures on earth."

XI

Much that Lady Gregory has gathered seems but the broken bread of old philosophers, or else of the one sort with the dough they made into their loaves. Were I not ignorant, my Greek gone and my meagre Latin all but gone, I do not doubt that I could find much to the point in Greek, perhaps in old writers on medicine, much in Renaissance or Medieval Latin. As it is, I must be content with what has been translated or with the seventeenth-century Platonists who are the handier for my purpose because they found in the affidavits and confessions of the witch trials, descriptions like those in our Connaught stories. I have Henry More in his verse and in his prose and I have Henry More's two friends, Joseph Glanvil, and Cudworth in his *Intellectual System of the Universe,* three volumes violently annotated by an opposed theologian; and two essays by Mr. G. R. S. Meade clipped out of his magazine, *The Quest.* These writers quote much from Plotinus and Porphyry and Plato and from later writers, especially Synesius and John Philoponus in whom the School of Plato came to an end in the seventh century.

We should not suppose that our souls began at birth, for as Henry More has said, a man might as well think "from souls new souls" to bring as "to press the sunbeams in his fist" or "wring the rainbow till it dye his hands." We have within us an "airy body" or "spirit body" which was our only body before our birth as it will be again when we are dead and its "plastic power" has shaped our terrestrial body as some day it may shape apparition and ghost. Porphyry is quoted by Mr. Meade as saying that "Souls who love the body attach a moist spirit to them and condense it like a cloud," and so become visible, and so are all apparitions of the dead made visible; though necromancers, according to Henry More, can ease and quicken this condensation "with reek of oil, meal, milk, and such like gear, wine, water, honey." One remembers that Dr. Ochorowicz's naked imp once described how she filled out an appearance of herself by putting a piece of blotting paper where her stomach should have been and that the blotting paper became damp because, as she said, a materialization, until it is completed, is a damp vapour. This airy body which so compresses vapour, Philoponus says, "takes the shape of the physical body as water takes the shape of the vessel that it has been frozen in," but it is capable of endless transformations, for "in itself it has no especial form," but Henry More believes that it has an especial form, for "its plastic power" cannot but find the human form most "natural," though "vehemency of desire to alter the figure into another representation may make the appearance to resemble some other creature; but no forced thing can last long." "The better genii" therefore prefer to show "in a human shape yet not it may be with all the lineaments" but with such as are "fit for this separate state" (separate from the body that is) or are "requisite to perfect the visible features of a person," desire and imagination adding clothes and ornament. The materialization,

331

as we would say, has but enough likeness for recognition. It may be that More but copies Philoponus who thought the shade's habitual form, the image that it was as it were frozen in for a time, could be again "coloured and shaped by fantasy," and that "it is probable that when the soul desires to manifest it shapes itself, setting its own imagination in movement, or even that it is probable with the help of daemonic co-operation that it appears and again becomes invisible, becoming condensed and rarefied." Porphyry, Philoponus adds, gives Homer as his authority for the belief that souls after death live among images of their experience upon earth, phantasms impressed upon the spirit body. While Synesius, who lived at the end of the fourth century and had Hypatia among his friends, also describes the spirit body as capable of taking any form and so of enabling us after death to work out our purgation; and says that for this reason the oracles have likened the state after death to the images of a dream. The seventeenth century English translation of Cornelius Agrippa's *De Occulta Philosophia* was once so famous that it found its way into the hands of Irish farmers and wandering Irish tinkers, and it may be that Agrippa influenced the common thought when he wrote that the evil dead see represented "in the fantastic reason" those shapes of life that are "the more turbulent and furious ... sometimes of the heavens falling upon their heads, sometimes of their being consumed with the violence of flames, sometimes of being drowned in a gulf, sometimes of being swallowed up in the earth, sometimes of being changed into divers kinds of beasts ... and sometimes of being taken and tormented by demons ... as if they were in a dream." The ancients, he writes, have called these souls "hobgoblins," and Orpheus has called them "the people of dreams" saying "the gates of Pluto cannot be unlocked; within is a people of dreams." They are a dream indeed that has place and weight and measure, and seeing that their bodies are of an actual air, they cannot, it was held, but travel in wind and set the straws and the dust twirling; though being of the wind's weight they need not, Dr. Henry More considers, so much as feel its ruffling, or if they should do so, they can shelter in a house or behind a wall, or gather into themselves as it were, out of the gross wind and vapour. But there are good dreams among the airy people, though we cannot properly name that a dream which is but analogical of the deep unimaginable virtues and has, therefore, stability and a common measure. Henry More stays himself in the midst of the dry learned and abstract writing of his treatise *The Immortality of the Soul* to praise "their comely carriage ... their graceful dancing, their melodious singing and playing with an accent so sweet and soft as if we should imagine air itself to compose lessons and send forth musical sounds without the help of any terrestrial instrument" and imagines them at their revels in the thin upper air where the earth can but seem "a fleecy and milky light" as the moon to us, and he cries out that they "sing and play and dance together, reaping the lawful pleasures of the very animal life, in a far higher degree than we are capable of in this world, for everything here does, as it were, taste of the cask and has some measure of foulness in it."

There is, however, another birth or death when we pass from the airy to the shining or ethereal body, and "in the airy the soul may inhabit for many ages and in the ethereal for ever," and indeed it is the ethereal body which is the root "of all that natural warmth in all generations" though in us it can no longer shine. It lives while in its true condition an unimaginable life and is sometimes described as of "a round or oval figure" and as always circling among gods and among the stars, and sometimes as having more dimensions than our penury can comprehend.

Last winter Mr. Ezra Pound was editing the late Professor Fenollosa's translations of the Noh Drama of Japan, and read me a great deal of what he was doing. Nearly all that my fat old woman in Soho learns from her familiars is there in an unsurpassed lyric poetry and in strange and poignant fables once danced or sung in the houses of nobles. In one a priest asks his way of some girls who are gathering herbs. He asks if it is a long road to town; and the girls begin to lament over their hard lot gathering cress in a cold wet bog where they sink up to their knees and to compare themselves with ladies in the big town who only pull the cress in sport, and need not when the cold wind is flapping their sleeves. He asks what village he has come to and if a road near by leads to the village of Ono. A girl replies that nobody can know that name without knowing the road, and another says: "Who would not know that name, written on so many pictures, and know the pine trees they are always drawing." Presently the cold drives away all the girls but one and she tells the priest she is a spirit and has taken solid form that she may speak with him and ask his help. It is her tomb that has made Ono so famous. Conscience-struck at having allowed two young men to fall in love with her she refused to choose between them. Her father said he would give her to the best archer. At the match to settle it both sent their arrows through the same wing of a mallard and were declared equal. She being ashamed and miserable because she had caused so much trouble and for the death of the mallard, took her own life. That, she thought, would end the trouble, but her lovers killed themselves beside her tomb, and now she suffered all manner of horrible punishments. She had but to lay her hand upon a pillar to make it burst into flame; she was perpetually burning. The priest tells her that if she can but cease to believe in her punishments they will cease to exist. She listens in gratitude but she cannot cease to believe, and while she is speaking they come upon her and she rushes away enfolded in flames. Her imagination has created all those terrors out of a scruple, and one remembers how Lake Harris, who led Laurence Oliphant such a dance, once said to a shade, "How did you know you were damned?" and that it answered, "I saw my own thoughts going past me like blazing ships."

In a play still more rich in lyric poetry a priest is wandering in a certain ancient village. He describes the journey and the scene, and from time to time the chorus sitting at the side of the stage sings its comment. He meets with two ghosts, the one holding a red stick, the other a piece of coarse cloth and both dressed in the fashion of a past age, but as he is a stranger he supposes them villagers wearing the village fashion. They sing as if muttering, "We are entangled up—whose fault was it, dear? Tangled up as the grass patterns are tangled up in this coarse cloth, or that insect which lives and chirrups in dried seaweed. We do not know where are today our tears in the undergrowth of this eternal wilderness. We neither wake nor sleep and passing our nights in sorrow, which is in the end a vision, what are these scenes of spring to us? This thinking in sleep for some one who has no thought for you, is it more than a dream? And yet surely it is the natural way of love. In our hearts there is much, and in our bodies nothing, and we do nothing at all, and only the waters of the river of tears flow quickly." To the priest they seem two married people but he cannot understand why they carry the red stick and the coarse cloth. They ask him to listen to a story. Two young people had lived in that village long ago and night after night for three years the young man had offered a charmed red stick, the token of love, at the young girl's window, but she pretended not to see and went on weaving. So the young man died and was buried in a cave with his charmed red sticks, and presently the girl died too, and now because they were never married in life they were unmarried in their death. The priest, who does not yet understand that it is their own tale, asks to be shown the cave, and says it will be a fine tale to tell when he goes home. The chorus describes the journey to the cave. The lovers go in front, the priest follows. They are all day pushing through long grasses that hide the narrow paths. They ask the way of a farmer who is mowing. Then night falls and it is cold and frosty. It is stormy and the leaves are falling and their feet sink into the muddy places made by the autumn showers; there is a long shadow on the slope of the mountain, and an owl in the ivy of the pine tree. They have found the cave and it is dyed with the red sticks of love to the colour of "the orchids and chrysanthemums which hide the mouth of a fox's hole"; and now the two lovers have "slipped into the shadow of the cave." Left alone and too cold to sleep the priest decides to spend the night in prayer. He prays that the lovers may at last be one. Presently he sees to his wonder that the cave is lighted up "where people are talking and setting up looms for spinning and painted red sticks." The ghosts creep out and thank him for his prayer and say that through his pity "the love promises of long past incarnations" find fulfilment in a dream. Then he sees the love story unfolded in a vision and the chorus compares the sound of weaving to the clicking of crickets. A little later he is shown the bridal room and the lovers drinking from the bridal cup. The dawn is coming. It is reflected in the bridal cup and now singers, cloth, and stick break and dissolve like a dream, and there is nothing but "a deserted grave on a hill where morning winds are blowing through the pine."

I remember that Aran story of the lovers who came after death to the priest for marriage. It is not uncommon for a ghost, "a control" as we say, to come to a medium to discover some old earthly link to fit into a new chain. It wishes to meet a ghostly enemy to win pardon or to renew an old friendship. Our service to the dead is not narrowed to our prayers, but may be as wide as our imagination. I have known a control to warn a medium to unsay her promise to an old man, to whom, that she might be rid of him, she had promised herself after death. What is promised here in our loves or in a witch's bond may be fulfilled in a life which is a dream. If our terrestrial condition is, as it seems the territory of choice and of cause, the one ground for all seed sowing, it is plain why our imagination has command over the dead and why they must keep from sight and earshot. At the British Museum at the end of the Egyptian Room and near the stairs are two statues, one an august decoration, one a most accurate looking naturalistic portrait. The august decoration was for a public site, the other, like all the naturalistic art of the epoch, for burial beside a mummy. So buried it was believed, the Egyptologists tell us, to be of service to the dead. I have no doubt it helped a dead man to build out of his spirit-body a recognizable apparition, and that all boats or horses or weapons or their models buried in ancient tombs were helps for a flagging memory or a too weak fancy to imagine and so substantiate the old surroundings. A shepherd at Doneraile told me some years ago of an aunt of his who showed herself after death stark naked and bid her relatives to make clothes and to give them to a beggar, the while remembering her.† Presently she appeared again wearing the clothes and thanked them.

XII

Certainly in most writings before our time the body of an apparition was held for a brief, artificial, dreamy, half-living thing. One is always meeting such phrases as Sir Thomas Browne's "they steal or contrive a body." A passage in the *Paradiso* comes to mind describing Dante in conversation with the blessed among their spheres, although they are but in appearance there, being in truth in the petals of the yellow rose; and another in the Odyssey where Odysseus speaks not with "the mighty Heracles," but with his phantom, for he himself "hath joy at the banquet among the deathless gods and hath to wife Hebe of the fair ankles, child of Zeus, and Hero of the golden sandals," while all about the phantom "there was a clamour of the dead, as it were fowls flying everywhere in fear and he, like black night with bow uncased, and shaft upon the string, fiercely glancing around like one in the act to shoot."

W. B .Y.

14th October, 1914

† Herodotus has an equivalent tale. Periander, because the ghost of his wife complained that it was "cold and naked," got the women of Corinth together in their best clothes and had them stripped and their clothes burned.

NOTES

NOTE 1. THE FAERY PEOPLE. The first detailed account of the Faery People of the Gaelic race was made by the Reverend Robert Kirk in 1691. His book which remained in manuscript till it was discovered by Sir Walter Scott in 1815 was called *The Secret Commonwealth*, an essay "of the nature of the subterranean (and for the most part invisible people) heretofore going under the names of elves, fays, and faeries." Kirk was a Gaelic scholar, a translator into Gaelic of the Psalms. He is described upon his tomb as *Lingnæ hibernælumen*, for in his day little distinction was made between the Irish and the Scottish-Irish among whom he lived and whose words he has recorded. He died a year after he had finished his manuscript or, as the people of his parish say, was taken by the faeries. The Reverend William Taylor, the present incumbent of Abberfoyle, Kirk's old living, told Mr. Wentz that it was generally believed at the time of Kirk's death, that the faeries had carried him off because he had looked too deeply into their secrets. He seems to have fainted while walking upon a faery knoll, a little way from his own door, and to have died immediately. Mr. Wentz found one old Gaelic speaker who believed that his spirit had been taken, but others who said there was nothing in the grave but a coffin full of stones, for body and soul had been taken. Mr. Lang prints a tradition that Kirk appeared to his cousin Graham of Ducray and could have been saved if the cousin had dared to throw a knife over the apparition's head.

Kirk describes "the subterranean people" or "the abstruse people," as he sometimes calls them, much as they are described today in Galway or in Mayo. He is clear that they are not demons and like Father Sinistrari, a Catholic theologian of Padua, quotes the Scriptures in support of this opinion. The "abstruse people" are not indeed without sin though midway between men and angels, but being in no way "drenched into so gross and dredgy bodies as we, are especially given to the more spiritual and haughty sins." "Whatever their own laws, be sure according to ours and equity natural civil and revealed" they do wrong by "their stealing of nurses to their children and that other sort of Plaginism in catching our children away (may seem to heir some estate in those invisible dominions) which never return. For the inconvenience of their succubi who tryst with men it is abominable, but for swearing and intemperance they are not observed so subject to this irregularity as to envy, spite, hypocrisy, lying, and simulation." Some have thought the spirit controls of our best mediums no better. "They are not subject to sore sickness, but dwindle and decay at a certain period all about ane age" and "they pass after a long healthy life into one orb and receptacle fitted to their degree till they come under the general cognism at the last day." They are the "Sleagh Math or the good people" being called so by the "Irish" . . . "to prevent the dint of their ill-attempts" and being "of a middle nature betwixt man and angel" have "intelligent, studious spirits, and light changeable bodies (like those called astral) somewhat of the nature of a condensed cloud and best seen in twilight. Their bodies are so pliable through the subtlety of the spirits that agitate them that they can make them appear or disappear at pleasure. Some have bodies or vehicles so spongeous, thin, and desiccate, that they are fed by only sucking into some fine spirituous liquors that pierce like pure air and oil; others feed more gross on the foisone or substance of corns and liquors or corn itself that grows upon the surface of the earth which these faeries steal away, partly invisible, partly preying on the grain as do crows and mice." Lady Gregory has a story of the crying of new dropped lambs of faery in November and some evidence that there is a reversal of the seasons, our winter being their summer, and some such belief was known to Kirk for "when we have plenty they have scarcity at their homes; and on the contrary (for they are empowered to catch as much prey everywhere as they please)." "Their bodies of congealed air are sometimes carried aloft, other whiles grovel in different shapes and enter into any cranny or cleft of the earth where air enters to their ordinary dwellings, the earth being full of cavities and cells and there being no place nor creature but is supposed to have other animals greater or lesser, living in or upon it as inhabitants, and no such thing as a pure wilderness in the whole universe" and we must always "labour for that abstruse people as well as for ourselves." Unless Kirk is in error, as seems probable, they are unlike the Irish faeries who shift but twice a year in May and in November, when the ancient Irish perhaps shifted from their winter houses to summer pastures or home again, for they have formed the custom to "remove to other lodgings at the beginning of each quarter of the year, so traversing till doomsday some being impudent [impotent?] of staying in one place and finding some ease by so purning [turning] and changing habitations," and at these times they are much seen when "their chameleon-like bodies swim in the air near the earth with bag and baggage." He is evidently puzzled how to place them among the orders and admits that it is uncertain "What at the last revolution will become of them when they are locked up into ane unchangeable condition." He even believes that they are so beset with anxiety upon this subject that have they "any frolic fit for mirth 'tis as the confirmed grinning of a mort head."

Many of the second-sighted men about him would have nothing of this doctrine and still believed, it seems, the old Celtic theory of the rebirth of the soul, a Manichæan and gnostic doctrine, for being "unwary in their observations" they believed what the "abstruse people" themselves declared "one averring those subterranean people to be departed souls attending awhile in this inferior state and clothed with bodies procured through their alms deeds in this life; fluid, active ethereal vehicles to hold them that they may not scatter or wander or be lost in the totum or the first nothing; but if any were so impious as to have given no alms they say when the souls of such do depart, they sleep in an uncertain state till they resume the terrestrial body." These bodies, come at by the giving of alms, suggest to one that body of Christ which, as Boehme taught, alone enables the shade to escape from *turba magna* the great wrath and dream-like transformation into the shape of beasts. One remembers also the celestial body of the seventeenth century Platonists. The power attributed to almsgiving calls to mind those tales of clothes given to the poor in some ghost's name thereby enabling the ghost to be decked out in their double. Lady Gregory has found the idea of rebirth in Aran, but in what seems the Cabalistic form not the Celtic; and it occurs again and again in the Gaelic romances. Cuchulain was the rebirth of Lug; and Mongan who was killed by Arthur of Britain was the rebirth of Finn Mac Cool. Here and there through the seventeenth-century Platonists, Kirk's contemporaries, one finds some story that might have been in Lady Gregory's book. Glanvill in the second part of his *Sadducismus Triumphatus* published in 1674 has an Irish tale where the dead and the faeries are associated as in Galway today. "A gentleman in Ireland near to the Earl of Orrery's seat sending his butler one afternoon to buy cards; as he passed a field, he, to his wonder, espied a company of people sitting round a table, with a deal of good cheer before them in the midst of a field. And he going up towards them, they all arose and saluted him, and desired him to sit down with them." But one of them said these words in his ear: "Do nothing this company invites you to." "He therefore refused to sit down at the table, and immediately the table and all that belonged to it were gone; and the company are now dancing and playing upon musical instruments, and the butler being desired to join himself to them; but he refusing this also, they fall all to work, and he not being to be prevailed with to accompany them in working, any more than in feasting and dancing, they all disappeared, and the butler is now alone." For some days attempts are made to carry away the butler. During one of these he is levitated in the presence of the Earl of Orrery and certain of his guests. Then the man who warned him to do nothing he was bid, came to his bedside. " 'I have been dead,' said the spectre or ghost, 'seven years and you know that I lived a loose life. And ever since have been hurried up and down in a restless condition with the company you saw and shall be till the Day of Judgment.' "

Throughout the Middle Ages, there must have been many discussions upon those questions that divided Kirk's Highlanders. Were these beings but the shades of men? Were they a separate race? Were they spirits of evil? Above all, perhaps, were they capable of salvation? Father Sinistrari in De Dæmonialitate et Incubis, et Succubis, reprinted in Paris with an English translation in 1879, tells a story which must have been familiar through the Irish Middle Ages, and the seed of many discussions. The Abbot Anthony went once upon a journey to visit St. Paul, the first hermit. After travelling for some days into the desert, he met a centaur of whom he asked his road and the centaur, muttering barbarous and unintelligible words, pointed to the road with his outstretched hand and galloped away and hid himself in a wood. St. Anthony went some way further and presently went into a valley and met there a little man with goat's feet and horns upon his forehead. St. Anthony stood still and made the sign of the cross being afraid of some devil's trick. But the sign of the cross did not alarm the little man who went nearer and offered some dates very respectfully as it seemed to make peace. When the old Saint asked him who he was, he said: "I am a mortal, one of those inhabitants of the desert called fauns, satyrs, and incubi, by the Gentiles. I have come as an ambassador from my people. I ask you to pray for us to our common God who came as we know for the salvation of the world and who is praised throughout the world." We are not told whether St. Anthony prayed but merely that he thought of the glory of Christ and thereafter of Christ's enemies and turning towards Alexandria said: "Woe upon you harlots worshipping animals as God." This tale so artfully arranged as it seems to set the pious by the ears may have been the original of a tale one hears in Ireland today. I heard or read that tale somewhere before I was twenty, for it is the subject of one of my first poems. But the priest in the Irish tale, as I remember it, tells the little man that there is no salvation for such as he and it ends with the wailing of the faery host. Sometimes too, one reads in Irish stories of hoof-footed creatures, and it may well be that the Irish theologians who read of St. Anthony in Sinistrari's authority, St. Hieronymus, thought centaur and homunculus were of like sort with the shades haunting their own raths and barrows. Father Sinistrari draws the moral that those inhabitants of the desert called "fauns and satyrs and incubi by the Gentiles" had souls that could be shrived, but Irish theologians in a country full of poems very upsetting to youth about the women of the Sidhe who could pass, it may be even monastic walls, may have turned the doubtful tale the other way. Sometimes we are told following the traditions of the eleventh-century poems that the Sidhe are "the ancient inhabitants of the country" but more often still they are fallen angels who, because they were too bad for heaven and not bad enough for hell, have been sent into the sea and into the waste places. More probably still the question was never settled, sometimes Christ was represented as throwing them into hell till someone said he would empty the whole paradise, and thereupon his hand slackened and some fell in this place and some in that other, as though providence itself were undecided. Father Sinistrari is conscious of weighty opponents but believes that Scripture is upon his side. He quotes St. John, Chapter x., verse 16: "And other sheep I have which are not of this fold; them also I must bring and they shall hear my voice and there shall be one fold and one shepherd." He argues that the commentators are wrong who say that the fold is the synagogue and the other sheep the Gentiles, because the true church has been from the beginning of the world, and has had nothing to do with Jewish observances, for its revelations were made to the first man and Jews and Gentiles have belonged to it. If the Gentiles were not also of Christ's fold, he would not have sent them prodigies to announce his birth, the star of the Magi, the silencing of their oracle, a miraculous spring of oil at Rome, the falling down of the images of Egyptian gods and so on. The other fold should therefore, he thinks, refer to those "rational animals" who sent their ambassador to St. Anthony and who were to hear Christ's voice "either directly through Himself or through His apostles." He argues that they are a race superior to the human and must not be confused with angels and devils who are pure spirits being in a final state of salvation or of judgment. He has written his book as a guide to confessors who have frequently, it seems, to protect men and women, often nuns or monks, who are plagued by spirits or tempted by spirit lovers, and to apportion penalties to those who have fallen. It is a great sin should they confuse their lovers with devils, for then they "sin through intention," but otherwise it is a venal sin, and seeing that incubi and succubi by reason of their "rational and immortal" spirits are the equal of man and by reason of their bodies being "more noble because more subtle," "more dignified than man," a commerce that does not "degrade but rather dignify our nature" (*et hoc homo jungens se incubo non vilificat, immo dignificat suam naturam*). The incubus, (or succuba) however, does, he holds, commit a very great sin considering that we belong to an inferior species. It is difficult to drive them away, for unlike devils they are no more subject to exorcism than we are ourselves, but just as we cannot breathe in the higher peaks of the Alps because of the thinness of the air, so they cannot come near to us if we make certain conditions of the air. They are of different kinds but always one or other of the four elements predominates, and those who are predominantly fiery cannot come if we make the air damp, and those that are watery cannot come if we use hot fumigations and so on. You can generally judge the kind by remembering that a man attracts spirits according to his own temperament, the sanguine, the spirits of fire, and the lymphatic, those of watery nature, and those of a mixed nature, mixed spirits; but it is easy to make mistakes. He tells of the case that came into his own experience. He was asked to drive a spirit away that was troubling a young monk and advised hot fumigations because it was by their means "a very erudite theologian" drove away a spirit who made passionate love in the form of "a very handsome young man to a certain young nun" after holy candles burning all night and "a crowd of relics and many exorcisms" had proved of but as little value as her own vows and fasts. A vessel made of "glass-like earth" containing "cubeb seed, roots of both aristolochies, great and small cardamon, ginger, long pepper, caryophylias, cinnamon, cloves, mace, nutmeg, calamite, storax, benzoin, aloes wood root, one ounce of triasandates and three pounds of half brandy and water," was set upon hot ashes to make it fume, and the door and window of the cell were closed. The young friar, a deacon of the great Carthusian priory of Padua, was further advised to carry about with him perfumes of musk, amber, chive, peruvian bark, and the like, and to smoke tobacco and drink brandy perfumed with musk. All was to no purpose for the spirit appeared to him in many forms such as "a skeleton, a pig, an ass, an angel, a bird" or "in the figure of one or other of the friars." These appearances seem to have had no object except that like the Irish faeries the spirit was pleased to make game of somebody. Presently it came in the likeness of the abbot and heard the young deacon's confession and recited with him the psalms *Exsurgat Deus* and *Qui habitat* and the Gospel according to St. John, and bent its knee at the words *Verbum caro factum est*, and then after sprinkling with holy water and blessing bed and cell and commanding the spirit to come there no more, it vanished. Presently in the likeness of the young friar, it called at the vicar's room and asked for some tobacco and brandy perfumed with musk of which it was, it said, extremely fond, and having received them "disappeared in the twinkling of an eye." Sinistrari, however, having decided that the demon must be igneous or "at the very least aërial, since he delighted in hot substances" and since the monk's temperament seemed "choleric and sanguine," advised the vicar to direct his penitent to strew about the cell and hang by the window and door bundles of "water-lily, liverwort, spurge, mandrake, house-leek, plantain," and henbane and other herbs of a damp nature which drove the spirit away though it came once to the cell door to speak of Sinistrari all the evil it could. He has other like stories; one to show the uselessness of mere sacred places and objects, describes a woman followed to the steps of the Cathedral altar and there stripped by invisible hands.

One remembers a passage in PLUTARCH: "But to believe the

gods have carnal knowledge, and do delight in the outward beauty of creatures, that seemeth to carry a very hard belief. Yet the wise Egyptians think it probable enough and likely, that the spirit of the gods hath given original of generation to women, and does beget fruits of their bodies; howbeit they hold that a man can have no corporal company with any divine nature."

One hears today in Galway, stories of love adventures between countrywomen or countrymen and the People of Faery—there are several in this book and these adventures have been always a principal theme to Gaelic poets. A goddess came to Cuchulain upon the battlefield, but sometimes it is the mortal who must go to them. "Oh beautiful woman, will you come with me to the wonderful country that is mine? It is pleasant to be looking at the people there: beautiful people without any blemish; their hair is of the colour of the flag flower, their fair body is as white as snow, the colour of the foxglove is on every cheek. The young never grow old there, the fields and the flowers are as pleasant to be looking at as the blackbird's eggs; warm and sweet streams of mead and wine flow through that country; there is no care and no sorrow upon any person; we see others, but we ourselves are not seen." Did Dame Kettler, a great lady of Kilkenny who was accused of witchcraft early in the fifteenth century, find such a lover when she offered up the combs of cocks and the bronzed tail feathers of nine peacocks; or had she indeed, as her enemies affirmed at the trial, been enamoured with "one of the meaner sort of hell"?

NOTE 2. This light occurs again and again in modern spiritism as in old legends. It shows in some form in almost every dark séance. Grettir the Strong saw it over buried treasure. It surrounded the head of Hereward the Wake in childhood, and in the middle of the nineteenth century, Baron Reichenbach called it "odic light" and published much evidence taken down from his "sensitives" who saw it about crystals, magnets, and one another, and over new-made graves. Holman Hunt represents in his *Flight into Egypt* the souls of the Innocents encircled by creeping and clinging fire. When his fire encircles a good spirit it is generally described as white and brilliant, but about the evil as lurid and smoky.

NOTE 3. When I was a boy, there was a countryman in a Sligo madhouse who was sane in all ways except that he saw, in

344

pools and rivers, beings who called and beckoned. I have myself known a landscape painter who after painting a certain stagnant pool was nightly afflicted by a dream of strange shapes, bidding him to drown himself there. The obsession was so strong that he could not throw it off during his waking hours, and for some days struggled with the temptation. I was with him at the time and had noticed his growing gloom and had questioned him about it.

NOTE 4. Bran, in the *Voyage of Bran*, when sailing, meets Manannan the sea-god. "And Manannan spoke to him in a song, and this is what he said:

"It is what Bran thinks, he is going in his curragh over the wonderful, beautiful, clear sea; but to me, from far off in my chariot, it is a flowery plain he is riding on.

"What is a clear sea to the good boat Bran is in, is a happy plain with many flowers to me in my two-wheeled chariot.

"It is what Bran sees, many waves beating across the clear sea; it is what I myself see, red flowers without any fault.

"The sea-horses are bright in summer-time, as far as Bran's eyes can reach; there is a wood of beautiful acorns under the head of your little boat.

"A wood with blossom and with fruit, that has the smell of wine; a wood without fault, without withering, with leaves of the colour of gold." (*Gods and Fighting Men*, by Lady Gregory.)

NOTE 5. Swedenborg describes these colours and I have a note of similar visions as seen by a fellow-student of mine at the Dublin Art School. Mrs Besant in her *Ancient Wisdom* and other writers of the Modern Theosophical School describe them and moralize about them.

NOTE 6. There are constant stories in the history of modern spiritism of people carried through the air often for considerable distances. It is not my business to weigh the evidence at this moment, for I am concerned only with similarity of belief. The medium, Mrs. Guppy, somewhere in the "sixties" was believed to have been carried from Hampstead, a pen in one hand and an account book in the other, and dropped on to the middle of a table in South Conduit Street. Lord Dunraven was one of a number of witnesses who testified to having seen the medium Hume float out of one window of the upper room, where they were sitting, and in at another window. I read the other day in a spiritistic paper, of two boys carried through the air in Italy and dropped in front of a bishop who immediately handed them over to the police. And of course the folk-lore of all countries and the legends of the saints are full of such tales.

NOTE 7. The offering to the Sidhe is generally made at Hallowe'en, the old beginning of winter, and upon that night I was told when a boy the offering was still made in the slums of Dublin.

NOTE 8. Father Sinistrari speaks of a like commerce between beasts and spirits. "Et non solum hoc evenit cum mulieribus, sed etiam cum equabus, cum quibus commicetur; quæ si libenter coitum admittunt, ab eo curantur optime, ac ipsarum jubæ varie artificiosis et inextricabilibus nodis texuntur; si autem illum adversentur, eas male tractat, percutit, macras reddit, et tandem necat, ut quotidiana constat experienta."

NOTE 9. Houses built upon faery paths are thought to be unlucky. Often the thatch will be blown away, or their inhabitants die or suffer misfortune.

NOTE 10. The number of quotations I can find to prove the universality of the thought that the dead and other spirits change their shape as they please is but lessened by the fewness of the books that are near my hand in the country where I am writing. John Heydon, "a servant of God and secretary of nature," writing in 1662 in *The Rosie Cross Uncovered* which is the last book of his *Holy Guide* says that a man may become one of the heroes: "A hero," he writes, "is a dæmon, or good genius, and a genius a partaker of divine things and a companion of the holy company of unbodied souls and immortal angels who live according to their vehicles a versatile life, turning themselves proteus-like into any shape."

And Mrs. Besant, a typical writer of the modern Theosophical School, insists upon these changes of form, especially among those spirits that are most free from the terrestrial body and explains it by saying that, "astral matter takes form under every impulse of thought." Swedenborg I have already quoted in my long essay, but to prove that the shape-changer is a part of general literature—I have but Wordsworth and Milton under my hand. When the white doe of Rylstone shows itself at the church door according to its Sunday custom, one has one tale to tell, another another, but an Oxford student will have it that it is the faery that loved a certain "shepherd-lord."

" 'Twas said that she all shapes could wear."

And Milton writes like any Platonist of his time:

> "For Spirits, when they please,
> Can either sex assume, or both; so soft
> And uncompounded is their essence pure,
> Not ty'd or manacled with joint or limb,
> Nor founded on the brittle strength of bones,
> Like cumbrous flesh; but, in what shape they choose,
> Dilated or condensed, bright or obscure,
> Can execute their aery purposes,
> And works of love or enmity fulfil."

NOTE 11. The seers and healers in this section differ but little from clairvoyants and spirit mediums of the towns, and explain their powers in much the same way. Indeed one of Lady Gregory's story-tellers will have it that America is more full than Ireland of faeries, and describes the mediums there to prove it. It is often through some virtue in these country seers and healers that the faeries or spirits are able to affect men and women and natural objects. Mrs. Sheridan says that a child could not have been taken if she had not been looking on, and one hears again and again that even when the faeries fight among themselves or play at hurley, there must be a man upon either side. We are all in a sense mediums, if the village seer speaks truth, for through any unsanctified emotion, love, affection, admiration, the spirits may attain power over a child or horse or whatever is before our eyes, and perhaps, as the controls of mediums will sometimes say, they can only see the world through our eyes. Albert de Rochas, borrowing a theory from the seventeenth century, has suggested with the general assent of spiritists that the fluidic or sidereal body of the medium, the mould upon which the physical body is, it may be, built up, is more detachable than in persons who are not mediums, and that the spirits make themselves visible by transforming it into

347

their own shape or into what shape they please and attain by its means a power over physical objects. (See *L'Extériorisation de la Motricité*.) Instead of the expensive crystal of the Bond Street clairvoyant, Biddy Early gazed into her bottle, but that is almost the whole difference. If the dreams and visions of Connacht have more richness and beauty than those of Camberwell, it is that Connacht, having no doubts as to our survival of death, is not always looking for but one sort of evidence, and so can let things happen as they will. The brother or sister or the like who comes to the knowledgeable man or woman after death is but the "guide" that has been so common in England and America, since the Rochester rappings, and a country form of Plutarch's "dæmon." At other moments, however, "seer" or "healer" resembles a witch or wizard rather than a modern medium.

In one thing, however, they always resemble the medium and not the witch. They seem to have no dealings with the devil. The Irish Trials for witchcraft of the English and continental type took place among the English settlers. I have never come across a case of a "compact" nor has Lady Gregory, nor have I read of one.

NOTE 12. It is almost unthinkable to Lady Gregory and myself, who know Mrs. Sheridan, that she can ever have seen a drawbridge in a picture or heard one spoken of. Nor does this instance stand alone. I have had in my own family what seemed the accurate calling up of an unknown past but failing a link of difficult evidence still unfound, coincidence, though exceedingly unlikely, is still a possible explanation. I have come upon a number of other cases which are, though no one case is decisive, a powerful argument taken altogether. In *The Adventure* (Macmillan), an elaborate vision of this kind is recorded in detail and, accepting the record as accurate, the verification is complete. Two ladies found themselves in the garden of the Petit Trianon in the midst of what seemed to be the court of Marie Antoinette, in just the same sudden way in which some countryman finds himself among ladies and gentlemen dressed in what seem the clothes of a long passed time. The record purports to have been made in November and December 1901, whereas the vision occurred in August. This lapse of time does not seem to me to destroy the value of the evidence, if the record was made before its corroboration by long and difficult research.[1] Accepting the good faith of the narrators, both well-known women and of established character, its evidence for some more obscure cause than unconscious memory can only be weakened by the discovery in some book or magazine accessible to the visionaries before their visit to the Trianon, of historical information on such minute points as the dress Marie Antoinette wore in a particular month, and the position of ornamental buildings and rock work not now in existence. There is a great mass of similar evidence in Denton's *Soul of Things* though its value is weakened by his not sufficiently allowing for thought transference from his own mind to that of his sensitives.

A "theosophist" or "occultist" of almost any modern school explains such visions by saying they are "pictures in the astral light" and that all objects and events leave their images in the astral light as upon a photographic plate, and that we must distinguished between spirits and these unintelligent pictures. I was once at Madame Blavatsky's when she tried to explain predestination, our freedom and God's full knowledge of the use that we should make of it. All things, past and to come were present to the mind of God and yet all things were free. She soon saw that she had carried us out of our depth and said to one of her followers with a mischievous, mocking voice: "You with your impudence and your spectacles will be sitting there in the Akasa to all eternity" and then in a more meditative voice, "No, not to all eternity for a day will come when even the Akasa will pass away and there will be nothing but God, chaos, that which every man is seeking in his heart." Akasa, she was accustomed to explain as some Indian word for the astral light. Perhaps that theory of the astral pictures came always from the despair of some visionary to find understanding for a more metaphysical theory. It is, however, ancient. To Cornelius Agrippa it is the air that reflects, but the air is something more than what the word means for us. "It is a vital spirit passing through all beings giving life and substance to all things . . . it immediately receives into itself the influences of all celestial bodies, and the communicates them to the other elements as also to all mixed bodies. Also it receives into itself as if it were a divine

1. Since writing the above the authors of *The Adventure* have shown me a mass of letters proving that they spoke of the visions to various correspondents before the corroboration, and showing the long and careful research that the corroboration involved. W. B. Y.

looking-glass the species of all things, as well natural as artificial," it enters into men and animals "through their pores" and "makes an impression upon them as well when they sleep as when they awake and affords matter to divers strange dreams and divinations... Hence it is that a man passing by a place where a man was slain and the carcass newly laid is moved by fear and dread; because the air in that place being full of the dread species of man-slaughter does being breathed in, move and trouble the spirit of the man with a like species... whence it is that many philosophers were of the opinion that the air is the cause of dreams." Henry More is more precise and philosophical and believes that this air which he calls *Spiritus Mundi*, contains all forms, so that the parents when a child is begotten, or a witch when the double is projected as a hare, but as it were, call upon the *Spiritus Mundi* for the form they need. The name "Astral Light" was given to this air or spirit by the Abbé Constant who wrote under the pseudonym of Elephas Lévi and like Madame Blavatsky, claimed to be the voice of an ancient magical society. In his *Dogma et Rituel de la Haute Magie* published in the fifties, he described in vague, eloquent words, influenced perhaps by the recent discovery of the daguerreotype these pictures which we continually confuse with the still animate shades. A more clear exposition of a perhaps always incomprehensible idea is that of Swedenborg who says that when we die, we live over again the events that lie in all their minute detail in our memory, and this is the explanation of the authors of *The Adventure* who believe, as it seems, that they were entangled in the memory of Marie Antoinette. I have met students who claimed to have had knowledge of Lévi's sources and who believed that when at last a spirit has been, as it were, pulled out of its coil, other spirits may use its memory, not only of events but of words and of thoughts. Did Cornelius Agrippa identify soul with memory when, after quoting Ovid to prove that the flesh cleaves to earth, the ghost hovers over the grave, the soul sinks to Oxos, and the spirit rises to the stars, he explains that if the soul has done well it rejoices with the almost faultless spirit, but if it has done ill, the spirit judges it and leaves it for the devil's prey and "the sad soul wanders about hell without a spirit and like an image?" Remembering these writings and sayings, I find new meaning in that description of death taken down by Lady Gregory in some cottage: "The shadow goes wandering and the soul is tired and the body is taking a rest."

I was once talking with Professor James of experiences like to those in *The Adventure* and said that I found it easiest to understand them by believing in a memory of nature distinguished from individual memory, though including and enclosing it. He would, however, have none of my explanation and preferred to think the past, present and future were only modes of our perception and that all three were in the divine mind, present at once. It was Madame Blavatsky's thought, and Shelley's in the *Sensitive Plant:*

> "That garden sweet, that lady fair,
> And all sweet shapes and odours there,
> In truth have never passed away;
> 'Tis we, 'tis ours, are changed, not they.

> "For love, and beauty, and delight,
> There is no death nor change; their light
> Exceeds our organs, which endure
> No light, being themselves obscure."

NOTE 13. The ancient Irish had quadrilateral houses built of logs, and round houses of clay and wattles. O'Sullivan, in his introduction to O'Curry's *Manners and Customs*, writes: "The houses built in *Duns* and in *stone caiseal*, and those surrounded by mounds of earth, were, probably in all cases round houses." A *Bo Aires*, or farmer with ten cows was supposed to have a house at least twenty-seven feet wide but the houses of better off men must have made one room of considerable size, a whole household sleeping on beds, sometimes with low partitions between, raying out from the wall like spokes of a wheel. Petrie thought the great quadrilateral banqueting hall of Tara was once ninety feet wide.

NOTE 14. In *The Roman Ritual*, there is an exorcism for evil spirits and a ceremony for the succour of the sick (*cura infirmorum*). And in the beginning of the chapter containing this ceremony (Caput IV., verse 12), it is stated that images of Christ, the Virgin, and of saints especially in veneration of the sick man, may cure him if brought into the room. In the ceremony of exorcism, the priest is directed to make numerous signs of the cross over the possessed person (*sic. rubric: Tres cruces sequentes fiant in pectore dæmoniaci*). The spirit is commanded to be gone in the name of the Father, of the Son, and of the Holy Spirit. The ceremony with psalms covers twenty-six pages of my copy. The exorcism is described as a driving out of the "most unclean spirit" of every phantasm and every legion. It commands the "most evil dragon, in the name of the immaculate lamb who walked upon the asp and the basilisk and cast down the lion and the dragon" to "go down out of this man."

In the ceremony for the sick, the priest places his hand on the head of the sick man and says:

"Let them place their hands on the sick and they shall be well [*Super ægros manus imponent, et bene habebunt*]. May Christ Son of Mary, Saviour of the world and Lord, by the merits and intercession of his holy apostles Peter and Paul and of all the saints be clement and propitious to you."

The ceremony is ten pages and contains various psalms and selections from the Gospels.

Round these two ceremonies have gathered in the minds of the country people, at least, many traditional ideas. When any one is cured, there is a victim, some other human being or some animal will die. If one remembers that diseases were very commonly considered to be the work of demons, one sees how the story of the Gadarene swine would support the tradition. I know not into what subtlety the dreaming mind may not carry the thought, for some few months ago in France, an excommunicated miracle-working priest said in my hearing: "There is always a victim; so-and-so was the victim for France," naming a holy Italian nun who had just died. "And so-and-so," naming a living holy woman, "is the victim for my own village." Various medieval saints, and even certain witches, cured sick persons by taking the disease upon themselves.

Christian Scientists and Mental Healers are often afraid of themselves acquiring the disease which they drive out of their patient; they sometimes speak of the effort that it costs them to shake it off. I was told a story the other day, which I have proved not to be true, but which is evidence of the belief. A woman said to me some such words as these: "My friend so-and-so, who is a Mental Healer, was staying in the country. She saw a woman there with a strange look. She asked what was wrong, and found that this woman was expecting a periodical fit of madness. She offered to undertake her cure, and brought her to her own house. The patient became violent, but my friend was able by faith and prayer to soothe her till she fell asleep. My

352

friend went downstairs exhausted, and lay upon the sofa. Presently she saw strange shadows coming into the room and knew they had come from the patient upstairs, and these shadows, taking the form of swine, threw themselves upon her and only after a long struggle could she throw them off." The swine and their attack were all moonshine, but the healer, whom I found and questioned, did believe that she saw shadows leaving the patient.

The transference of disease was a generally recognized part of medieval and ancient medicine; and Albert de Rochas gives considerable space to it in his *L'Extériorisation de la Sensibilité,* Paris, 1909. He quotes from a seventeenth-century writer, Abbé de Vellemort, many examples from medical and scientific writers of that time who believed themselves to have transferred diseases from their patients to animals and to trees and to various substances, "Mumia" as they called them, which absorb *des esprits qui résident dans le sang* and then describes various experiments made in 1885 by Dr. Babinski "Chef de Clinique de M. Charcot" in transferring now by magnets, now by suggestion various forms of nervous disease from one patient to another. Where these diseases were produced in the first instance by suggestion, the patient from whom the disease was transferred, was freed from it, but where the disease was natural and the cause of the patient being at the hospital, there was no cure although in one case there was improvement. Albert de Rochas then quotes as follows from a lecture given by Dr. Luys to la Société de Biologie in 1894.

"M. D'Arsonval has, according to a communication from an English physician, given an account at the last meeting of the Société de Biologie, of the persistent action in a magnetized iron bar of the magnetic fluid, which to a certain extent, kept a memory of its former state.

"My researches of the same kind have given me proofs some time since of analogous phenomena with the help of magnetized crowns placed on the head of a subject in an hypnotic state.

"In this case, it is a question not only of storing vibrations of magnetic nature, but of really living nature, of real cerebral vibrations through the coating of the brain, stored in a magnetic crown, in which they remain for a greater or less length of time.

"To arrive at this phenomenon, instead of using an unresponsive physical instrument, I use a reacting living being—an hypnotized subject, who has thus become sensitive to living magnetic vibrations. I am presenting to the Society the magnetized crown, like several other models which I have already shown. It is adapted to the head by means of a system of straps, encircles it and leaves the frontal region free.

"It also forms a bent magnet with a positive and a negative pole. This crown was put, more than a year ago, on the head of a woman suffering from melancholia with ideas of persecution, agitation, and a tendency to suicide, etc. The application of the crown lead to the patient's getting slowly better after five or six séances; and at the end of ten days I thought I could send her back to the hospital without any danger. At the end of a fortnight, the crown having been isolated, the idea came to me quite empirically of placing it on the head of the 'subject' now before you.

"He is a male, hypnotizable, *hystérique*, given to frequent fits of lethargy. What was my surprise to see this subject, put into the somnambulistic state, complaining in exactly the same terms as those the cured patient had used a fortnight before.

"*He* first of all took the sex of the patient; *he* spoke in the feminine gender; *he* complained of violent headache; *he* said he was going mad, that his neighbours came into his room to do him harm. In a word, the hypnotic subject had, thanks to the magnetized crown, taken on the cerebral state of the melancholic patient. The magnetized crown had been powerful enough to draw off the morbid cerebral influx of the patient (who got well), which had persisted, like a memory, in the intimate (or innermost) texture of the magnetic strip of metal.

"This is a phenomenon we have produced many times, for several years; not only with the subject now present, but with others.

"This communication is, amongst physiological phenomena, on a line with M. D'Arsonval's on the persistence of certain anterior states in inorganic bodies; it will no doubt cause much astonishment and scepticism amongst those who are not accustomed to hypnologic research.

"Doubts will be cast on the sincerity of the subject, on his tendency to produce wonders, to being carried away, and also on what may perhaps seem too easy an acquiescence on the part of the operator.

"To all these objections I will only answer: that this phenomenon of the transmission of the psychical states of a subject by means of a magnetized crown which keeps given impressions is quite in the order of the phenomena formerly communicated by M. D'Arsonval. And, further, the first time I made this experiment, it was done without my knowing, in an entirely empirical way. The impregnated crown was put on the head of the hypnotic subject about a fortnight after it had been put on the patient's head. There has therefore necessarily been a first operation, of which I did not foreknow the results; for we did not know any more than the hypnotized subject, what was going to happen, and the subject reacted, *motu proprio*, without any excitant other than the magnetic crown.

"So one can assert, without trying to draw any other conclusions, that certain vibratory states of the brain, and probably of the nervous system, are capable of storing themselves in a magnetized bent strip of metal, as the magnetic fluid is stored in the soft bar of iron, and of leaving persistent traces; still further, that one can only destroy this persistent magnetic property by fire. The crown has to be red-hot before it ceases to act, as M. D'Arsonval found to be the case with the iron bar."

Albert de Rochas makes this notable comment:

"The same phenomenon would certainly have been produced had the patient been dead, and so one might by this means have a sort of evocation of a personality no longer of this world."

NOTE 15. As late as the sixteenth and seventeenth centuries the Irish were accustomed to leave their houses on the plains and valleys in spring and live with their cattle on the uplands, returning to the valleys and plains in time to reap the harvest. Before tillage became general they may not have returned till the chill of Autumn. From this perhaps came the faery flittings of May and November.

NOTE 16. The pictures shown were drawings of spirits "A.E." made from his own visions. The yellow thing upon the head was, I suppose, some sort of crown. These countrywomen have seen so little gold that they do not describe anything as "of gold" or "like gold." They will say of yellow hair that it is "bright like silver."

NOTE 17. The death-coach or more properly *coiste-bodhar* or "deaf-coach," so called from its rumbling sound. It is usually an omen of death.

NOTE 18. The thing "yellow and slippery, not hair but like marble" is evidently a crown of gold. Are these spirits in dress of ancient authority the shepherds of the more recent dead?

NOTE 19. I have read somewhere, but cannot remember where, that ragweed was once used to make some medicine for horses. This would account for its association with them in the half-fantasy, half-vision of the country seers. In the same way, the mushroom ring of the faeries is, it seems, a memory of some intoxicating liquor made of mushrooms, when intoxication was mysterious. The storyteller speaks of "those red flowers," showing how vague her sense of colour, or her knowledge of English, for ragweed is, of course, yellow.

NOTE 20. "Bracket" is Irish for "speckled" and seems to me a description of the plaids and stripes of medieval Ireland.

NOTE 21. Bodin in his *De Magorum Dæmonomania* speaks of salt as a spell against spirits because a "symbol of eternity."

NOTE 22. Tir-nan-og, the country of the young, the paradise of the ancient Irish. It is sometimes described as under the earth, sometimes all about us, and sometimes as an enchanted island. This island paradise has given rise to many legends; sailors have bragged of meeting it. A Dutch pilot settled in Dublin in 1614, claimed to have seen it off the coast of Greenland in 61° of latitude. It vanished as he came near, but sailing in an opposite direction he came upon it once more, but Giraldus Cambrensis claimed that shortly before he came to Ireland such a phantom island was discovered off the west coast of Ireland and made habitable. Some young men saw it from the shore; when they came near it, it sank into the water. The next day it reappeared and again mocked the same youths with the like delusion. At length, on their rowing towards it on the third day, they followed the advice of an older man, and let fly an arrow, barbed with red-hot steel, against the island; and then landing, found it stationary and habitable.

NOTE 23. Supernatural strength is often spoken of by the people as a sign of faery power. It is also enumerated in *The Roman Ritual* among the signs of possession. I have read somewhere that the priests of Apollo showed it in their religious transports.

NOTE 24. "Materializations" are generally imperfect. The spirit makes just enough of mind and form for its purpose. Even when the form is only visible to the clairvoyant there may still be materialization, though not carried far enough to affect ordinary sight.

NOTE 25. The picture was made by "A.E." of one of the forms he sees in vision.

NOTE 26. The barrel which contained a brew that made the spirits invisible is probably the cauldron of the god Dagda, called "The Undry" "because it was never empty." The Tuatha-de-Danaan, the old Irish divine race, brought with them to Ireland four talismans, the sword, the spear, the stone, and the cauldron. Rhys, in his *Celtic Heathendom*, compares it with the Irish well of wisdom, overhung by nine hazels, and the Welsh "Cauldron of the Head of Hades," set over a fire, blown into a flame by the breath of nine young girls. Girls and hazels were alike, he thinks, symbols of time because of the nine days of the old Celtic week, and comparable with the nine Muses, daughters of Memory. Nutt thought the Celtic cauldron the first form of the Holy Grail.

NOTE 27. In my record of this conversation I find a sentence that has dropped out in Lady Gregory's. The old man used these words: "And I took down a fork from the rafters and asked her was it a broom and she said it was," and it was that answer that proved her in the power of the faeries. She was "suggestible" and probably in a state of trance.

NOTE 28. The Dundonians are, of course, the Tuatha-de-Danaan, and those with the bag are the "firbolg' or bag-men;" we have now, it may be, a true explanation of a name Professor Rhys has interpreted with intricate mythology. I wonder if these bags are related to the Sporran of the Highlanders.

NOTE 29. Here though maybe but in seeming, spiritism and folk-lore are at issue with one another. The spirit of the séance room is described as growing to maturity and remaining in that state. In Swedenborg it moves toward "the day-spring of its youth." Among the country people too, one sometimes hears of the dead growing to the likeness of thirty years in heaven and remaining so. Thirty years, I suppose, because at that age Christ began his ministry. The idea that underlies Mrs. Fagan's statement seems to be that we have a certain measure of life to live out on earth or in some intermediate state. Are the inhabitants of this "intermediate state" the "earthbound" of the spiritists?

NOTE 30. Professor Lombroso quotes from Professor Faffofer the following description of how he received news of the death of Carducci: "On the 18th of February, in the evening, our spirit-friends did not at once give us notice of their presence at our sitting, and we waited for them about half an hour. 'Remigo,' on being asked the reason why they had delayed, replied: 'We are in a state of agitation and confusion here. We have just come from a festival—of grief for you and joy for us. We have been present at the death-bed of Carducci.' He had died that day and in that very hour and the news had not yet arrived by the ordinary channels."

NOTE 31. I was the patient; it seemed to be the only way of coming to intimate speech with the knowledgeable man.

NOTE 32. The ghosts of "spiritism" are constantly changing place or state. Sometimes for this reason they must say "good-bye" to a medium. That they are passing to a "higher state" seems to be the usual phrase. See for instance the account signed by A. I. Smart and a number of witnesses, published in *The Medium and Daybreak*, of June 15, 1877.

NOTE 33. I have been several times told that a great battle for the potatoes preceded the great famine. What decays with us seems to come out, as it were, on the other side of the picture and is spirits' property.

NOTE 34. This is true, but he might have guessed it from the difference of my glasses; one is plain glass.

NOTE 35. They are only small when "upon certain errands," but when small, three feet or thereabouts seems to be the almost invariable height. Mary Battle, my uncle George Pollexfen's second-sighted servant, told me that "it is something in our eyes makes them big or little." People in trance often see objects reduced. Mrs. Piper when half awakened will sometimes see the people about her very small.

NOTE 36. The same story as that in one of the most beautiful of the "Noh" plays of Japan. I tell the Japanese story in my long terminal essay.

NOTE 37. Mediums have often said that the spirits see this world through our eyes. John Heydon, upon the other hand, calls good spirits "The eyes and ears of God."

NOTE 38. The herbs were gathered before dawn, probably that the dew might be upon them. Dew, a signature or symbol of the philosopher's stone, was held once to be a secretion from dawning light.

NOTE 39. The most puzzling thing in Irish folk-lore is the number of countrymen and countrywomen who are "away." A man or woman or child will suddenly take to the bed, and from that on, perhaps for a few weeks, perhaps for a lifetime, will be at times unconscious, in a state of dream, in trance, as we say. According to the peasant theory these persons are, during these times, with the faeries, riding through the country, eating or dancing, or suckling children. They may even, in that other world, marry, bring forth, and beget, and may when cured of their trances mourn for the loss of their children in faery. This state generally commences by their being "touched" or "struck" by a spirit. The country people do not say that the soul is away and the body in the bed, as a spiritist would, but that body and soul have been taken and somebody or something put in their place so bewitched that we do not know the difference. This thing may be some old person who was taken years ago and having come near his allotted term is put back to get the rites of the church, or as a substitute for some more youthful and more helpful person. The old man may have grown too infirm even to drive cattle. On the other hand, the thing may be a broomstick or a heap of shavings. I imagine that an explanatory myth arose at a very early age when men had not learned to distinguish between the body and the soul, and was perhaps once universal. The fact itself is certainly "possession" and "trance" precisely as we meet them in spiritism, and was perhaps once an inseparable part of religion. Mrs. Piper surrenders her body to the control of her trance personality but her soul, separated from the body, has a life of its own, of which, however, she is little if at all conscious.

There are two books which describe with considerable detail a like experience in China and Japan respectively: *Demon Possession and Allied Themes*, by the Rev. John L. Nevius, D.D. (Fleming H. Revell & Co., 1894); *Occult Japan*, by Percival Lowell (Houghton, Mifflin, 1895). In both countries, however, the dualism of body and soul is recognized, and the theory is therefore identical with that of spiritism. Dr. Nevius is a missionary who gradually became convinced, after much doubt and perplexity, of the reality of possession by what he believes to be evil spirits precisely similar to that described in the New Testament. These spirits take possession of some Chinese man or woman who falls suddenly into a trance, and announce through their medium's mouth, that when they lived on earth they had such and such a name, sometimes if they think a false name will make them more pleasing they will give a false name and history. They demand certain offerings and explain that they are seeking a home; and if the offerings are refused, and the medium seeks to drive them from body and house they turn persecutors; the house may catch fire suddenly; but if they have their way, they are ready to be useful, especially to heal the sick. The missionaries expel them in the name of Christ, but the Chinese exorcists adopt a method familiar to the west of Ireland —tortures or threats of torture. They will light tapers which they stick upon the fingers. They wish to make the body uncomfortable for its tenant. As they believe in the division of soul and body they are not likely to go too far. A man actually did burn his wife to death, in Tipperary a few years ago, and is no doubt still in prison for it. My uncle, George Pollexfen, had an old servant Mary Battle, and when she spoke of the case to me, she described that man as very superstitious. I asked what she meant by that and she explained that everybody knew that you must only threaten, for whatever injury you did to the changeling the faeries would do to the living person they had carried away. In fact mankind and spiritkind have each their hostage. These explanatory myths are not a speculative but a practical wisdom. And one can count perhaps, when they are rightly remembered, upon their preventing the more gross practical errors. The Tipperary witch-burner only half knew his own belief. "I stand here in the door," said Mary Battle, "and I hear them singing over there in the field, but I have never given in to them yet." And by "giving in" I understood her to mean losing her head.

The form of possession described in Lowell's book is not involuntary like that the missionary describes. And the possessing spirits are believed to be those of holy hermits or of the gods. He saw it for the first time on a pilgrimage to the top of Mount Ontaké. Close on the border of the snow he came to a rest house which was arranged to enclose the path, that all, it would seem, might stop and rest and eat and give something to its keeper. Presently he saw three young men dressed in white who passed on in spite of the entreaties of the keeper. He followed and presently found them praying before a shrine cut in the side of a cliff. When the prayer was finished one of them took from his sleeve a stick that had hanging from it pieces of zigzag paper, and sat himself on a bench opposite the shrine. One of the others sat facing upon another bench, clasping his hands over his breast and closing his eyes. Then the first young man began a long evocation, chanting and twisting and untwisting his fingers all the time. Presently he put the wand with the zigzag paper into the other's hands and the other's hands began to twitch, and that twitching grew more and more. Then the man was possessed. A spirit spoke through his mouth and called itself the God, Hakkai.

Now the evoker became very respectful and asked if the peak would be clear of clouds, and the pilgrimage a lucky one, and if the god would take care of those left at home. The god answered that the peak would be clear until the afternoon of the day following and all else go well. The voice ceased and the evoker offered a prayer of adoration. The entranced man was awakened by being touched on the breast and slapped upon the back and now another of the three took his place. And all was gone through afresh; and when that was over the third young man was entranced in his turn.

Mr. Lowell made considerable further investigation and records many cases, and was told that the god or spirit would sometimes speak in a tongue unknown to the possessed man, or gave useful medical advice. He is one of the few Europeans who have witnessed what seems to be an important rite of Shinto religion. Shintoism, or the Way of the Gods, until its revival in the last half of the nineteenth century remained lost and forgotten in the roots of Japanese life. It had been superseded by Buddhism, if Mr. Lowell was correctly informed, as completely as this old faery faith of Ireland has been superseded by Christianity. Buddhism, however, having no Christian hostility to friendly spirits, does not seem to have done anything to discourage a revival which was one of the causes that brought Japan under the single rule of the Mikado. It had always indeed in certain of its sects practised ceremonies that had for their object the causing of possession.

There is a story in *The Book of the Dun Cow* which certainly describes a like experience, though Prof. Rhys interprets it as a solar myth. I will take the story from Lady Gregory's *Cuchulain of Muirthemne*. The people of Ulster were celebrating the festival of the beginning of winter, held always at the beginning of November. The first of November is still a very haunted day and night. A flock of wild birds lit upon the waters near to Cuchulain and certain fair women. "In all Ireland there were not birds to be seen that were more beautiful."

One woman said: " 'I must have a bird of these birds on each of my two shoulders.' 'We must all have the same,' said the other women. 'If any one is to get them, it is I that must first get them,' said Eithne Inguba, who loved Cuchulain. 'What shall we do?' said the women. 'It is I will tell you that,' said Levarcham, 'for I will go to Cuchulain from you to ask him to get them.' "

So she went to Cuchulain and said: " 'The women of Ulster desire that you will get these birds for them.' Cuchulain put his hand upon his sword as if to strike her, and he said: 'Have the idle women of Ulster nothing better to do than to send me catching birds today?' 'It is not for you,' said Levarcham, 'to be angry with them; for there are many of them are half blind today with looking at you, from the greatness of their love for you.' "

After this Cuchulain catches the birds and divides them amongst the women, and to every woman there are two birds, but when he comes to his mistress, Eithne Inguba, he has no birds left. " 'It is vexed you seem to be,' he said, 'because I have given the birds to the other women.' 'You have good reason for that,' she said, 'for there is not a woman of them but would share her love and her friendship with you; while as for me no person shares my love but you alone.' " Cuchulain promises her whatever birds come, and presently there come two birds who are linked together with a chain of gold and "singing soft music that went near to put sleep on the whole gathering." Cuchulain went in their pursuit, though Eithne and his charioteer tried to dissuade him, believing them enchanted. Twice he casts a stone from his sling and misses, and then he throws his spear but merely pierces the wing of one bird. Thereupon the birds dive and he goes away in great vexation, and he lies upon the ground and goes to sleep, and while he sleeps two women come to him and put him under enchantment. In the Connacht stories the enchantment begins with a stroke, or with a touch from some person of faery and it is so the women deal with Cuchulain. "The woman with the green cloak went up to him and smiled at him and she gave him a stroke of a rod. The other went up to him then and smiled at him and gave him a stroke in the same way; and they went on doing this for a long time, each of them striking him in turn till he was more dead than alive. And then they went away and left him there." The men of Ulster found him and they carried him to a house and to a bed and there he lay till the next November came round. They were sitting about the bed when a strange man came in and sat amongst them. It was the God, Ængus, and he told how Cuchulain could be healed. A king of the other world, Labraid, wished for Cuchulain's help in a war, and if he would give it, he would have the love of Fand the wife of the sea god Manannan. The women who gave him the strokes of the rods were Fand and her sister Liban, who was Labraid's wife They had sought his help as the Connacht faeries will ask the help of some good hurler. Were they too like our faeries "shadows" until they found it? When the god was gone, Cuchulain awoke, and Conchubar, the King of Ulster, who had been watching by his bedside, told him that he must go again to the rock where the enchantment was laid upon him. He goes there and sees the woman with the green cloak. She is Liban and pleads with him that he may accept the love of Fand and give his help to Labraid. If he will only promise, he will become strong again. Cuchulain will not go at once but sends his charioteer into the other world. When he has his charioteer's good report, he consents, and wins the fight for Labraid and is the lover of Fand. In the Connacht stories a wife can sometimes get back her husband by throwing some spell-breaking object over the heads of the faery cavalcade that keeps him spellbound. Emir, in much the same way, recovers her husband Cuchulain, for she and her women go armed with knives

363

to the yew tree upon Baile's strand where he had appointed a meeting with Fand and outface Fand and drive her away.

We have here certainly a story of trance and of the soul leaving the body, but probably after it has passed through the minds of story-tellers who have forgotten its original meaning. There is no mention of any one taking Cuchulain's place, but Prof. Rhys in his reconstruction of the original form of the story of "Cuchulain and the Beetle of Forgetfulness,' a visit also to the other world, makes the prince who summoned him to the adventure take his place in the court of Ulster. There are many stories belonging to different countries, of people whose places are taken for a time by angels or spirits or gods, the best known being that of the nun and the Virgin Mary, and all may have once been stories of changelings and entranced persons. Pwyll and Arawyn in the Mabinogion change places for a year, Pwyll going to the court of the dead in the shape of Arawyn to overcome his enemies, and Arawyn going to the court of Dyved. Pwyll overcomes Arawyn's enemies with one blow and the changeling's rule at Dyved was marvellous for its wisdom. In all these stories strength comes from men and wisdom from among gods who are but shadows. I have read somewhere of a Norse legend of a false Odin that took the true Odin's place, when the sun of summer became the wintry sun. When we say a man has had a stroke of paralysis or that he is touched we refer perhaps to a once universal faery belief.

NOTE 40. I suppose this woman who was glad to "pick a bit of what was in the pigs' trough" had passed along the roads in a state of semi-trance, living between two worlds. Boehme had for seven days what he called a walking trance that began by his gazing at a gleam of light on a copper pot and in that trance truth fell upon him "like a bursting shower."

NOTE 41. A village beauty of Ballylee. Raftery praised her in lines quoted in my *Celtic Twilight*, and Lady Gregory speaks of her in her essay on Raftery in *Poets and Dreamers*.

NOTE 42. An old, second-sighted servant to an uncle of mine used to say that dreams were no longer true "when the sap began to rise" and when I asked her how she knew that, she said; "What is the use of having an intellect unless you know a thing like that."

NOTE 43. "In the faeries" is plainly a misspeaking of the old phrase "in faery" that is to say "in glamour" "under enchantment." The word "faery" as used for an individual is a modern corruption. The right word is "fay."

NOTE 44. The sudden filling of the air by a sweet odour is a common event of the Séance room. It is mentioned several times in the 'Diary" of Stainton Moses.

NOTE 45. A woman from the North would probably be a faery woman or at any rate a "knowledgeable" woman, one who was "in the faeries" and certainly not necessarily at all a woman from Ulster. The North where the old Celtic other world was thought to lie is the quarter of spells and faeries. A visionary student, who was at the Dublin Art School when I was there, described to me a waking dream of the North Pole. There were luxuriant vegetation and overflowing life though still but ice to the physical eye. He added thereto his conviction that wherever physical life was abundant, the spiritual life was vague and thin, and of the converse truth.

NOTE 46. St. Patrick prayed, in *The Breastplate of St. Patrick*, to be delivered from the spells of smiths and women.

ST. MARY'S COLLEGE OF MARYLAND

ST. MARY'S CITY, MARYLAND

45316